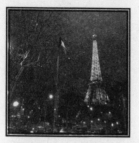

Yuto Tsukuda

For the first time in my life, I went to France. It was one surprise after another.

- Everyone is huge.
- All the security people at the airport and elsewhere look really strong and intimidating.
- The flush handles on toilets are strangely fashionable.
- If you look at someone, they smile at you.
- Or they might say “bonjour” to you.
- Advertisements displayed in town have nude women on them for no reason. (Woo-hoo!)

Man, the world sure is large.

Shun Saeki

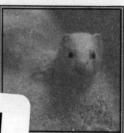

Wow, *Food Wars!* is going to be an anime. Amazing! There’s bound to be a lot of exciting stuff in it! I just bought a new DVR too. I'll be sure to watch each e…

p…

About the authors

Yuto Tsukuda won the 34th Jump Juniketsu Newcomers’ Manga Award for his one-shot story *Kiba ni Naru*. He made his *Weekly Shonen Jump* debut in 2010 with the series *Shonen Shikku*. His follow-up series, *Food Wars!: Shokugeki no Soma*, is his first English-language release.

Shun Saeki made his *Jump NEXT!* debut in 2011 with the one-shot story *Kimi to Watashi no Renai Soudan. Food Wars!: Shokugeki no Soma* is his first *Shonen Jump* series.

Food Wars!
SHOKUGEKI NO SOMA

Volume 12
Shonen Jump Advanced Manga Edition
Story by Yuto Tsukuda, Art by Shun Saeki
Contributor Yuki Morisaki

Translation: Adrienne Beck
Touch-Up Art & Lettering: Mara Coman
Design: Izumi Evers
Editor: Jennifer LeBlanc

Printed in the U.S.A.

Published by VIZ Media, LLC
P.O. Box 77010
San Francisco, CA 94107

10 9 8 7 6 5 4 3 2 1
First printing, June 2016

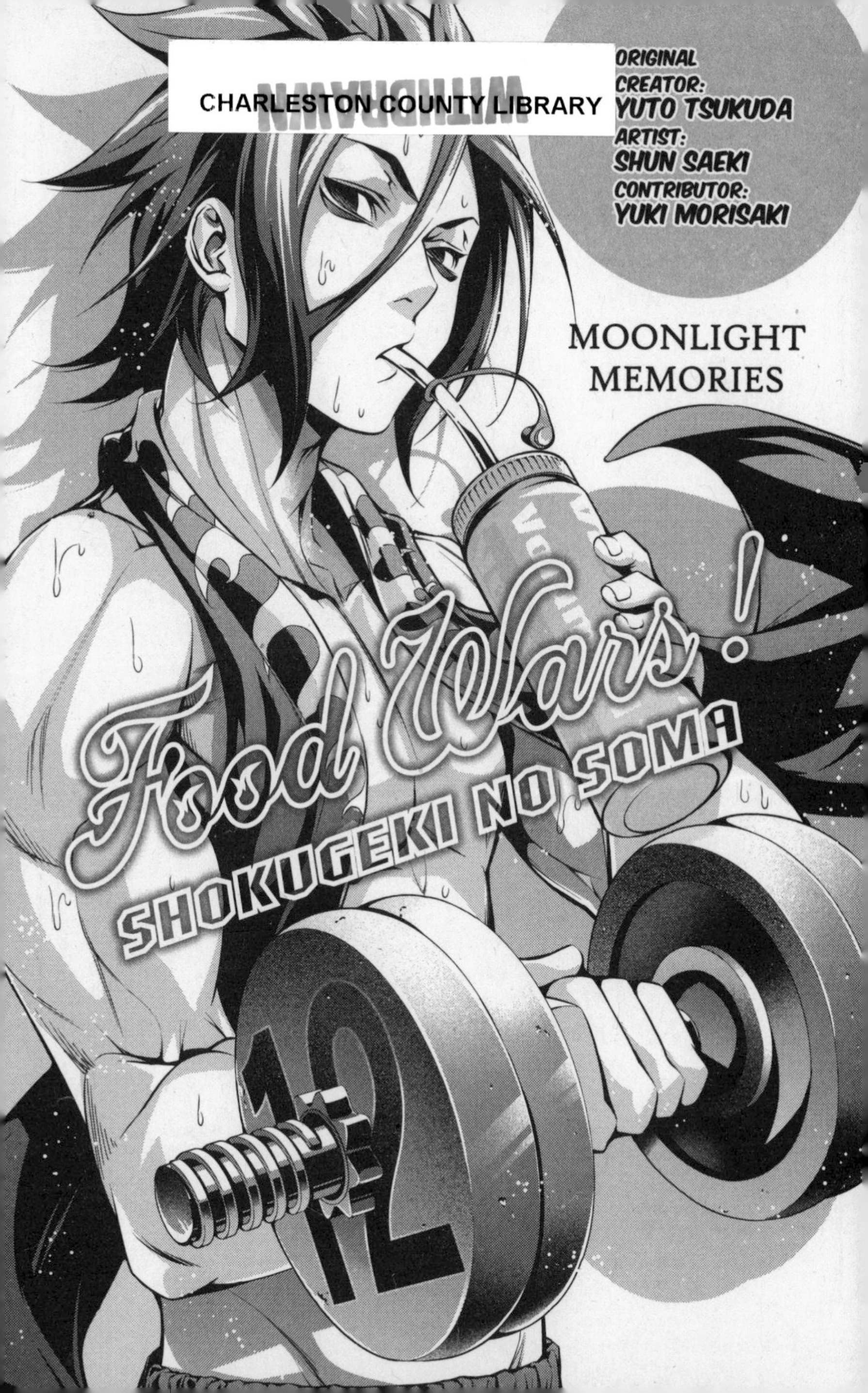
ORIGINAL CREATOR: YUTO TSUKUDA
ARTIST: SHUN SAEKI
CONTRIBUTOR: YUKI MORISAKI
MOONLIGHT MEMORIES
Food Wars!
SHOKUGEKI NO SOMA
12

CHARACTERS

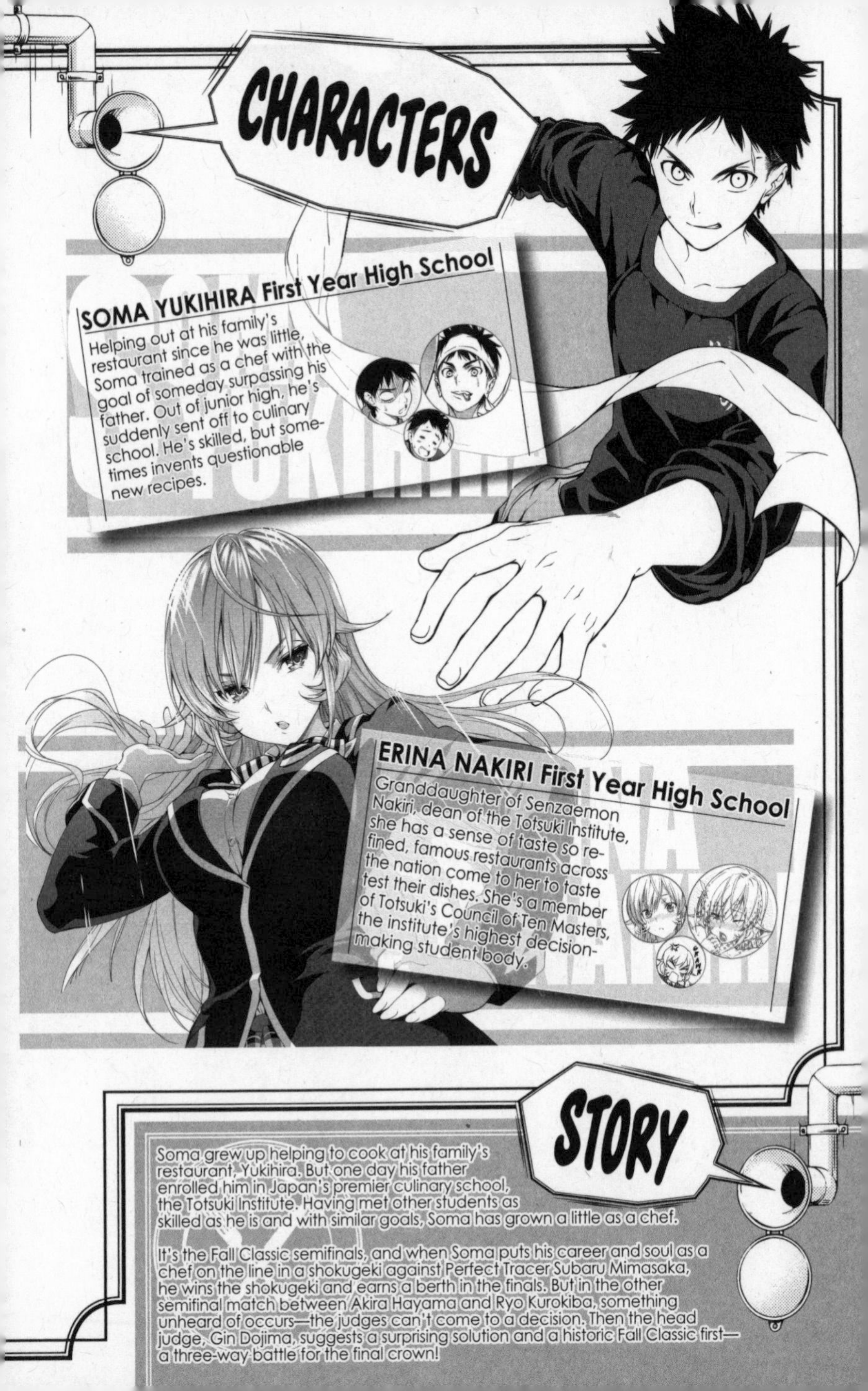

SOMA YUKIHIRA First Year High School

Helping out at his family's restaurant since he was little, Soma trained as a chef with the goal of someday surpassing his father. Out of junior high, he's suddenly sent off to culinary school. He's skilled, but sometimes invents questionable new recipes.

ERINA NAKIRI First Year High School

Granddaughter of Senzaemon Nakiri, dean of the Totsuki Institute, she has a sense of taste so refined, famous restaurants across the nation come to her to taste test their dishes. She's a member of Totsuki's Council of Ten Masters, the institute's highest decision-making student body.

STORY

Soma grew up helping to cook at his family's restaurant, Yukihira. But one day his father enrolled him in Japan's premier culinary school, the Totsuki Institute. Having met other students as skilled as he is and with similar goals, Soma has grown a little as a chef.

It's the Fall Classic semifinals, and when Soma puts his career and soul as a chef on the line in a shokugeki against Perfect Tracer Subaru Mimasaka, he wins the shokugeki and earns a berth in the finals. But in the other semifinal match between Akira Hayama and Ryo Kurokiba, something unheard of occurs—the judges can't come to a decision. Then the head judge, Gin Dojima, suggests a surprising solution and a historic Fall Classic first—a three-way battle for the final crown!

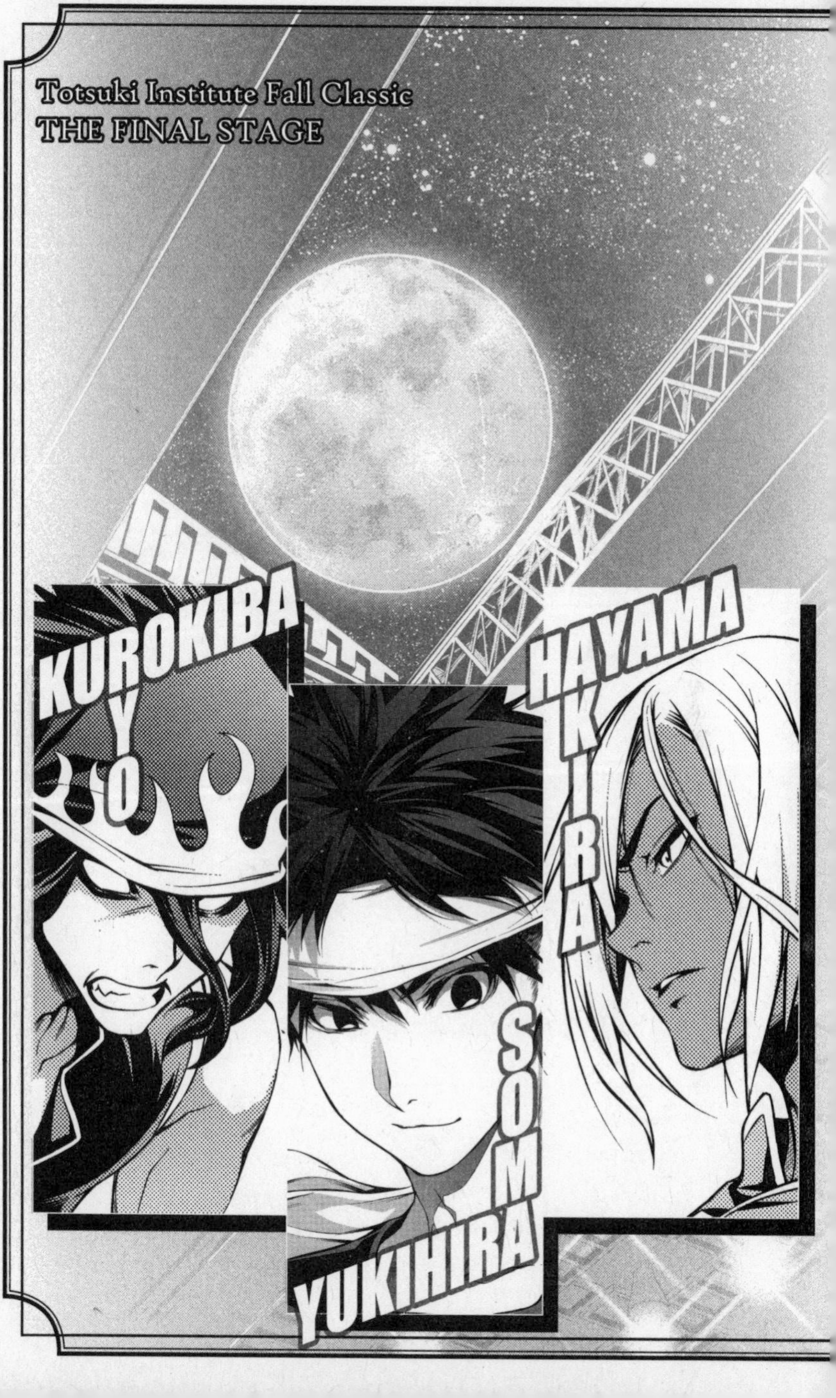
Totsuki Institute Fall Classic
THE FINAL STAGE
HAYAMA
AKIRA
SOMA
YUKIHIRA
KUROKIBA
RYO

Food Wars!
SHOKUGEKI NO SOMA

12

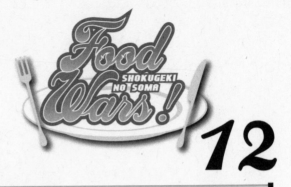

Table of Contents

193 AUTUMN'S "PIKE"

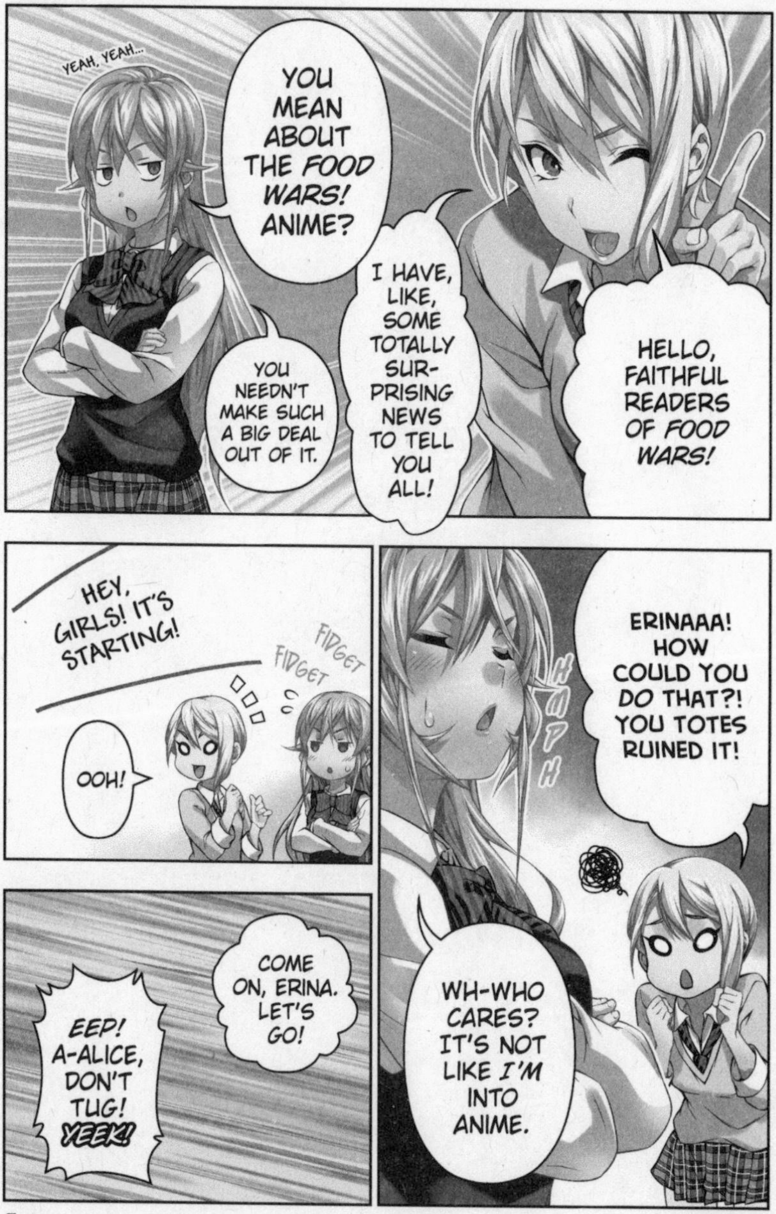
HELLO, FAITHFUL READERS OF FOOD WARS!
I HAVE, LIKE, SOME TOTALLY SUR-PRISING NEWS TO TELL YOU ALL!
YOU MEAN ABOUT THE FOOD WARS! ANIME?
YOU NEEDN'T MAKE SUCH A BIG DEAL OUT OF IT.
YEAH, YEAH...
ERINAAA! HOW COULD YOU DO THAT?! YOU TOTES RUINED IT!
HMMPH
WH-WHO CARES? IT'S NOT LIKE I'M INTO ANIME.
HEY, GIRLS! IT'S STARTING!
FIDGET FIDGET
OOH!
COME ON, ERINA. LET'S GO!
EEP! A-ALICE, DON'T TUG! YEEK!

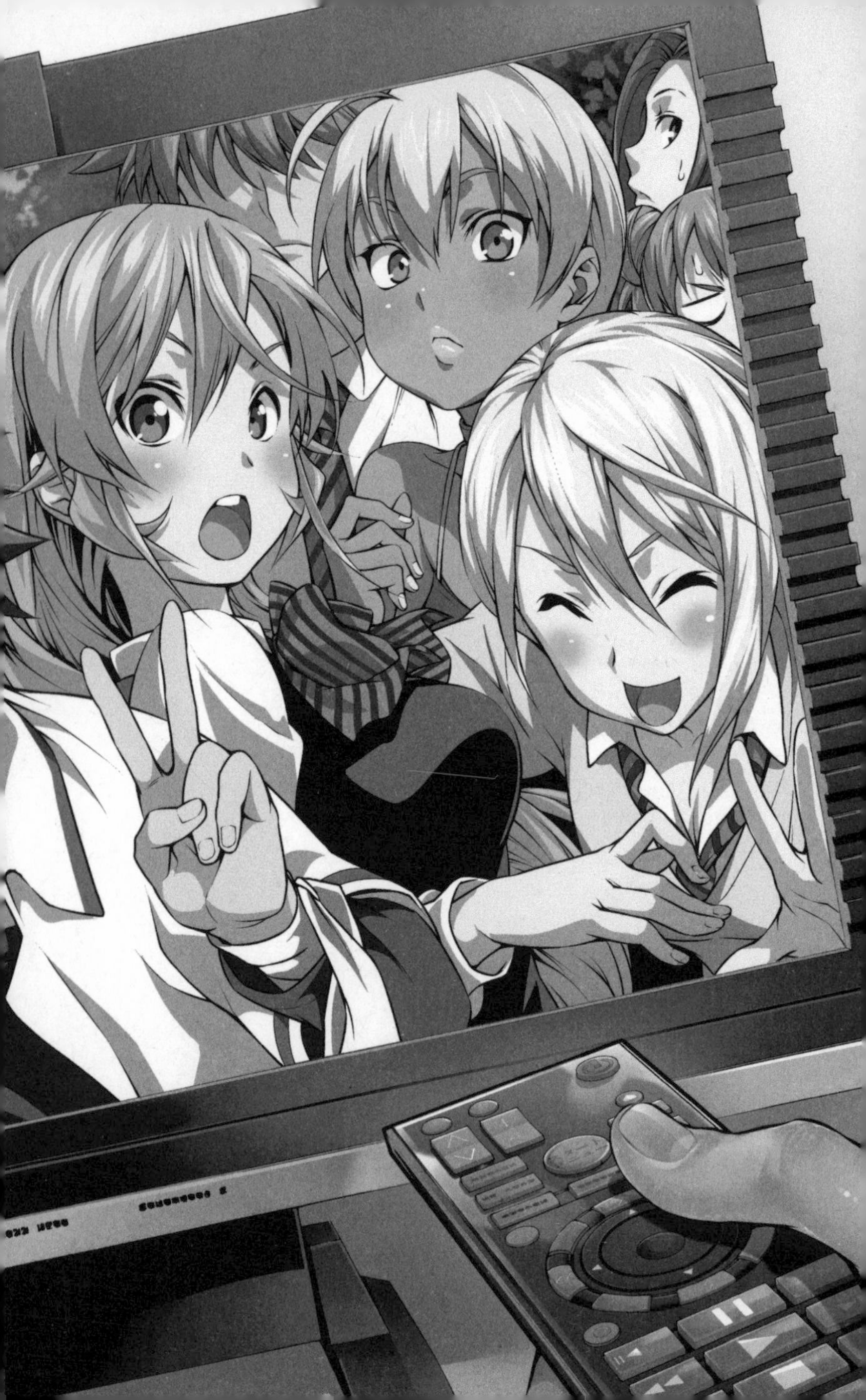

93 AUTUMN'S "PIKE"

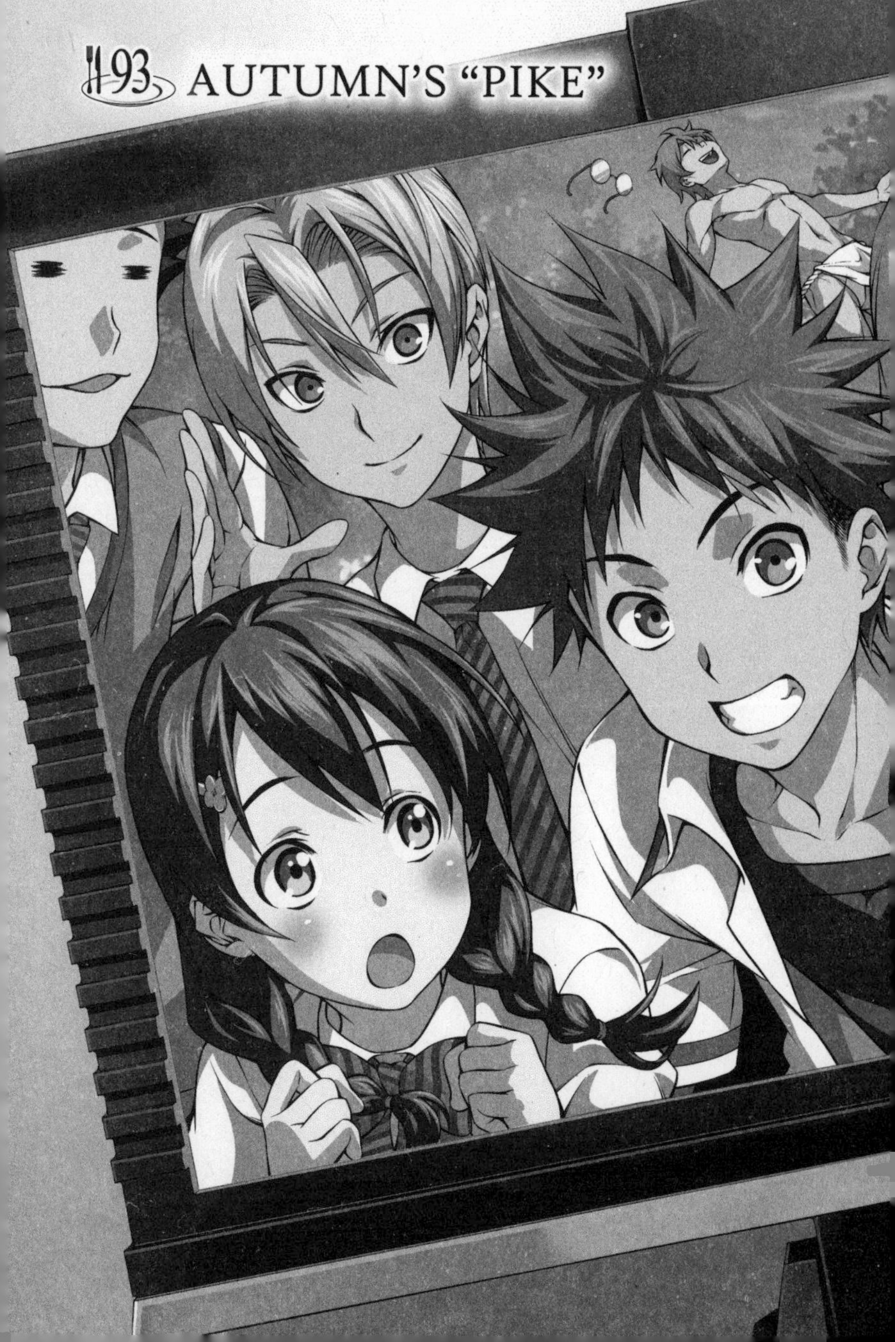

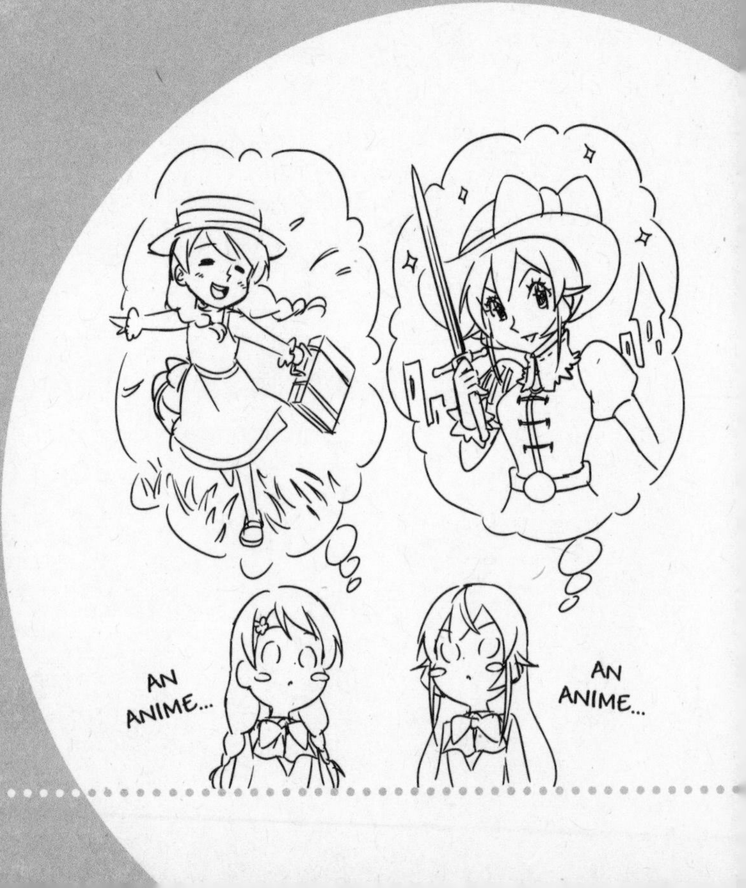
AN ANIME...
AN ANIME...

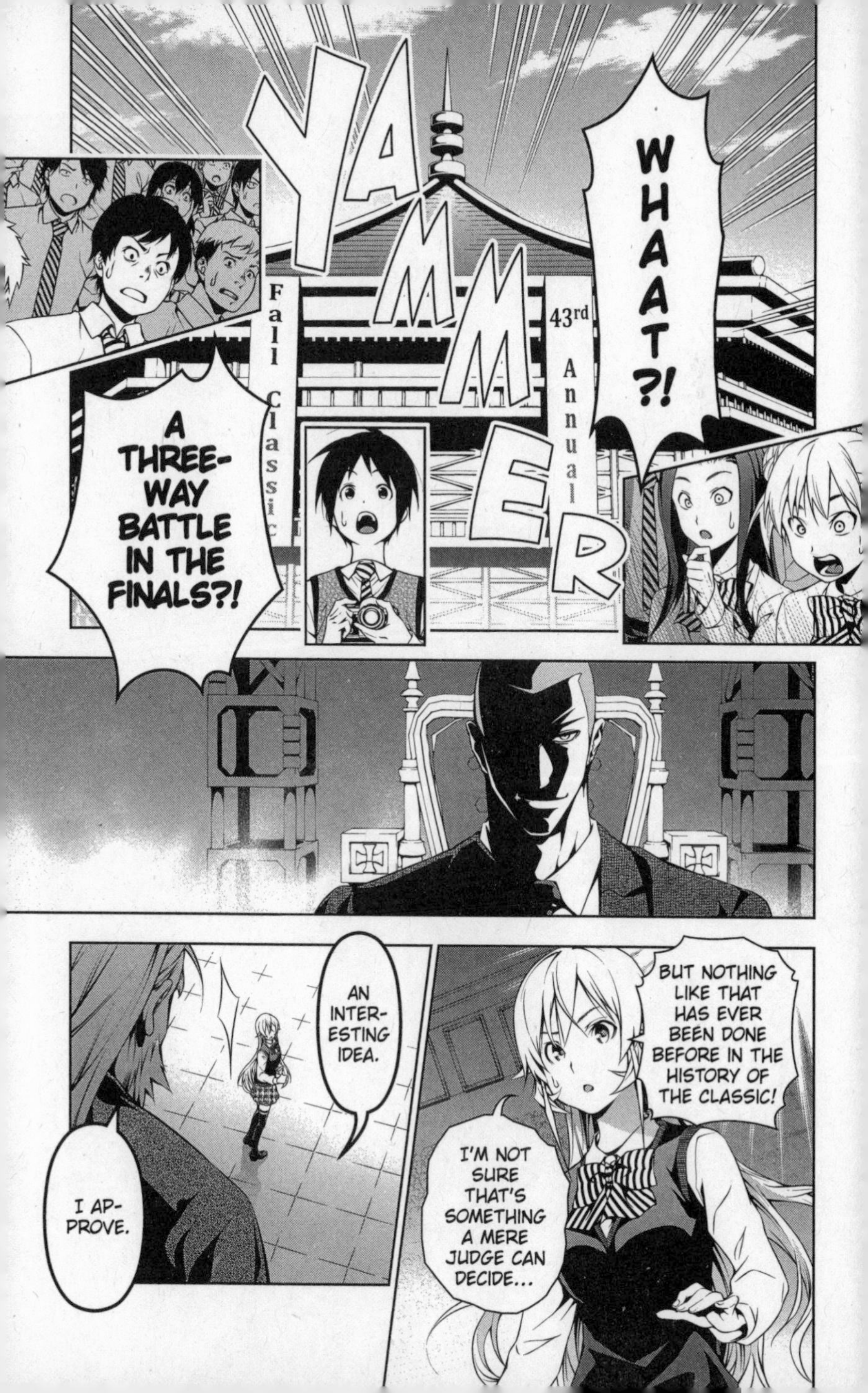
WHAAT?!
YAMMMMER
43rd Annual
Fall Classic
A THREE-WAY BATTLE IN THE FINALS?!
BUT NOTHING LIKE THAT HAS EVER BEEN DONE BEFORE IN THE HISTORY OF THE CLASSIC!
I'M NOT SURE THAT'S SOMETHING A MERE JUDGE CAN DECIDE...
AN INTERESTING IDEA.
I APPROVE.

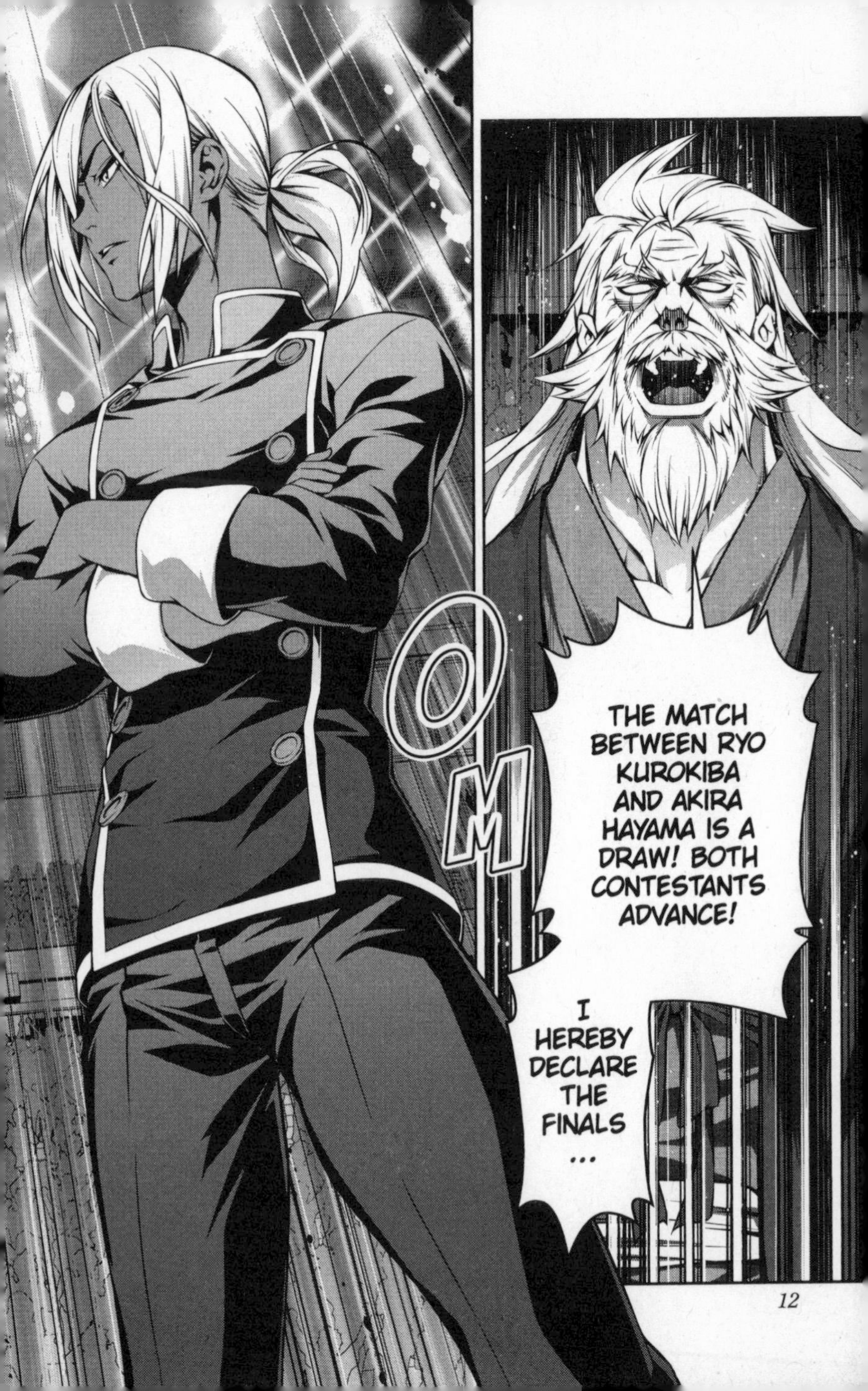
THE MATCH BETWEEN RYO KUROKIBA AND AKIRA HAYAMA IS A DRAW! BOTH CONTESTANTS ADVANCE!
I HEREBY DECLARE THE FINALS ...
M

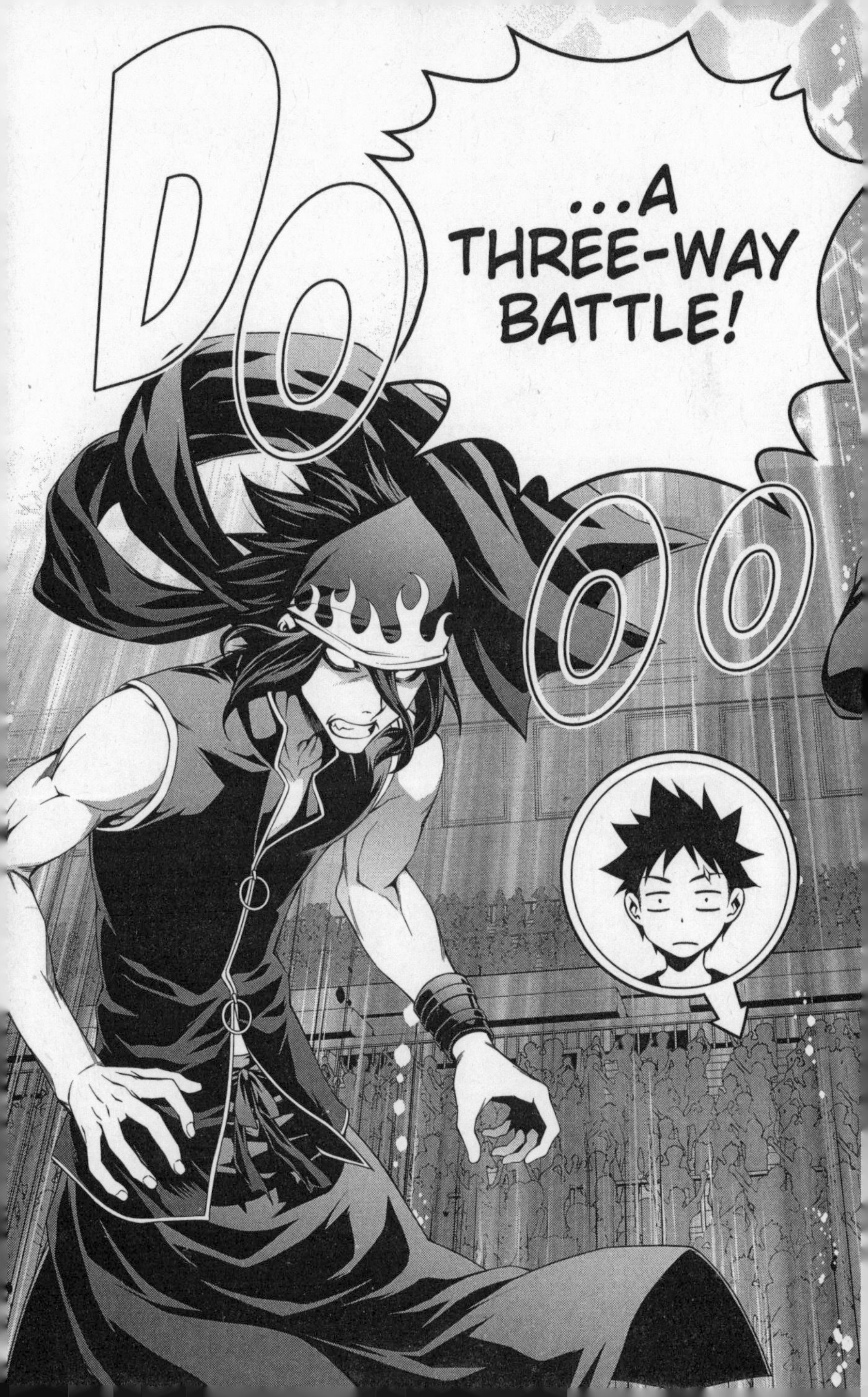
...A THREE-WAY BATTLE!
DOOOO

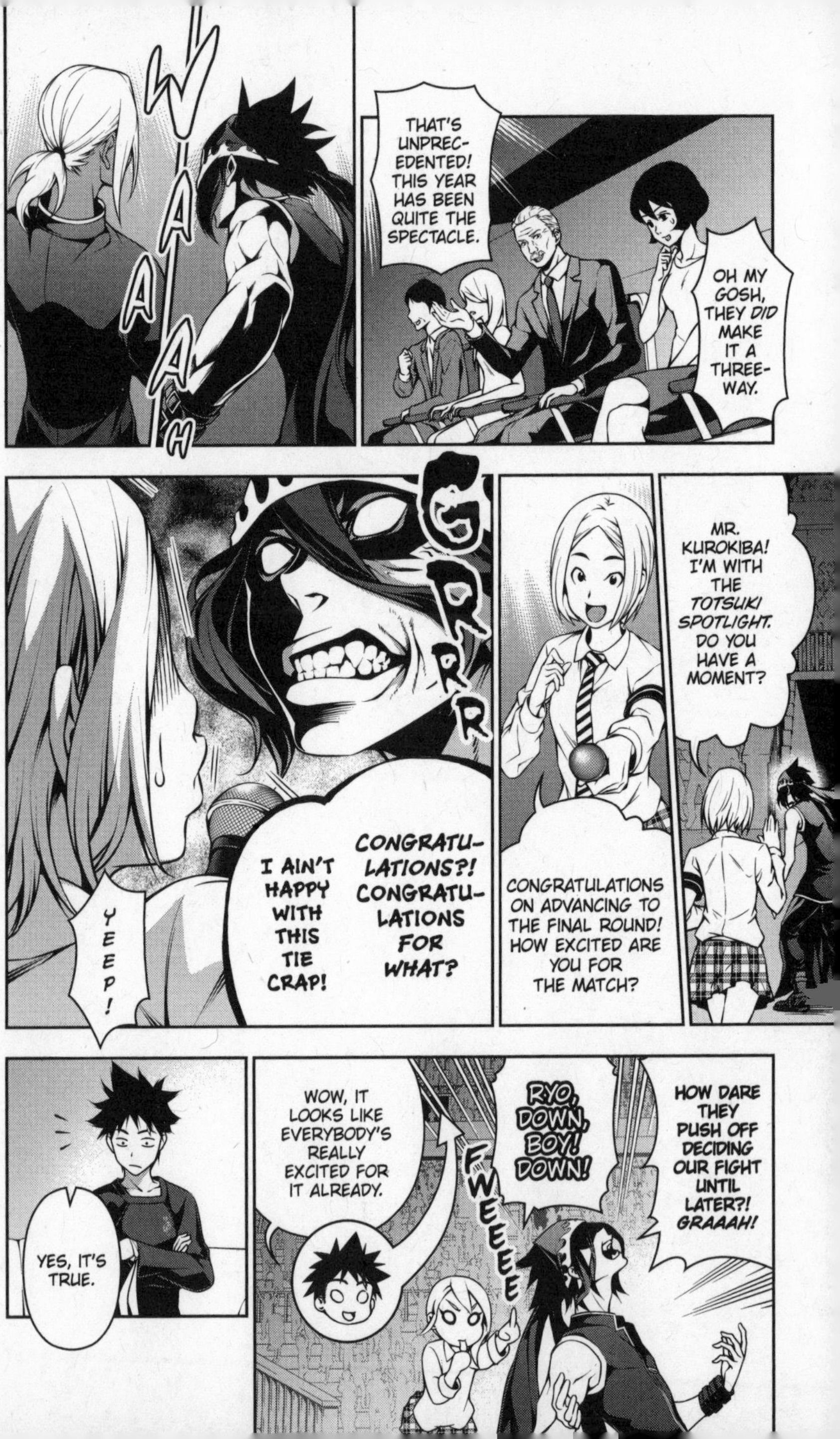
OH MY GOSH, THEY *DID* MAKE IT A THREE-WAY.
THAT'S UNPRECEDENTED! THIS YEAR HAS BEEN QUITE THE SPECTACLE.
WAAAAH
MR. KUROKIBA! I'M WITH THE *TOTSUKI SPOTLIGHT*. DO YOU HAVE A MOMENT?
CONGRATULATIONS ON ADVANCING TO THE FINAL ROUND! HOW EXCITED ARE YOU FOR THE MATCH?
GRRRR
CONGRATULATIONS?! CONGRATULATIONS FOR WHAT?
I AIN'T HAPPY WITH THIS TIE CRAP!
YEEEP!
HOW DARE THEY PUSH OFF DECIDING OUR FIGHT UNTIL LATER?! *GRAAAH!*
RYO, DOWN, BOY! DOWN!
FWEEEE
WOW, IT LOOKS LIKE EVERYBODY'S REALLY EXCITED FOR IT ALREADY.
YES, IT'S TRUE.

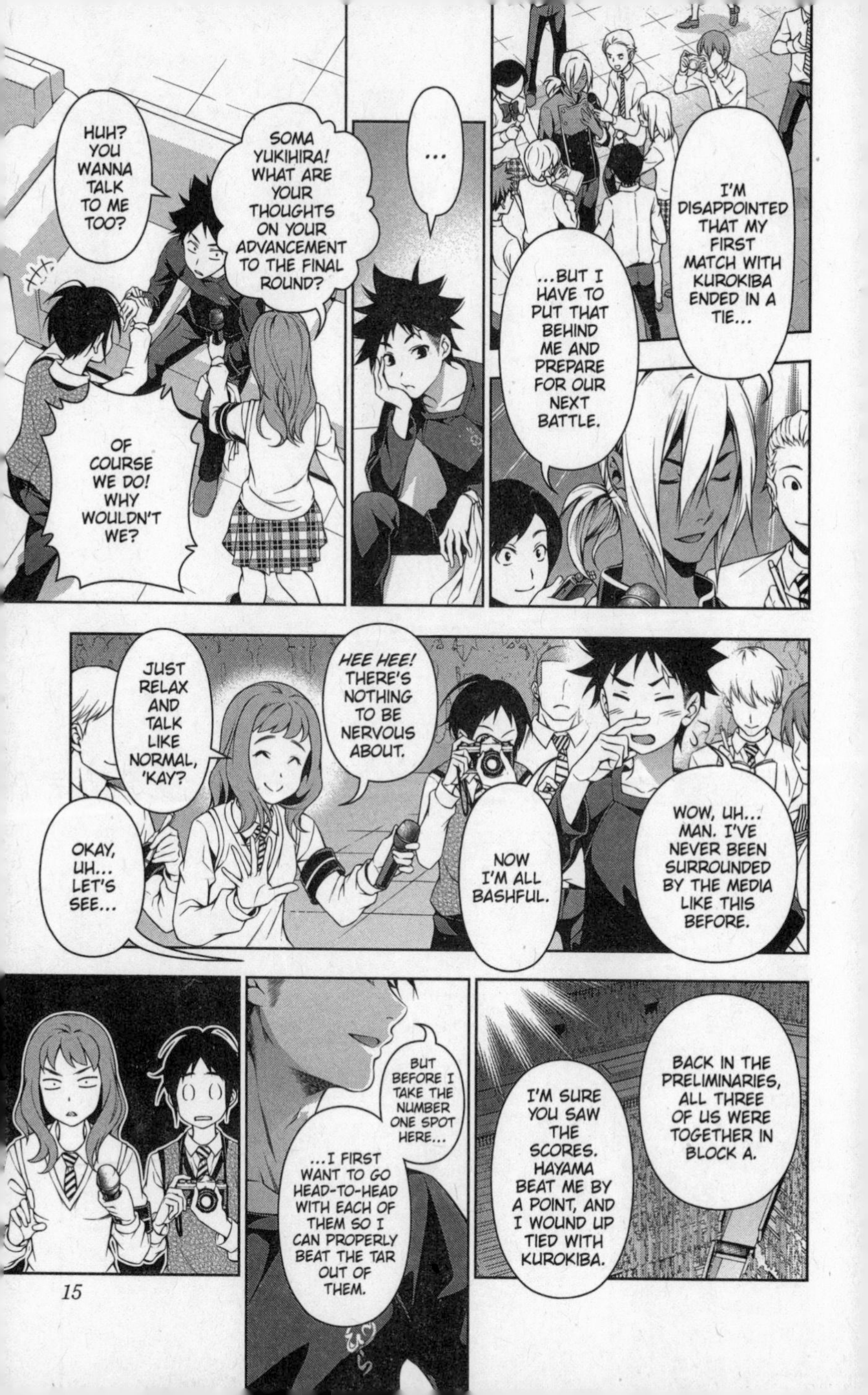
I'M DISAPPOINTED THAT MY FIRST MATCH WITH KUROKIBA ENDED IN A TIE...
...BUT I HAVE TO PUT THAT BEHIND ME AND PREPARE FOR OUR NEXT BATTLE.
...
SOMA YUKIHIRA! WHAT ARE YOUR THOUGHTS ON YOUR ADVANCEMENT TO THE FINAL ROUND?
HUH? YOU WANNA TALK TO ME TOO?
OF COURSE WE DO! WHY WOULDN'T WE?
WOW, UH... MAN. I'VE NEVER BEEN SURROUNDED BY THE MEDIA LIKE THIS BEFORE.
NOW I'M ALL BASHFUL.
HEE HEE! THERE'S NOTHING TO BE NERVOUS ABOUT.
JUST RELAX AND TALK LIKE NORMAL, 'KAY?
OKAY, UH... LET'S SEE...
BACK IN THE PRELIMINARIES, ALL THREE OF US WERE TOGETHER IN BLOCK A.
I'M SURE YOU SAW THE SCORES. HAYAMA BEAT ME BY A POINT, AND I WOUND UP TIED WITH KUROKIBA.
BUT BEFORE I TAKE THE NUMBER ONE SPOT HERE...
...I FIRST WANT TO GO HEAD-TO-HEAD WITH EACH OF THEM SO I CAN PROPERLY BEAT THE TAR OUT OF THEM.

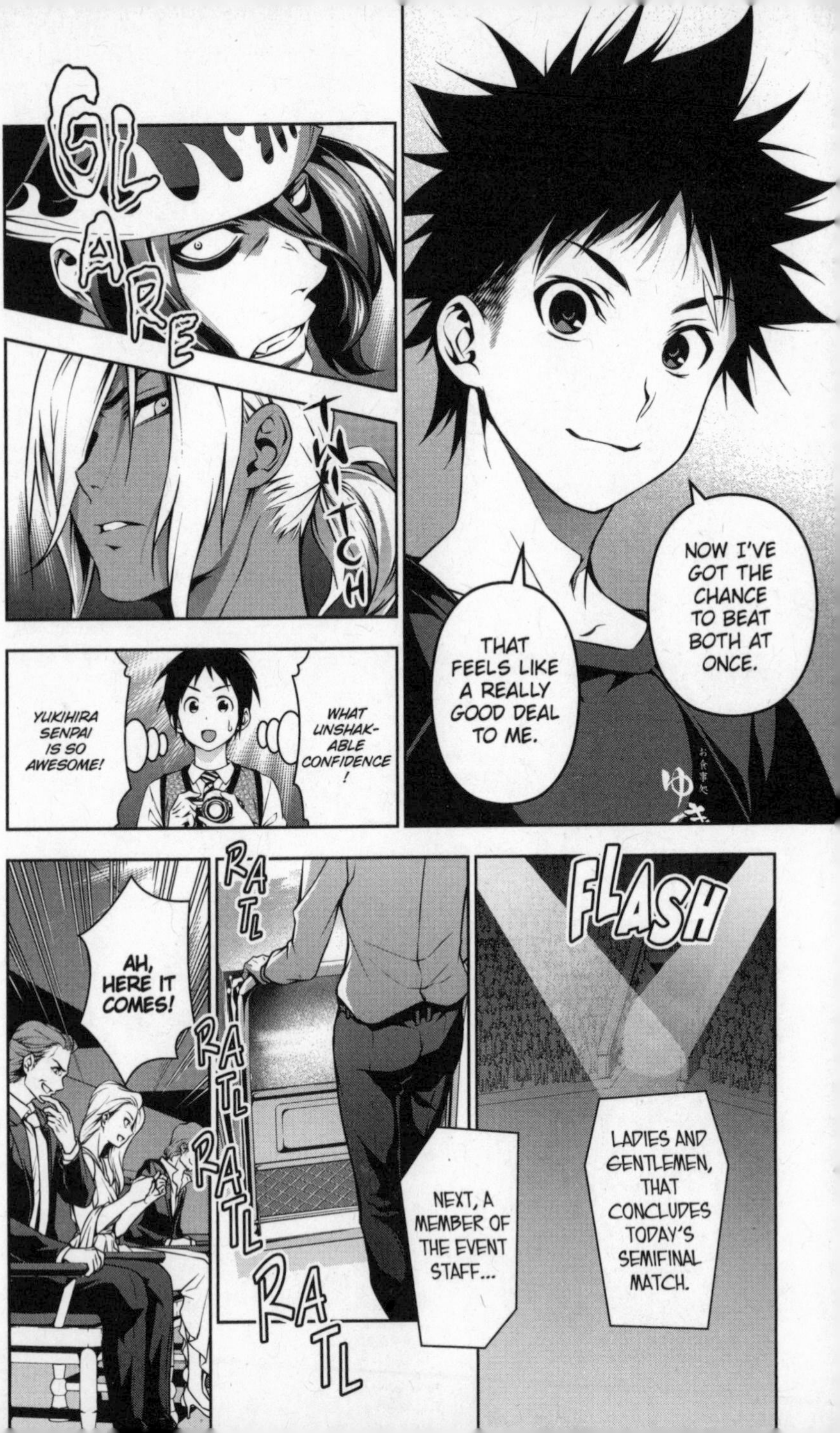
NOW I'VE GOT THE CHANCE TO BEAT BOTH AT ONCE.
THAT FEELS LIKE A REALLY GOOD DEAL TO ME.
GLARE
TWITCH
WHAT UNSHAK-ABLE CONFIDENCE!
YUKIHIRA SENPAI IS SO AWESOME!
FLASH
LADIES AND GENTLEMEN, THAT CONCLUDES TODAY'S SEMIFINAL MATCH.
RATL
NEXT, A MEMBER OF THE EVENT STAFF...
AH, HERE IT COMES!
RATL
RATL
RATL

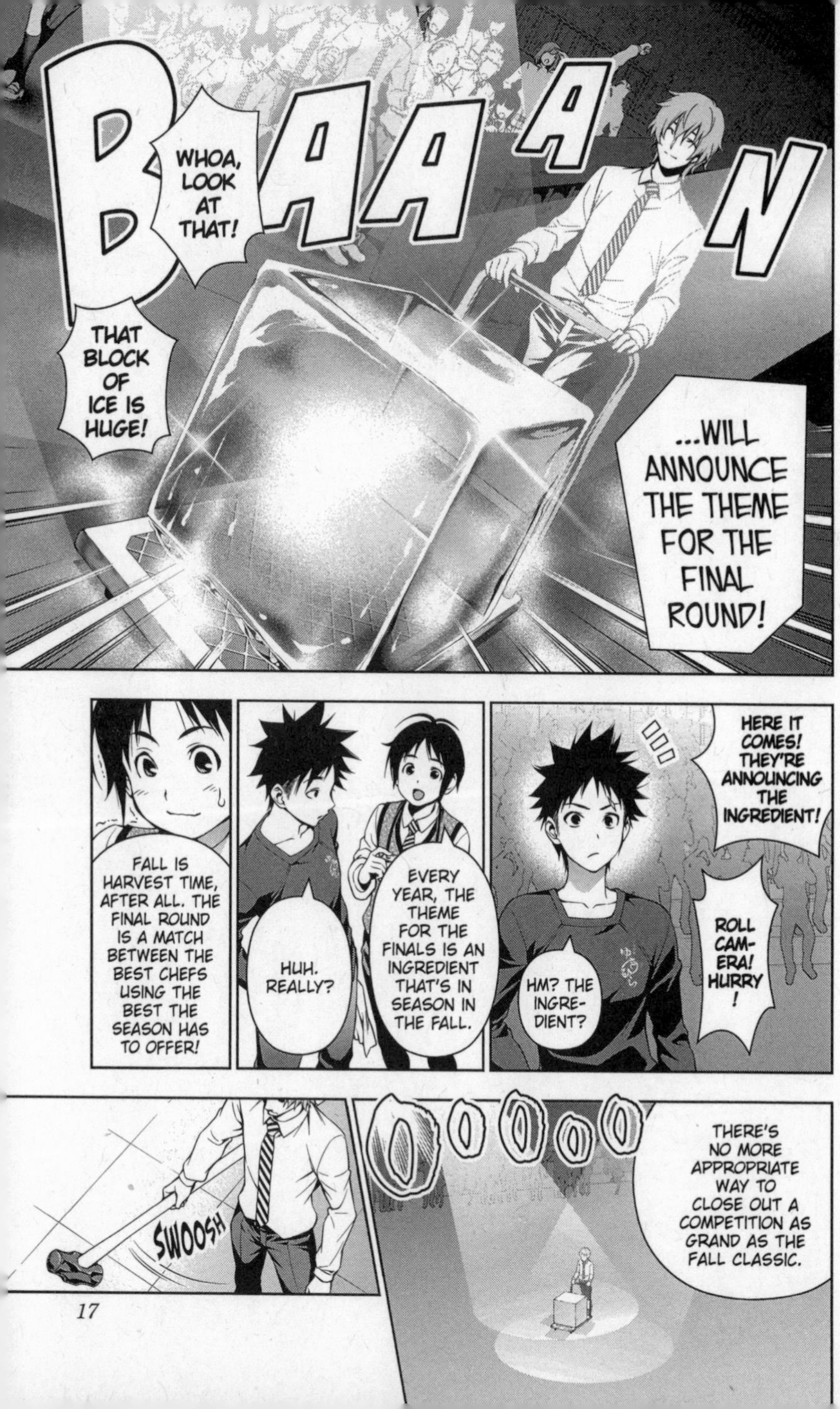
BAAAAN
...WILL ANNOUNCE THE THEME FOR THE FINAL ROUND!
WHOA, LOOK AT THAT!
THAT BLOCK OF ICE IS HUGE!
!!!
HERE IT COMES! THEY'RE ANNOUNCING THE INGREDIENT!
ROLL CAMERA! HURRY!
HM? THE INGREDIENT?
EVERY YEAR, THE THEME FOR THE FINALS IS AN INGREDIENT THAT'S IN SEASON IN THE FALL.
HUH. REALLY?
FALL IS HARVEST TIME, AFTER ALL. THE FINAL ROUND IS A MATCH BETWEEN THE BEST CHEFS USING THE BEST THE SEASON HAS TO OFFER!
THERE'S NO MORE APPROPRIATE WAY TO CLOSE OUT A COMPETITION AS GRAND AS THE FALL CLASSIC.
OOOOOO
SWOOSH

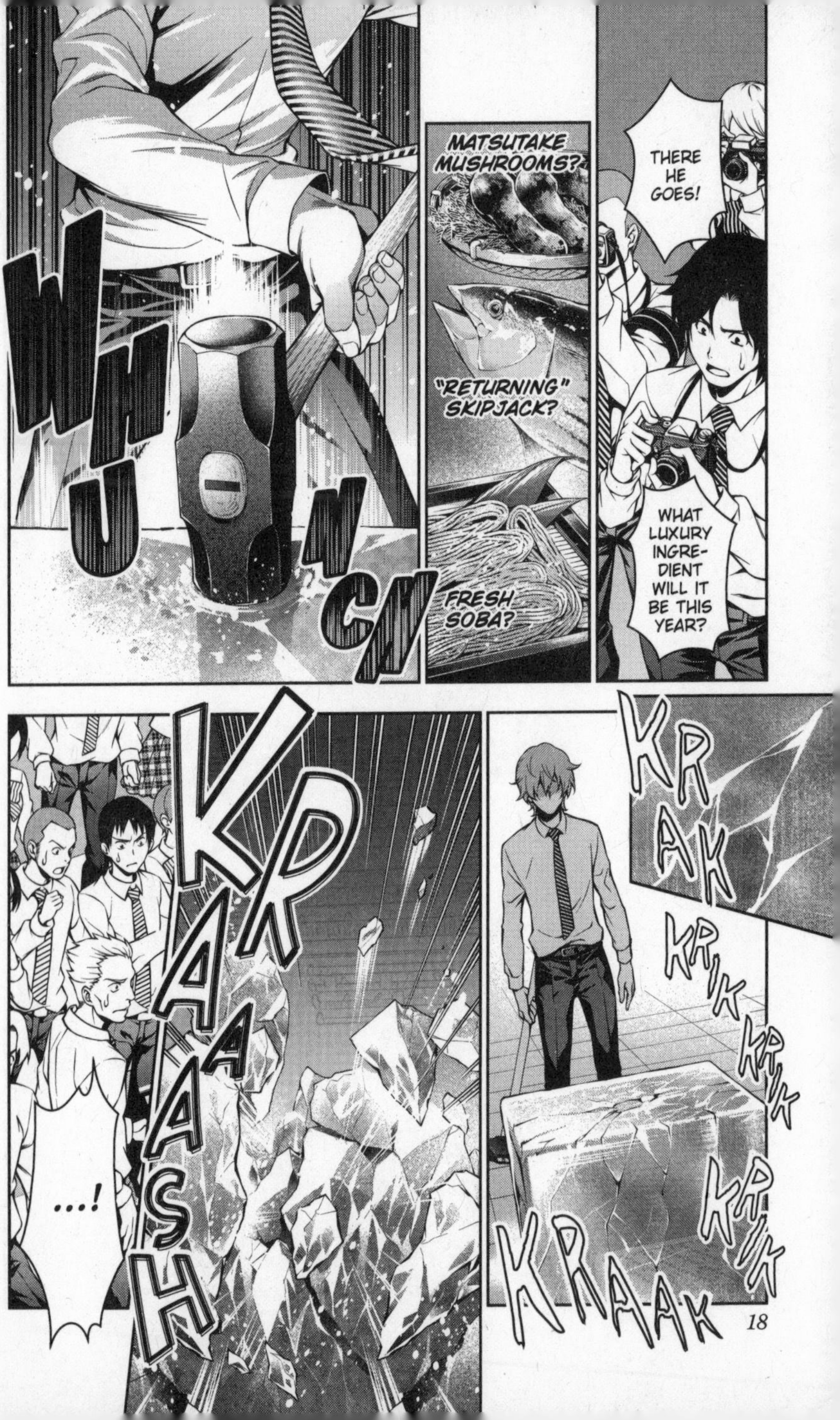
THERE HE GOES!
WHAT LUXURY INGRE-DIENT WILL IT BE THIS YEAR?
MATSUTAKE MUSHROOMS?
"RETURNING" SKIPJACK?
FRESH SOBA?
WHUNCH
KRAK
KRIK
KRIK
KRIK
KRAAAK
KRAAASH
...!

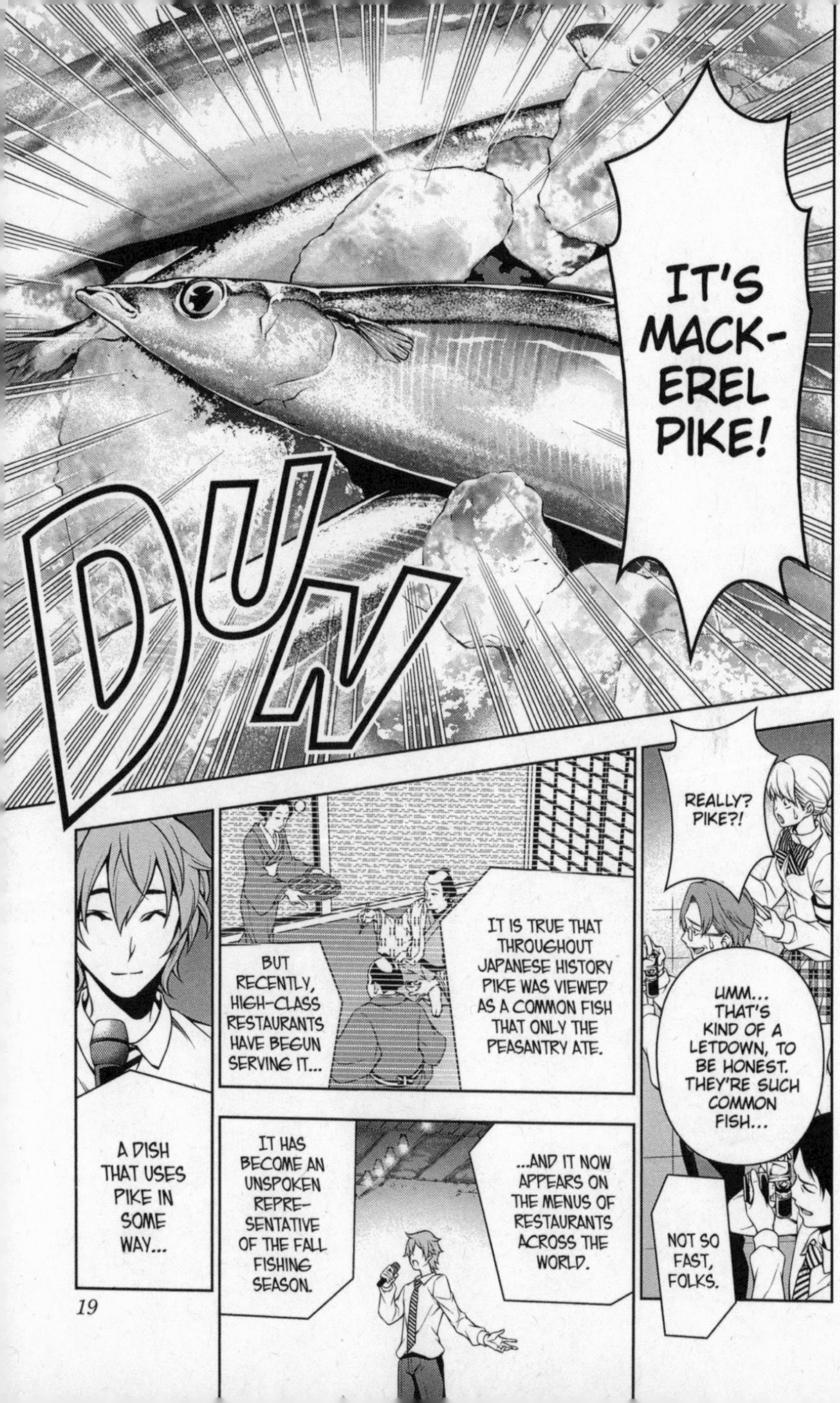
IT'S MACK-ERE PIKE!
DUN
REALLY? PIKE?!
UMM... THAT'S KIND OF A LETDOWN, TO BE HONEST. THEY'RE SUCH COMMON FISH...
NOT SO FAST, FOLKS.
IT IS TRUE THAT THROUGHOUT JAPANESE HISTORY PIKE WAS VIEWED AS A COMMON FISH THAT ONLY THE PEASANTRY ATE.
BUT RECENTLY, HIGH-CLASS RESTAURANTS HAVE BEGUN SERVING IT...
...AND IT NOW APPEARS ON THE MENUS OF RESTAURANTS ACROSS THE WORLD.
IT HAS BECOME AN UNSPOKEN REPRE-SENTATIVE OF THE FALL FISHING SEASON.
A DISH THAT USES PIKE IN SOME WAY...

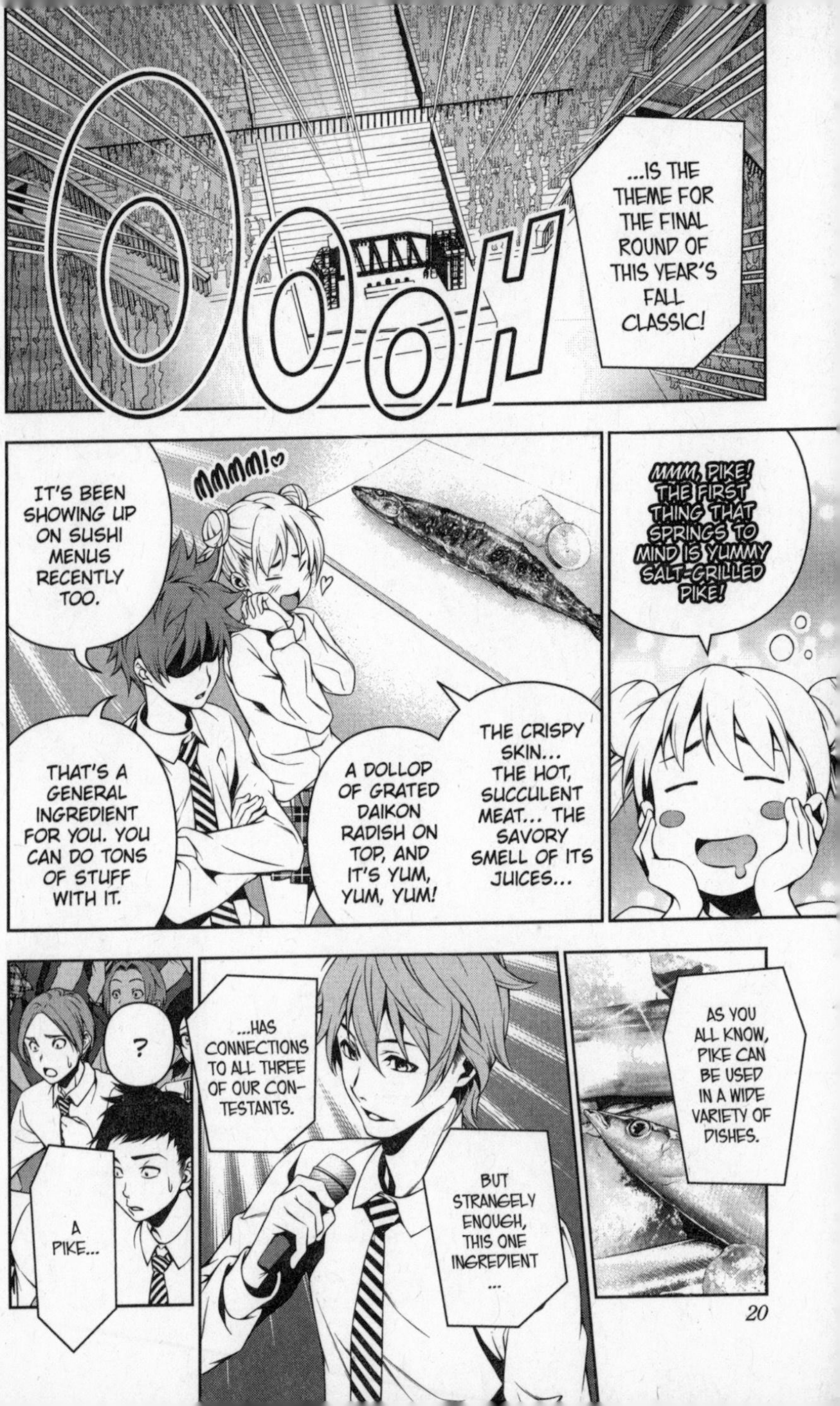
...IS THE THEME FOR THE FINAL ROUND OF THIS YEAR'S FALL CLASSIC!
OOOOH
MMM, PIKE! THE FIRST THING THAT SPRINGS TO MIND IS YUMMY SALT-GRILLED PIKE!
MMMM!♡
IT'S BEEN SHOWING UP ON SUSHI MENUS RECENTLY TOO.
THE CRISPY SKIN... THE HOT, SUCCULENT MEAT... THE SAVORY SMELL OF ITS JUICES...
A DOLLOP OF GRATED DAIKON RADISH ON TOP, AND IT'S YUM, YUM, YUM!
THAT'S A GENERAL INGREDIENT FOR YOU. YOU CAN DO TONS OF STUFF WITH IT.
AS YOU ALL KNOW, PIKE CAN BE USED IN A WIDE VARIETY OF DISHES.
BUT STRANGELY ENOUGH, THIS ONE INGREDIENT ...
...HAS CONNECTIONS TO ALL THREE OF OUR CON-TESTANTS.
?
A PIKE...

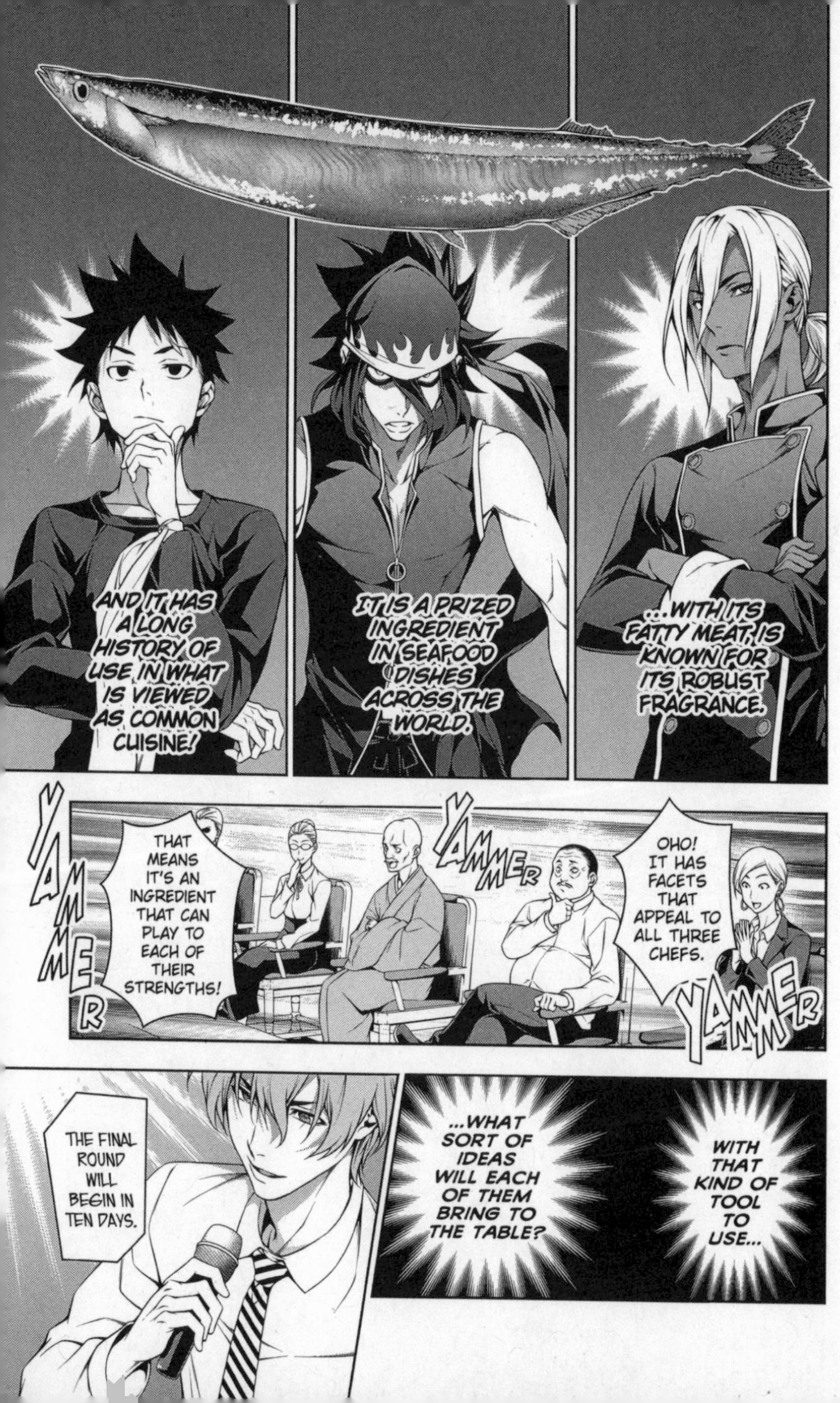
...WITH ITS FATTY MEAT, IS KNOWN FOR ITS ROBUST FRAGRANCE.
IT IS A PRIZED INGREDIENT IN SEAFOOD DISHES ACROSS THE WORLD.
AND IT HAS A LONG HISTORY OF USE IN WHAT IS VIEWED AS COMMON CUISINE!
YAMMER
OHO! IT HAS FACETS THAT APPEAL TO ALL THREE CHEFS.
YAMMER
THAT MEANS IT'S AN INGREDIENT THAT CAN PLAY TO EACH OF THEIR STRENGTHS!
YAMMER
WITH THAT KIND OF TOOL TO USE...
...WHAT SORT OF IDEAS WILL EACH OF THEM BRING TO THE TABLE?
THE FINAL ROUND WILL BEGIN IN TEN DAYS.

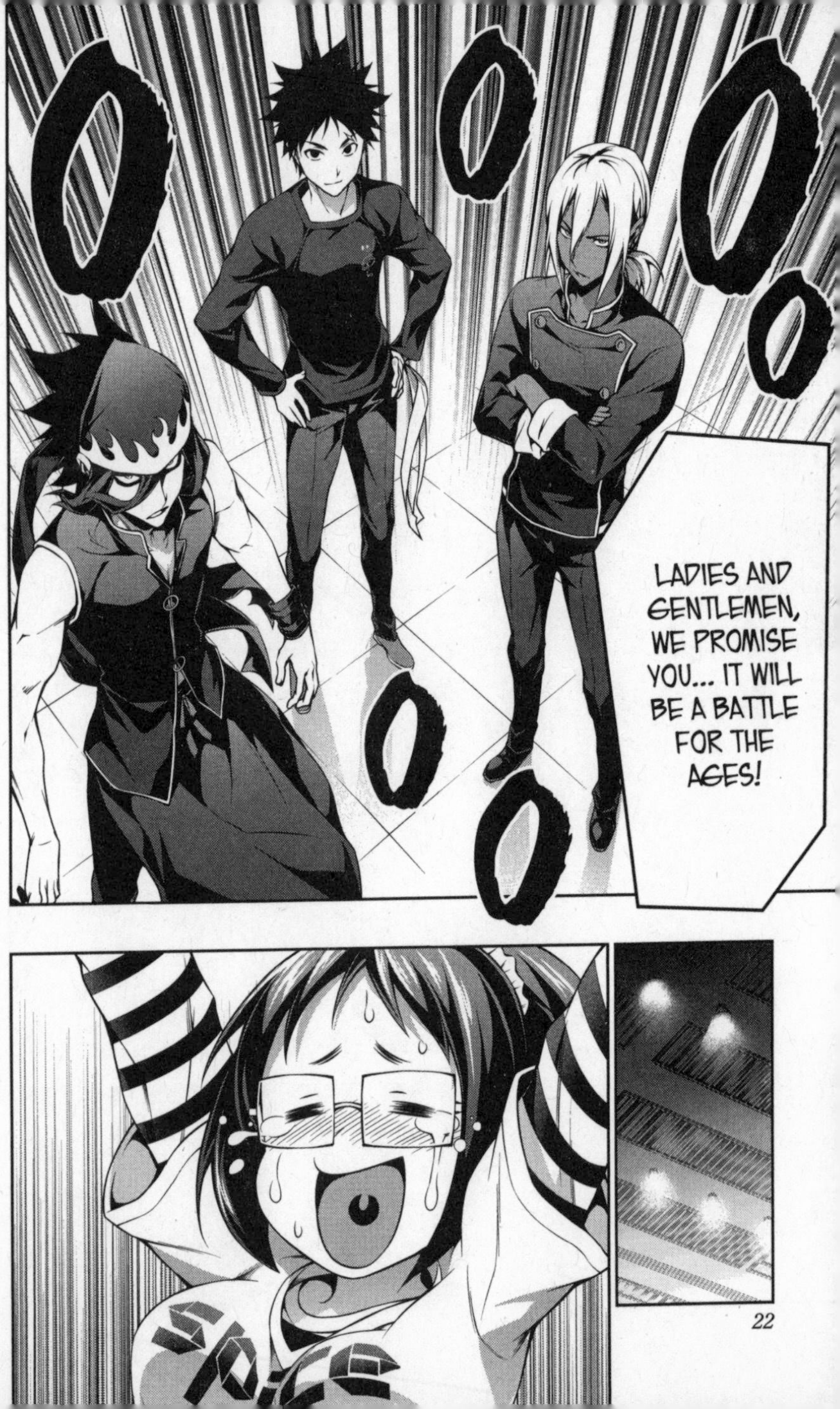
LADIES AND GENTLEMEN, WE PROMISE YOU... IT WILL BE A BATTLE FOR THE AGES!

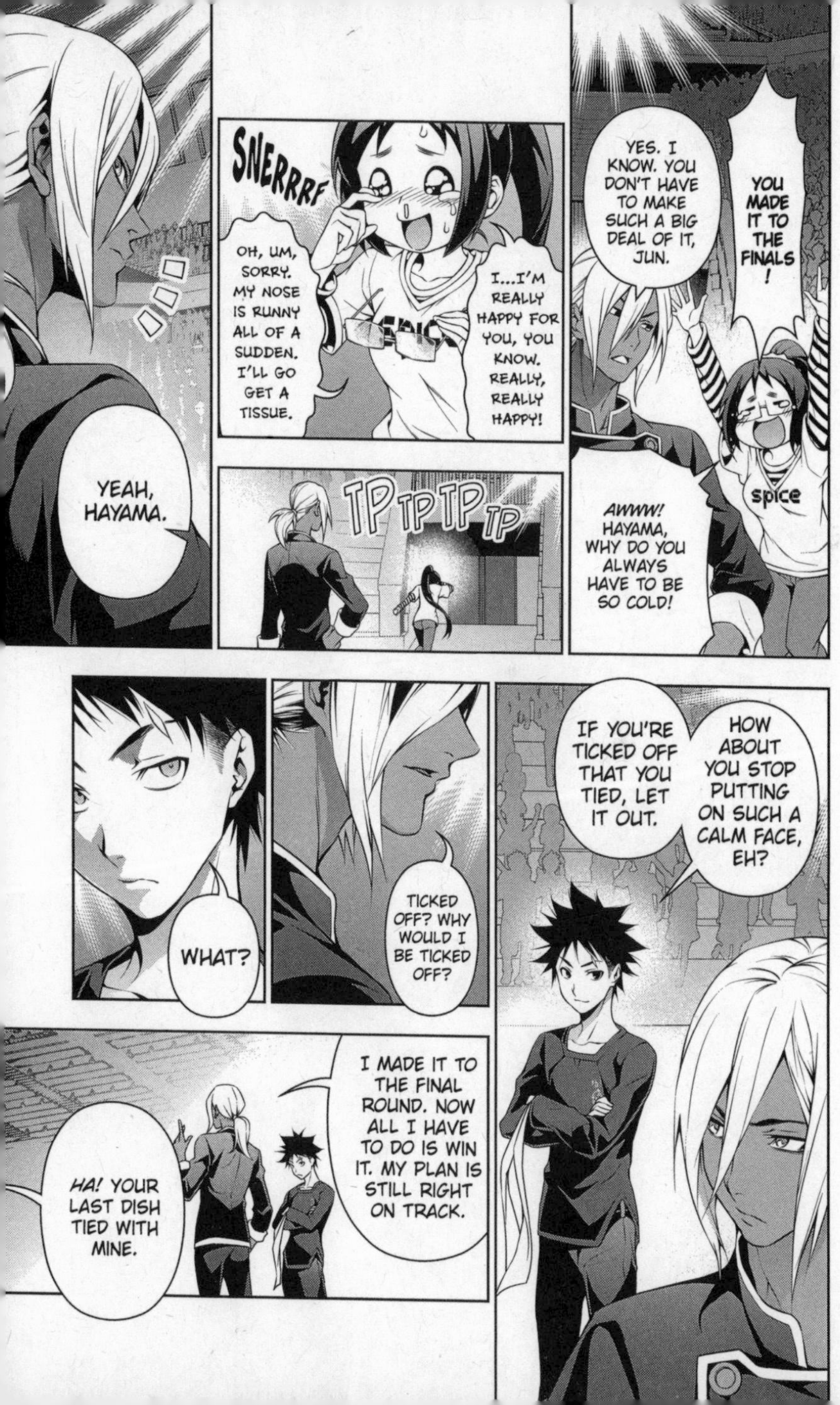
YOU MADE IT TO THE FINALS!
YES. I KNOW. YOU DON'T HAVE TO MAKE SUCH A BIG DEAL OF IT, JUN.
AWWW! HAYAMA, WHY DO YOU ALWAYS HAVE TO BE SO COLD!
I...I'M REALLY HAPPY FOR YOU, YOU KNOW. REALLY, REALLY HAPPY!
SNERRRF
OH, UM, SORRY. MY NOSE IS RUNNY ALL OF A SUDDEN. I'LL GO GET A TISSUE.
TP TP TP TP
YEAH, HAYAMA.
HOW ABOUT YOU STOP PUTTING ON SUCH A CALM FACE, EH?
IF YOU'RE TICKED OFF THAT YOU TIED, LET IT OUT.
TICKED OFF? WHY WOULD I BE TICKED OFF?
WHAT?
I MADE IT TO THE FINAL ROUND. NOW ALL I HAVE TO DO IS WIN IT. MY PLAN IS STILL RIGHT ON TRACK.
HA! YOUR LAST DISH TIED WITH MINE.

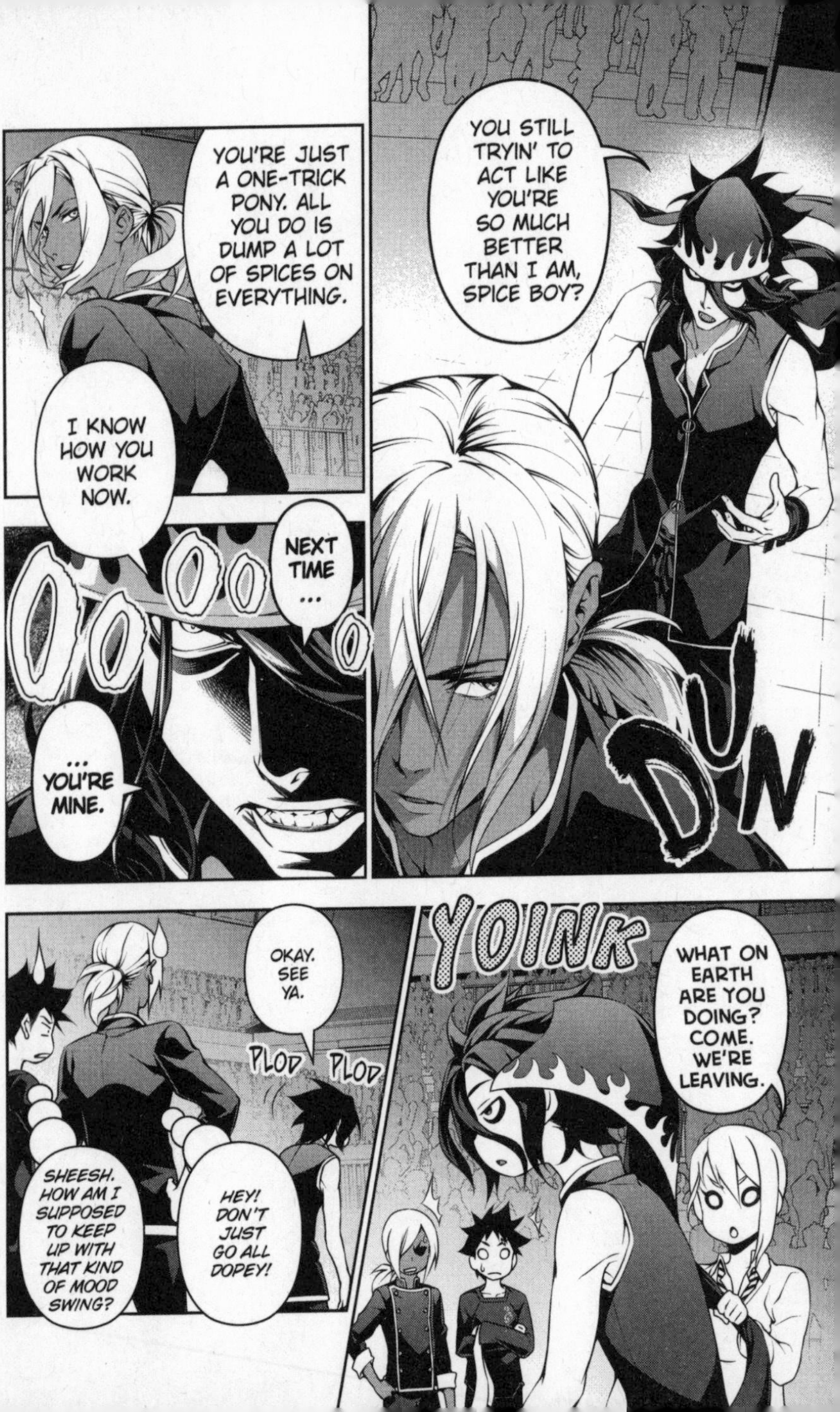
YOU STILL TRYIN' TO ACT LIKE YOU'RE SO MUCH BETTER THAN I AM, SPICE BOY?
DUN
YOU'RE JUST A ONE-TRICK PONY. ALL YOU DO IS DUMP A LOT OF SPICES ON EVERYTHING.
I KNOW HOW YOU WORK NOW.
NEXT TIME ...
... YOU'RE MINE.
YOINK
WHAT ON EARTH ARE YOU DOING? COME. WE'RE LEAVING.
OKAY. SEE YA.
PLOD PLOD
HEY! DON'T JUST GO ALL DOPEY!
SHEESH. HOW AM I SUPPOSED TO KEEP UP WITH THAT KIND OF MOOD SWING?

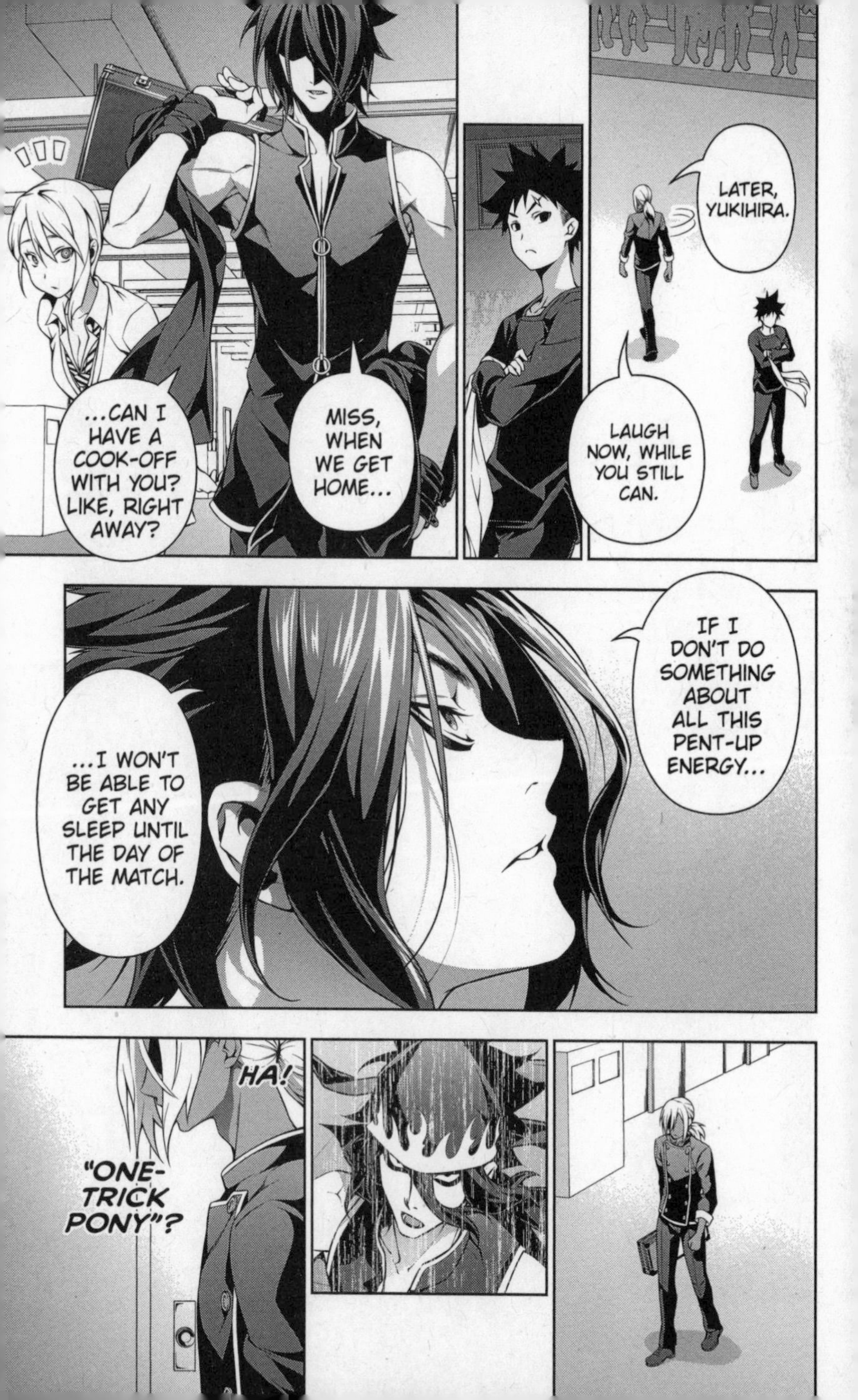
LATER, YUKIHIRA.
LAUGH NOW, WHILE YOU STILL CAN.
MISS, WHEN WE GET HOME...
...CAN I HAVE A COOK-OFF WITH YOU? LIKE, RIGHT AWAY?
IF I DON'T DO SOMETHING ABOUT ALL THIS PENT-UP ENERGY...
...I WON'T BE ABLE TO GET ANY SLEEP UNTIL THE DAY OF THE MATCH.
HA!
"ONE-TRICK PONY"?

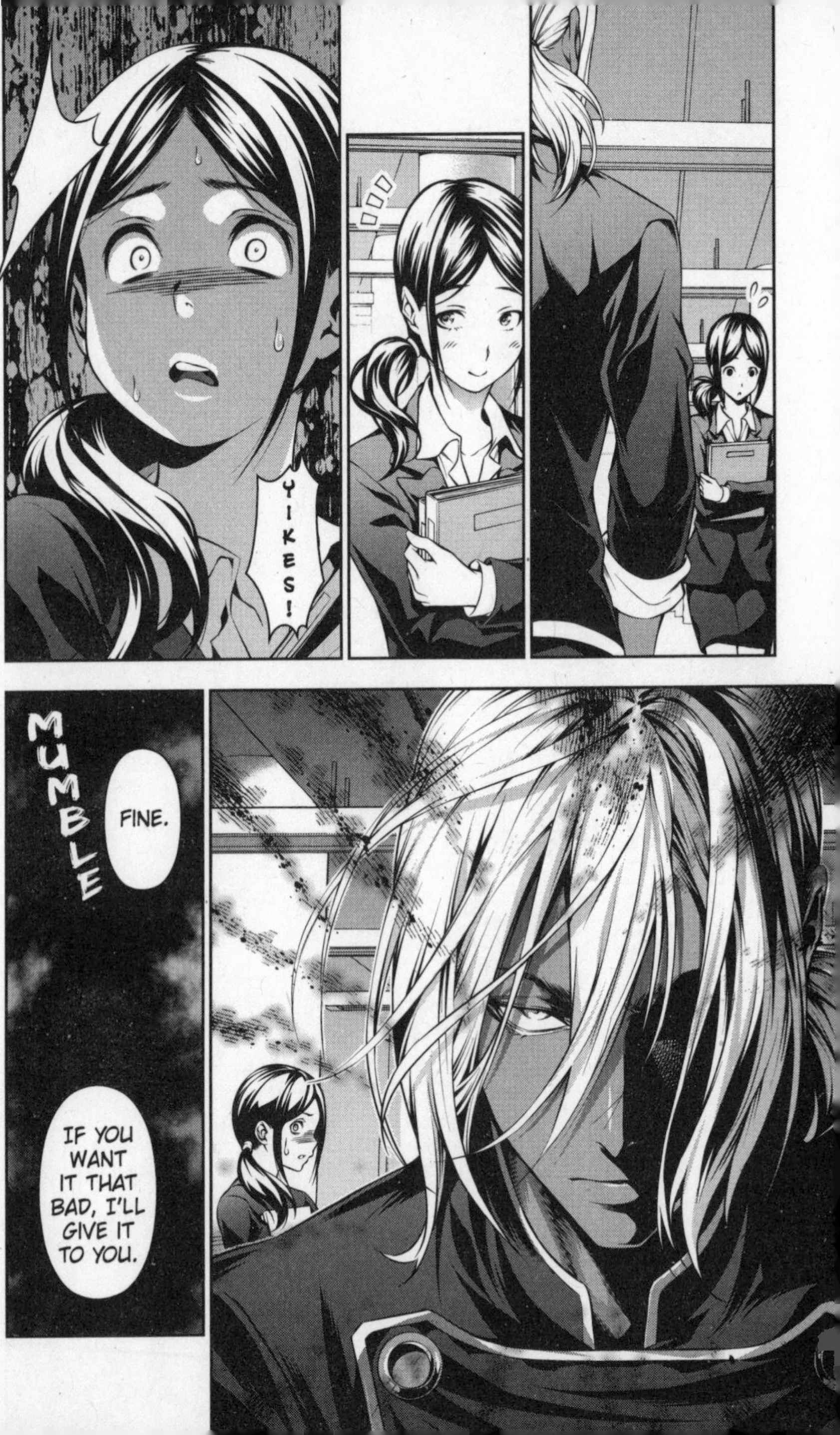
YIKES!
MUMBLE
FINE.
IF YOU WANT IT THAT BAD, I'LL GIVE IT TO YOU.

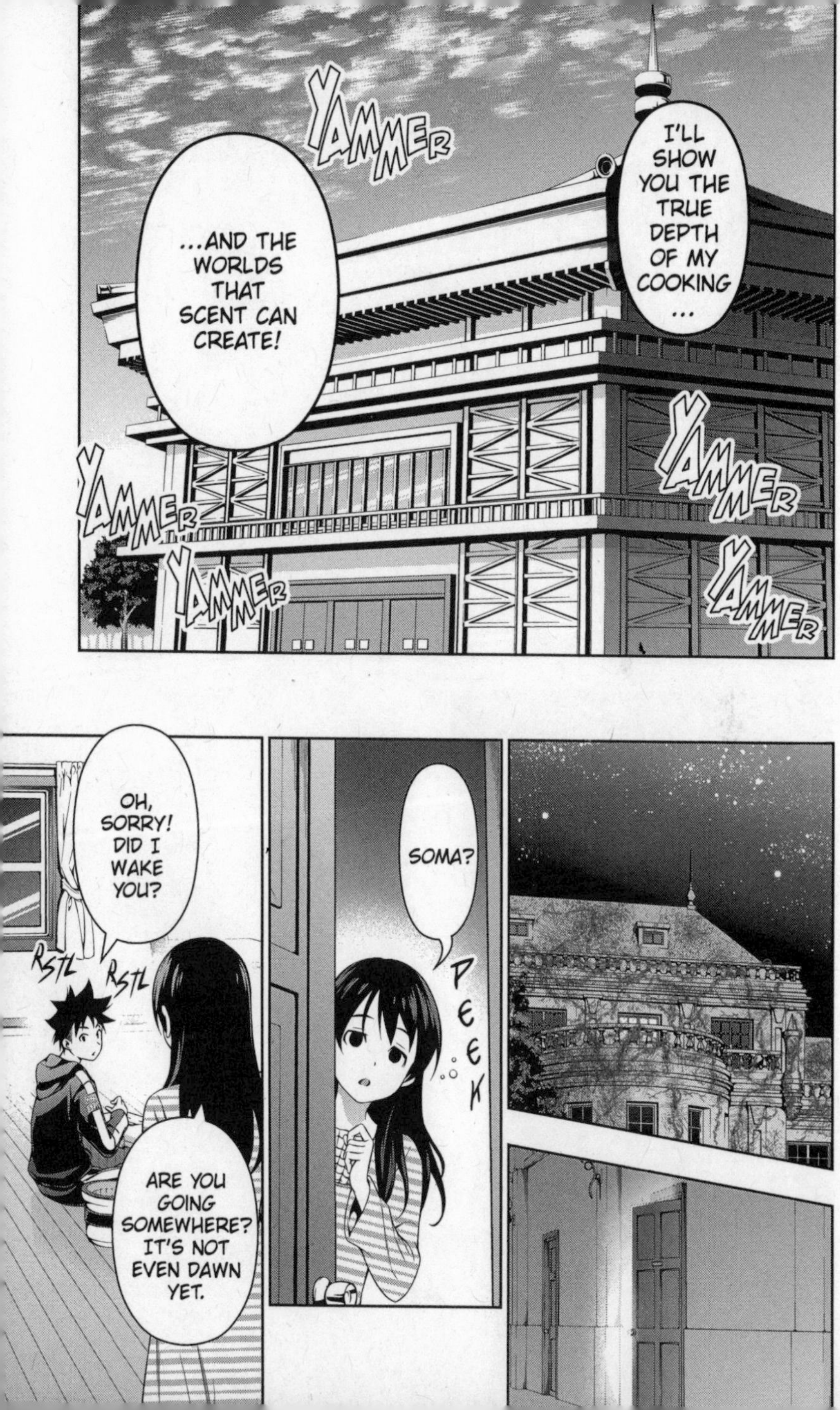
YAMMER
I'LL SHOW YOU THE TRUE DEPTH OF MY COOKING ...
...AND THE WORLDS THAT SCENT CAN CREATE!
YAMMER
YAMMER
YAMMER
YAMMER
SOMA?
PEEK
OH, SORRY! DID I WAKE YOU?
RSTL RSTL
ARE YOU GOING SOMEWHERE? IT'S NOT EVEN DAWN YET.

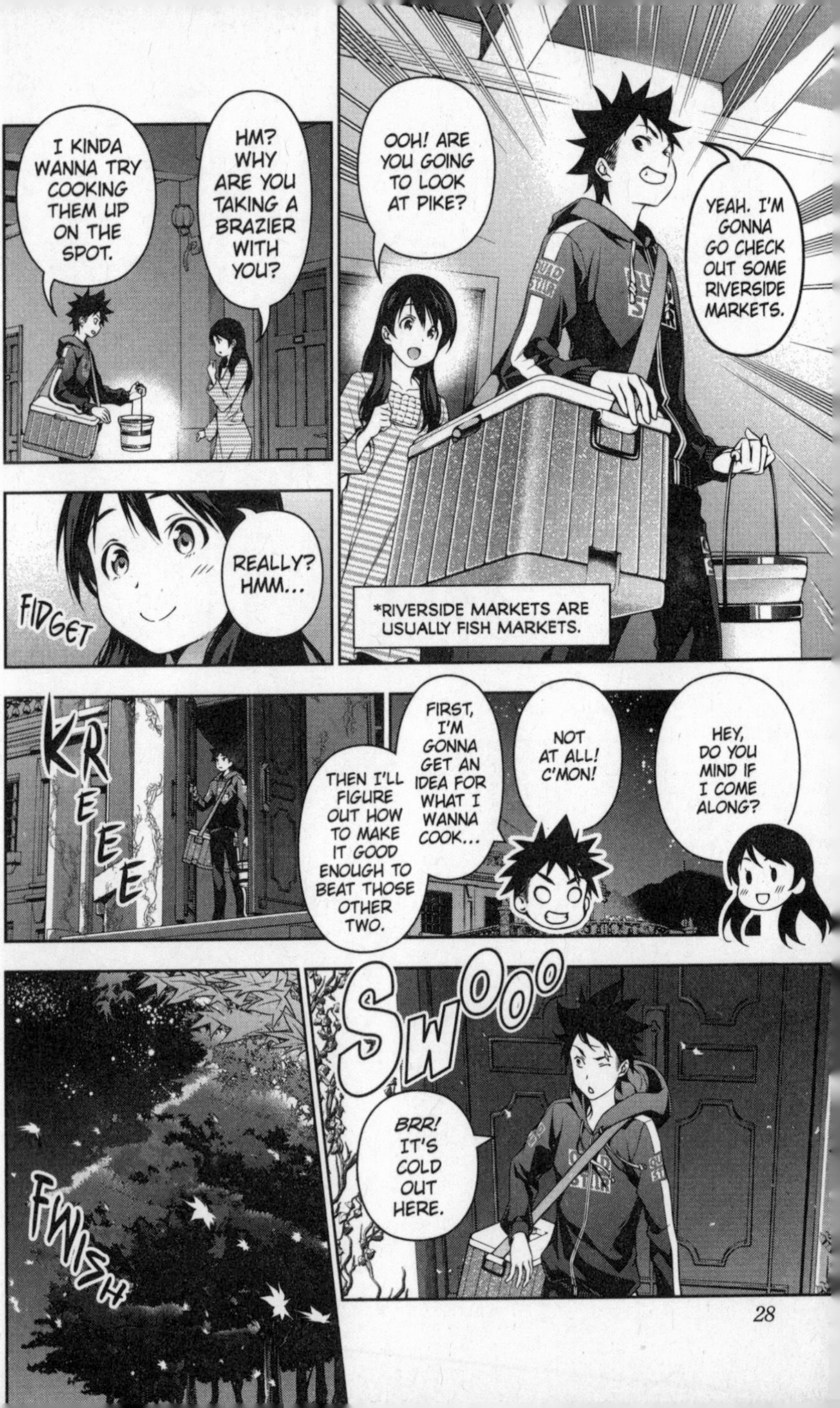
YEAH. I'M GONNA GO CHECK OUT SOME RIVERSIDE MARKETS.
OOH! ARE YOU GOING TO LOOK AT PIKE?
*RIVERSIDE MARKETS ARE USUALLY FISH MARKETS.
HM? WHY ARE YOU TAKING A BRAZIER WITH YOU?
I KINDA WANNA TRY COOKING THEM UP ON THE SPOT.
REALLY? HMM...
FIDGET
HEY, DO YOU MIND IF I COME ALONG?
NOT AT ALL! C'MON!
FIRST, I'M GONNA GET AN IDEA FOR WHAT I WANNA COOK...
THEN I'LL FIGURE OUT HOW TO MAKE IT GOOD ENOUGH TO BEAT THOSE OTHER TWO.
KREEE-E
SWOOO
BRR! IT'S COLD OUT HERE.
FWISH

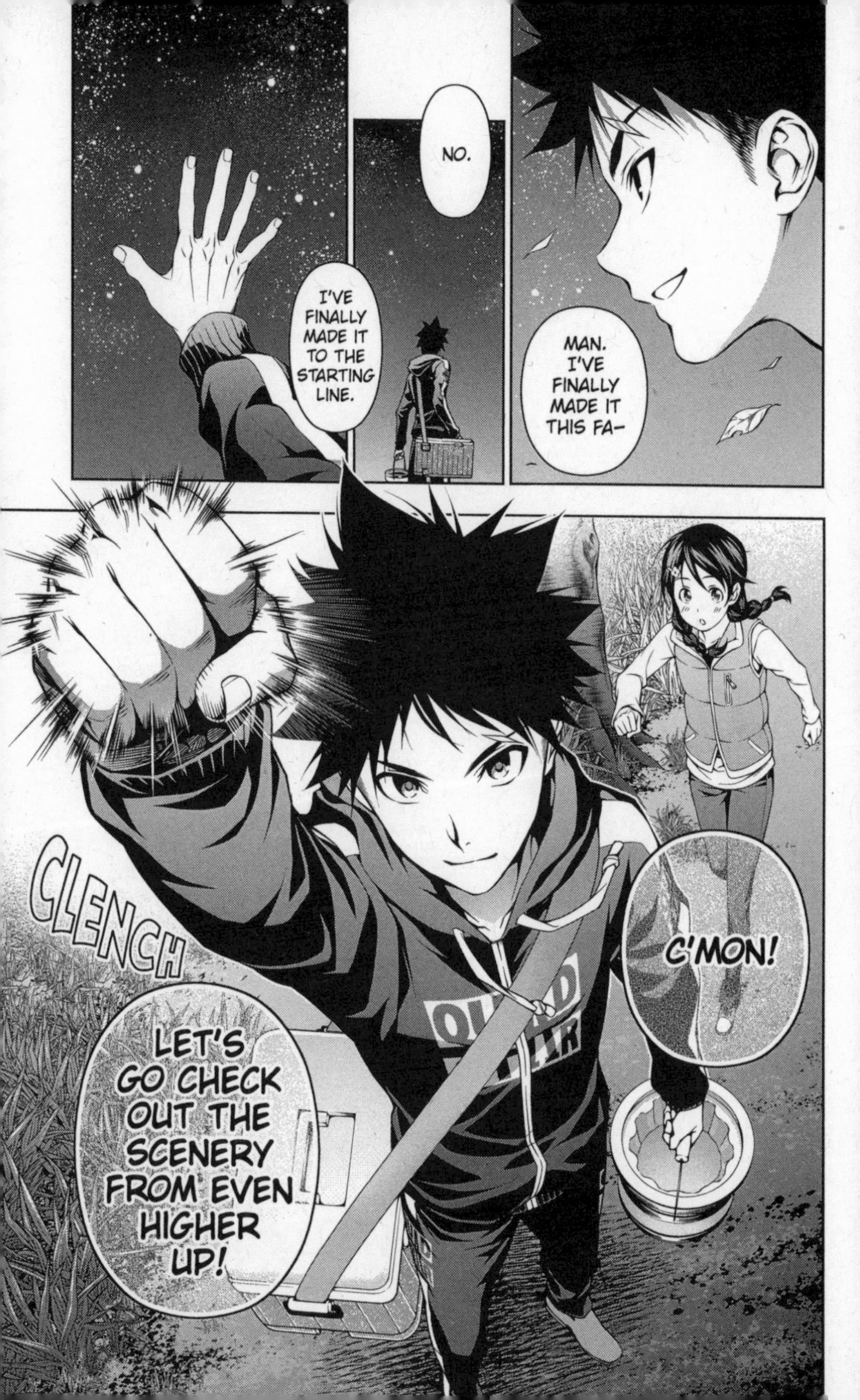
MAN. I'VE FINALLY MADE IT THIS FA-
NO.
I'VE FINALLY MADE IT TO THE STARTING LINE.
C'MON!
CLENCH
LET'S GO CHECK OUT THE SCENERY FROM EVEN HIGHER UP!

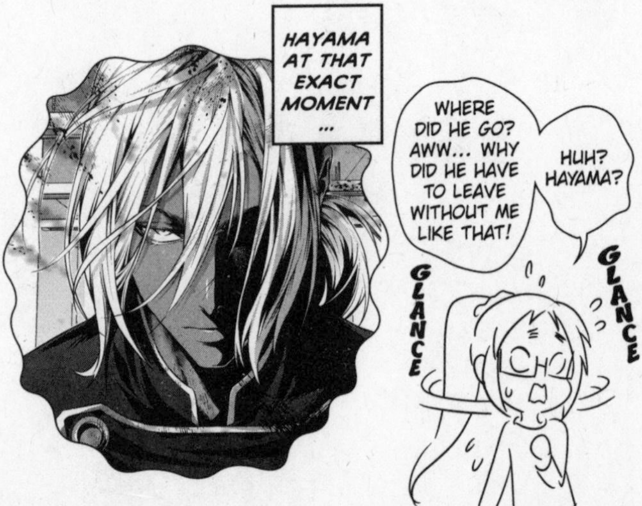
HUH? HAYAMA?
GLANCE
WHERE DID HE GO? AWW... WHY DID HE HAVE TO LEAVE WITHOUT ME LIKE THAT!
GLANCE
HAYAMA AT THAT EXACT MOMENT ...

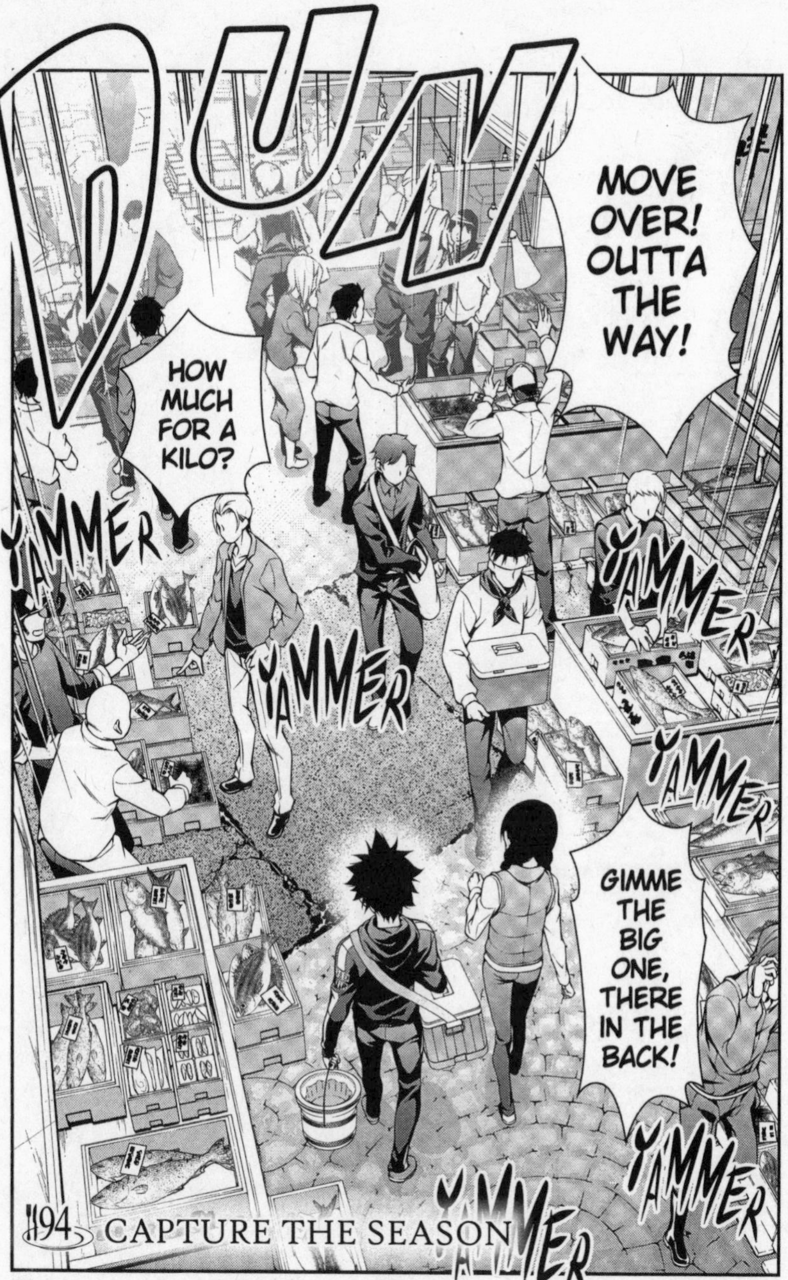
DUN
MOVE OVER! OUTTA THE WAY!
HOW MUCH FOR A KILO?
YAMMER
YAMMER
YAMMER
YAMMER
GIMME THE BIG ONE, THERE IN THE BACK!
YAMMER
YAMMER

194 CAPTURE THE SEASON

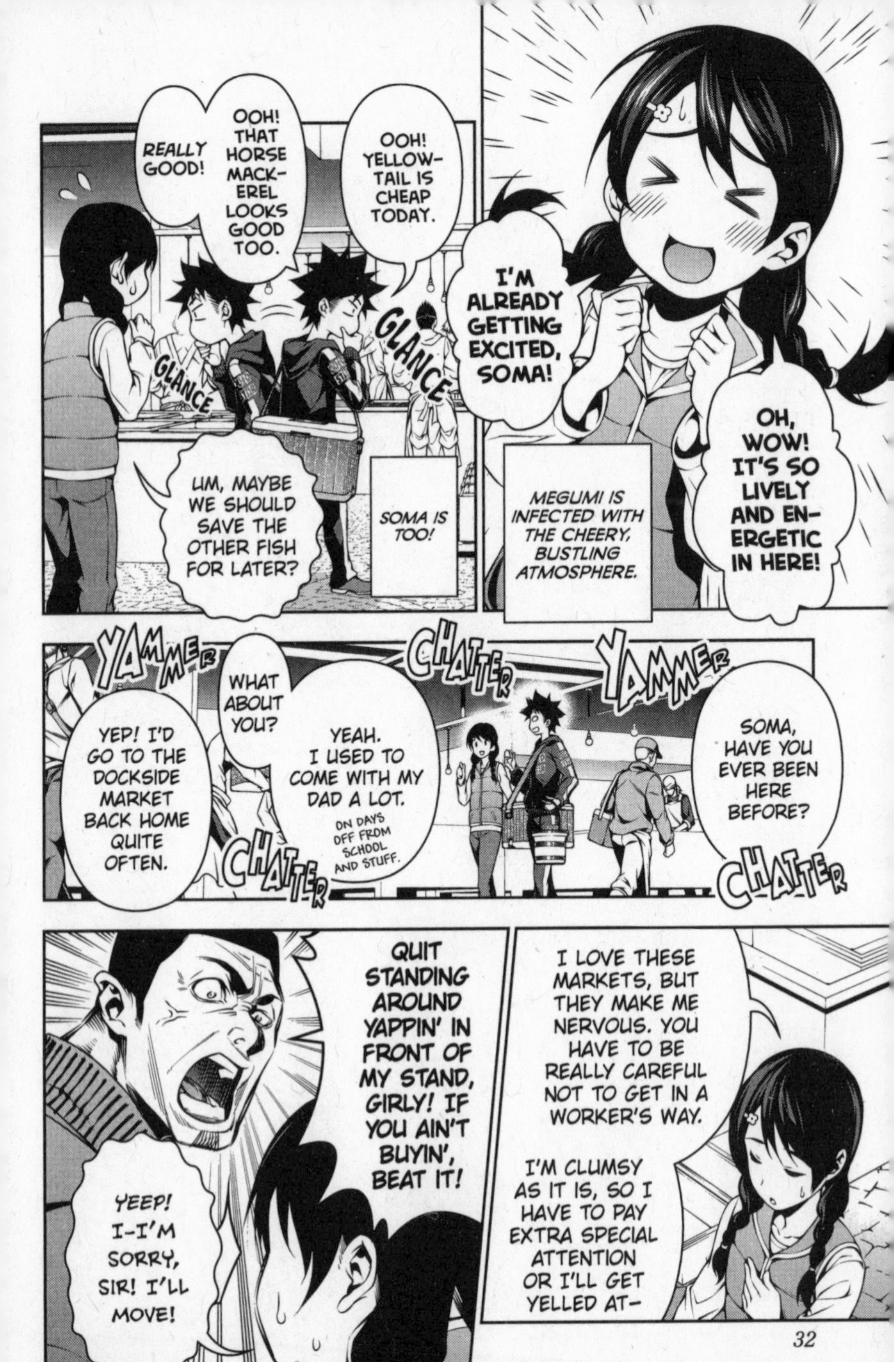
OH, WOW! IT'S SO LIVELY AND ENERGETIC IN HERE!
I'M ALREADY GETTING EXCITED, SOMA!
MEGUMI IS INFECTED WITH THE CHEERY, BUSTLING ATMOSPHERE.
OOH! YELLOWTAIL IS CHEAP TODAY.
OOH! THAT HORSE MACKEREL LOOKS GOOD TOO.
REALLY GOOD!
GLANCE
GLANCE
SOMA IS TOO!
UM, MAYBE WE SHOULD SAVE THE OTHER FISH FOR LATER?
YAMMER
CHATTER
SOMA, HAVE YOU EVER BEEN HERE BEFORE?
CHATTER
YEAH. I USED TO COME WITH MY DAD A LOT.
ON DAYS OFF FROM SCHOOL AND STUFF.
WHAT ABOUT YOU?
YAMMER
YEP! I'D GO TO THE DOCKSIDE MARKET BACK HOME QUITE OFTEN.
CHATTER
I LOVE THESE MARKETS, BUT THEY MAKE ME NERVOUS. YOU HAVE TO BE REALLY CAREFUL NOT TO GET IN A WORKER'S WAY.
I'M CLUMSY AS IT IS, SO I HAVE TO PAY EXTRA SPECIAL ATTENTION OR I'LL GET YELLED AT–
QUIT STANDING AROUND YAPPIN' IN FRONT OF MY STAND, GIRLY! IF YOU AIN'T BUYIN', BEAT IT!
YEEP! I-I'M SORRY, SIR! I'LL MOVE!

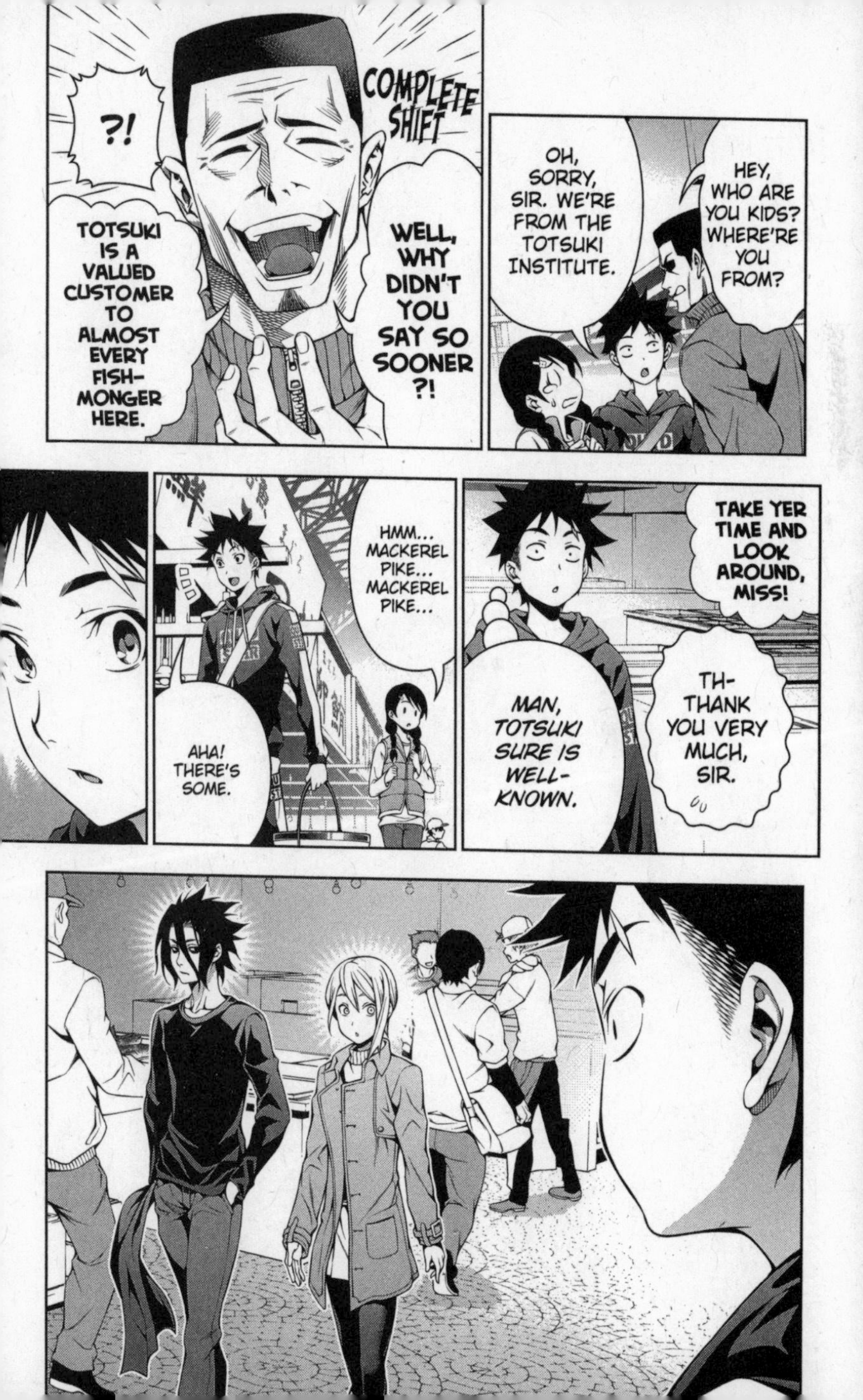
HEY, WHO ARE YOU KIDS? WHERE'RE YOU FROM?
OH, SORRY, SIR. WE'RE FROM THE TOTSUKI INSTITUTE.
COMPLETE SHIFT
WELL, WHY DIDN'T YOU SAY SO SOONER ?!
?!
TOTSUKI IS A VALUED CUSTOMER TO ALMOST EVERY FISH-MONGER HERE.
TAKE YER TIME AND LOOK AROUND, MISS!
TH-THANK YOU VERY MUCH, SIR.
MAN, TOTSUKI SURE IS WELL-KNOWN.
HMM... MACKEREL PIKE... MACKEREL PIKE...
AHA! THERE'S SOME.

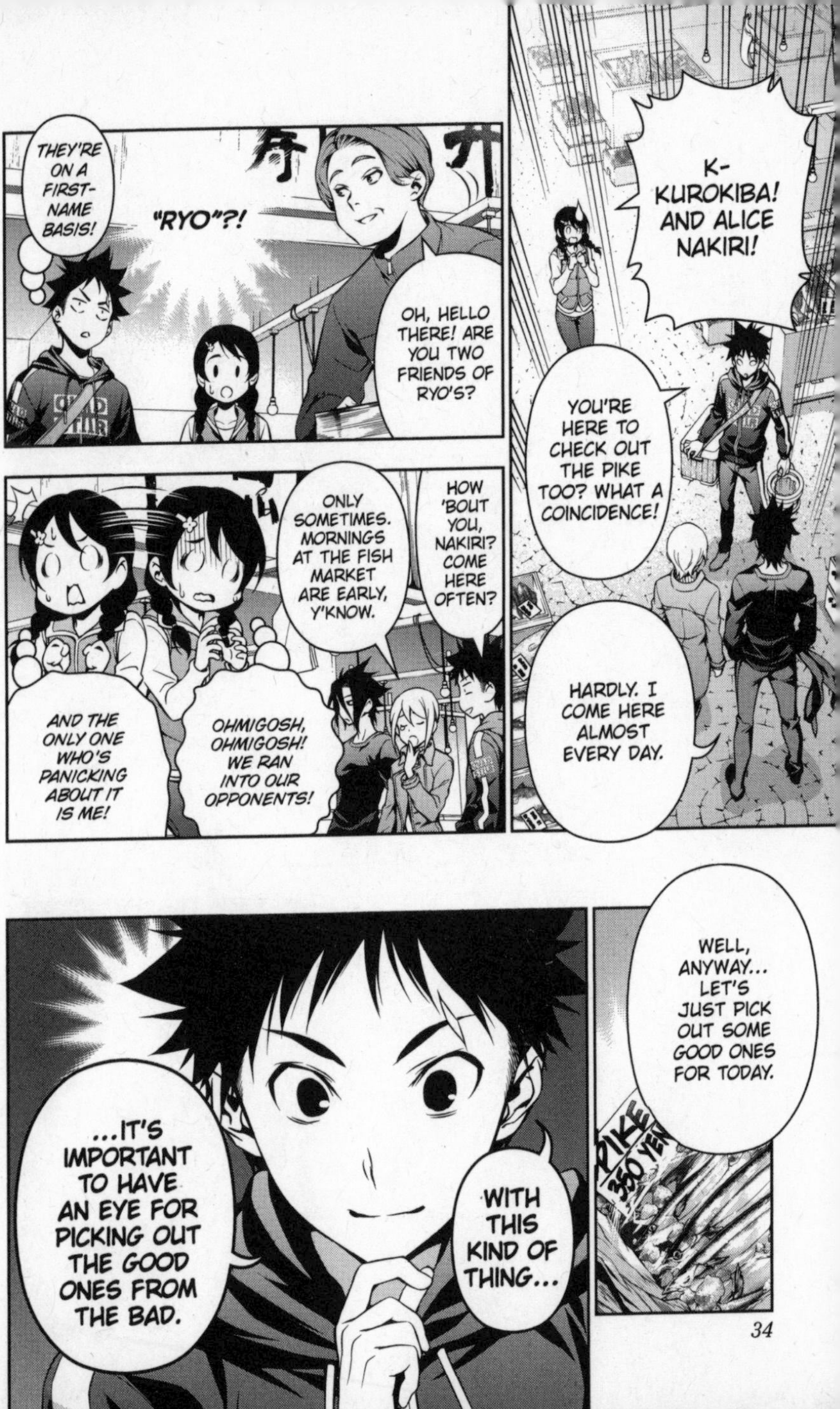
K-KUROKIBA! AND ALICE NAKIRI!
YOU'RE HERE TO CHECK OUT THE PIKE TOO? WHAT A COINCIDENCE!
HARDLY. I COME HERE ALMOST EVERY DAY.
OH, HELLO THERE! ARE YOU TWO FRIENDS OF RYO'S?
"RYO"?!
THEY'RE ON A FIRST-NAME BASIS!
HOW 'BOUT YOU, NAKIRI? COME HERE OFTEN?
ONLY SOMETIMES. MORNINGS AT THE FISH MARKET ARE EARLY, Y'KNOW.
OHMIGOSH, OHMIGOSH! WE RAN INTO OUR OPPONENTS!
AND THE ONLY ONE WHO'S PANICKING ABOUT IT IS ME!
WELL, ANYWAY... LET'S JUST PICK OUT SOME GOOD ONES FOR TODAY.
PIKE 350 YEN
WITH THIS KIND OF THING...
...IT'S IMPORTANT TO HAVE AN EYE FOR PICKING OUT THE GOOD ONES FROM THE BAD.

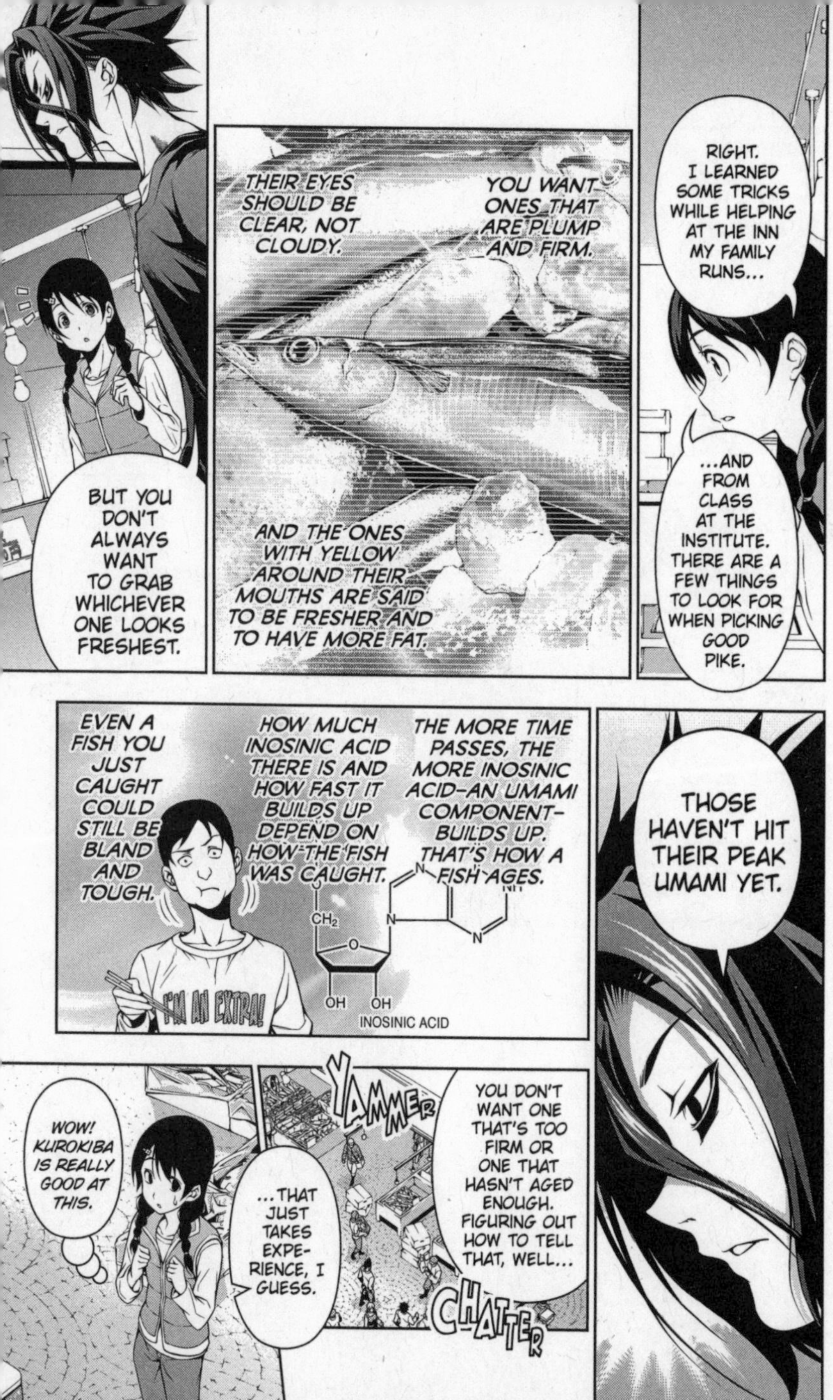
RIGHT. I LEARNED SOME TRICKS WHILE HELPING AT THE INN MY FAMILY RUNS...
...AND FROM CLASS AT THE INSTITUTE. THERE ARE A FEW THINGS TO LOOK FOR WHEN PICKING GOOD PIKE.
YOU WANT ONES THAT ARE PLUMP AND FIRM.
THEIR EYES SHOULD BE CLEAR, NOT CLOUDY.
AND THE ONES WITH YELLOW AROUND THEIR MOUTHS ARE SAID TO BE FRESHER AND TO HAVE MORE FAT.
BUT YOU DON'T ALWAYS WANT TO GRAB WHICHEVER ONE LOOKS FRESHEST.
THOSE HAVEN'T HIT THEIR PEAK UMAMI YET.
THE MORE TIME PASSES, THE MORE INOSINIC ACID–AN UMAMI COMPONENT–BUILDS UP. THAT'S HOW A FISH AGES.
HOW MUCH INOSINIC ACID THERE IS AND HOW FAST IT BUILDS UP DEPEND ON HOW THE FISH WAS CAUGHT.
EVEN A FISH YOU JUST CAUGHT COULD STILL BE BLAND AND TOUGH.
I'M AN EXTRA!
CH2
OH
OH
INOSINIC ACID
YAMMER
YOU DON'T WANT ONE THAT'S TOO FIRM OR ONE THAT HASN'T AGED ENOUGH. FIGURING OUT HOW TO TELL THAT, WELL...
CHATTER
...THAT JUST TAKES EXPE-RIENCE, I GUESS.
WOW! KUROKIBA IS REALLY GOOD AT THIS.

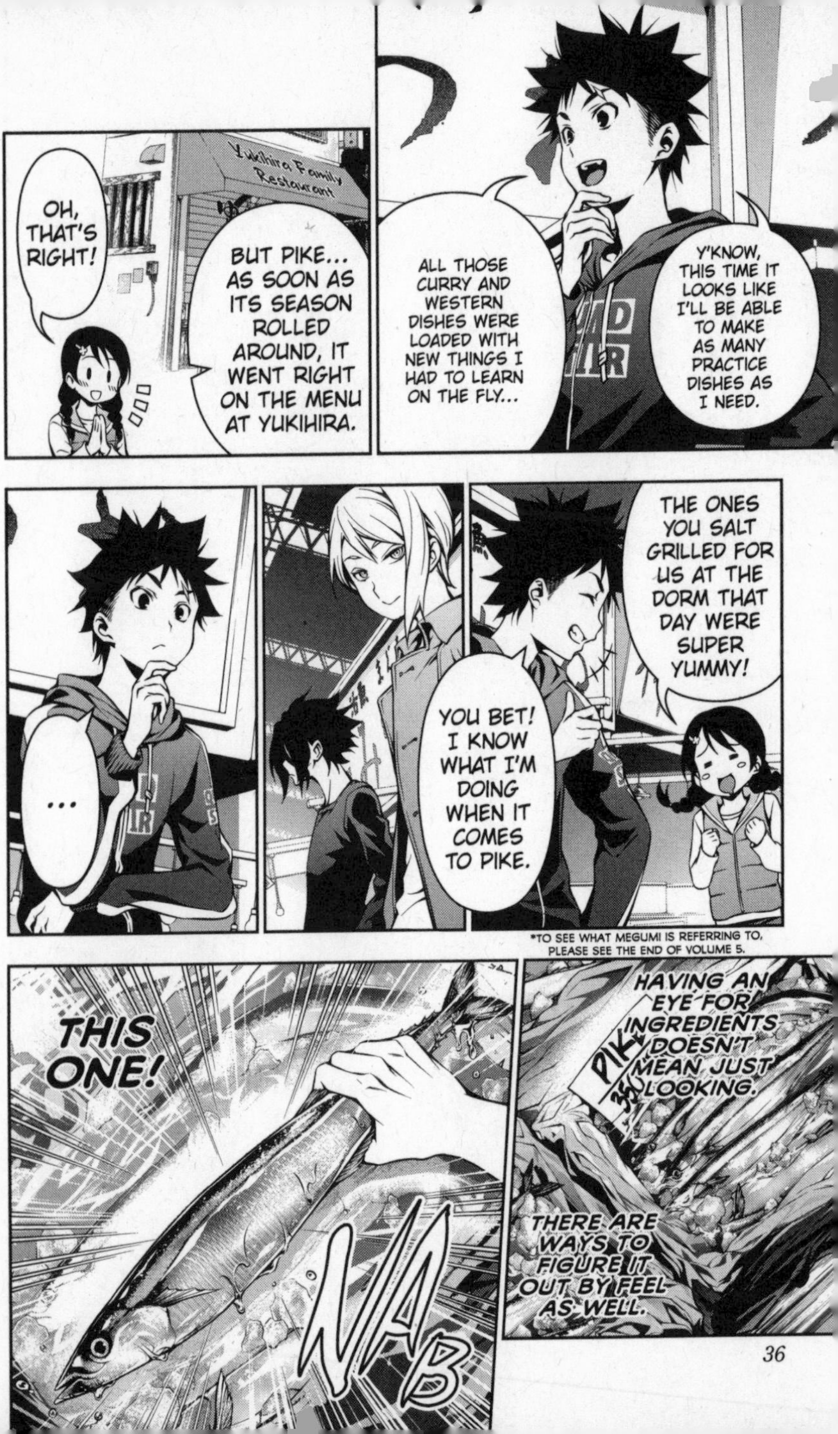
Y'KNOW, THIS TIME IT LOOKS LIKE I'LL BE ABLE TO MAKE AS MANY PRACTICE DISHES AS I NEED.
ALL THOSE CURRY AND WESTERN DISHES WERE LOADED WITH NEW THINGS I HAD TO LEARN ON THE FLY...
BUT PIKE... AS SOON AS ITS SEASON ROLLED AROUND, IT WENT RIGHT ON THE MENU AT YUKIHIRA.
OH, THAT'S RIGHT!
Yukihira Family Restaurant
THE ONES YOU SALT GRILLED FOR US AT THE DORM THAT DAY WERE SUPER YUMMY!
YOU BET! I KNOW WHAT I'M DOING WHEN IT COMES TO PIKE.
...
*TO SEE WHAT MEGUMI IS REFERRING TO, PLEASE SEE THE END OF VOLUME 5.
HAVING AN EYE FOR INGREDIENTS DOESN'T MEAN JUST LOOKING.
THERE ARE WAYS TO FIGURE IT OUT BY FEEL AS WELL.
THIS ONE!
NAB

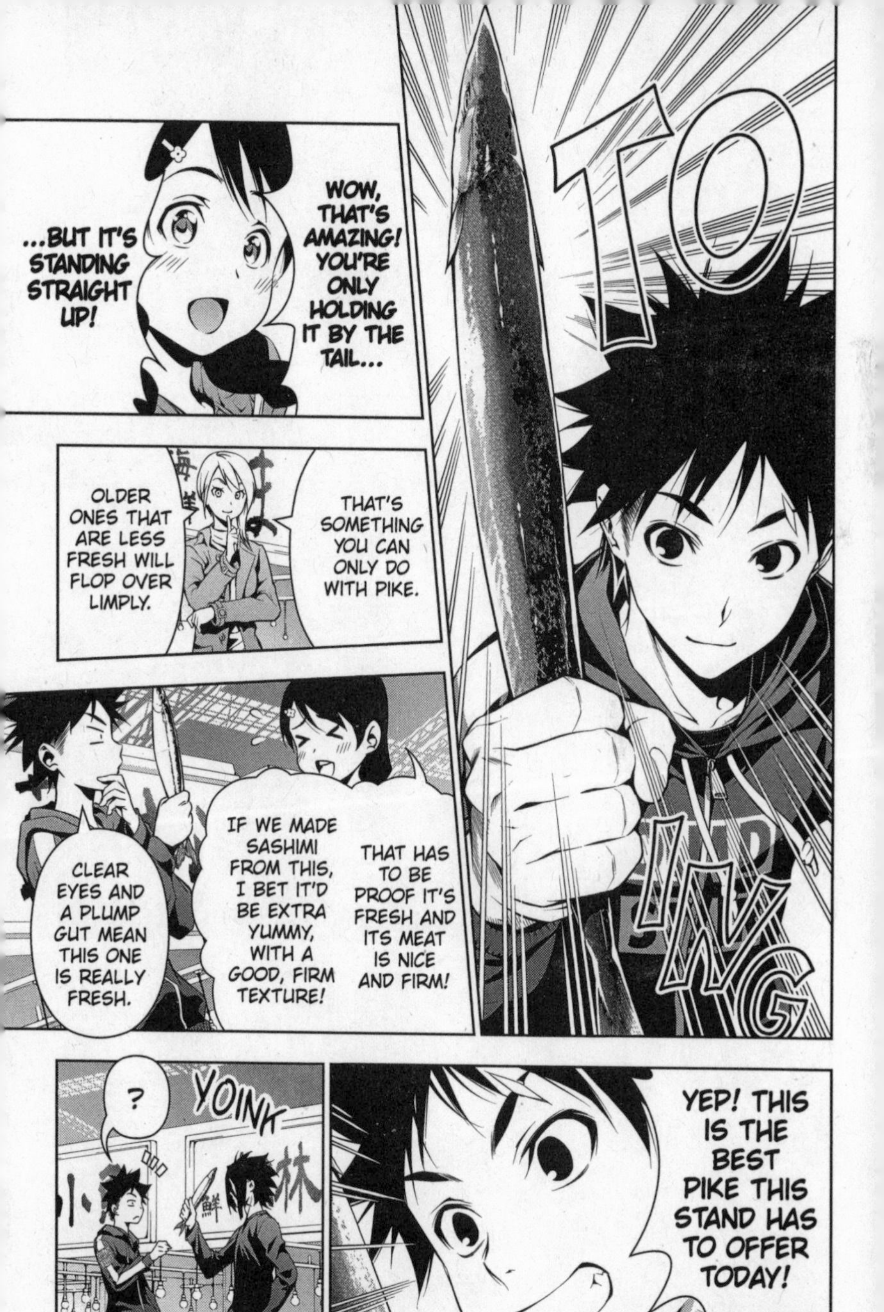
TO
ING
WOW, THAT'S AMAZING! YOU'RE ONLY HOLDING IT BY THE TAIL...
...BUT IT'S STANDING STRAIGHT UP!
THAT'S SOMETHING YOU CAN ONLY DO WITH PIKE.
OLDER ONES THAT ARE LESS FRESH WILL FLOP OVER LIMPLY.
THAT HAS TO BE PROOF IT'S FRESH AND ITS MEAT IS NICE AND FIRM!
IF WE MADE SASHIMI FROM THIS, I BET IT'D BE EXTRA YUMMY, WITH A GOOD, FIRM TEXTURE!
CLEAR EYES AND A PLUMP GUT MEAN THIS ONE IS REALLY FRESH.
YEP! THIS IS THE BEST PIKE THIS STAND HAS TO OFFER TODAY!
YOINK
?

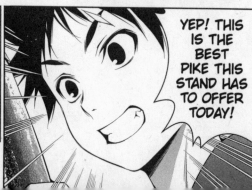

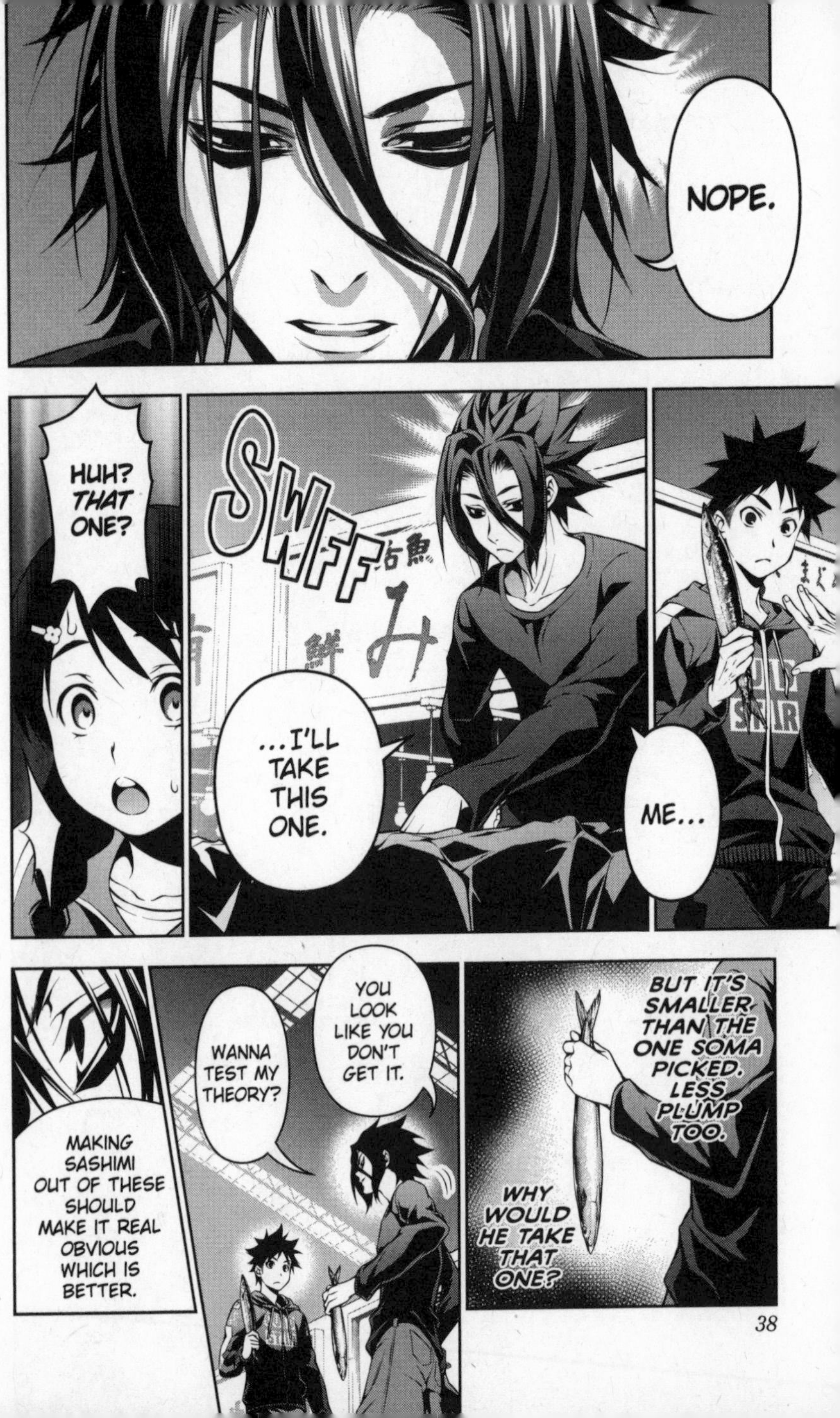
NOPE.
ME...
SWFF
...I'LL TAKE THIS ONE.
HUH? THAT ONE?
BUT IT'S SMALLER THAN THE ONE SOMA PICKED. LESS PLUMP TOO.
WHY WOULD HE TAKE THAT ONE?
YOU LOOK LIKE YOU DON'T GET IT.
WANNA TEST MY THEORY?
MAKING SASHIMI OUT OF THESE SHOULD MAKE IT REAL OBVIOUS WHICH IS BETTER.

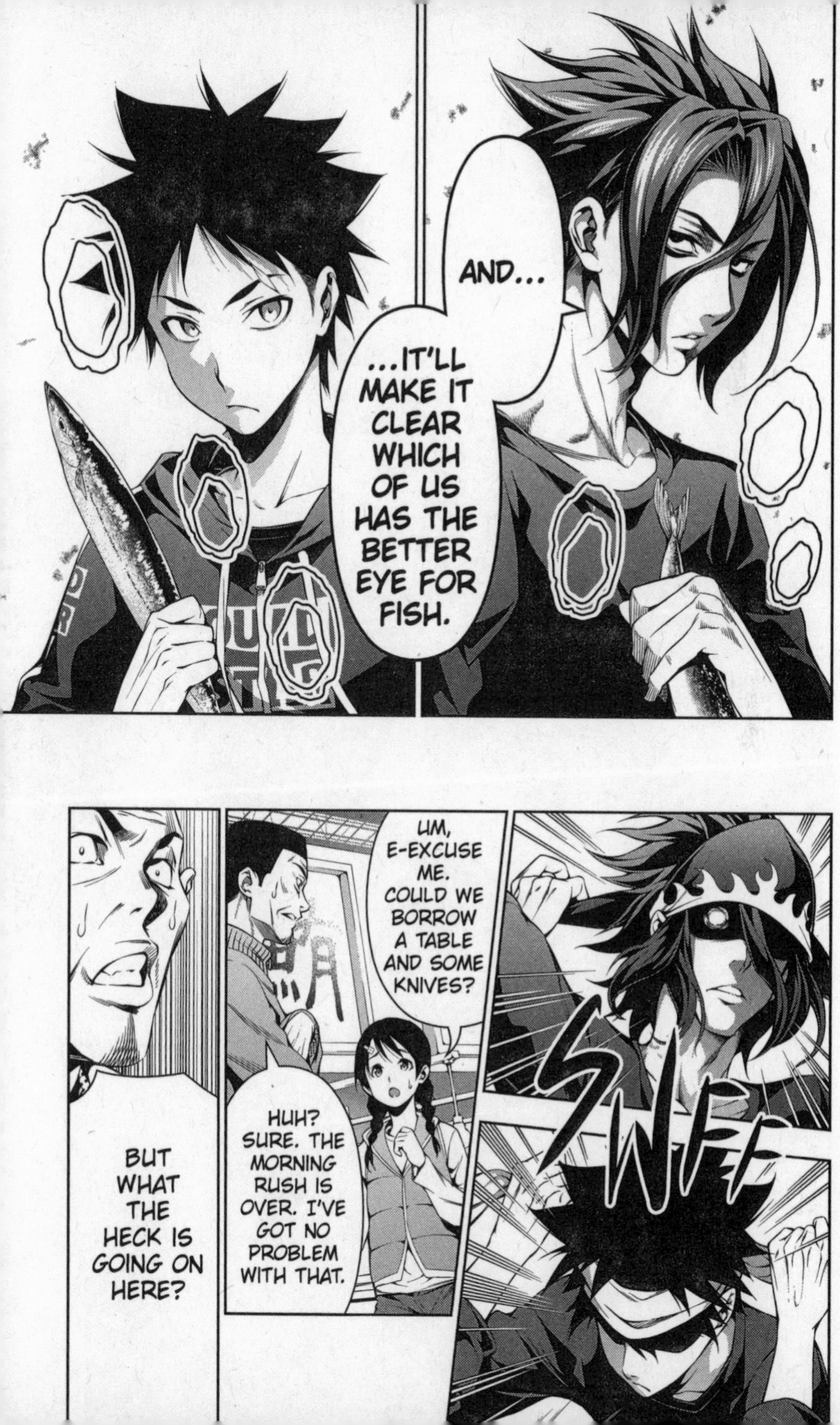
AND...
...IT'LL MAKE IT CLEAR WHICH OF US HAS THE BETTER EYE FOR FISH.
SWFF
UM, E-EXCUSE ME. COULD WE BORROW A TABLE AND SOME KNIVES?
HUH? SURE. THE MORNING RUSH IS OVER. I'VE GOT NO PROBLEM WITH THAT.
BUT WHAT THE HECK IS GOING ON HERE?

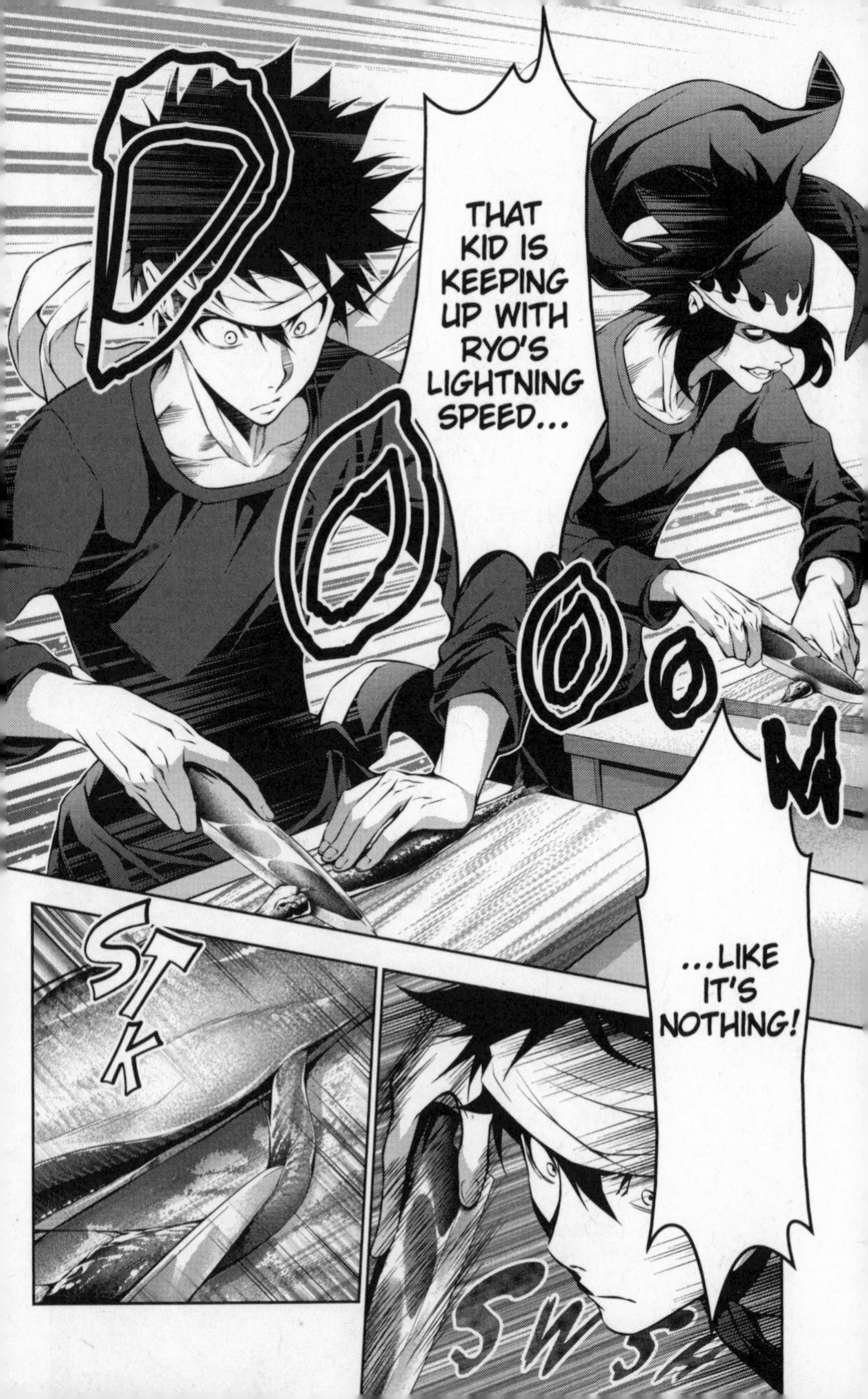
THAT KID IS KEEPING UP WITH RYO'S LIGHTNING SPEED...
...LIKE IT'S NOTHING!
STK

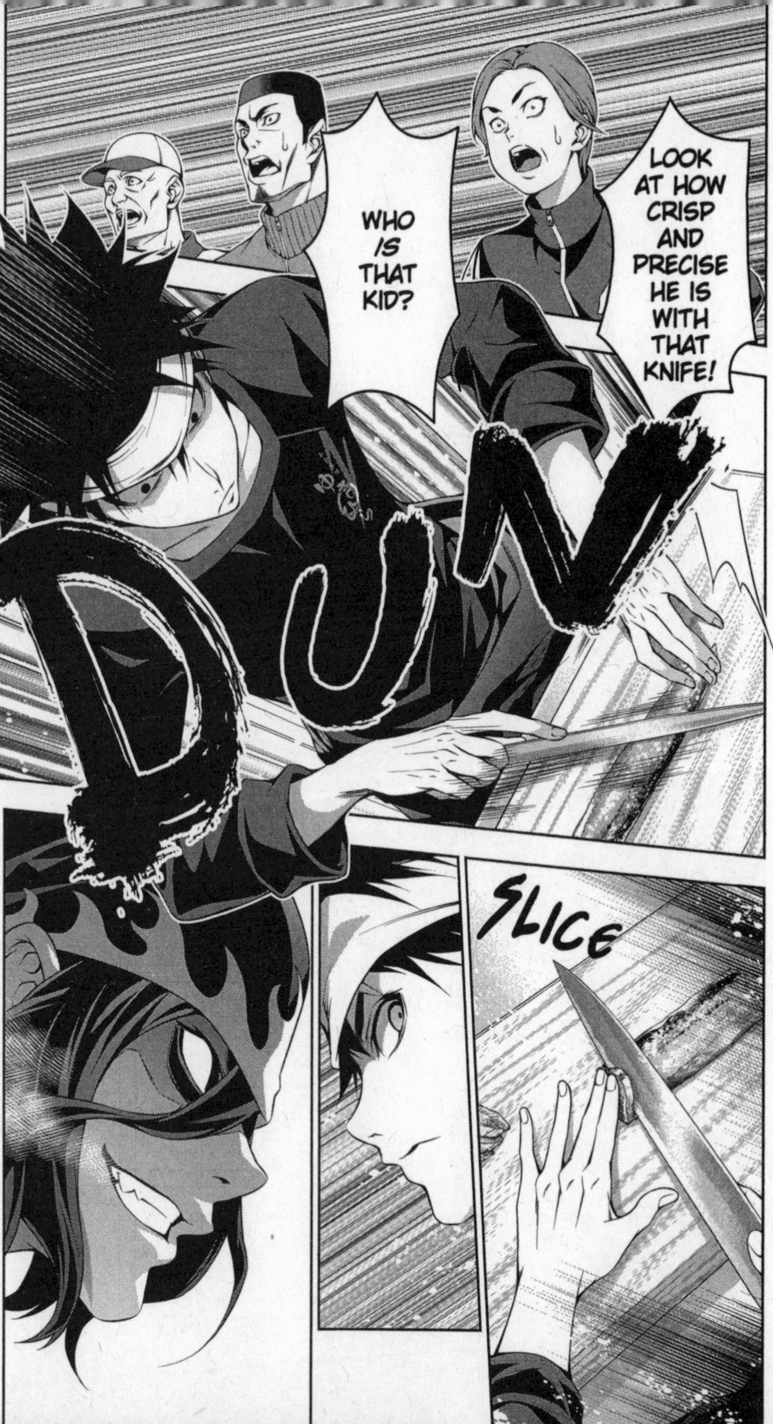
LOOK AT HOW CRISP AND PRECISE HE IS WITH THAT KNIFE!
WHO IS THAT KID?
DUN
SLICE

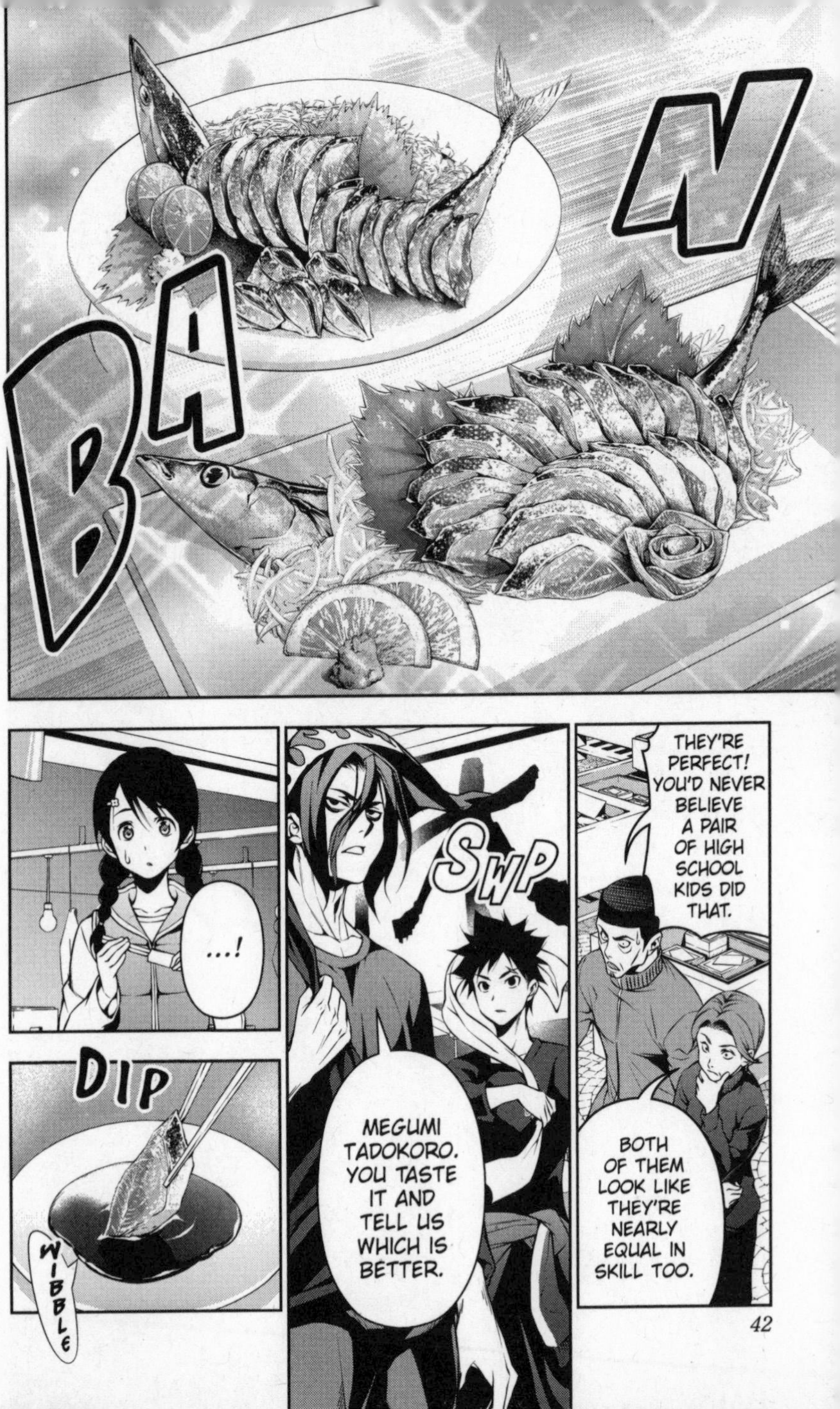
BAN
THEY'RE PERFECT! YOU'D NEVER BELIEVE A PAIR OF HIGH SCHOOL KIDS DID THAT.
BOTH OF THEM LOOK LIKE THEY'RE NEARLY EQUAL IN SKILL TOO.
SWP
MEGUMI TADOKORO. YOU TASTE IT AND TELL US WHICH IS BETTER.
...!
DIP
WIBBLE

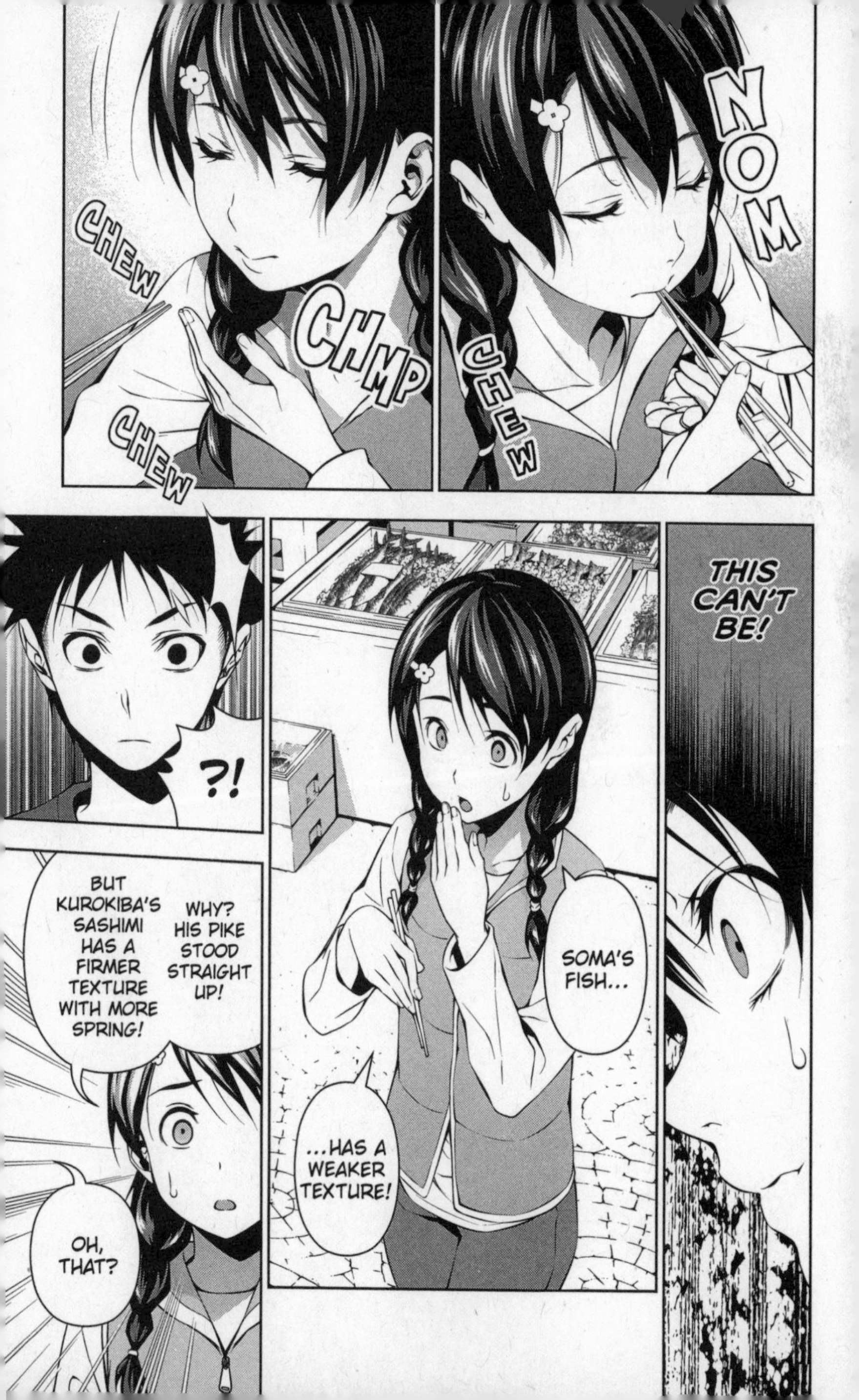
NOM
CHEW
CHEW
CHMP
CHEW
THIS CAN'T BE!
SOMA'S FISH...
...HAS A WEAKER TEXTURE!
?!
BUT KUROKIBA'S SASHIMI HAS A FIRMER TEXTURE WITH MORE SPRING!
WHY? HIS PIKE STOOD STRAIGHT UP!
OH, THAT?

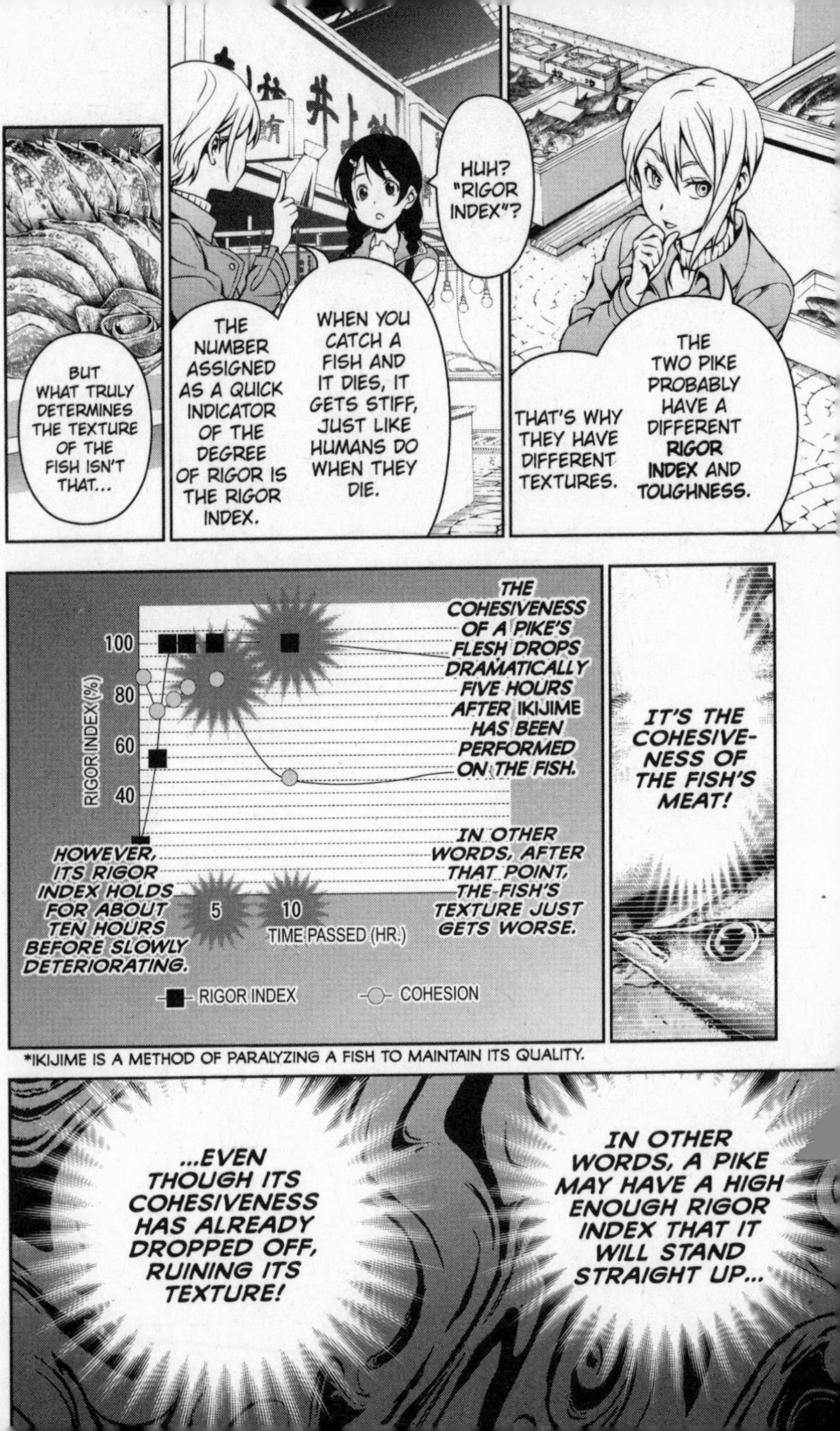
THE TWO PIKE PROBABLY HAVE A DIFFERENT **RIGOR INDEX** AND TOUGHNESS.
THAT'S WHY THEY HAVE DIFFERENT TEXTURES.
HUH? "RIGOR INDEX"?
WHEN YOU CATCH A FISH AND IT DIES, IT GETS STIFF, JUST LIKE HUMANS DO WHEN THEY DIE.
THE NUMBER ASSIGNED AS A QUICK INDICATOR OF THE DEGREE OF RIGOR IS THE RIGOR INDEX.
BUT WHAT TRULY DETERMINES THE TEXTURE OF THE FISH ISN'T THAT...
IT'S THE COHESIVENESS OF THE FISH'S MEAT!
THE COHESIVENESS OF A PIKE'S FLESH DROPS DRAMATICALLY FIVE HOURS AFTER IKIJIME HAS BEEN PERFORMED ON THE FISH.
IN OTHER WORDS, AFTER THAT POINT, THE FISH'S TEXTURE JUST GETS WORSE.
HOWEVER, ITS RIGOR INDEX HOLDS FOR ABOUT TEN HOURS BEFORE SLOWLY DETERIORATING.
RIGOR INDEX (%)
100
80
60
40
5
10
TIME PASSED (HR.)
RIGOR INDEX
COHESION
IN OTHER WORDS, A PIKE MAY HAVE A HIGH ENOUGH RIGOR INDEX THAT IT WILL STAND STRAIGHT UP...
...EVEN THOUGH ITS COHESIVENESS HAS ALREADY DROPPED OFF, RUINING ITS TEXTURE!

*IKIJIME IS A METHOD OF PARALYZING A FISH TO MAINTAIN ITS QUALITY.

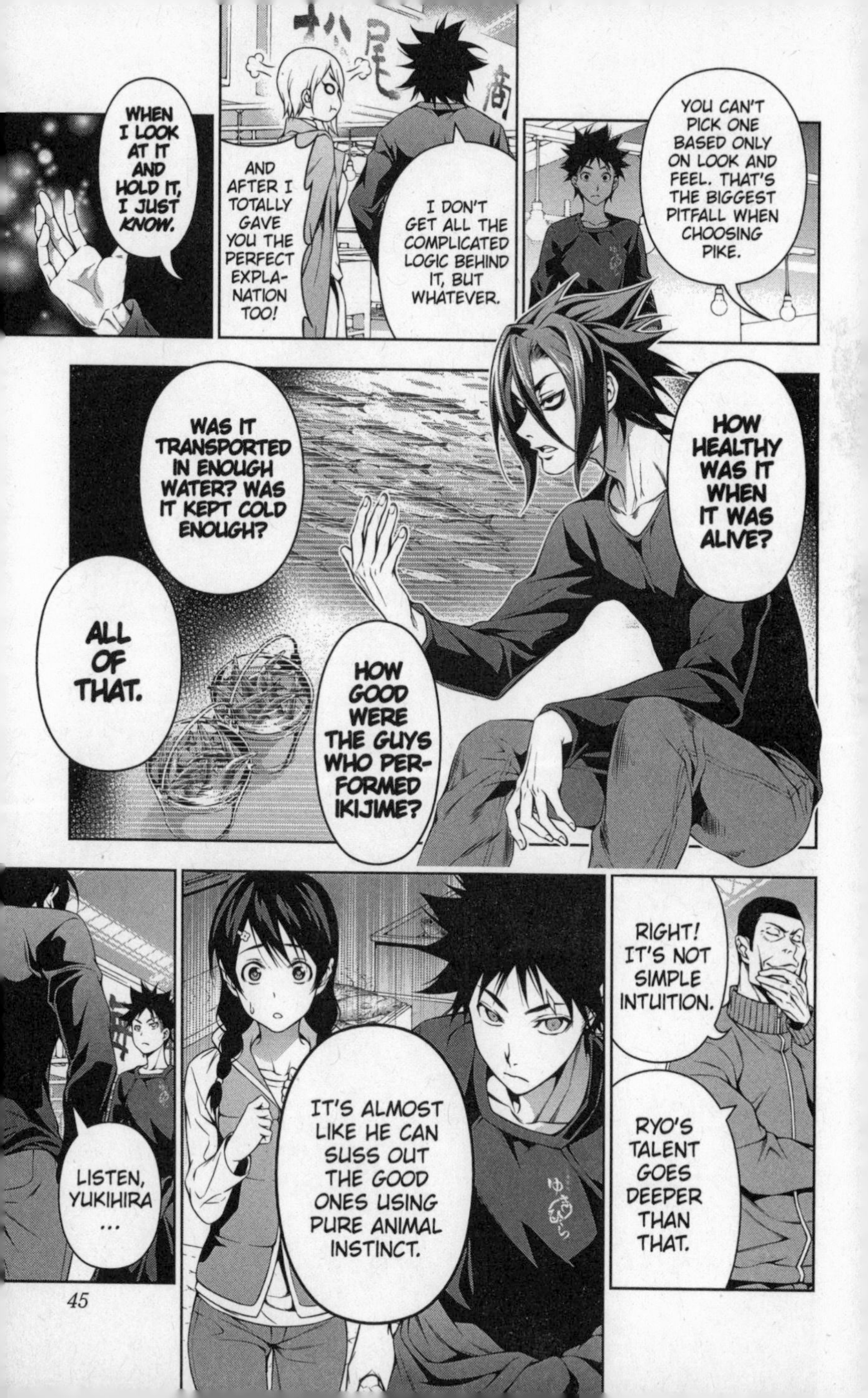
YOU CAN'T PICK ONE BASED ONLY ON LOOK AND FEEL. THAT'S THE BIGGEST PITFALL WHEN CHOOSING PIKE.
I DON'T GET ALL THE COMPLICATED LOGIC BEHIND IT, BUT WHATEVER.
AND AFTER I TOTALLY GAVE YOU THE PERFECT EXPLANATION TOO!
WHEN I LOOK AT IT AND HOLD IT, I JUST *KNOW*.
HOW HEALTHY WAS IT WHEN IT WAS ALIVE?
WAS IT TRANSPORTED IN ENOUGH WATER? WAS IT KEPT COLD ENOUGH?
HOW GOOD WERE THE GUYS WHO PERFORMED IKIJIME?
ALL OF THAT.
RIGHT! IT'S NOT SIMPLE INTUITION.
RYO'S TALENT GOES DEEPER THAN THAT.
IT'S ALMOST LIKE HE CAN SUSS OUT THE GOOD ONES USING PURE ANIMAL INSTINCT.
LISTEN, YUKIHIRA...

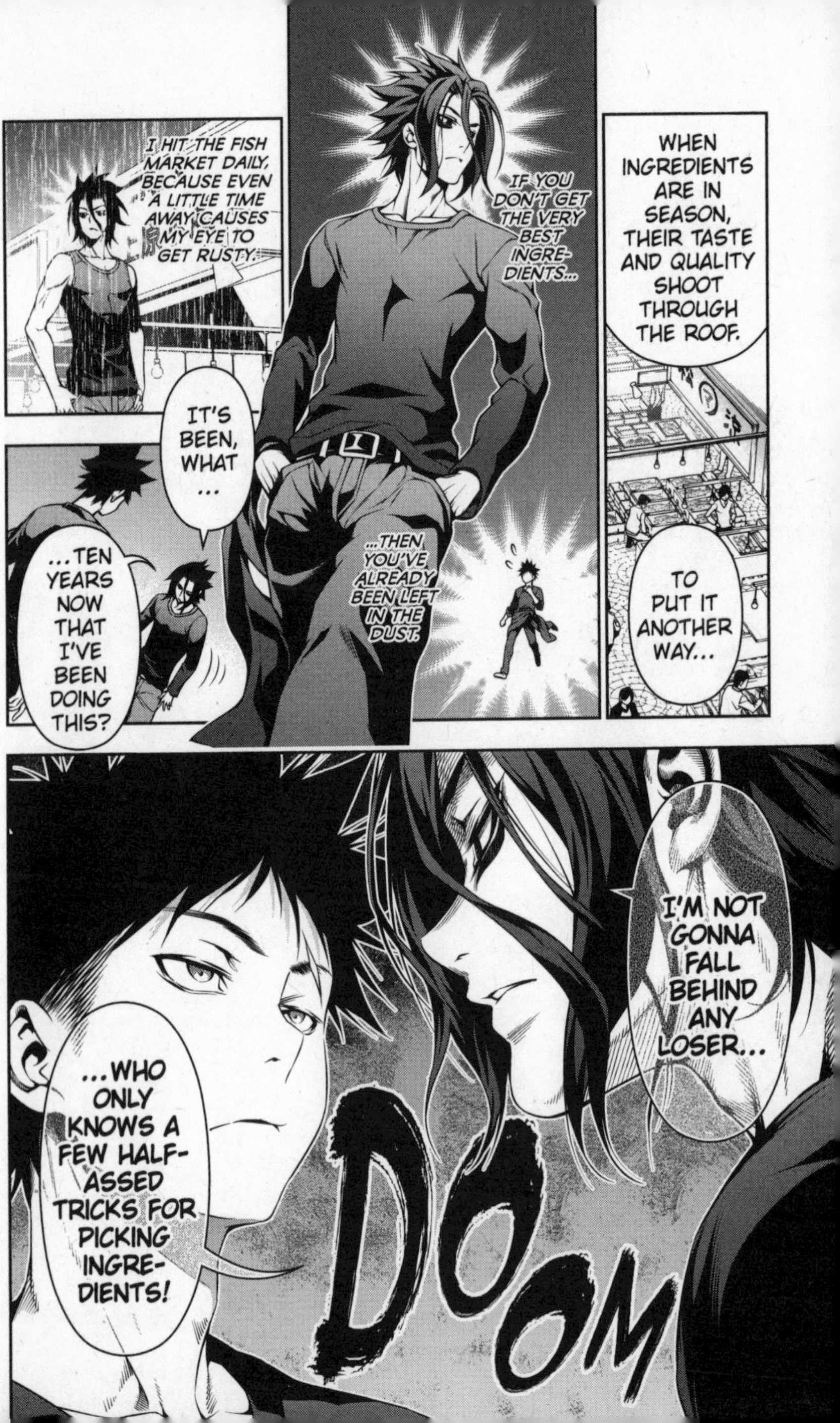
WHEN INGREDIENTS ARE IN SEASON, THEIR TASTE AND QUALITY SHOOT THROUGH THE ROOF.
TO PUT IT ANOTHER WAY...
IF YOU DON'T GET THE VERY BEST INGRE-DIENTS...
...THEN YOU'VE ALREADY BEEN LEFT IN THE DUST.
I HIT THE FISH MARKET DAILY, BECAUSE EVEN A LITTLE TIME AWAY CAUSES MY EYE TO GET RUSTY.
IT'S BEEN, WHAT...
...TEN YEARS NOW THAT I'VE BEEN DOING THIS?
I'M NOT GONNA FALL BEHIND ANY LOSER...
...WHO ONLY KNOWS A FEW HALF-ASSED TRICKS FOR PICKING INGRE-DIENTS!
DOOOM

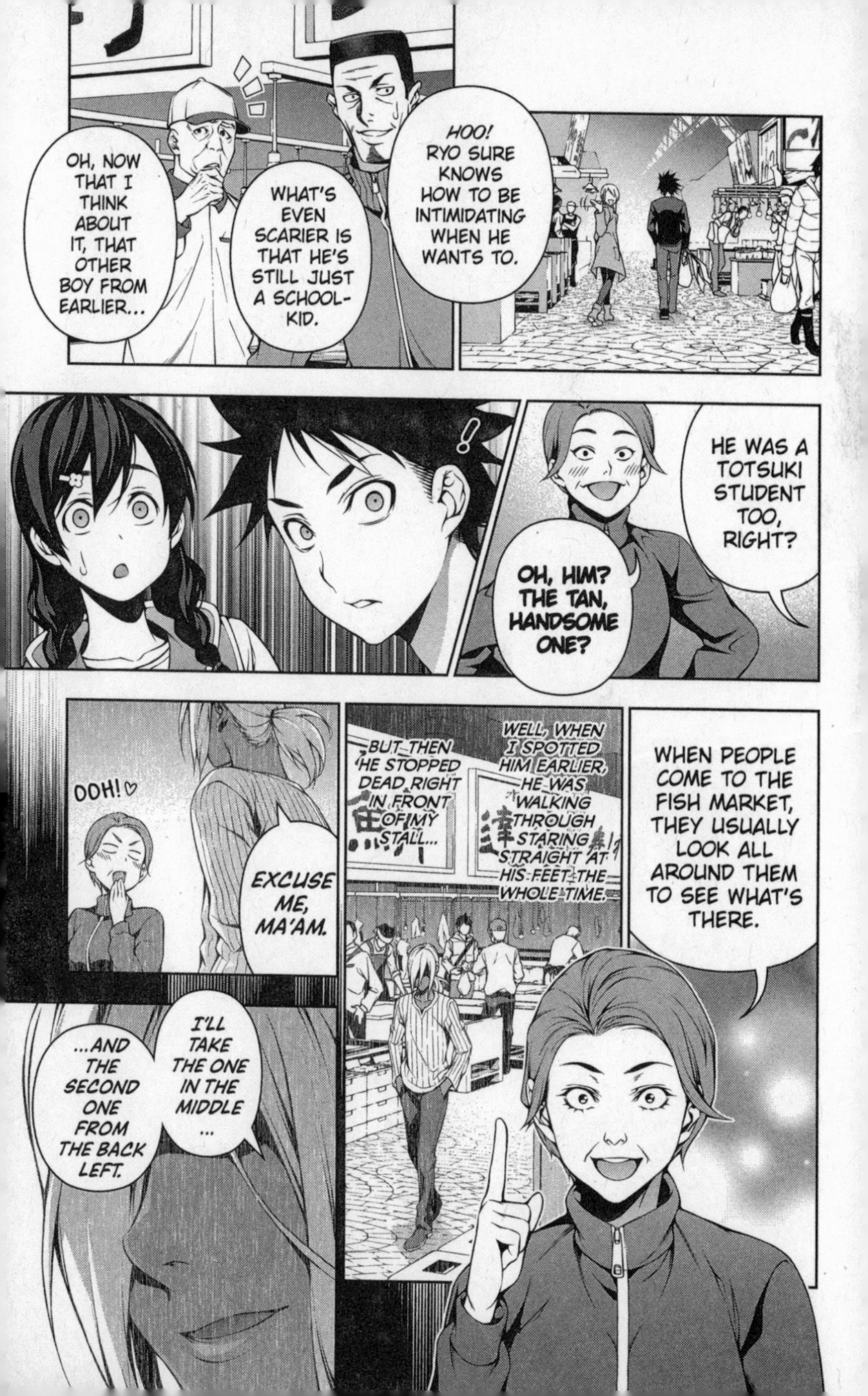

HOO! RYO SURE KNOWS HOW TO BE INTIMIDATING WHEN HE WANTS TO.
WHAT'S EVEN SCARIER IS THAT HE'S STILL JUST A SCHOOL-KID.
OH, NOW THAT I THINK ABOUT IT, THAT OTHER BOY FROM EARLIER...
HE WAS A TOTSUKI STUDENT TOO, RIGHT?
OH, HIM? THE TAN, HANDSOME ONE?
WHEN PEOPLE COME TO THE FISH MARKET, THEY USUALLY LOOK ALL AROUND THEM TO SEE WHAT'S THERE.
WELL, WHEN I SPOTTED HIM EARLIER, HE WAS WALKING THROUGH STARING STRAIGHT AT HIS FEET THE WHOLE TIME.
BUT THEN HE STOPPED DEAD RIGHT IN FRONT OF MY STALL...
OOH!♡
EXCUSE ME, MA'AM.
I'LL TAKE THE ONE IN THE MIDDLE...
...AND THE SECOND ONE FROM THE BACK LEFT.

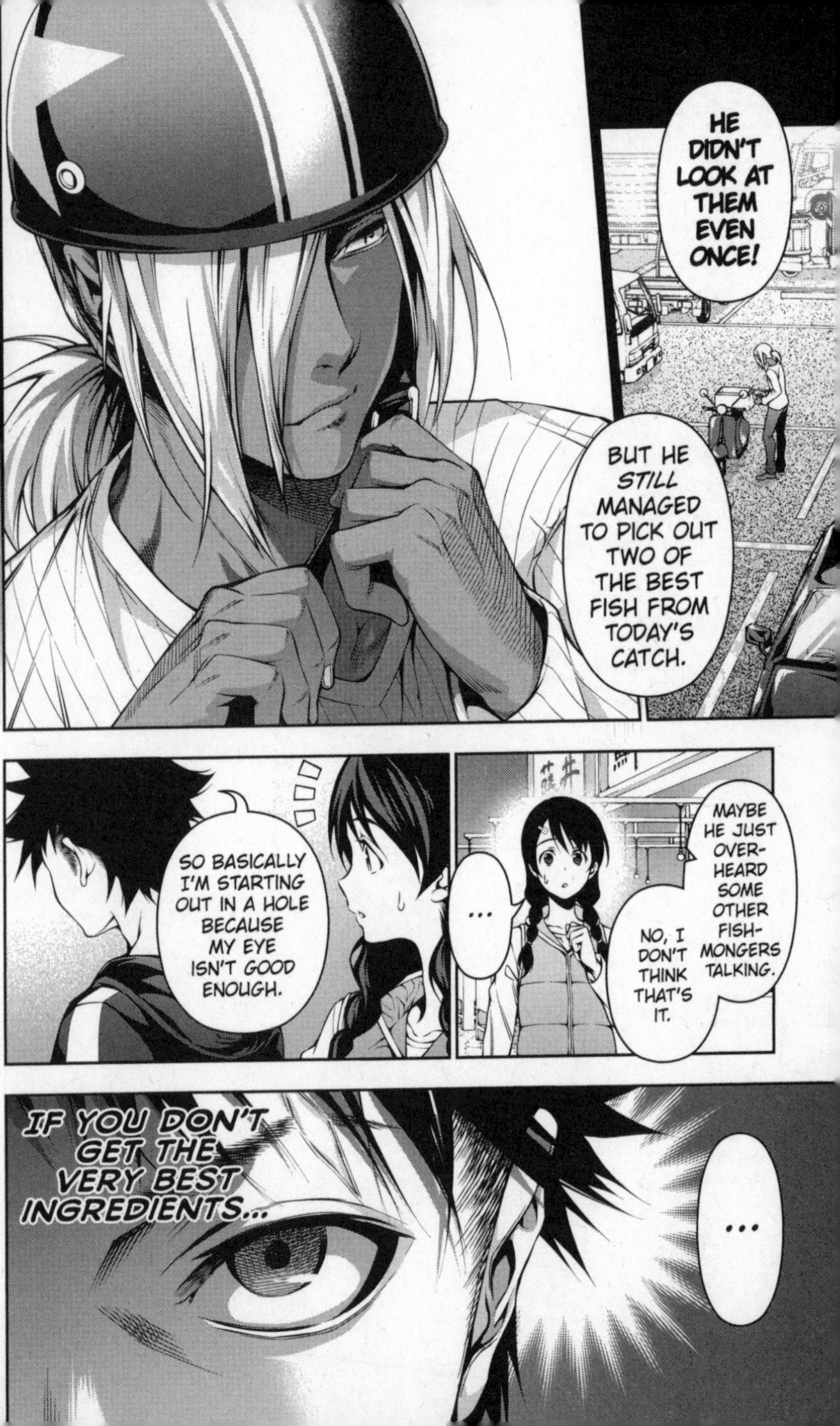
HE DIDN'T LOOK AT THEM EVEN ONCE!
BUT HE *STILL* MANAGED TO PICK OUT TWO OF THE BEST FISH FROM TODAY'S CATCH.
MAYBE HE JUST OVER-HEARD SOME OTHER FISH-MONGERS TALKING.
NO, I DON'T THINK THAT'S IT.
...
SO BASICALLY I'M STARTING OUT IN A HOLE BECAUSE MY EYE ISN'T GOOD ENOUGH.
...
IF YOU DON'T GET THE VERY BEST INGREDIENTS...

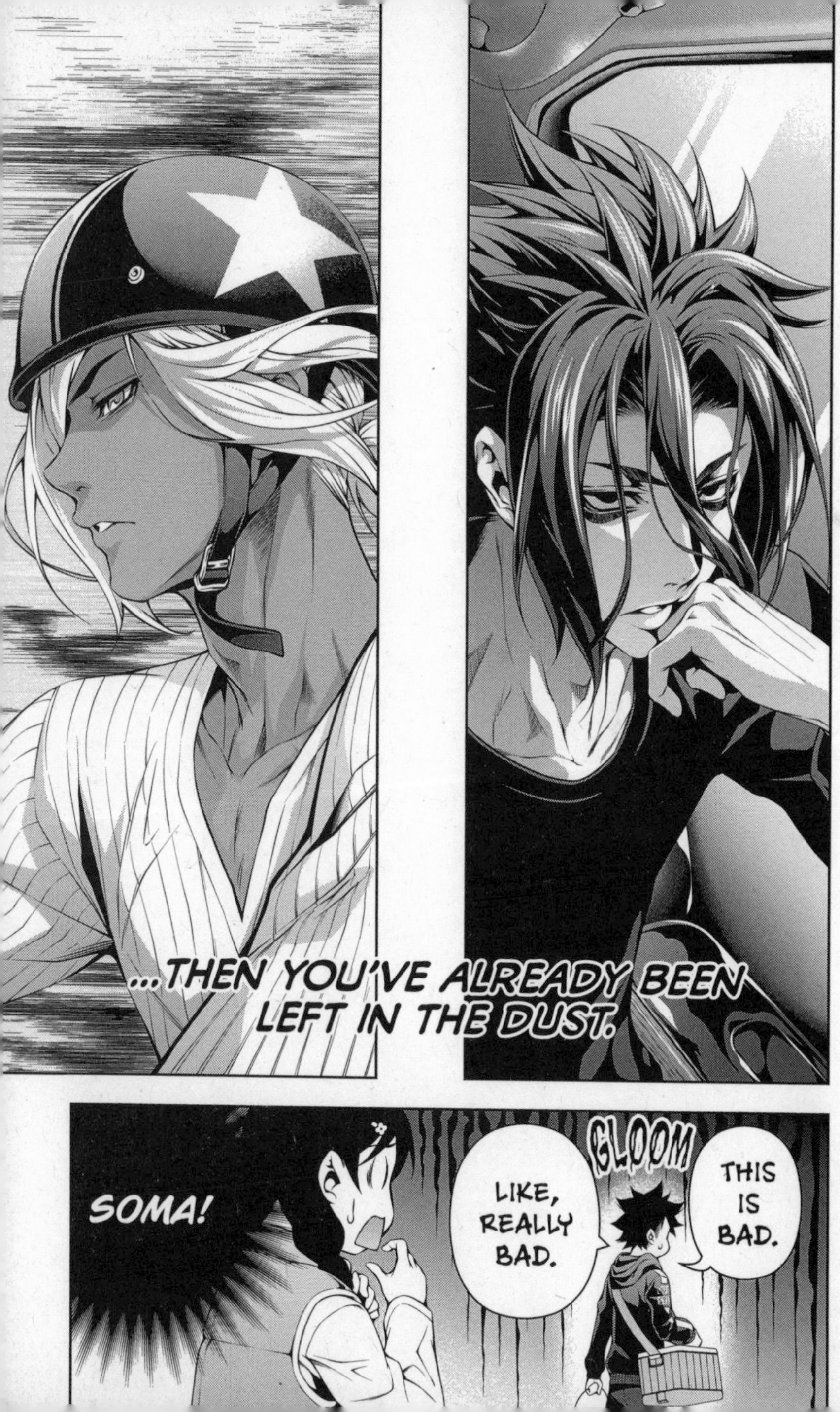
...THEN YOU'VE ALREADY BEEN LEFT IN THE DUST.
GLOOM
THIS IS BAD.
LIKE, REALLY BAD.
SOMA!

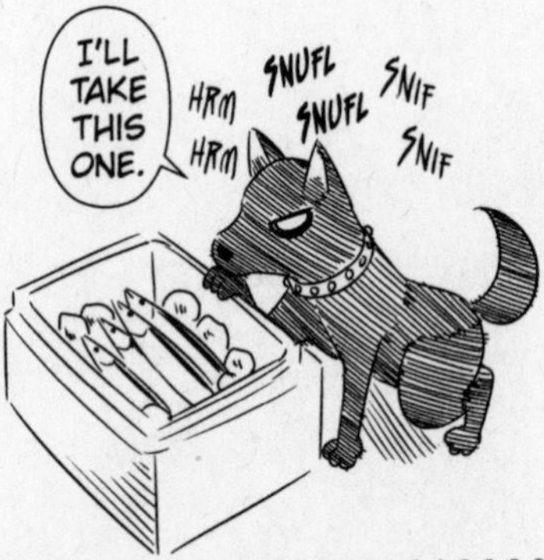

I'LL TAKE THIS ONE.
HRM HRM
SNUFL SNUFL
SNIF SNIF

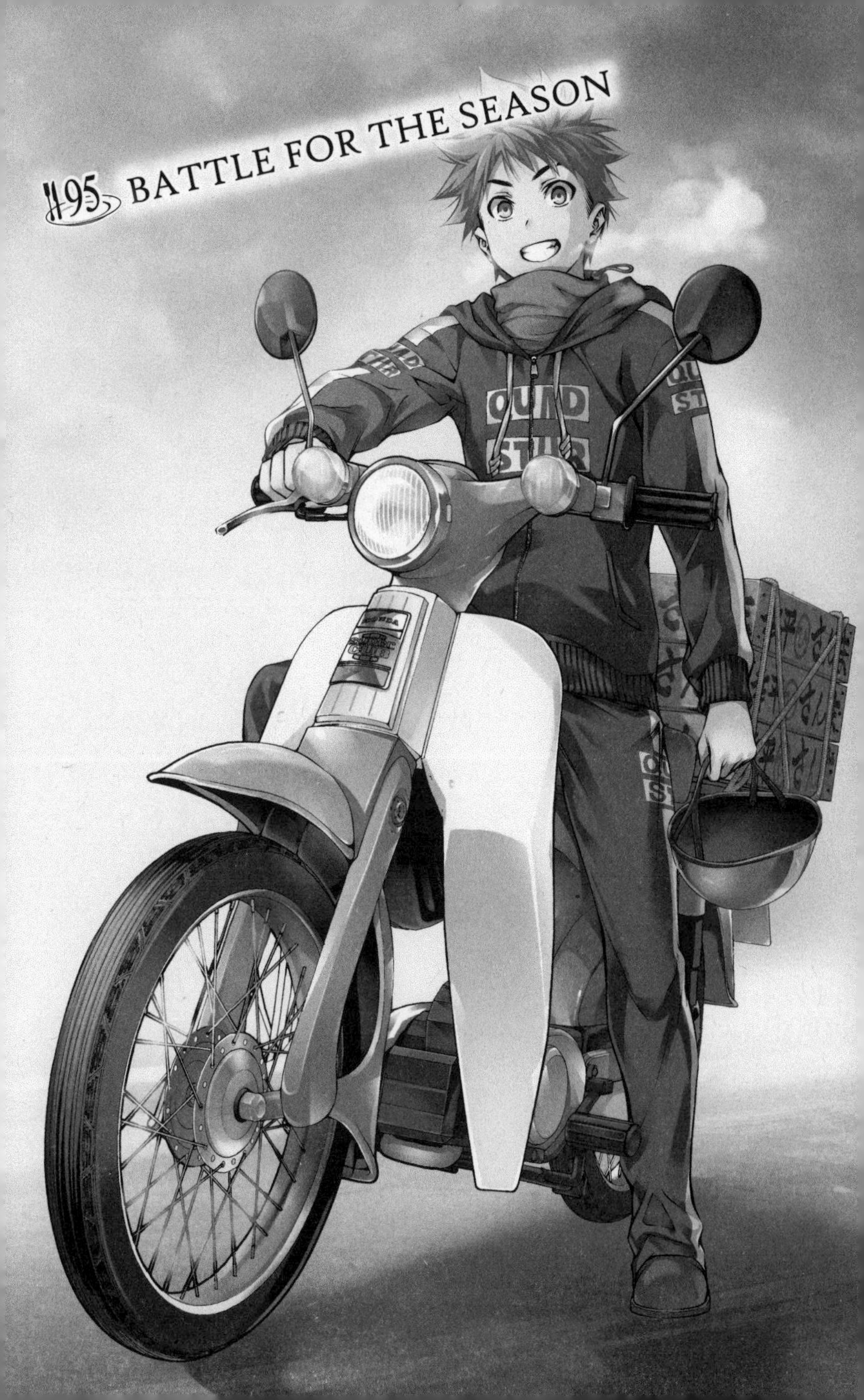
#95 BATTLE FOR THE SEASON

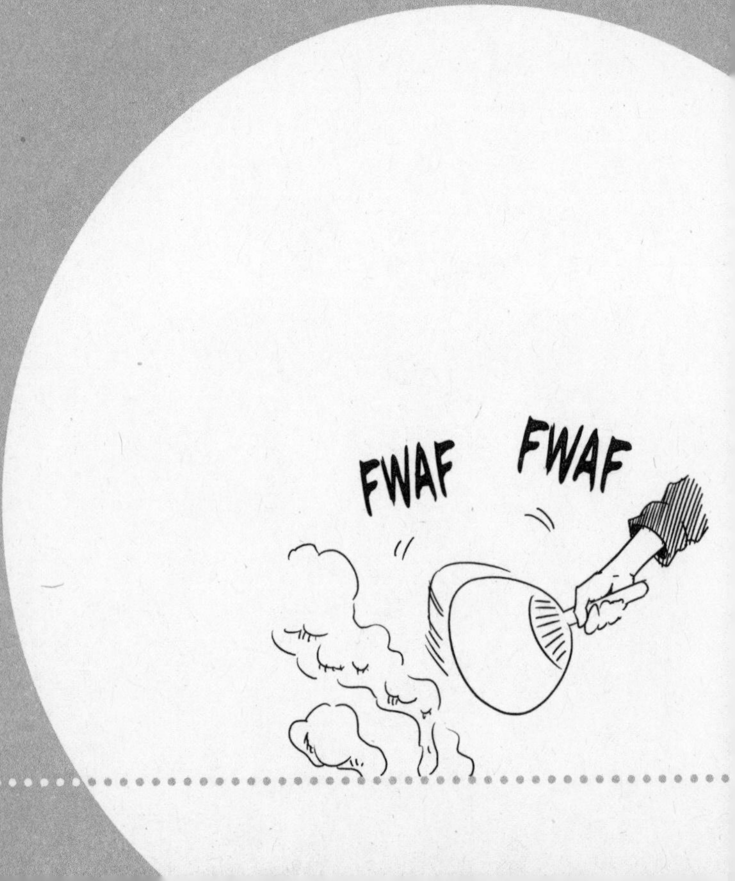
FWAF FWAF

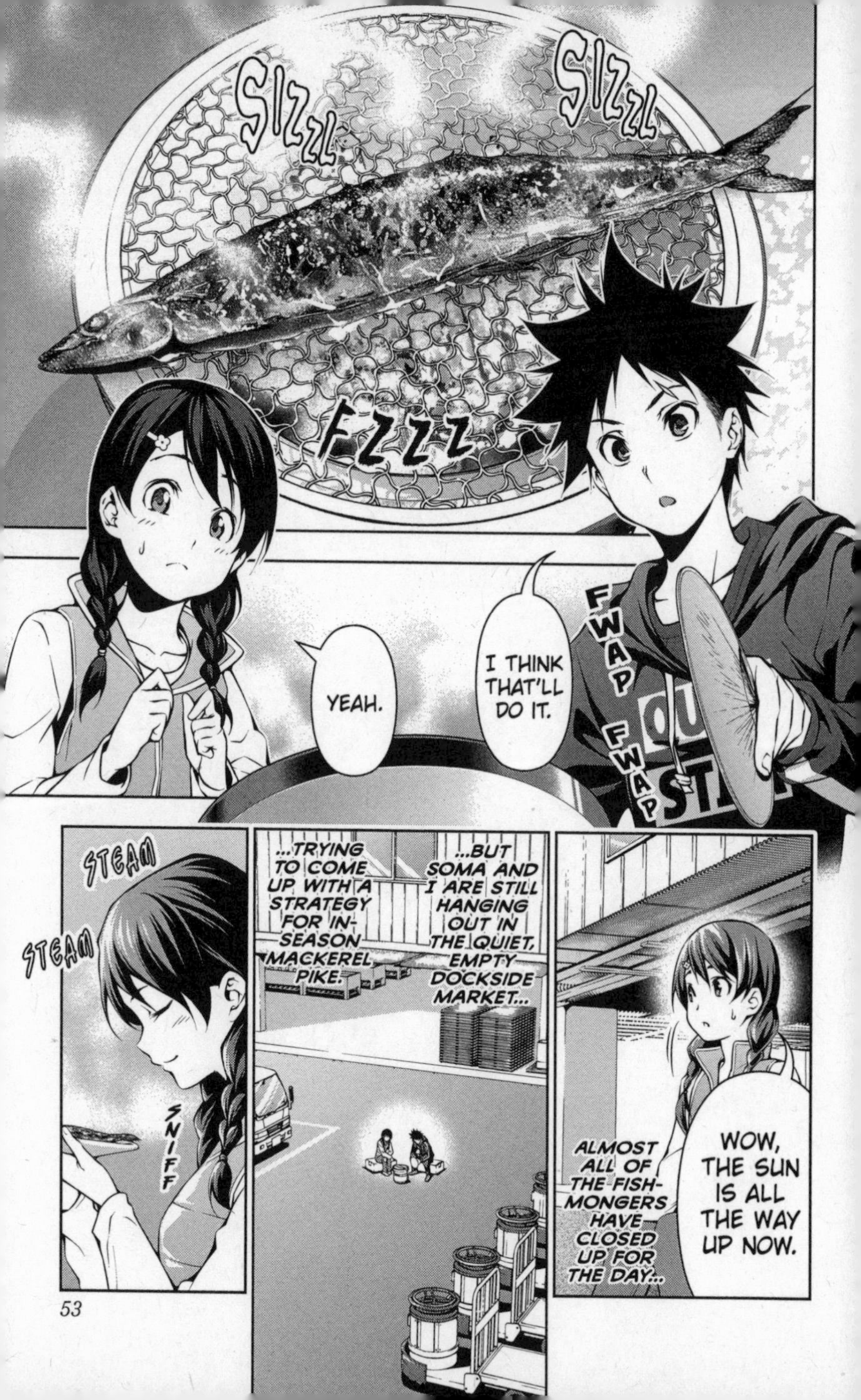
SIZZL
SIZZL
FZZZ
FWAP FWAP
I THINK THAT'LL DO IT.
YEAH.
WOW, THE SUN IS ALL THE WAY UP NOW.
ALMOST ALL OF THE FISH-MONGERS HAVE CLOSED UP FOR THE DAY...
...BUT SOMA AND I ARE STILL HANGING OUT IN THE QUIET, EMPTY DOCKSIDE MARKET...
...TRYING TO COME UP WITH A STRATEGY FOR IN-SEASON MACKEREL PIKE.
STEAM
STEAM
SNIFF

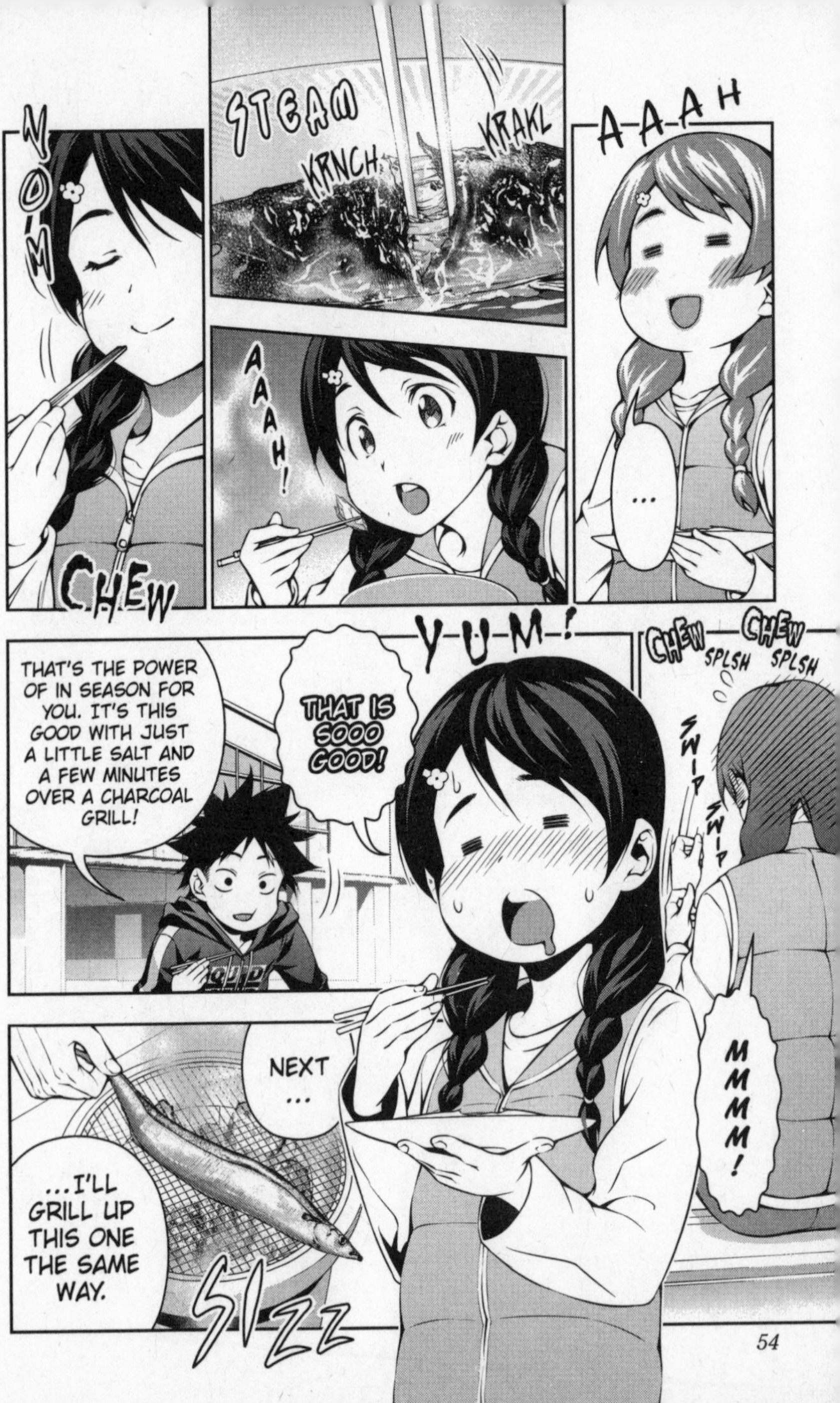
A-A-A-H
...
STEAM
KRAKL
KRNCH
AAAAH!
NOM
CHEW
CHEW CHEW
SPLSH SPLSH
SWIP SWIP
MMMMM!
YUM!
THAT IS SOOO GOOD!
THAT'S THE POWER OF IN SEASON FOR YOU. IT'S THIS GOOD WITH JUST A LITTLE SALT AND A FEW MINUTES OVER A CHARCOAL GRILL!
NEXT ...
...I'LL GRILL UP THIS ONE THE SAME WAY.
SIZZ

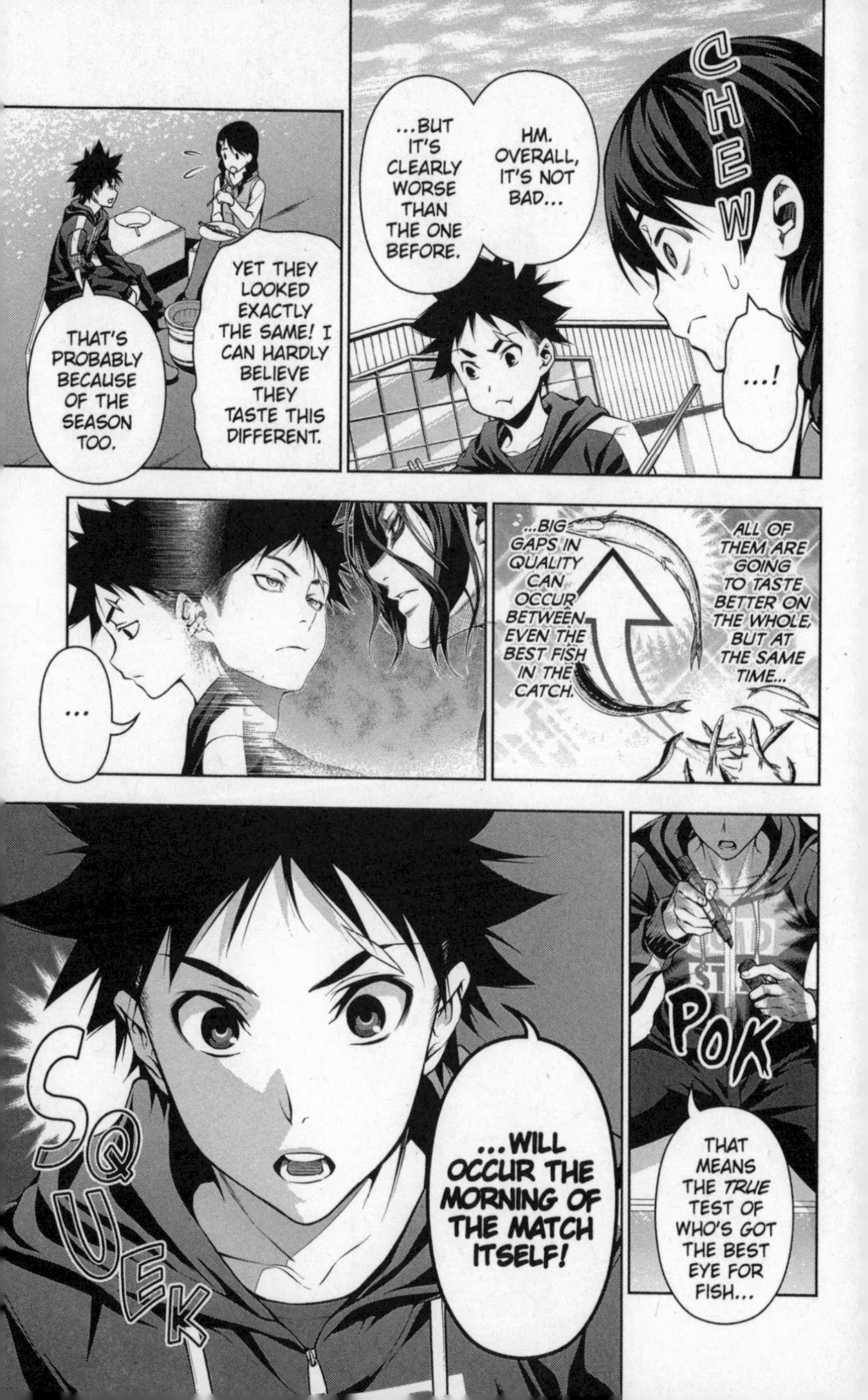
CHEW
HM. OVERALL, IT'S NOT BAD...
...BUT IT'S CLEARLY WORSE THAN THE ONE BEFORE.
...!
YET THEY LOOKED EXACTLY THE SAME! I CAN HARDLY BELIEVE THEY TASTE THIS DIFFERENT.
THAT'S PROBABLY BECAUSE OF THE SEASON TOO.
ALL OF THEM ARE GOING TO TASTE BETTER ON THE WHOLE, BUT AT THE SAME TIME...
...BIG GAPS IN QUALITY CAN OCCUR BETWEEN EVEN THE BEST FISH IN THE CATCH.
...
POK
THAT MEANS THE *TRUE* TEST OF WHO'S GOT THE BEST EYE FOR FISH...
...WILL OCCUR THE MORNING OF THE MATCH ITSELF!
SQUEK

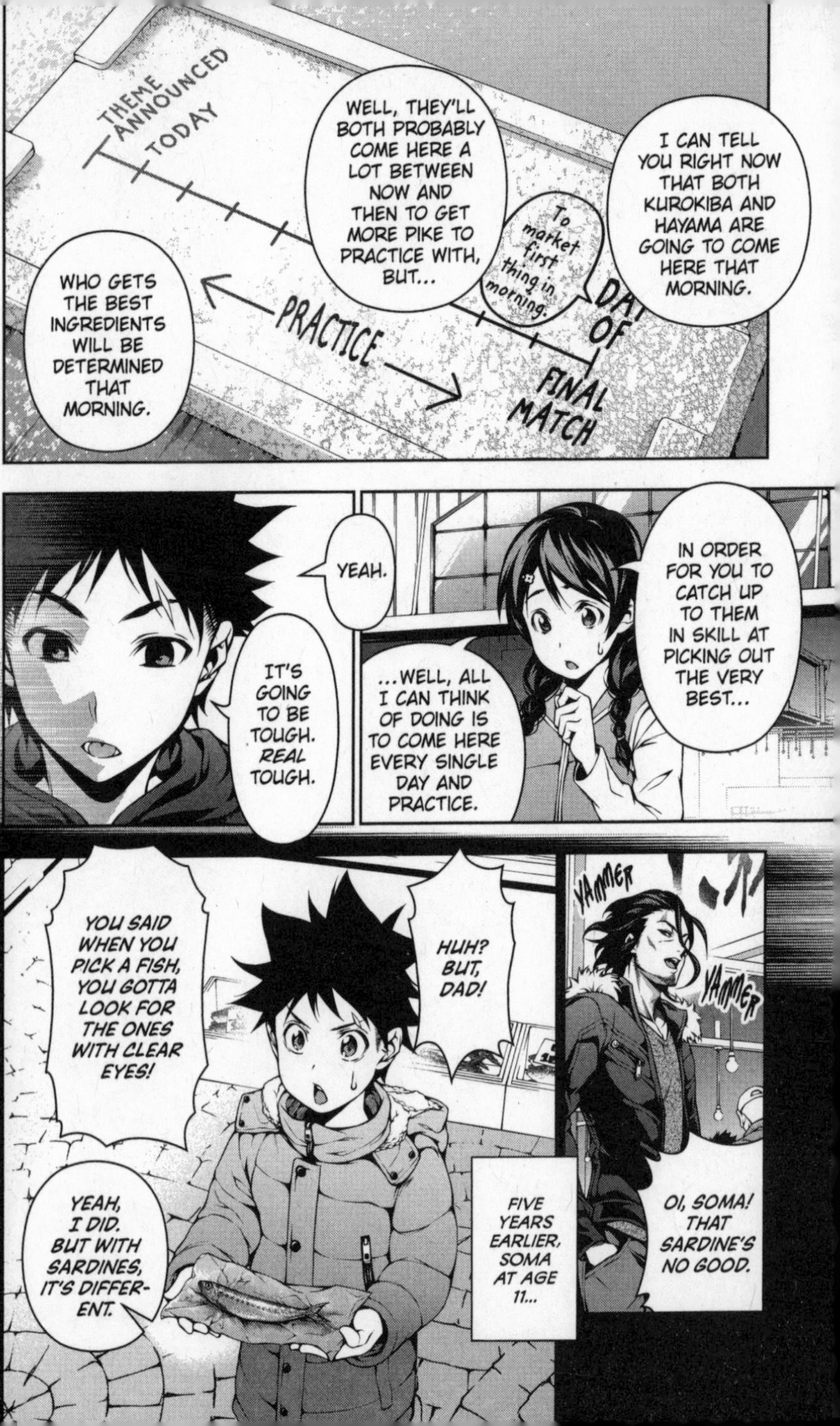

THEME ANNOUNCED
TODAY
PRACTICE
DAY OF FINAL MATCH
I CAN TELL YOU RIGHT NOW THAT BOTH KUROKIBA AND HAYAMA ARE GOING TO COME HERE THAT MORNING.
To market first thing in morning.
WELL, THEY'LL BOTH PROBABLY COME HERE A LOT BETWEEN NOW AND THEN TO GET MORE PIKE TO PRACTICE WITH, BUT...
WHO GETS THE BEST INGREDIENTS WILL BE DETERMINED THAT MORNING.
IN ORDER FOR YOU TO CATCH UP TO THEM IN SKILL AT PICKING OUT THE VERY BEST...
...WELL, ALL I CAN THINK OF DOING IS TO COME HERE EVERY SINGLE DAY AND PRACTICE.
YEAH.
IT'S GOING TO BE TOUGH. REAL TOUGH.
YAMMER
YAMMER
OI, SOMA! THAT SARDINE'S NO GOOD.
FIVE YEARS EARLIER, SOMA AT AGE 11...
HUH? BUT, DAD!
YOU SAID WHEN YOU PICK A FISH, YOU GOTTA LOOK FOR THE ONES WITH CLEAR EYES!
YEAH, I DID. BUT WITH SARDINES, IT'S DIFFER-ENT.

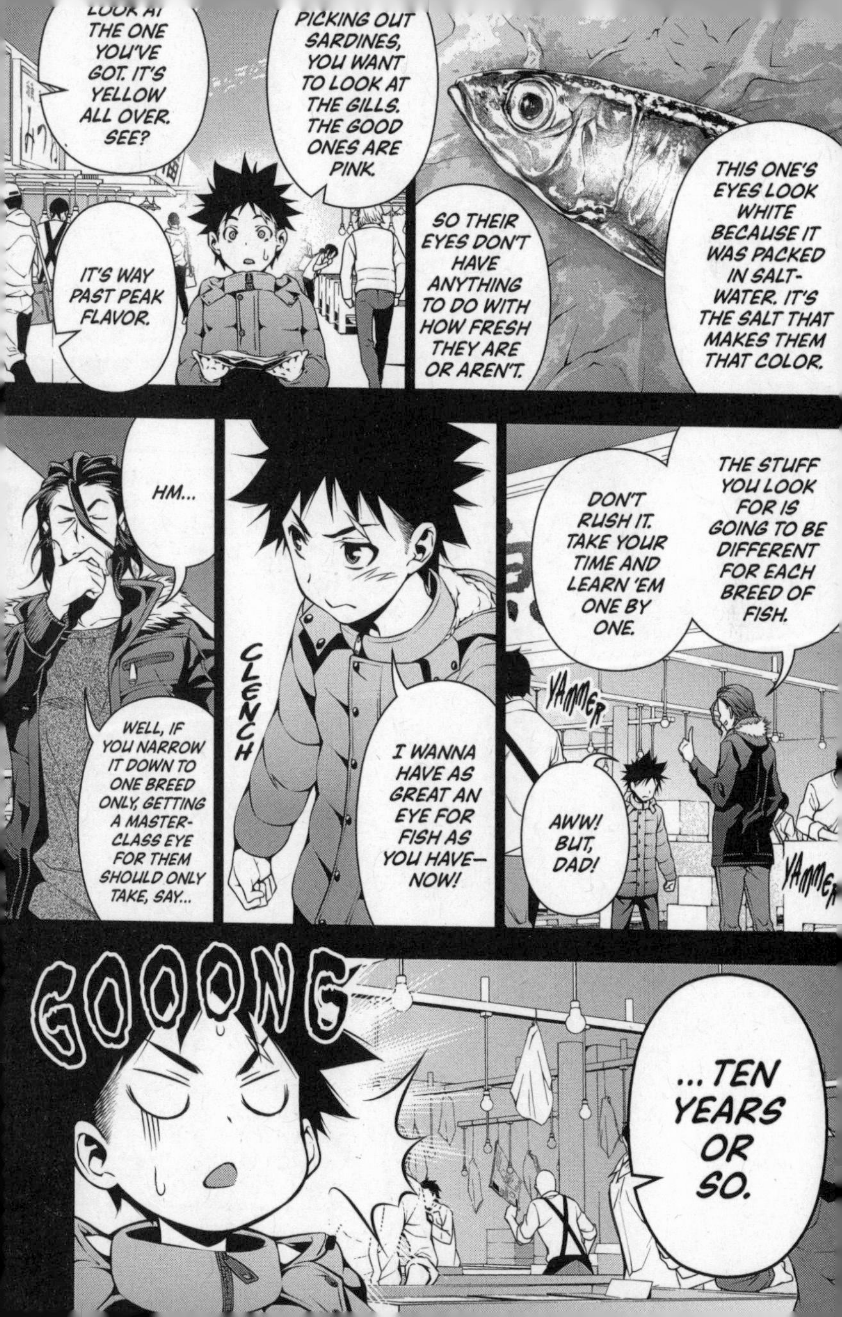
THIS ONE'S EYES LOOK WHITE BECAUSE IT WAS PACKED IN SALT-WATER. IT'S THE SALT THAT MAKES THEM THAT COLOR.
SO THEIR EYES DON'T HAVE ANYTHING TO DO WITH HOW FRESH THEY ARE OR AREN'T.
PICKING OUT SARDINES, YOU WANT TO LOOK AT THE GILLS. THE GOOD ONES ARE PINK.
LOOK AT THE ONE YOU'VE GOT. IT'S YELLOW ALL OVER. SEE?
IT'S WAY PAST PEAK FLAVOR.
THE STUFF YOU LOOK FOR IS GOING TO BE DIFFERENT FOR EACH BREED OF FISH.
DON'T RUSH IT. TAKE YOUR TIME AND LEARN 'EM ONE BY ONE.
YAMMER
AWW! BUT, DAD!
YAMMER
CLENCH
I WANNA HAVE AS GREAT AN EYE FOR FISH AS YOU HAVE—NOW!
HM...
WELL, IF YOU NARROW IT DOWN TO ONE BREED ONLY, GETTING A MASTER-CLASS EYE FOR THEM SHOULD ONLY TAKE, SAY...
...TEN YEARS OR SO.
GOOONG

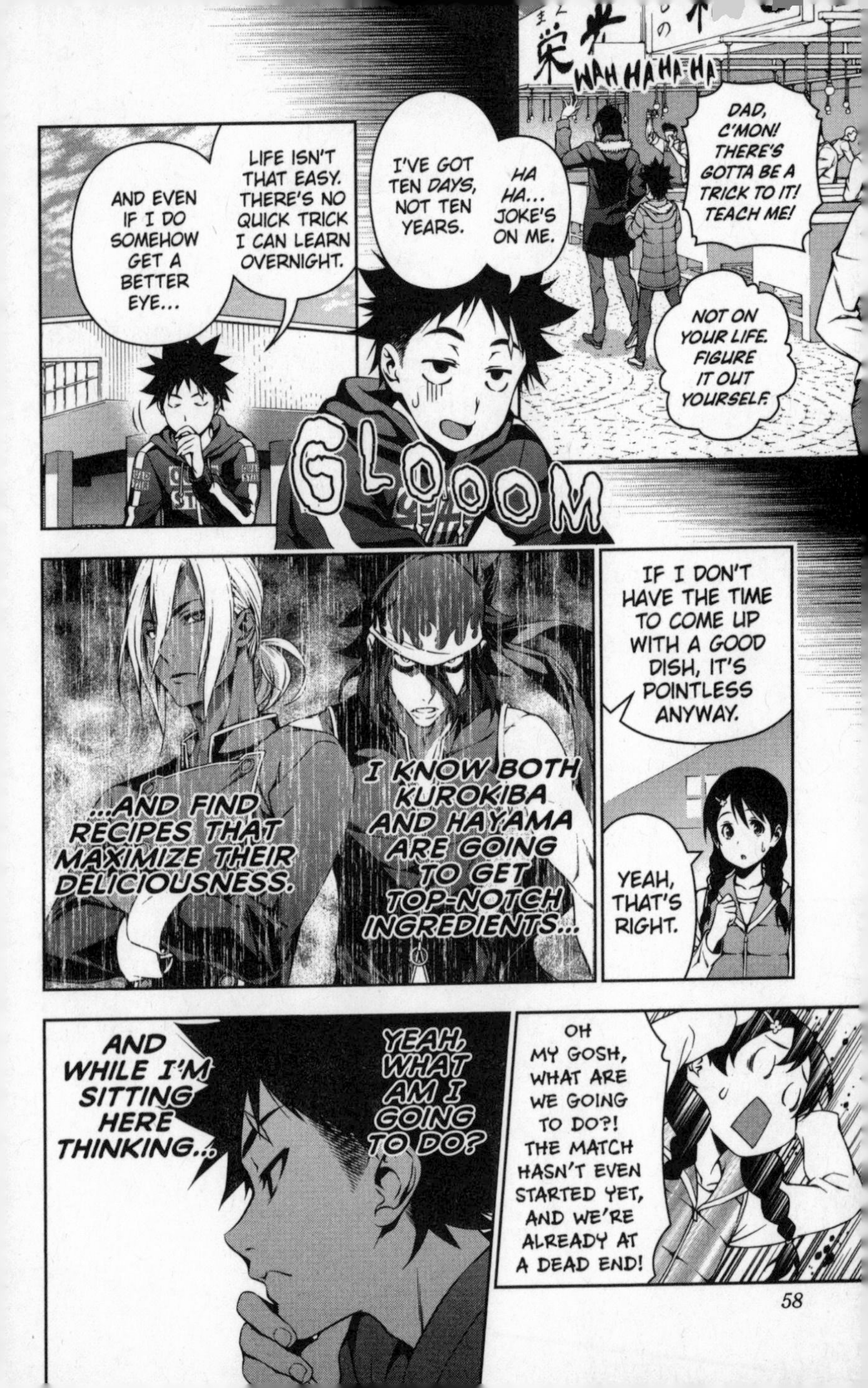
WAH HA HA HA
DAD, C'MON! THERE'S GOTTA BE A TRICK TO IT! TEACH ME!
NOT ON YOUR LIFE. FIGURE IT OUT YOURSELF.
HA HA... JOKE'S ON ME.
I'VE GOT TEN DAYS, NOT TEN YEARS.
LIFE ISN'T THAT EASY. THERE'S NO QUICK TRICK I CAN LEARN OVERNIGHT.
AND EVEN IF I DO SOMEHOW GET A BETTER EYE...
GLOOOM
IF I DON'T HAVE THE TIME TO COME UP WITH A GOOD DISH, IT'S POINTLESS ANYWAY.
YEAH, THAT'S RIGHT.
I KNOW BOTH KUROKIBA AND HAYAMA ARE GOING TO GET TOP-NOTCH INGREDIENTS...
...AND FIND RECIPES THAT MAXIMIZE THEIR DELICIOUSNESS.
OH MY GOSH, WHAT ARE WE GOING TO DO?! THE MATCH HASN'T EVEN STARTED YET, AND WE'RE ALREADY AT A DEAD END!
YEAH, WHAT AM I GOING TO DO?
AND WHILE I'M SITTING HERE THINKING...

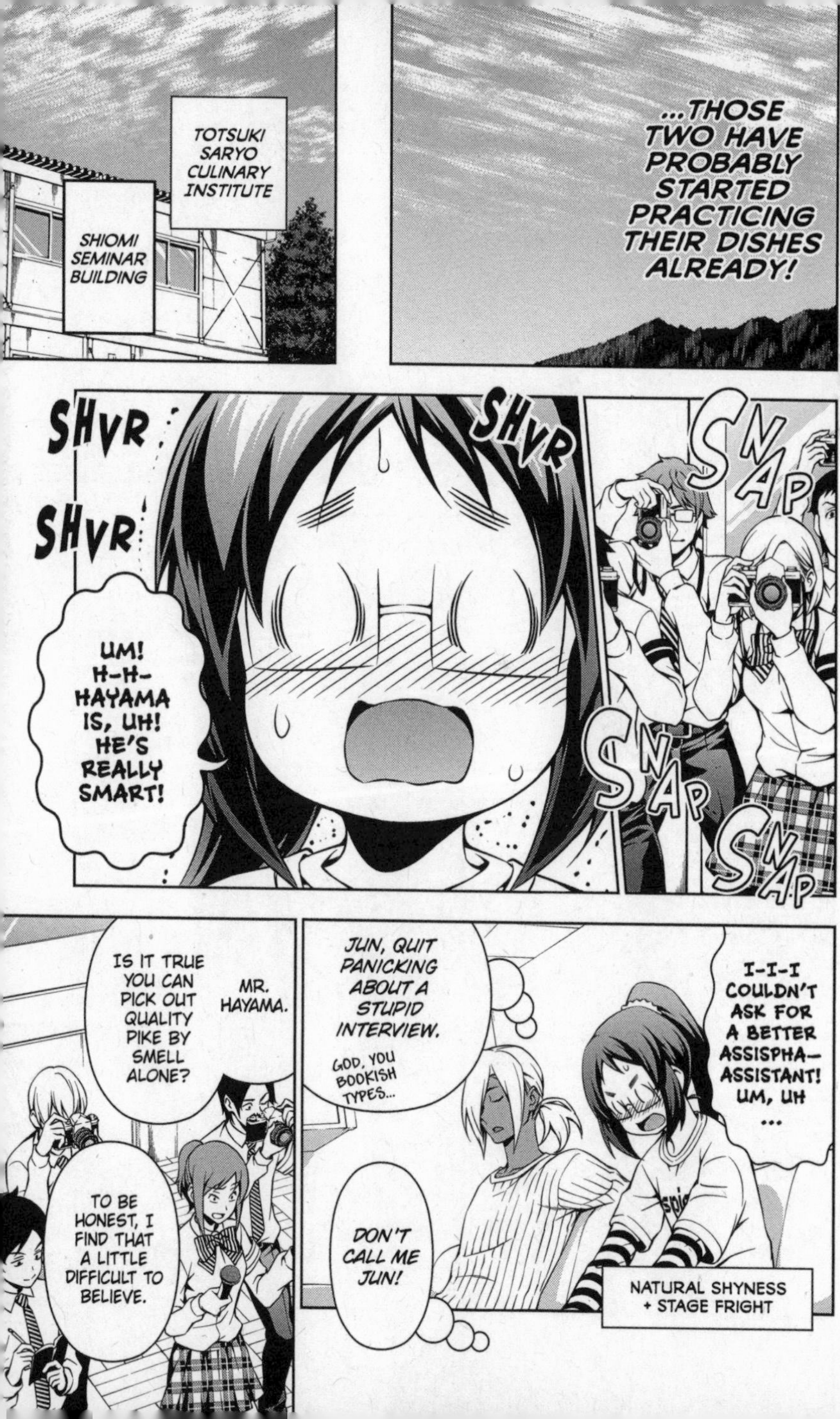
...THOSE TWO HAVE PROBABLY STARTED PRACTICING THEIR DISHES ALREADY!
TOTSUKI SARYO CULINARY INSTITUTE
SHIOMI SEMINAR BUILDING
SNAP
SNAP
SNAP
SHVR
SHVR
SHVR
UM! H-H-HAYAMA IS, UH! HE'S REALLY SMART!
I-I-I COULDN'T ASK FOR A BETTER ASSISPHA-ASSISTANT! UM, UH ...
JUN, QUIT PANICKING ABOUT A STUPID INTERVIEW.
GOD, YOU BOOKISH TYPES...
DON'T CALL ME JUN!
NATURAL SHYNESS + STAGE FRIGHT
IS IT TRUE YOU CAN PICK OUT QUALITY PIKE BY SMELL ALONE?
MR. HAYAMA.
TO BE HONEST, I FIND THAT A LITTLE DIFFICULT TO BELIEVE.

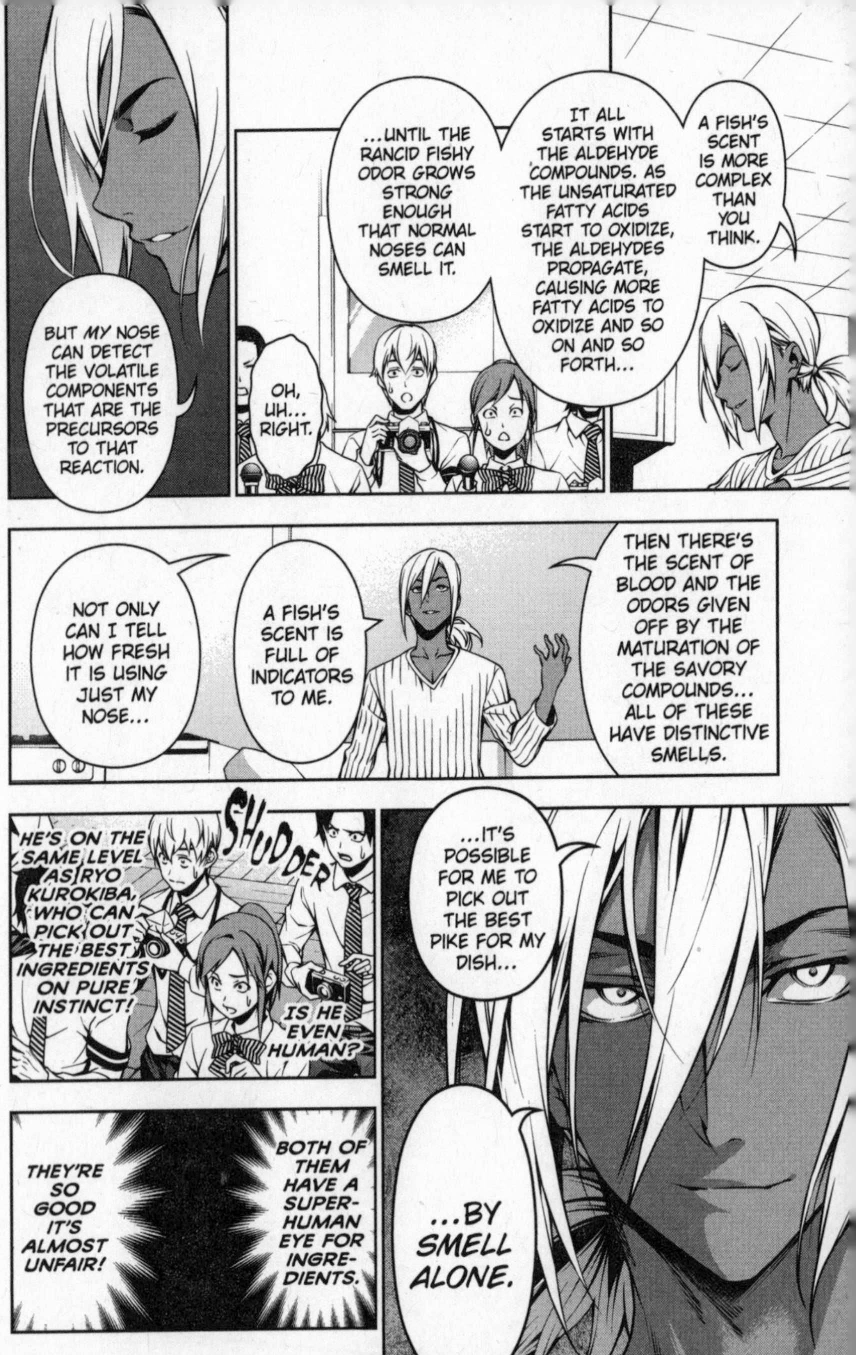
A FISH'S SCENT IS MORE COMPLEX THAN YOU THINK.
IT ALL STARTS WITH THE ALDEHYDE COMPOUNDS. AS THE UNSATURATED FATTY ACIDS START TO OXIDIZE, THE ALDEHYDES PROPAGATE, CAUSING MORE FATTY ACIDS TO OXIDIZE AND SO ON AND SO FORTH...
...UNTIL THE RANCID FISHY ODOR GROWS STRONG ENOUGH THAT NORMAL NOSES CAN SMELL IT.
OH, UH... RIGHT.
BUT MY NOSE CAN DETECT THE VOLATILE COMPONENTS THAT ARE THE PRECURSORS TO THAT REACTION.
THEN THERE'S THE SCENT OF BLOOD AND THE ODORS GIVEN OFF BY THE MATURATION OF THE SAVORY COMPOUNDS... ALL OF THESE HAVE DISTINCTIVE SMELLS.
A FISH'S SCENT IS FULL OF INDICATORS TO ME.
NOT ONLY CAN I TELL HOW FRESH IT IS USING JUST MY NOSE...
...IT'S POSSIBLE FOR ME TO PICK OUT THE BEST PIKE FOR MY DISH...
...BY SMELL ALONE.
SHUDDER
HE'S ON THE SAME LEVEL AS RYO KUROKIBA, WHO CAN PICK OUT THE BEST INGREDIENTS ON PURE INSTINCT!
IS HE EVEN HUMAN?
BOTH OF THEM HAVE A SUPER-HUMAN EYE FOR INGRE-DIENTS.
THEY'RE SO GOOD IT'S ALMOST UNFAIR!

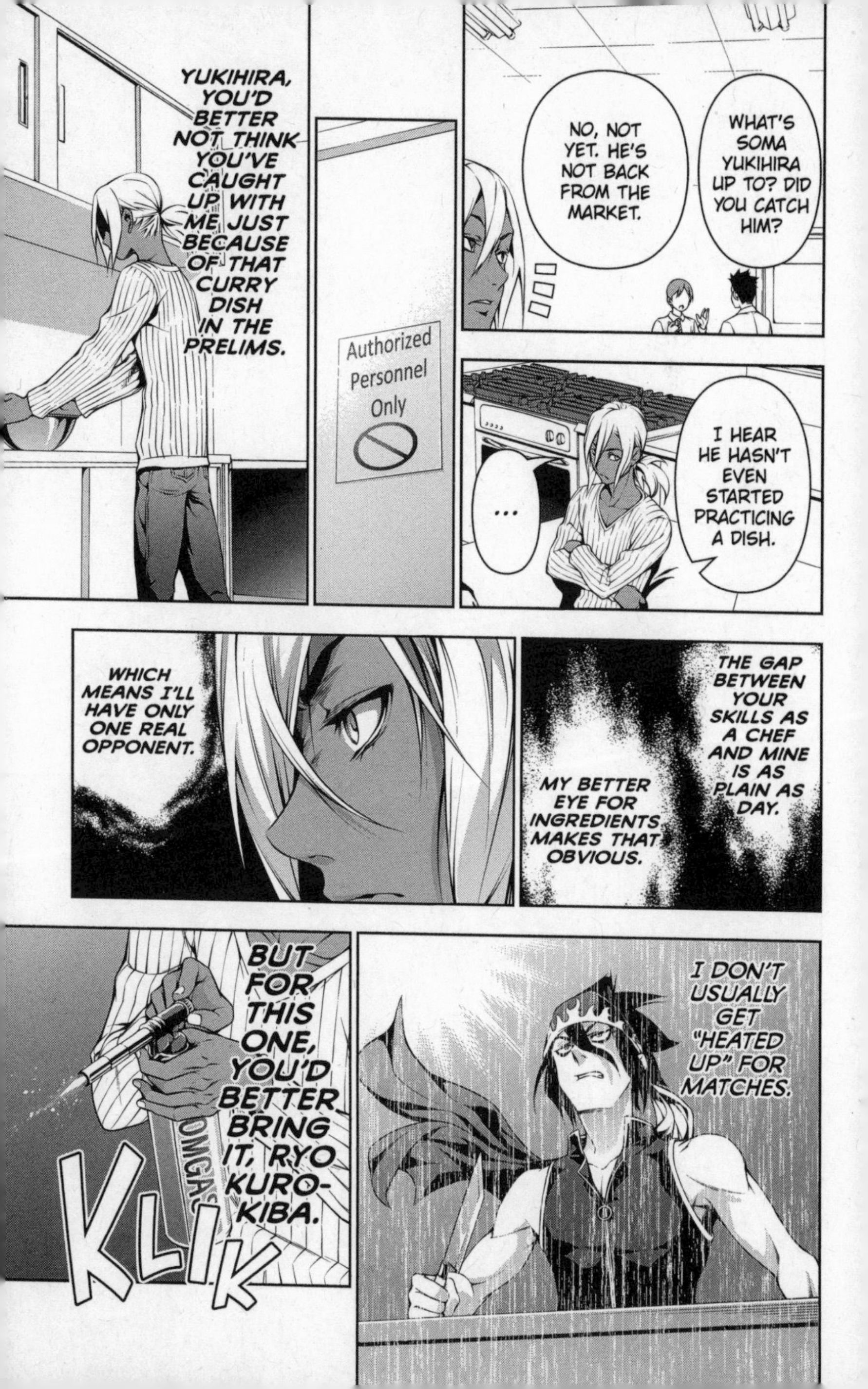
WHAT'S SOMA YUKIHIRA UP TO? DID YOU CATCH HIM?
NO, NOT YET. HE'S NOT BACK FROM THE MARKET.
I HEAR HE HASN'T EVEN STARTED PRACTICING A DISH.
...
Authorized Personnel Only
YUKIHIRA, YOU'D BETTER NOT THINK YOU'VE CAUGHT UP WITH ME JUST BECAUSE OF THAT CURRY DISH IN THE PRELIMS.
THE GAP BETWEEN YOUR SKILLS AS A CHEF AND MINE IS AS PLAIN AS DAY.
MY BETTER EYE FOR INGREDIENTS MAKES THAT OBVIOUS.
WHICH MEANS I'LL HAVE ONLY ONE REAL OPPONENT.
I DON'T USUALLY GET "HEATED UP" FOR MATCHES.
BUT FOR THIS ONE, YOU'D BETTER BRING IT, RYO KURO-KIBA.
KLIK

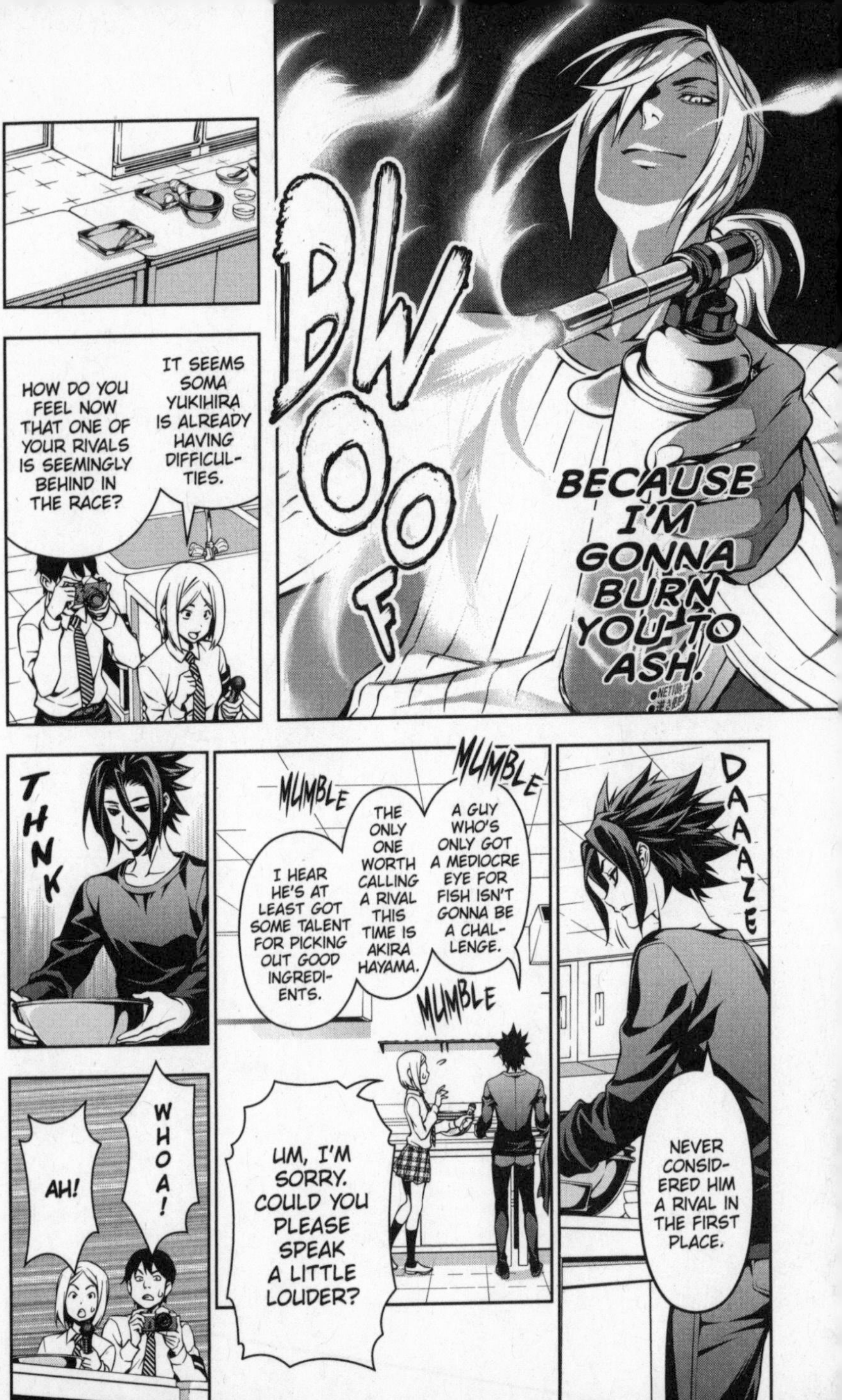
BWOOOF
BECAUSE I'M GONNA BURN YOU TO ASH.
IT SEEMS SOMA YUKIHIRA IS ALREADY HAVING DIFFICULTIES.
HOW DO YOU FEEL NOW THAT ONE OF YOUR RIVALS IS SEEMINGLY BEHIND IN THE RACE?
DAAAZE
NEVER CONSIDERED HIM A RIVAL IN THE FIRST PLACE.
MUMBLE
A GUY WHO'S ONLY GOT A MEDIOCRE EYE FOR FISH ISN'T GONNA BE A CHALLENGE.
MUMBLE
THE ONLY ONE WORTH CALLING A RIVAL THIS TIME IS AKIRA HAYAMA.
I HEAR HE'S AT LEAST GOT SOME TALENT FOR PICKING OUT GOOD INGREDIENTS.
MUMBLE
UM, I'M SORRY. COULD YOU PLEASE SPEAK A LITTLE LOUDER?
THNK
WHOA!
AH!

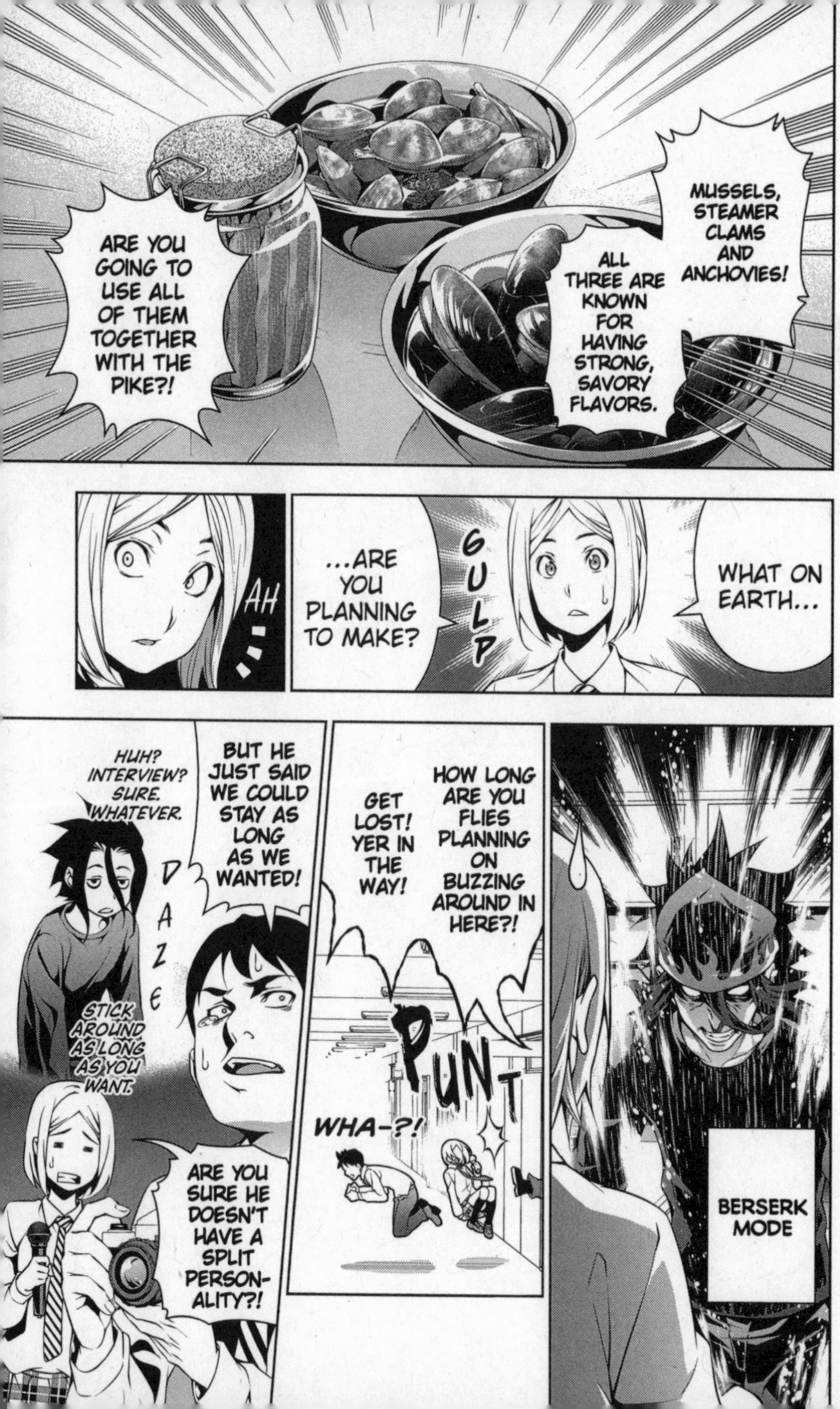
MUSSELS, STEAMER CLAMS AND ANCHOVIES!
ALL THREE ARE KNOWN FOR HAVING STRONG, SAVORY FLAVORS.
ARE YOU GOING TO USE ALL OF THEM TOGETHER WITH THE PIKE?!
WHAT ON EARTH...
GULP
...ARE YOU PLANNING TO MAKE?
AH...
BERSERK MODE
HOW LONG ARE YOU FLIES PLANNING ON BUZZING AROUND IN HERE?!
GET LOST! YER IN THE WAY!
PUNT
WHA-?!
BUT HE JUST SAID WE COULD STAY AS LONG AS WE WANTED!
HUH? INTERVIEW? SURE. WHATEVER.
DAZE
STICK AROUND AS LONG AS YOU WANT.
ARE YOU SURE HE DOESN'T HAVE A SPLIT PERSON-ALITY?!

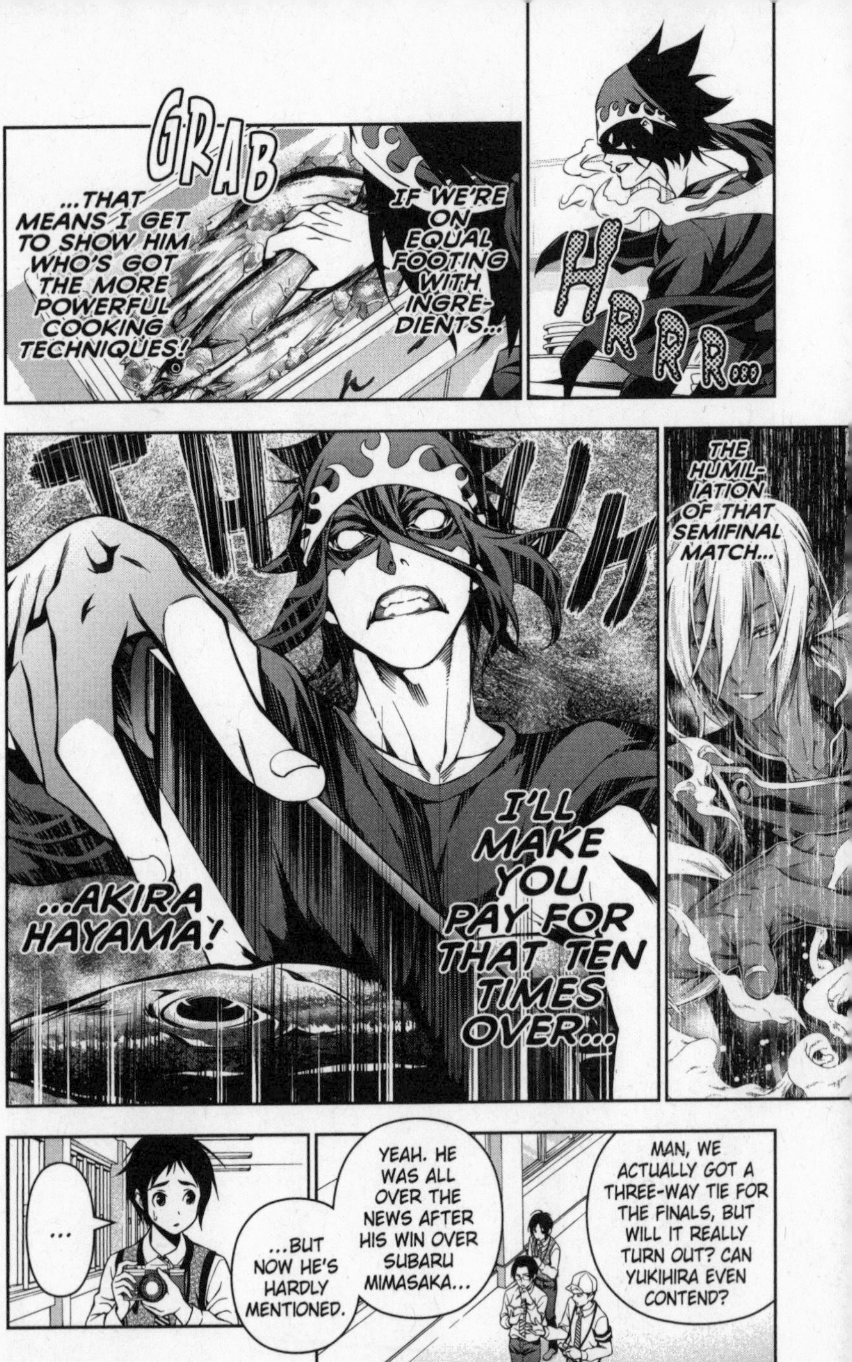
HRRRR...
GRAB
IF WE'RE ON EQUAL FOOTING WITH INGRE-DIENTS...
...THAT MEANS I GET TO SHOW HIM WHO'S GOT THE MORE POWERFUL COOKING TECHNIQUES!
THE HUMIL-IATION OF THAT SEMIFINAL MATCH...
I'LL MAKE YOU PAY FOR THAT TEN TIMES OVER...
...AKIRA HAYAMA!
MAN, WE ACTUALLY GOT A THREE-WAY TIE FOR THE FINALS, BUT WILL IT REALLY TURN OUT? CAN YUKIHIRA EVEN CONTEND?
YEAH. HE WAS ALL OVER THE NEWS AFTER HIS WIN OVER SUBARU MIMASAKA...
...BUT NOW HE'S HARDLY MENTIONED.
...

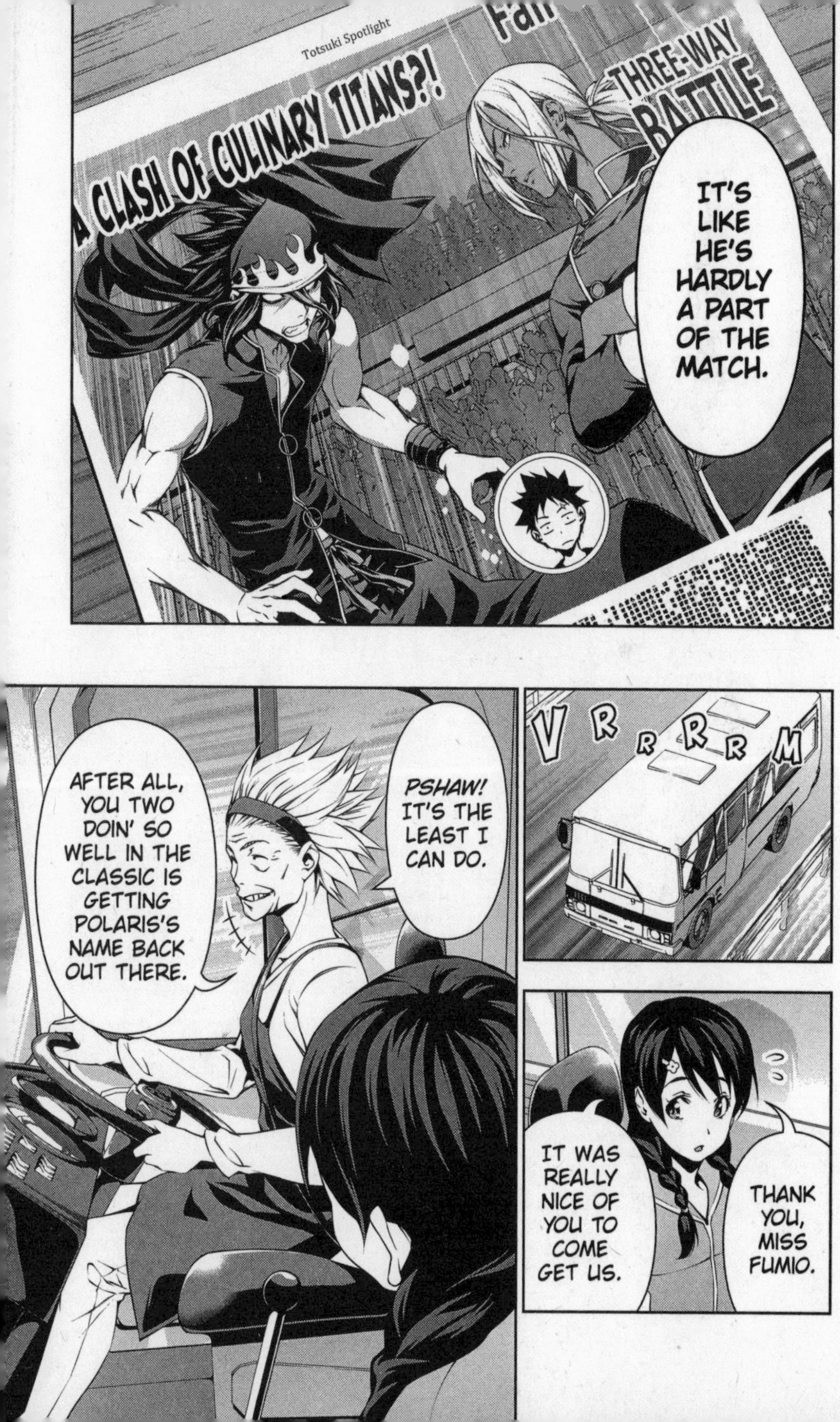
Totsuki Spotlight
THREE-WAY BATTLE
A CLASH OF CULINARY TITANS?!
IT'S LIKE HE'S HARDLY A PART OF THE MATCH.
VRRRRRM
THANK YOU, MISS FUMIO.
IT WAS REALLY NICE OF YOU TO COME GET US.
PSHAW! IT'S THE LEAST I CAN DO.
AFTER ALL, YOU TWO DOIN' SO WELL IN THE CLASSIC IS GETTING POLARIS'S NAME BACK OUT THERE.

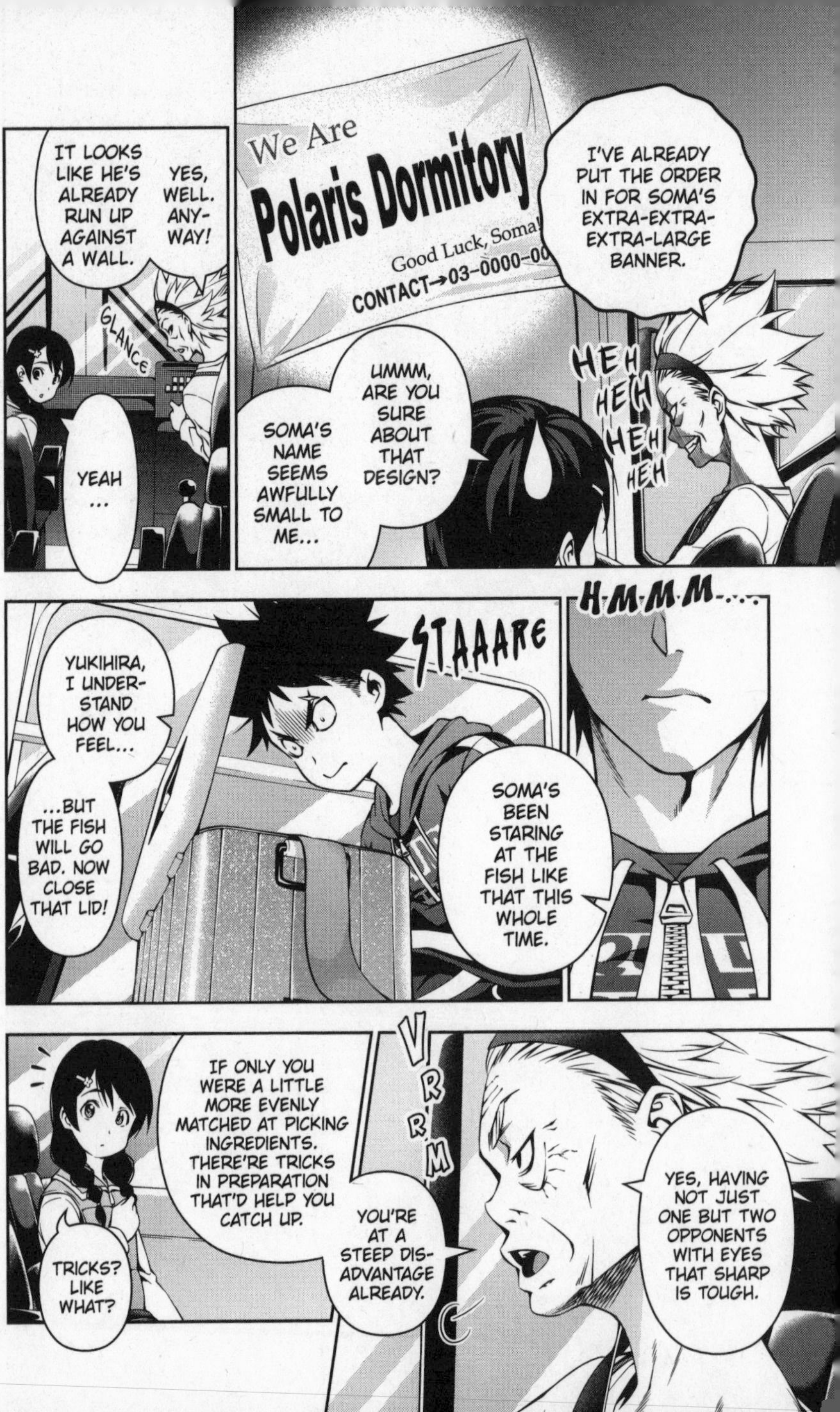
I'VE ALREADY PUT THE ORDER IN FOR SOMA'S EXTRA-EXTRA-EXTRA-LARGE BANNER.
We Are
Polaris Dormitory
Good Luck, Soma!
CONTACT→03-0000-00
HEH HEH HEH HEH
UMMM, ARE YOU SURE ABOUT THAT DESIGN?
SOMA'S NAME SEEMS AWFULLY SMALL TO ME...
IT LOOKS LIKE HE'S ALREADY RUN UP AGAINST A WALL.
YES, WELL. ANY-WAY!
GLANCE
YEAH ...
H-M-M-M-...
SOMA'S BEEN STARING AT THE FISH LIKE THAT THIS WHOLE TIME.
STAAARE
YUKIHIRA, I UNDER-STAND HOW YOU FEEL...
...BUT THE FISH WILL GO BAD. NOW CLOSE THAT LID!
VRRM
YES, HAVING NOT JUST ONE BUT TWO OPPONENTS WITH EYES THAT SHARP IS TOUGH.
YOU'RE AT A STEEP DIS-ADVANTAGE ALREADY.
IF ONLY YOU WERE A LITTLE MORE EVENLY MATCHED AT PICKING INGREDIENTS. THERE'RE TRICKS IN PREPARATION THAT'D HELP YOU CATCH UP.
TRICKS? LIKE WHAT?

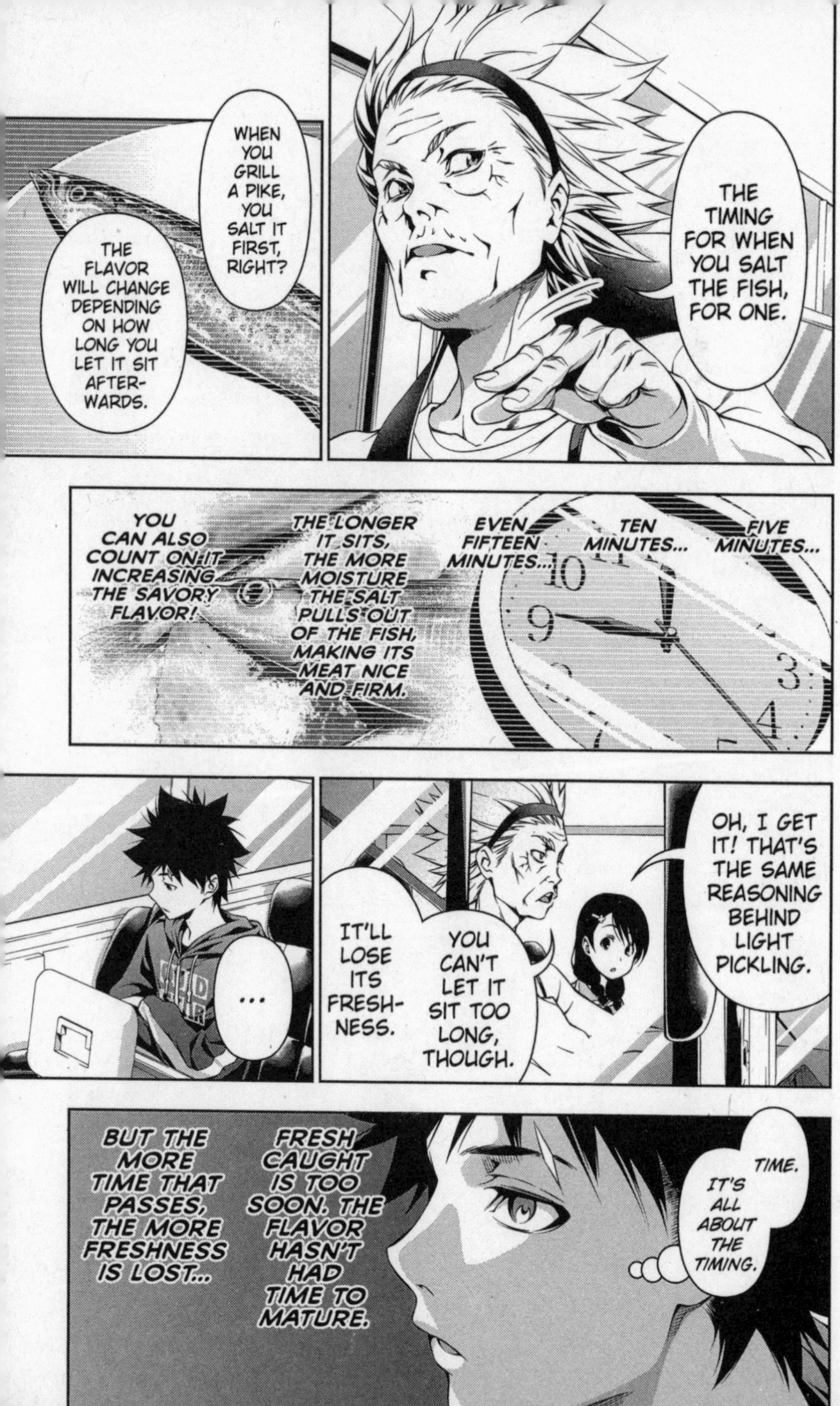
THE TIMING FOR WHEN YOU SALT THE FISH, FOR ONE.
WHEN YOU GRILL A PIKE, YOU SALT IT FIRST, RIGHT?
THE FLAVOR WILL CHANGE DEPENDING ON HOW LONG YOU LET IT SIT AFTER-WARDS.
FIVE MINUTES...
TEN MINUTES...
EVEN FIFTEEN MINUTES...
THE LONGER IT SITS, THE MORE MOISTURE THE SALT PULLS OUT OF THE FISH, MAKING ITS MEAT NICE AND FIRM.
YOU CAN ALSO COUNT ON IT INCREASING THE SAVORY FLAVOR!
OH, I GET IT! THAT'S THE SAME REASONING BEHIND LIGHT PICKLING.
YOU CAN'T LET IT SIT TOO LONG, THOUGH.
IT'LL LOSE ITS FRESH-NESS.
...
TIME. IT'S ALL ABOUT THE TIMING.
FRESH CAUGHT IS TOO SOON. THE FLAVOR HASN'T HAD TIME TO MATURE.
BUT THE MORE TIME THAT PASSES, THE MORE FRESHNESS IS LOST...

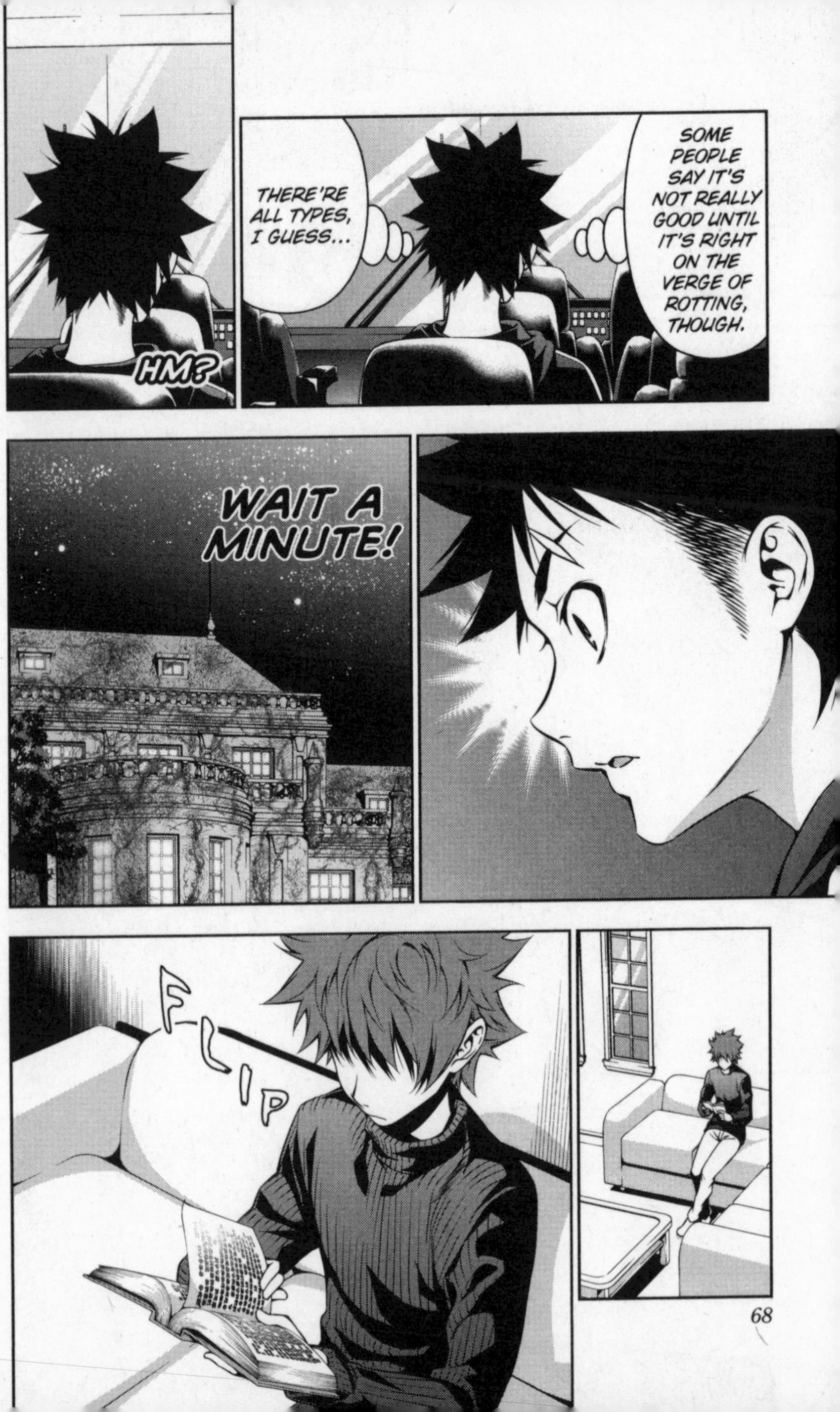
SOME PEOPLE SAY IT'S NOT REALLY GOOD UNTIL IT'S RIGHT ON THE VERGE OF ROTTING, THOUGH.
THERE'RE ALL TYPES, I GUESS...
HM?
WAIT A MINUTE!
FLIP

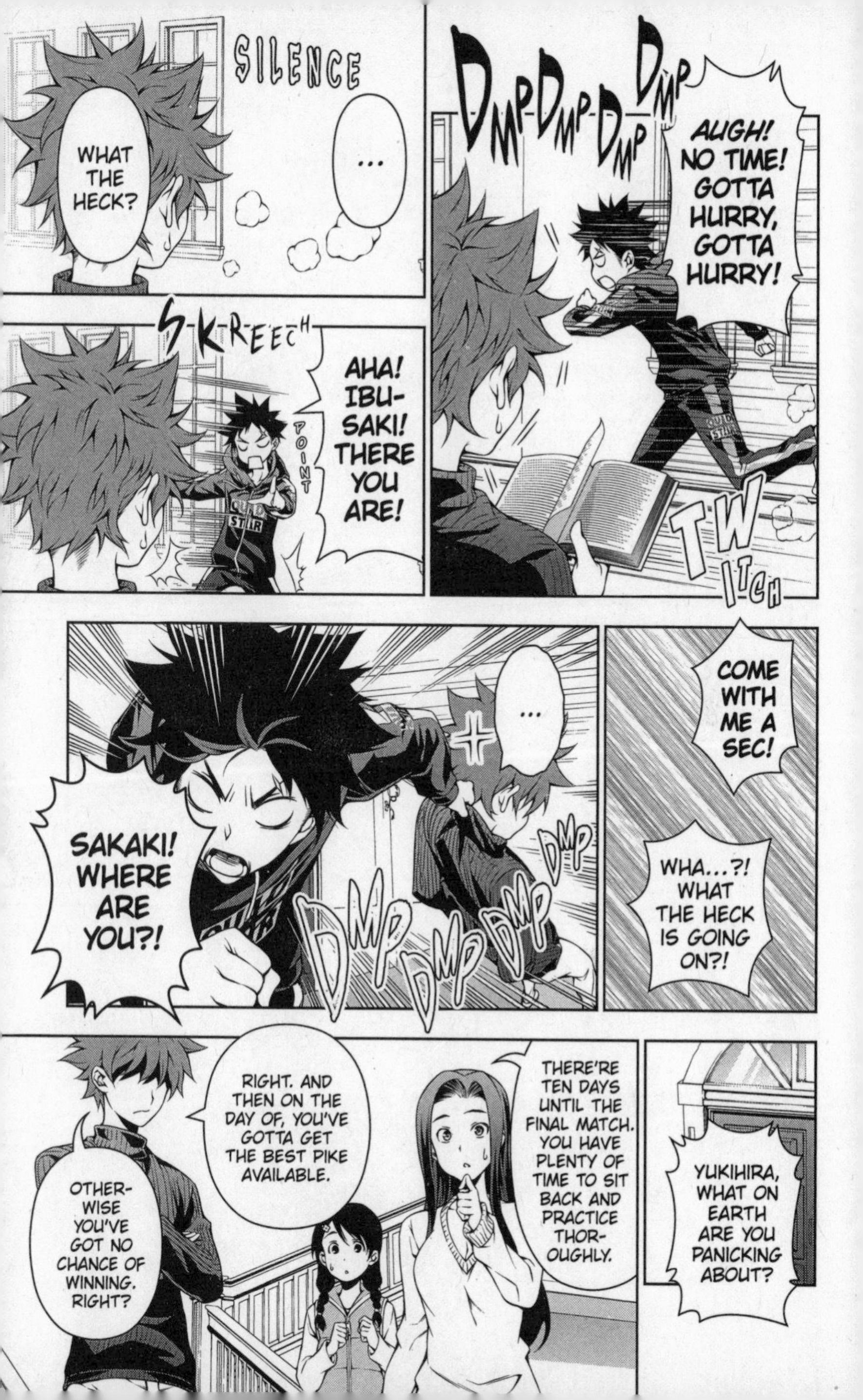
DMP-DMP-DMP-DMP-DMP
AUGH! NO TIME! GOTTA HURRY, GOTTA HURRY!
TWITCH
SILENCE
...
WHAT THE HECK?
SKREECH
AHA! IBUSAKI! THERE YOU ARE!
POINT
COME WITH ME A SEC!
WHA...?! WHAT THE HECK IS GOING ON?!
...
SAKAKI! WHERE ARE YOU?!
DMP DMP DMP DMP
YUKIHIRA, WHAT ON EARTH ARE YOU PANICKING ABOUT?
THERE'RE TEN DAYS UNTIL THE FINAL MATCH. YOU HAVE PLENTY OF TIME TO SIT BACK AND PRACTICE THOR-OUGHLY.
RIGHT. AND THEN ON THE DAY OF, YOU'VE GOTTA GET THE BEST PIKE AVAILABLE.
OTHER-WISE YOU'VE GOT NO CHANCE OF WINNING. RIGHT?

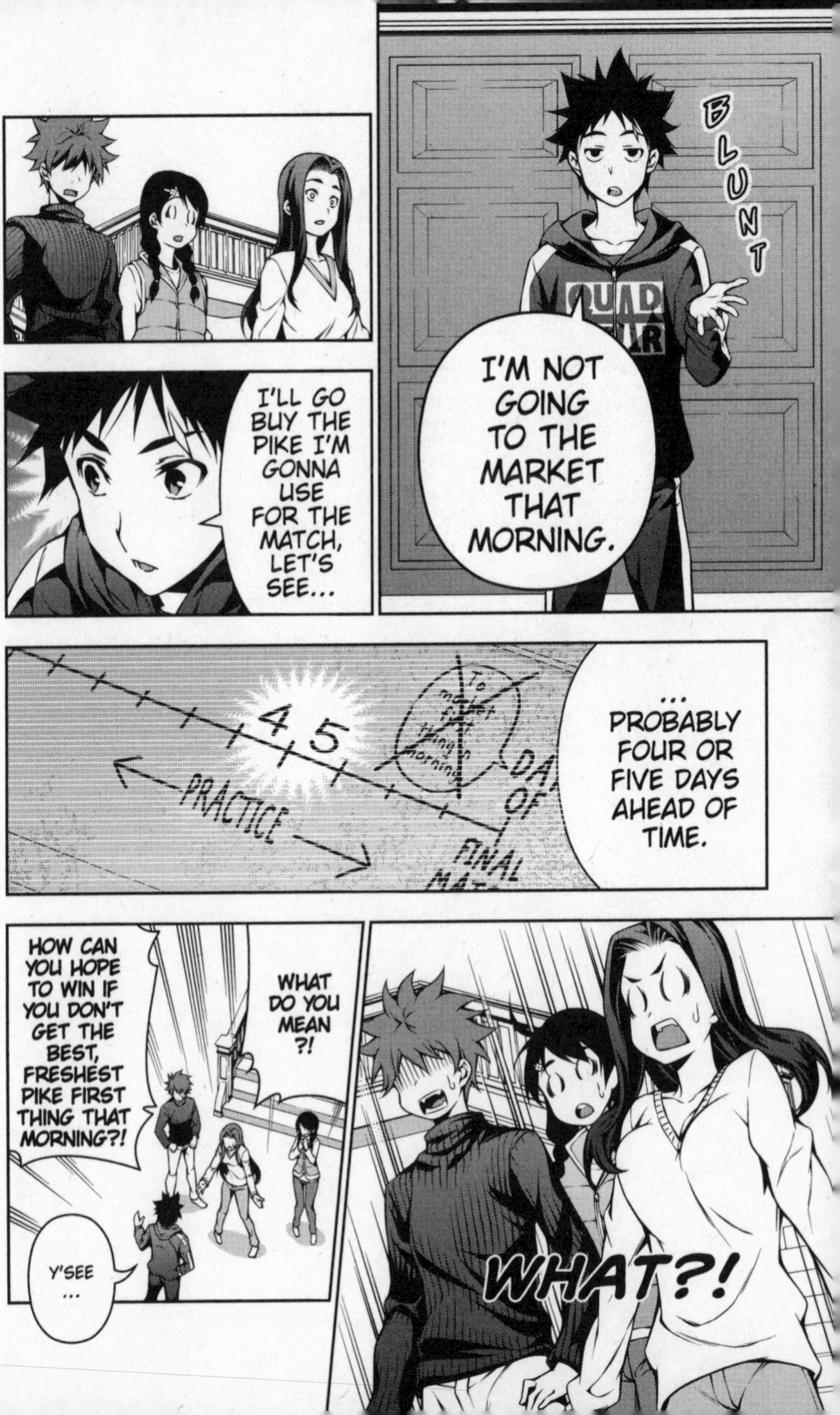
BLUNT
I'M NOT GOING TO THE MARKET THAT MORNING.
I'LL GO BUY THE PIKE I'M GONNA USE FOR THE MATCH, LET'S SEE...
... PROBABLY FOUR OR FIVE DAYS AHEAD OF TIME.
4 5
PRACTICE
DAY OF
FINAL
WHAT?!
WHAT DO YOU MEAN ?!
HOW CAN YOU HOPE TO WIN IF YOU DON'T GET THE BEST, FRESHEST PIKE FIRST THING THAT MORNING?!
Y'SEE ...

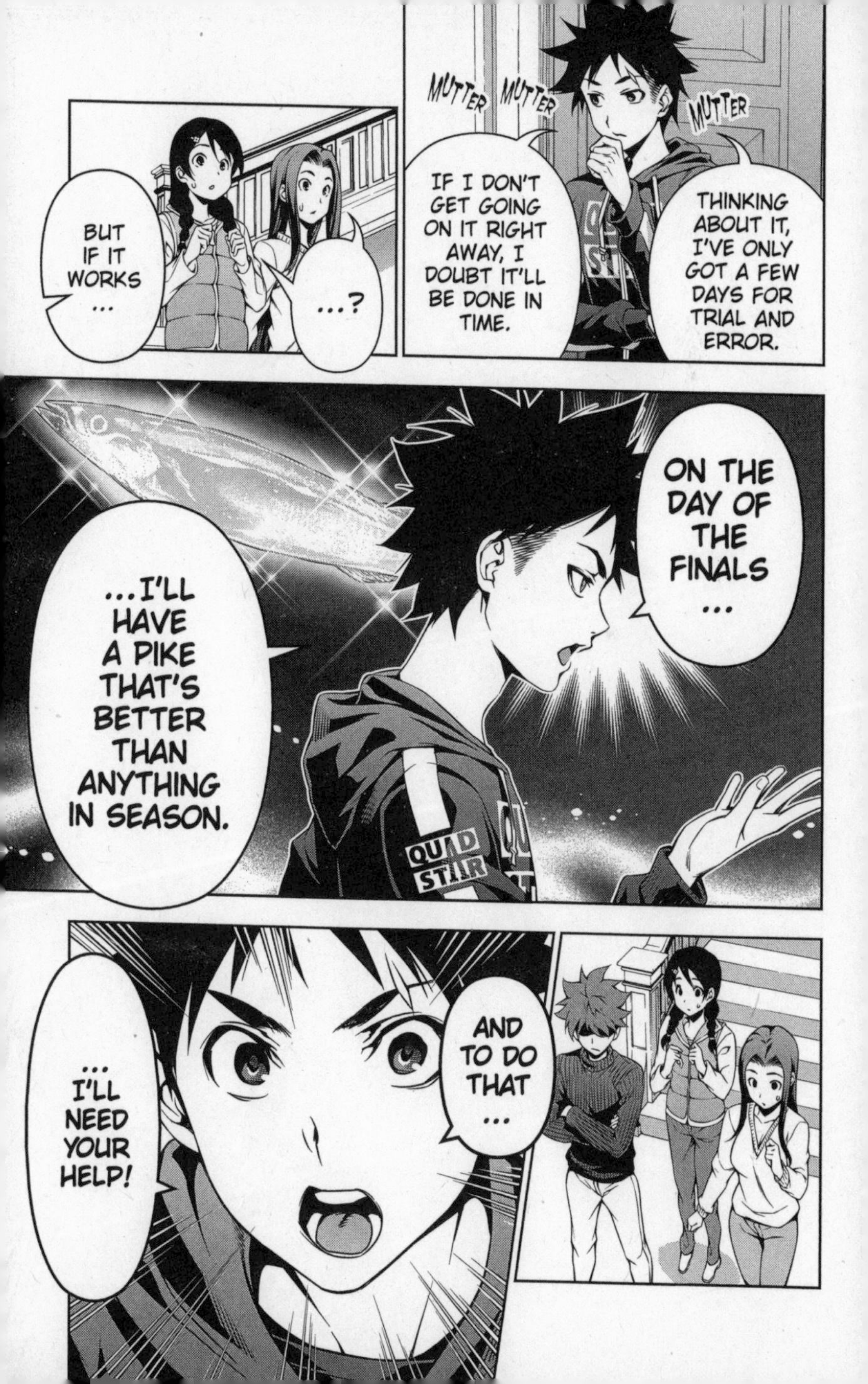
MUTTER MUTTER
MUTTER
THINKING ABOUT IT, I'VE ONLY GOT A FEW DAYS FOR TRIAL AND ERROR.
IF I DON'T GET GOING ON IT RIGHT AWAY, I DOUBT IT'LL BE DONE IN TIME.
...?
BUT IF IT WORKS ...
ON THE DAY OF THE FINALS ...
...I'LL HAVE A PIKE THAT'S BETTER THAN ANYTHING IN SEASON.
QUAD STAR
AND TO DO THAT ...
... I'LL NEED YOUR HELP!

EASY-TO-
CARRY
HANDLE

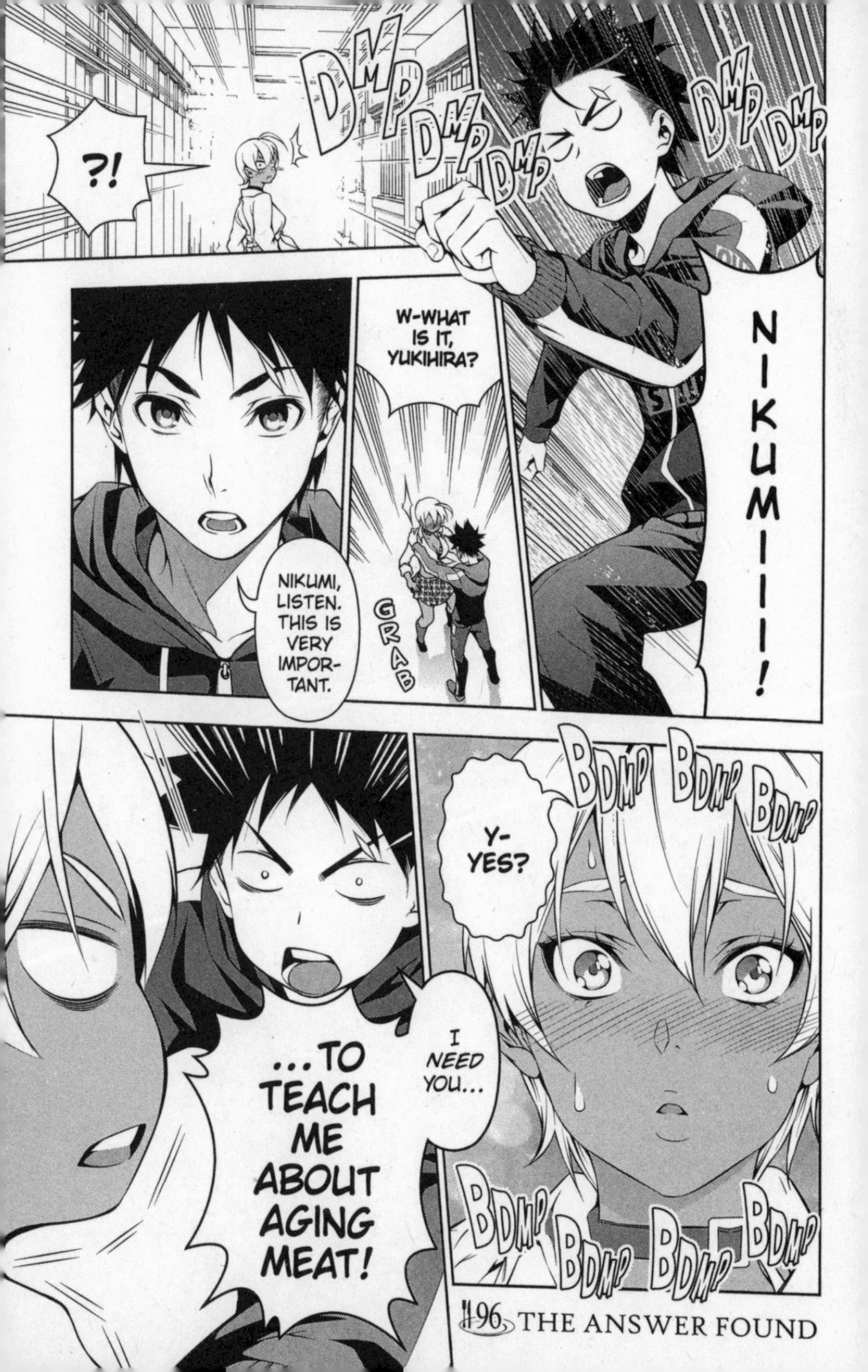
DMP DMP DMP DMP DMP DMP DMP
?!
NIKUMIIII!
W-WHAT IS IT, YUKIHIRA?
GRAB
NIKUMI, LISTEN. THIS IS VERY IMPOR-TANT.
BDMP BDMP BDMP
Y-YES?
BDMP BDMP BDMP BDMP
I NEED YOU...
...TO TEACH ME ABOUT AGING MEAT!

196 THE ANSWER FOUND

96 THE ANSWER FOUND

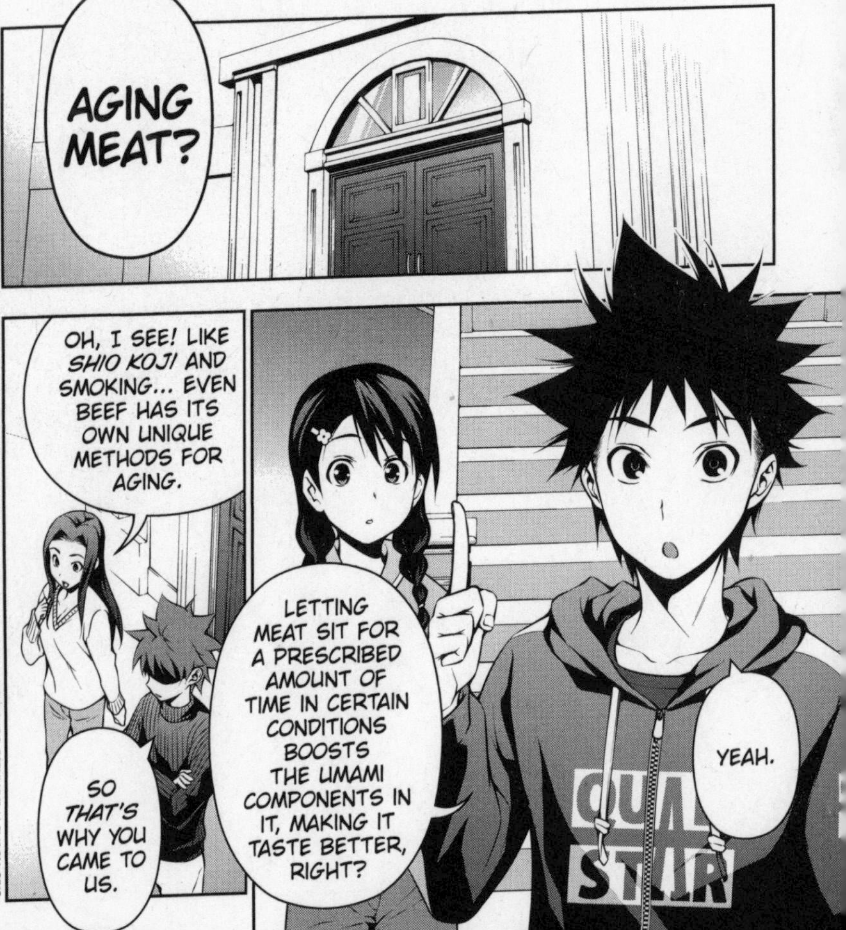
AGING MEAT?
LETTING MEAT SIT FOR A PRESCRIBED AMOUNT OF TIME IN CERTAIN CONDITIONS BOOSTS THE UMAMI COMPONENTS IN IT, MAKING IT TASTE BETTER, RIGHT?
YEAH.
OH, I SEE! LIKE *SHIO KOJI* AND SMOKING... EVEN BEEF HAS ITS OWN UNIQUE METHODS FOR AGING.
SO *THAT'S* WHY YOU CAME TO US.

*SHIO KOJI IS A JAPANESE CONDIMENT MADE FROM SALT AND RICE INOCULATED BY KOJI (A MOLD).

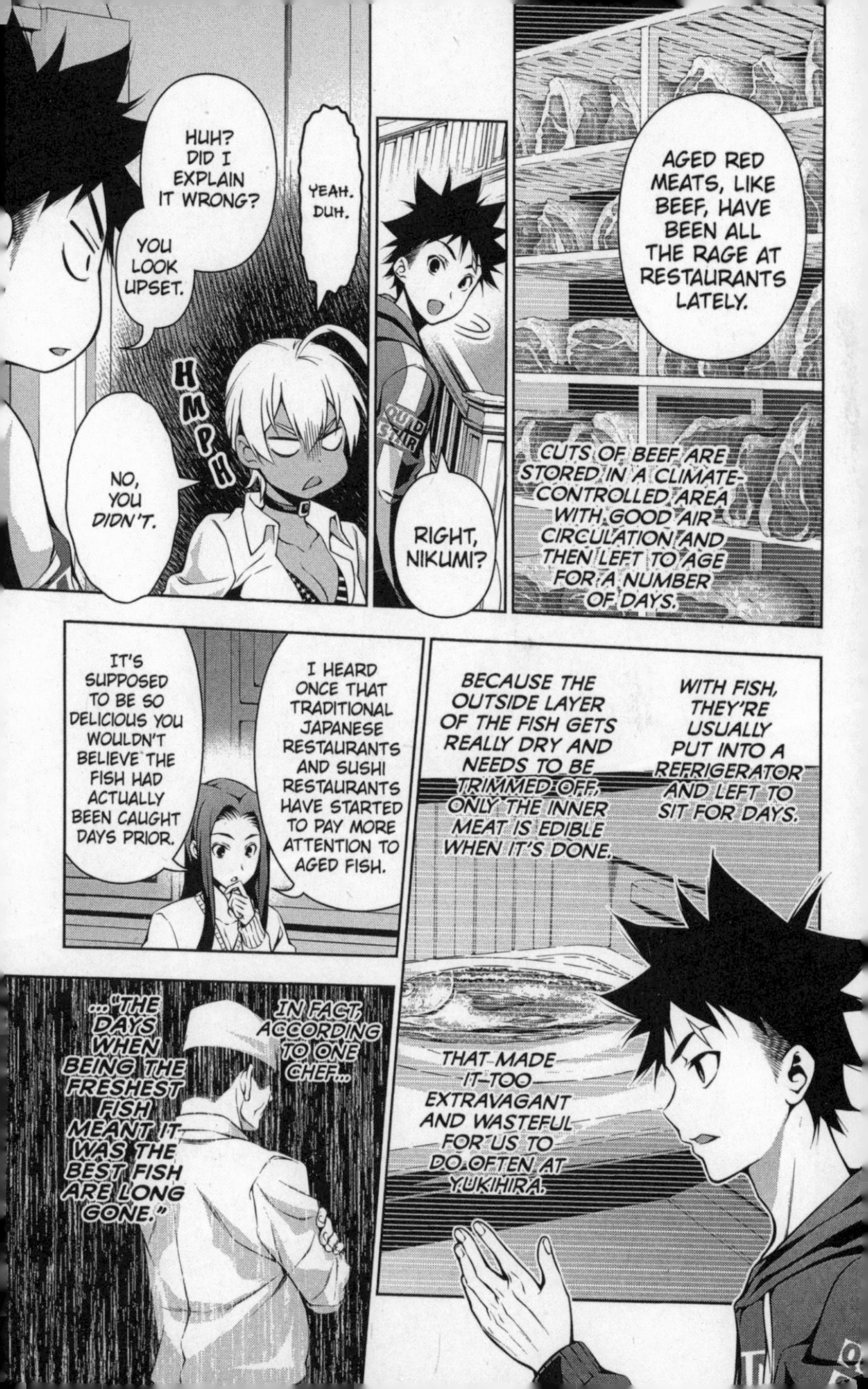
AGED RED MEATS, LIKE BEEF, HAVE BEEN ALL THE RAGE AT RESTAURANTS LATELY.
CUTS OF BEEF ARE STORED IN A CLIMATE-CONTROLLED AREA WITH GOOD AIR CIRCULATION AND THEN LEFT TO AGE FOR A NUMBER OF DAYS.
RIGHT, NIKUMI?
YEAH. DUH.
HUH? DID I EXPLAIN IT WRONG?
YOU LOOK UPSET.
HMPH
NO, YOU DIDN'T.
WITH FISH, THEY'RE USUALLY PUT INTO A REFRIGERATOR AND LEFT TO SIT FOR DAYS.
BECAUSE THE OUTSIDE LAYER OF THE FISH GETS REALLY DRY AND NEEDS TO BE TRIMMED OFF, ONLY THE INNER MEAT IS EDIBLE WHEN IT'S DONE.
THAT MADE IT TOO EXTRAVAGANT AND WASTEFUL FOR US TO DO OFTEN AT YUKIHIRA.
I HEARD ONCE THAT TRADITIONAL JAPANESE RESTAURANTS AND SUSHI RESTAURANTS HAVE STARTED TO PAY MORE ATTENTION TO AGED FISH.
IT'S SUPPOSED TO BE SO DELICIOUS YOU WOULDN'T BELIEVE THE FISH HAD ACTUALLY BEEN CAUGHT DAYS PRIOR.
IN FACT, ACCORDING TO ONE CHEF...
..."THE DAYS WHEN BEING THE FRESHEST FISH MEANT IT WAS THE BEST FISH ARE LONG GONE."

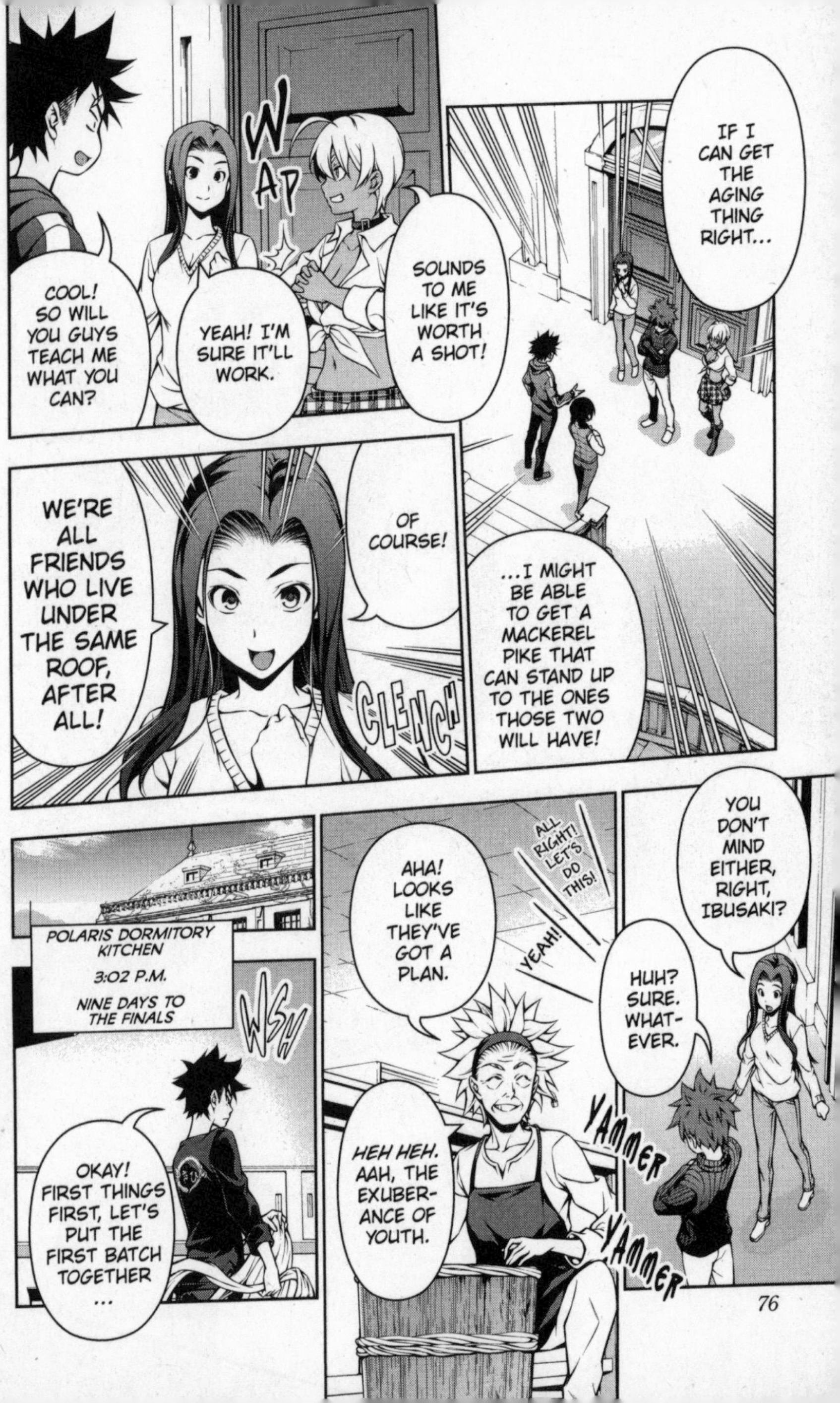

IF I CAN GET THE AGING THING RIGHT...
...I MIGHT BE ABLE TO GET A MACKEREL PIKE THAT CAN STAND UP TO THE ONES THOSE TWO WILL HAVE!
WAP
SOUNDS TO ME LIKE IT'S WORTH A SHOT!
YEAH! I'M SURE IT'LL WORK.
COOL! SO WILL YOU GUYS TEACH ME WHAT YOU CAN?
OF COURSE!
CLENCH
WE'RE ALL FRIENDS WHO LIVE UNDER THE SAME ROOF, AFTER ALL!
YOU DON'T MIND EITHER, RIGHT, IBUSAKI?
HUH? SURE. WHAT-EVER.
YAMMER
YAMMER
ALL RIGHT! LET'S DO THIS!
YEAH!
AHA! LOOKS LIKE THEY'VE GOT A PLAN.
HEH HEH. AAH, THE EXUBER-ANCE OF YOUTH.
POLARIS DORMITORY KITCHEN
3:02 P.M.
NINE DAYS TO THE FINALS
WSH
OKAY! FIRST THINGS FIRST, LET'S PUT THE FIRST BATCH TOGETHER ...

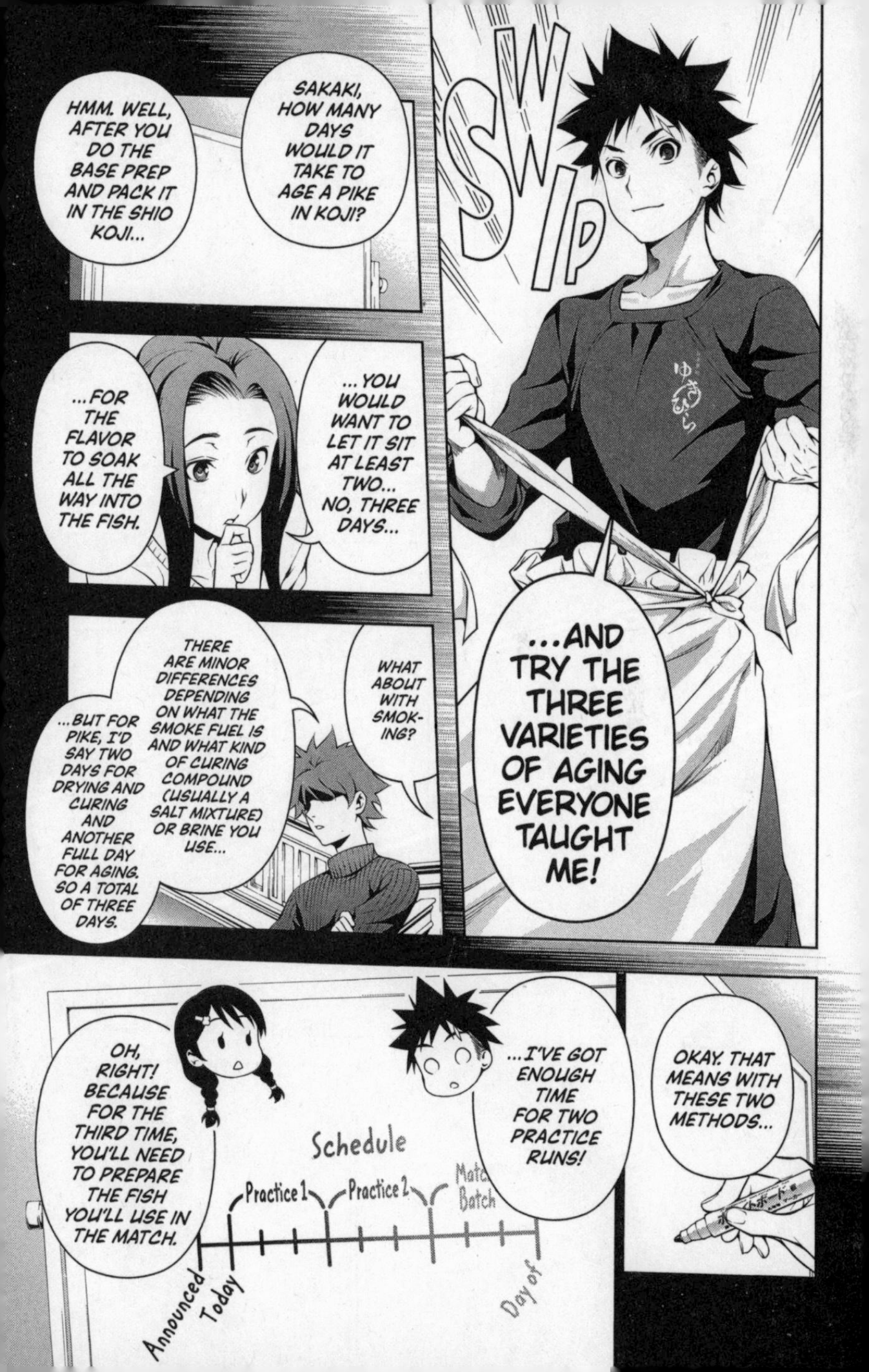
SWIP
...AND TRY THE THREE VARIETIES OF AGING EVERYONE TAUGHT ME!
SAKAKI, HOW MANY DAYS WOULD IT TAKE TO AGE A PIKE IN KOJI?
HMM. WELL, AFTER YOU DO THE BASE PREP AND PACK IT IN THE SHIO KOJI...
...YOU WOULD WANT TO LET IT SIT AT LEAST TWO... NO, THREE DAYS...
...FOR THE FLAVOR TO SOAK ALL THE WAY INTO THE FISH.
WHAT ABOUT WITH SMOKING?
THERE ARE MINOR DIFFERENCES DEPENDING ON WHAT THE SMOKE FUEL IS AND WHAT KIND OF CURING COMPOUND (USUALLY A SALT MIXTURE) OR BRINE YOU USE...
...BUT FOR PIKE, I'D SAY TWO DAYS FOR DRYING AND CURING AND ANOTHER FULL DAY FOR AGING. SO A TOTAL OF THREE DAYS.
OKAY. THAT MEANS WITH THESE TWO METHODS...
...I'VE GOT ENOUGH TIME FOR TWO PRACTICE RUNS!
OH, RIGHT! BECAUSE FOR THE THIRD TIME, YOU'LL NEED TO PREPARE THE FISH YOU'LL USE IN THE MATCH.
Schedule
Practice 1
Practice 2
Batch
Announced
Today
Day of

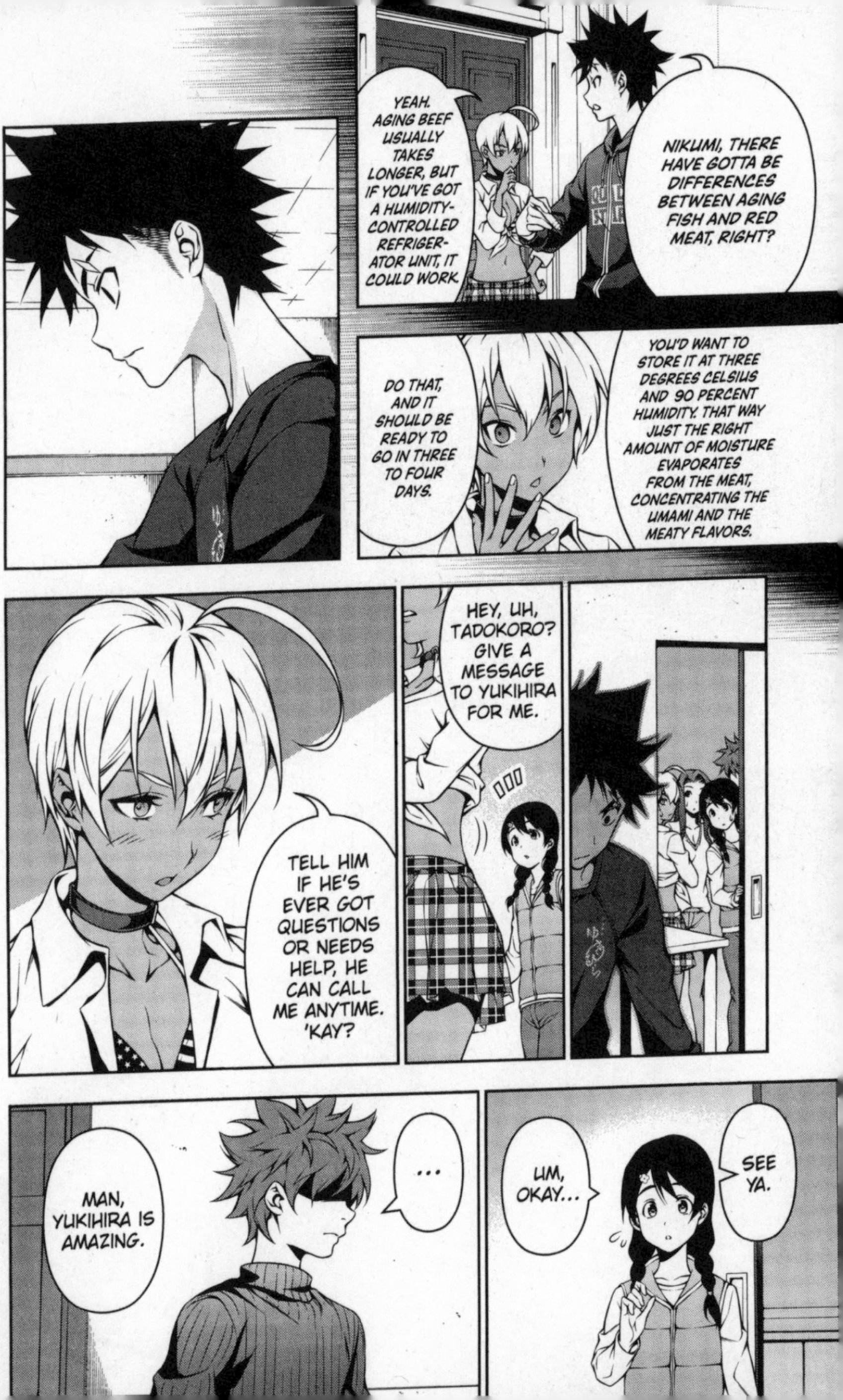
NIKUMI, THERE HAVE GOTTA BE DIFFERENCES BETWEEN AGING FISH AND RED MEAT, RIGHT?
YEAH. AGING BEEF USUALLY TAKES LONGER, BUT IF YOU'VE GOT A HUMIDITY-CONTROLLED REFRIGER-ATOR UNIT, IT COULD WORK.
YOU'D WANT TO STORE IT AT THREE DEGREES CELSIUS AND 90 PERCENT HUMIDITY. THAT WAY JUST THE RIGHT AMOUNT OF MOISTURE EVAPORATES FROM THE MEAT, CONCENTRATING THE UMAMI AND THE MEATY FLAVORS.
DO THAT, AND IT SHOULD BE READY TO GO IN THREE TO FOUR DAYS.
HEY, UH, TADOKORO? GIVE A MESSAGE TO YUKIHIRA FOR ME.
TELL HIM IF HE'S EVER GOT QUESTIONS OR NEEDS HELP, HE CAN CALL ME ANYTIME. 'KAY?
SEE YA.
UM, OKAY...
...
MAN, YUKIHIRA IS AMAZING.

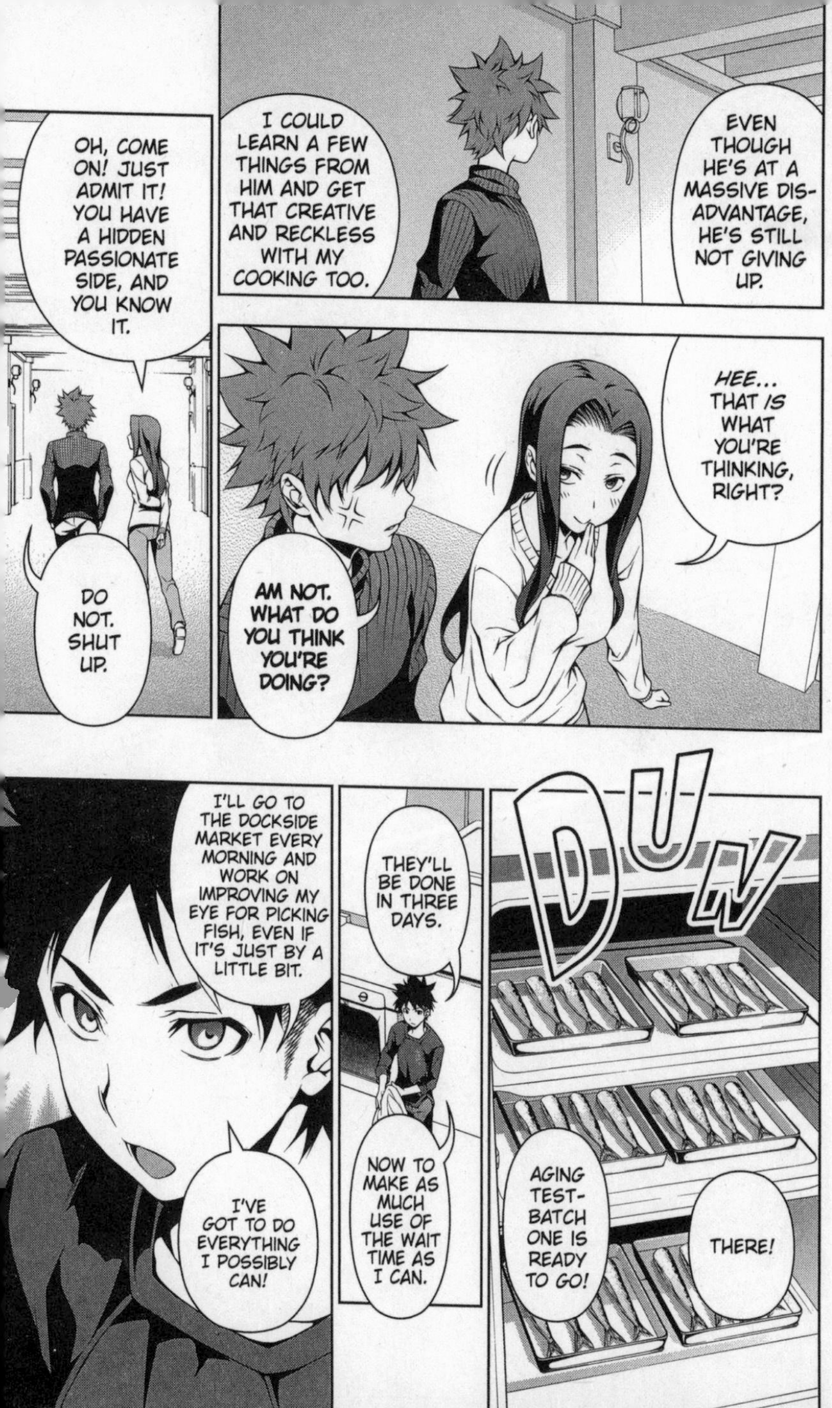
EVEN THOUGH HE'S AT A MASSIVE DIS-ADVANTAGE, HE'S STILL NOT GIVING UP.
I COULD LEARN A FEW THINGS FROM HIM AND GET THAT CREATIVE AND RECKLESS WITH MY COOKING TOO.
HEE... THAT *IS* WHAT YOU'RE THINKING, RIGHT?
AM NOT. WHAT DO YOU THINK YOU'RE DOING?
OH, COME ON! JUST ADMIT IT! YOU HAVE A HIDDEN PASSIONATE SIDE, AND YOU KNOW IT.
DO NOT. SHUT UP.
DUN
THERE!
AGING TEST-BATCH ONE IS READY TO GO!
THEY'LL BE DONE IN THREE DAYS.
NOW TO MAKE AS MUCH USE OF THE WAIT TIME AS I CAN.
I'LL GO TO THE DOCKSIDE MARKET EVERY MORNING AND WORK ON IMPROVING MY EYE FOR PICKING FISH, EVEN IF IT'S JUST BY A LITTLE BIT.
I'VE GOT TO DO EVERYTHING I POSSIBLY CAN!

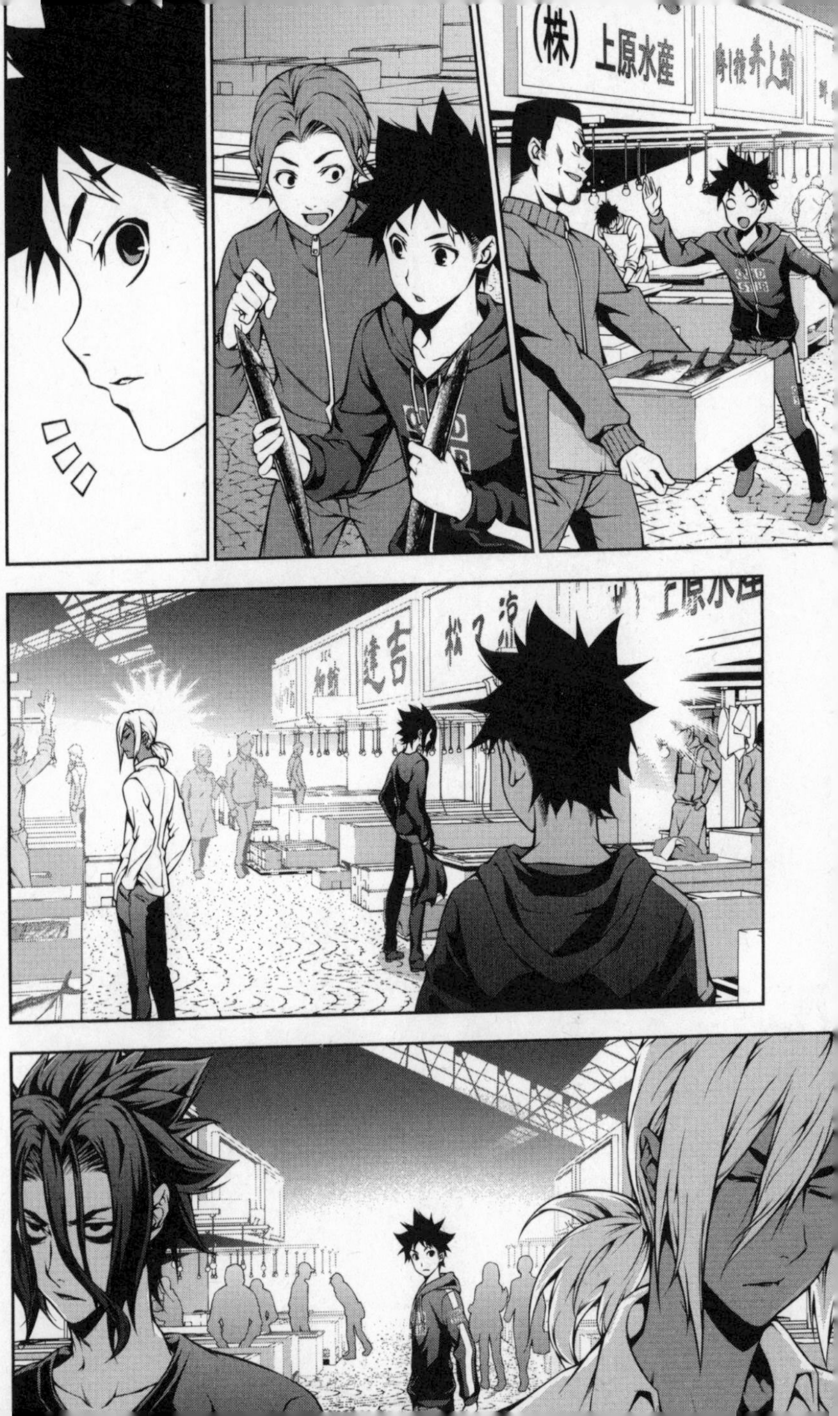
(株) 上原水産

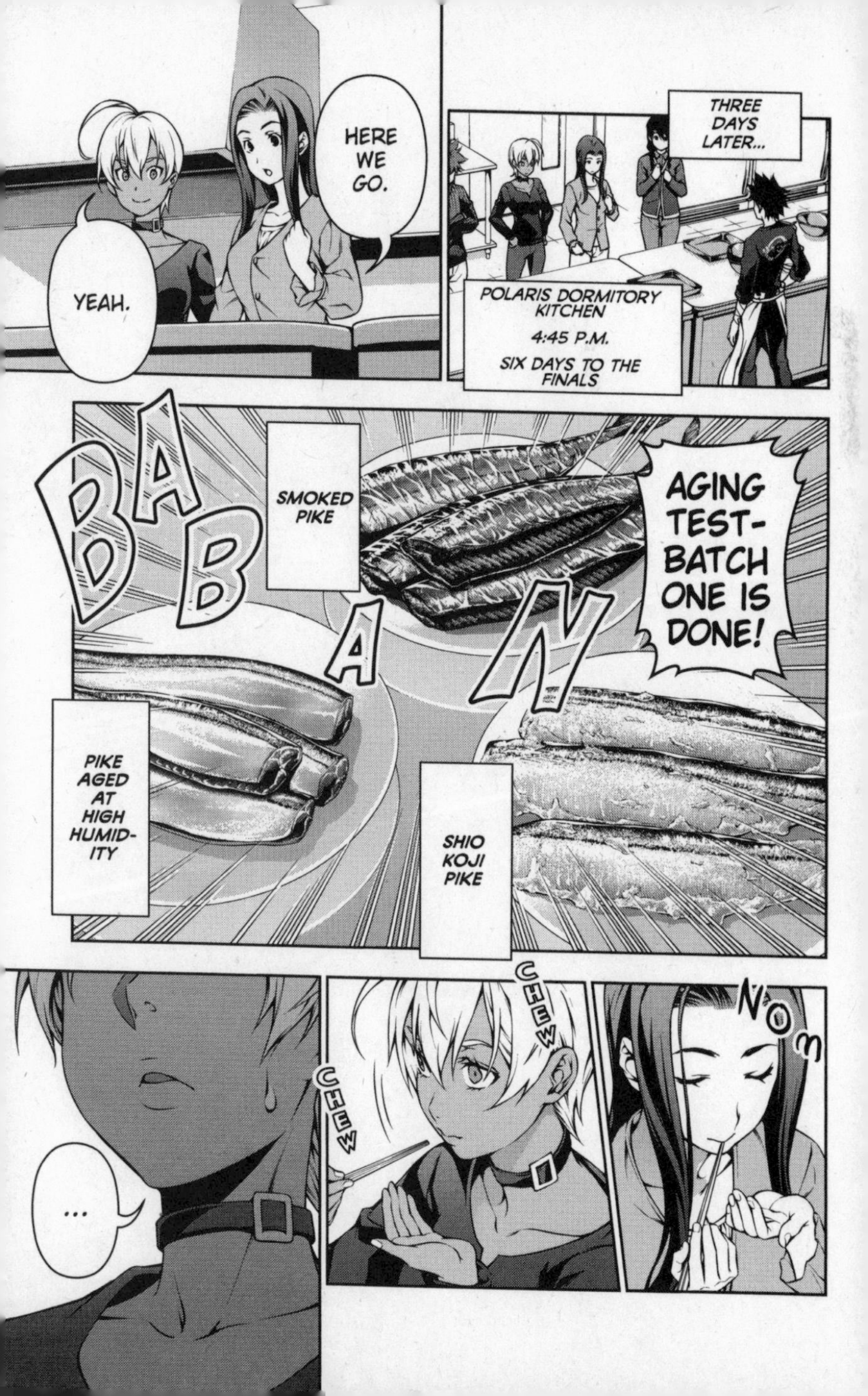
THREE DAYS LATER...
POLARIS DORMITORY KITCHEN
4:45 P.M.
SIX DAYS TO THE FINALS
HERE WE GO.
YEAH.
AGING TEST-BATCH ONE IS DONE!
SMOKED PIKE
BABAN
SHIO KOJI PIKE
PIKE AGED AT HIGH HUMIDITY
NOM
CHEW
CHEW
...

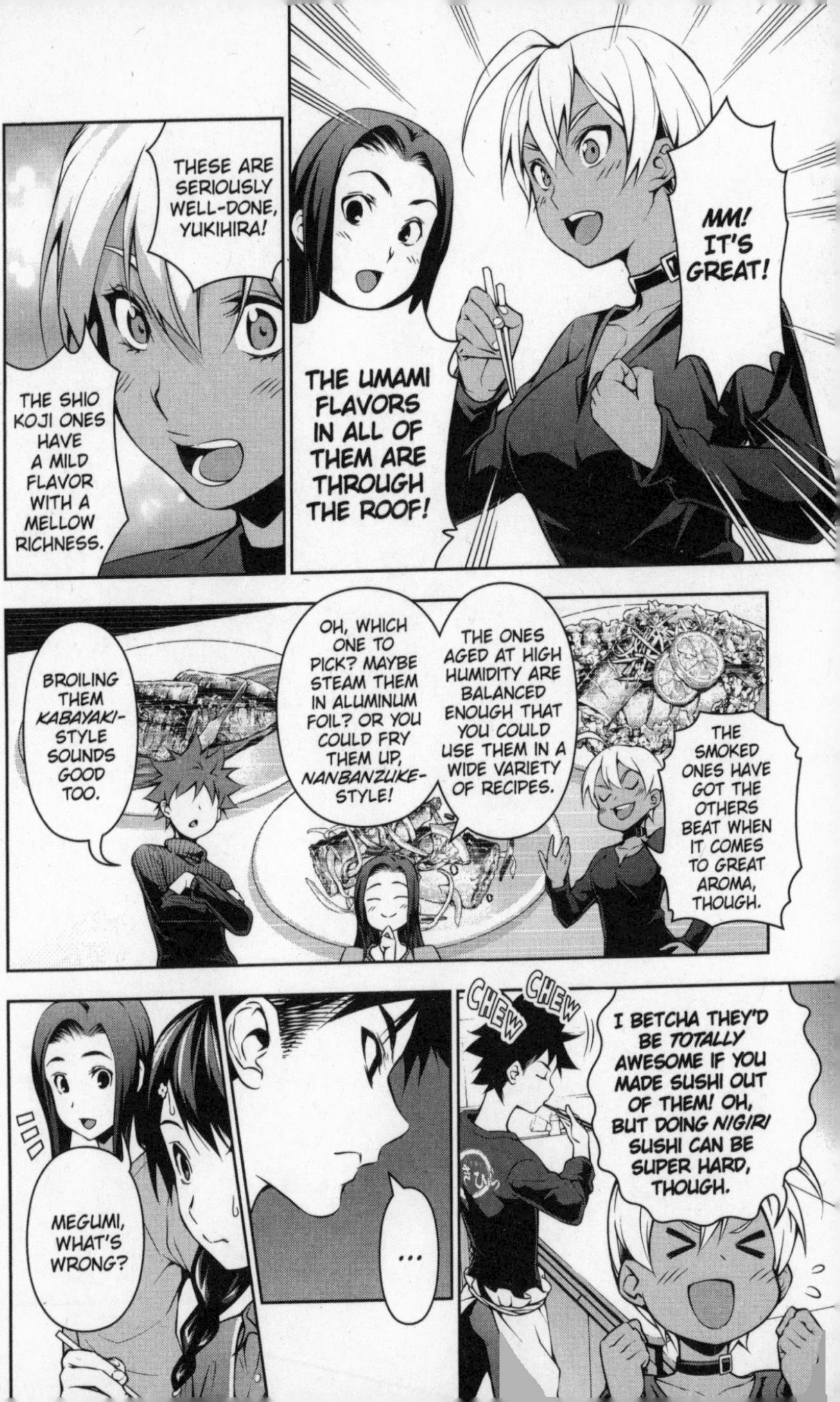
MM! IT'S GREAT!
THE UMAMI FLAVORS IN ALL OF THEM ARE THROUGH THE ROOF!
THESE ARE SERIOUSLY WELL-DONE, YUKIHIRA!
THE SHIO KOJI ONES HAVE A MILD FLAVOR WITH A MELLOW RICHNESS.
THE SMOKED ONES HAVE GOT THE OTHERS BEAT WHEN IT COMES TO GREAT AROMA, THOUGH.
THE ONES AGED AT HIGH HUMIDITY ARE BALANCED ENOUGH THAT YOU COULD USE THEM IN A WIDE VARIETY OF RECIPES.
OH, WHICH ONE TO PICK? MAYBE STEAM THEM IN ALUMINUM FOIL? OR YOU COULD FRY THEM UP, *NANBANZUKE*-STYLE!
BROILING THEM *KABAYAKI*-STYLE SOUNDS GOOD TOO.
CHEW CHEW
I BETCHA THEY'D BE *TOTALLY* AWESOME IF YOU MADE SUSHI OUT OF THEM! OH, BUT DOING *NIGIRI* SUSHI CAN BE SUPER HARD, THOUGH.
...
MEGUMI, WHAT'S WRONG?

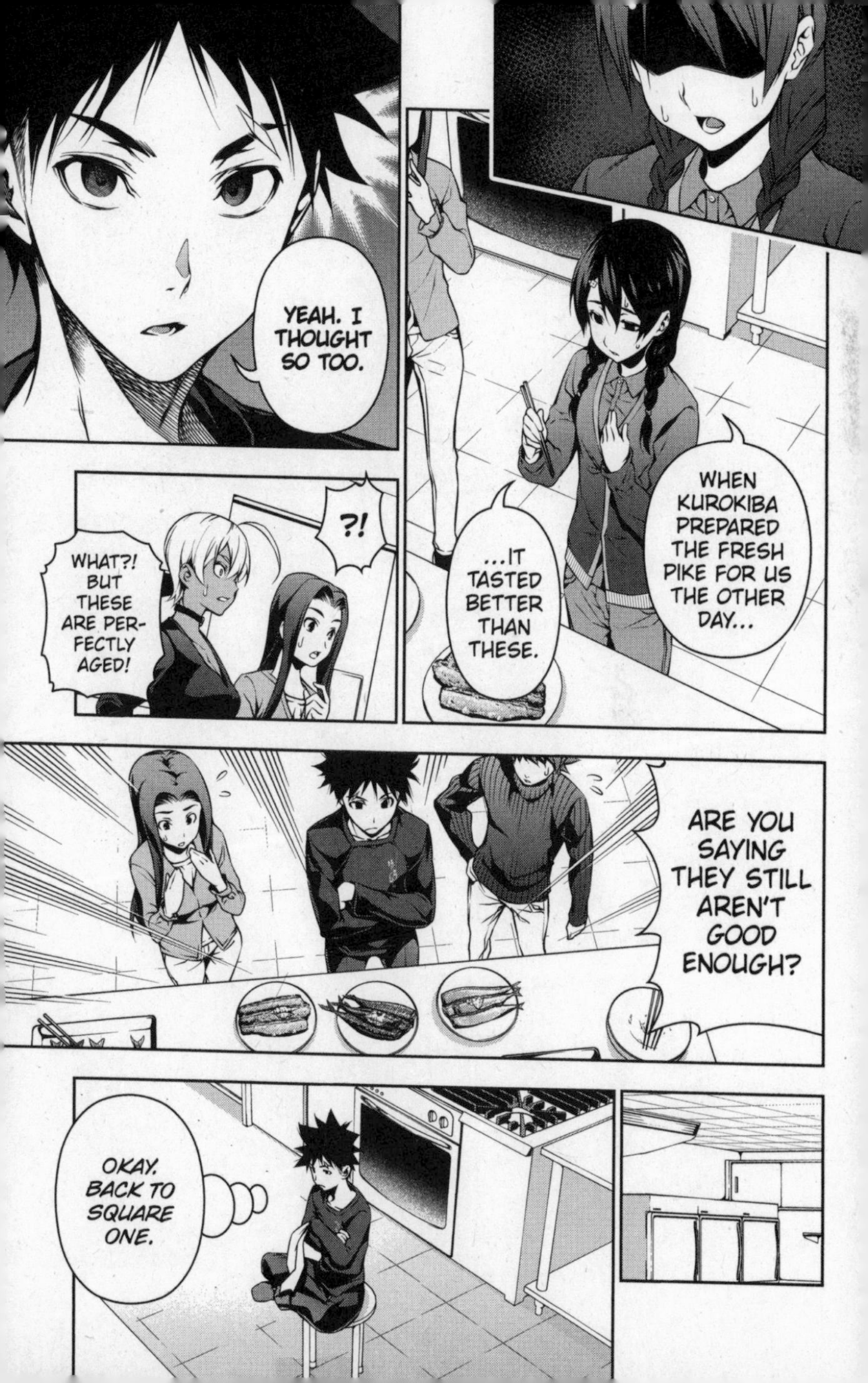
WHEN KUROKIBA PREPARED THE FRESH PIKE FOR US THE OTHER DAY...
...IT TASTED BETTER THAN THESE.
YEAH. I THOUGHT SO TOO.
?!
WHAT?! BUT THESE ARE PER-FECTLY AGED!
ARE YOU SAYING THEY STILL AREN'T GOOD ENOUGH?
OKAY. BACK TO SQUARE ONE.

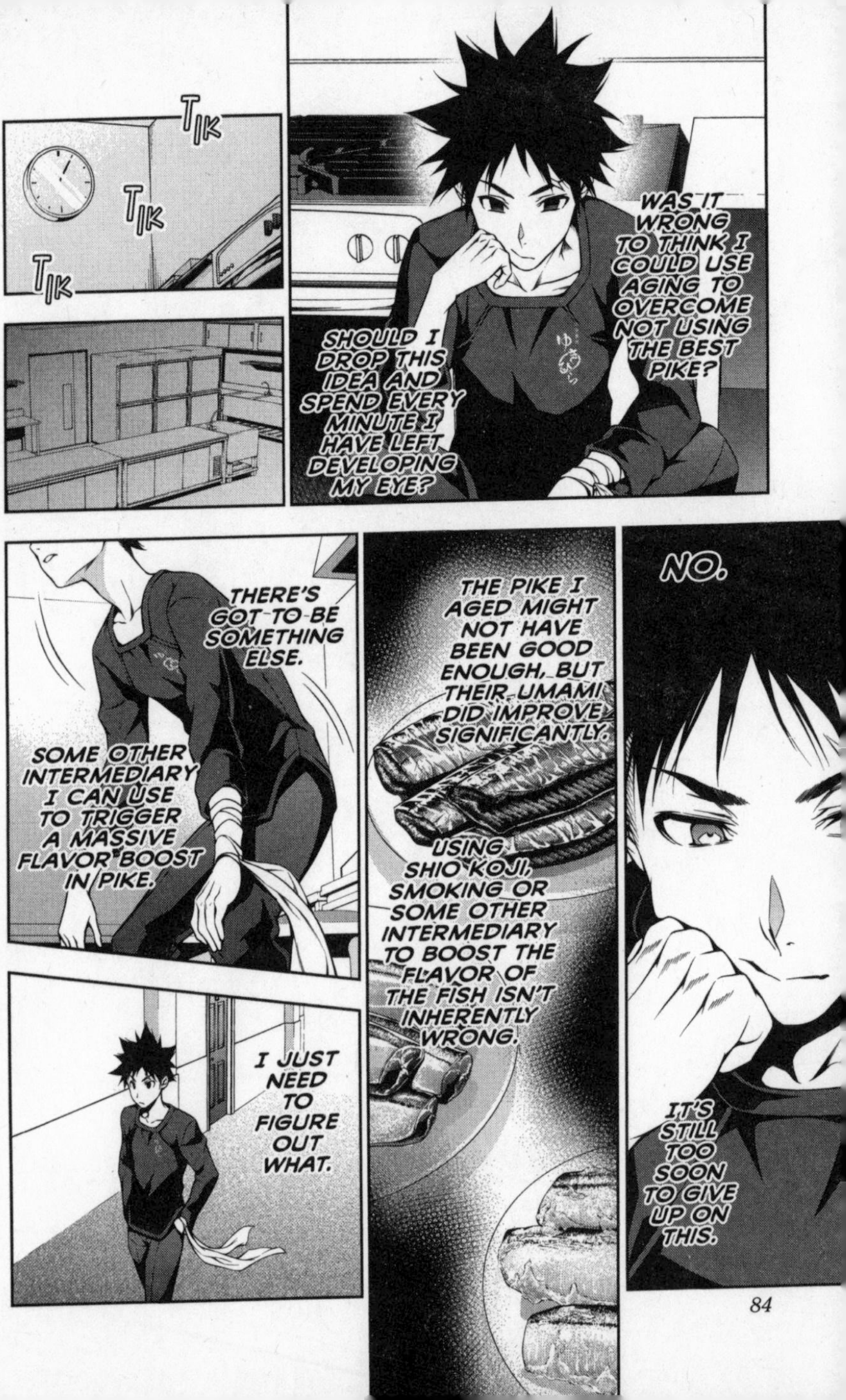
WAS IT WRONG TO THINK I COULD USE AGING TO OVERCOME NOT USING THE BEST PIKE?
SHOULD I DROP THIS IDEA AND SPEND EVERY MINUTE I HAVE LEFT DEVELOPING MY EYE?
TIK
TIK
TIK
NO.
IT'S STILL TOO SOON TO GIVE UP ON THIS.
THE PIKE I AGED MIGHT NOT HAVE BEEN GOOD ENOUGH, BUT THEIR UMAMI DID IMPROVE SIGNIFICANTLY.
USING SHIO KOJI, SMOKING OR SOME OTHER INTERMEDIARY TO BOOST THE FLAVOR OF THE FISH ISN'T INHERENTLY WRONG.
THERE'S GOT TO BE SOMETHING ELSE.
SOME OTHER INTERMEDIARY I CAN USE TO TRIGGER A MASSIVE FLAVOR BOOST IN PIKE.
I JUST NEED TO FIGURE OUT WHAT.

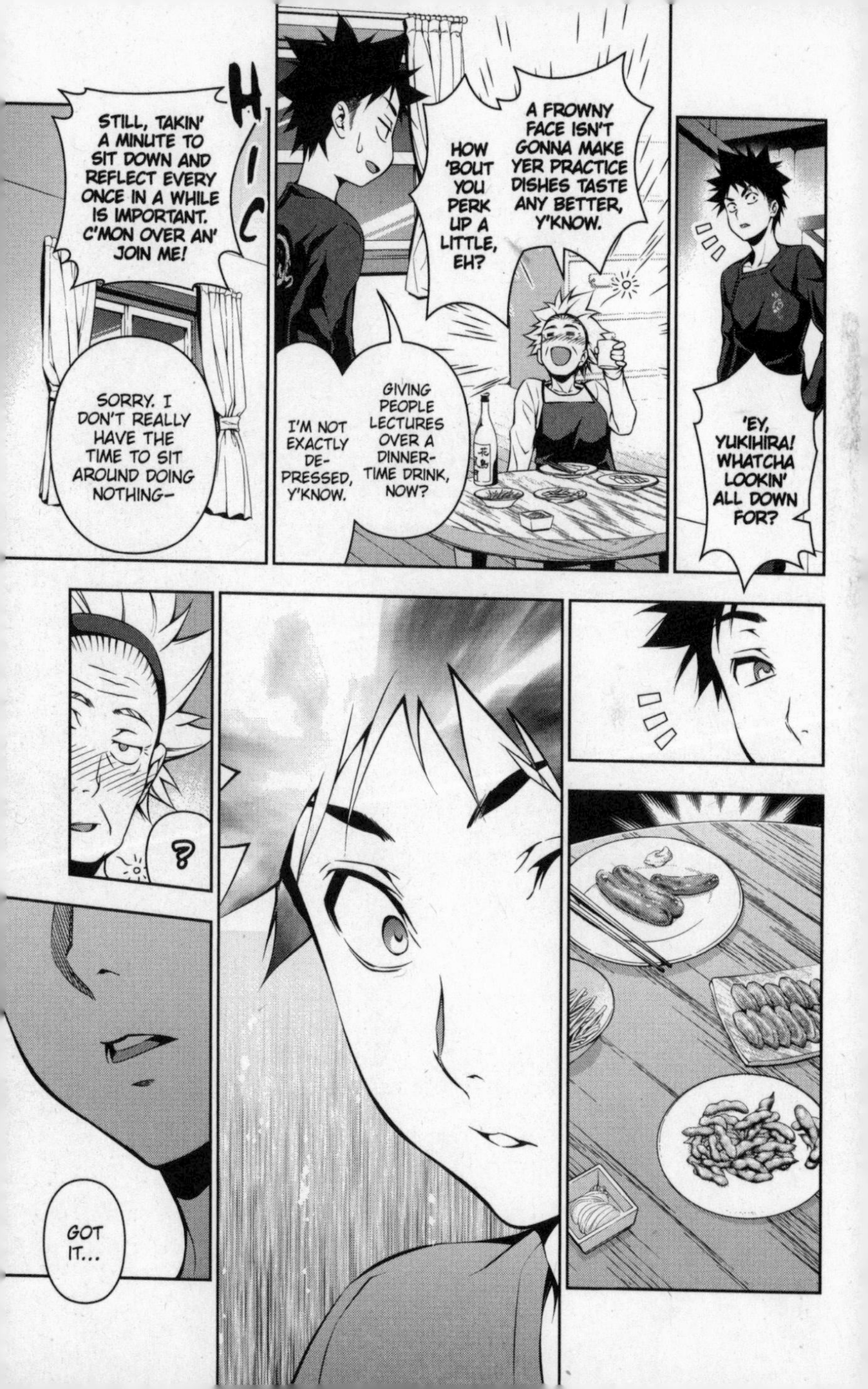
'EY, YUKIHIRA! WHATCHA LOOKIN' ALL DOWN FOR?
A FROWNY FACE ISN'T GONNA MAKE YER PRACTICE DISHES TASTE ANY BETTER, Y'KNOW.
HOW 'BOUT YOU PERK UP A LITTLE, EH?
GIVING PEOPLE LECTURES OVER A DINNER-TIME DRINK, NOW?
I'M NOT EXACTLY DE-PRESSED, Y'KNOW.
HIC
STILL, TAKIN' A MINUTE TO SIT DOWN AND REFLECT EVERY ONCE IN A WHILE IS IMPORTANT. C'MON OVER AN' JOIN ME!
SORRY. I DON'T REALLY HAVE THE TIME TO SIT AROUND DOING NOTHING-
?
GOT IT...

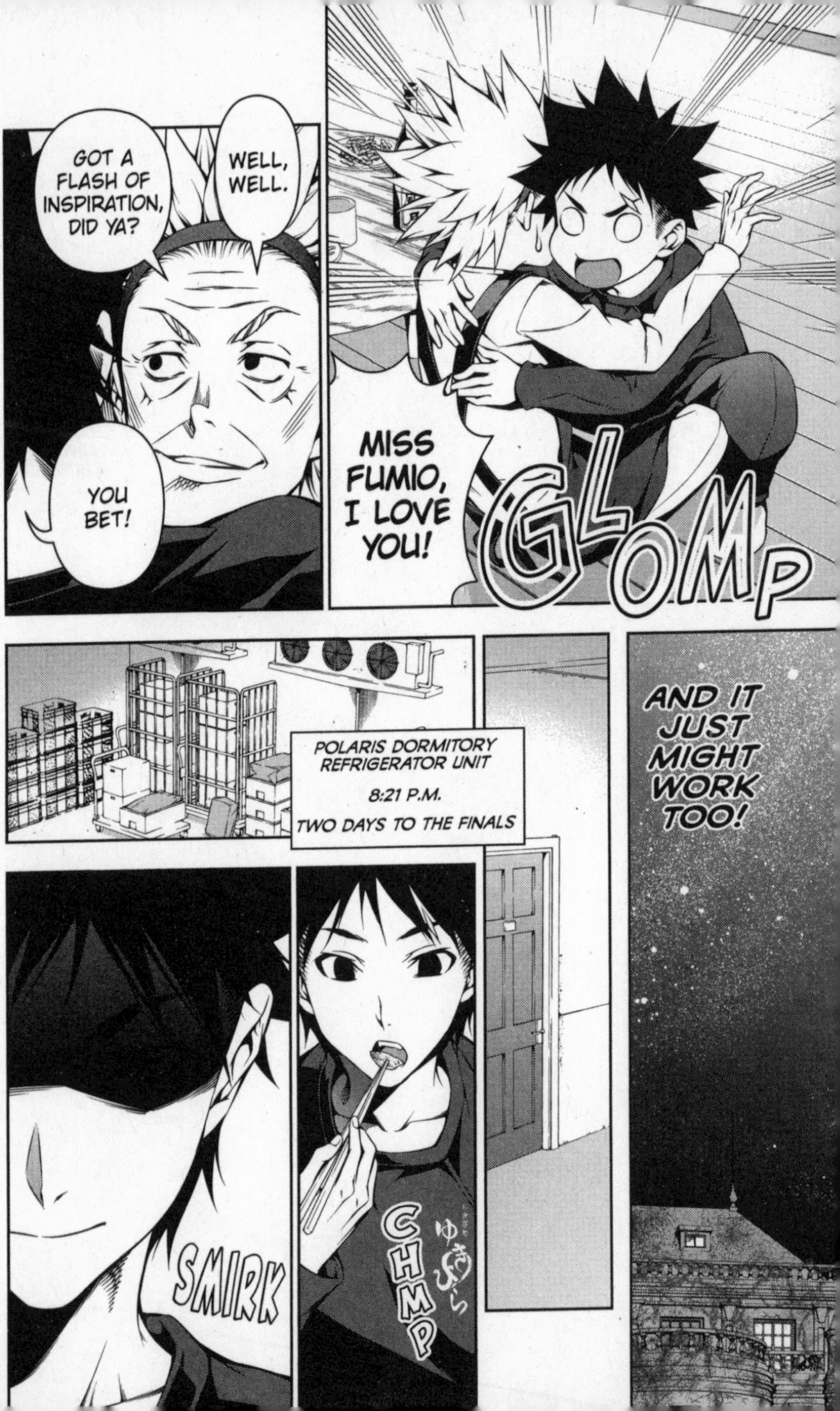
MISS FUMIO, I LOVE YOU!
GLOMP
WELL, WELL.
GOT A FLASH OF INSPIRATION, DID YA?
YOU BET!
AND IT JUST MIGHT WORK TOO!
POLARIS DORMITORY REFRIGERATOR UNIT
8:21 P.M.
TWO DAYS TO THE FINALS
ゆきひら
CHMP
SMIRK

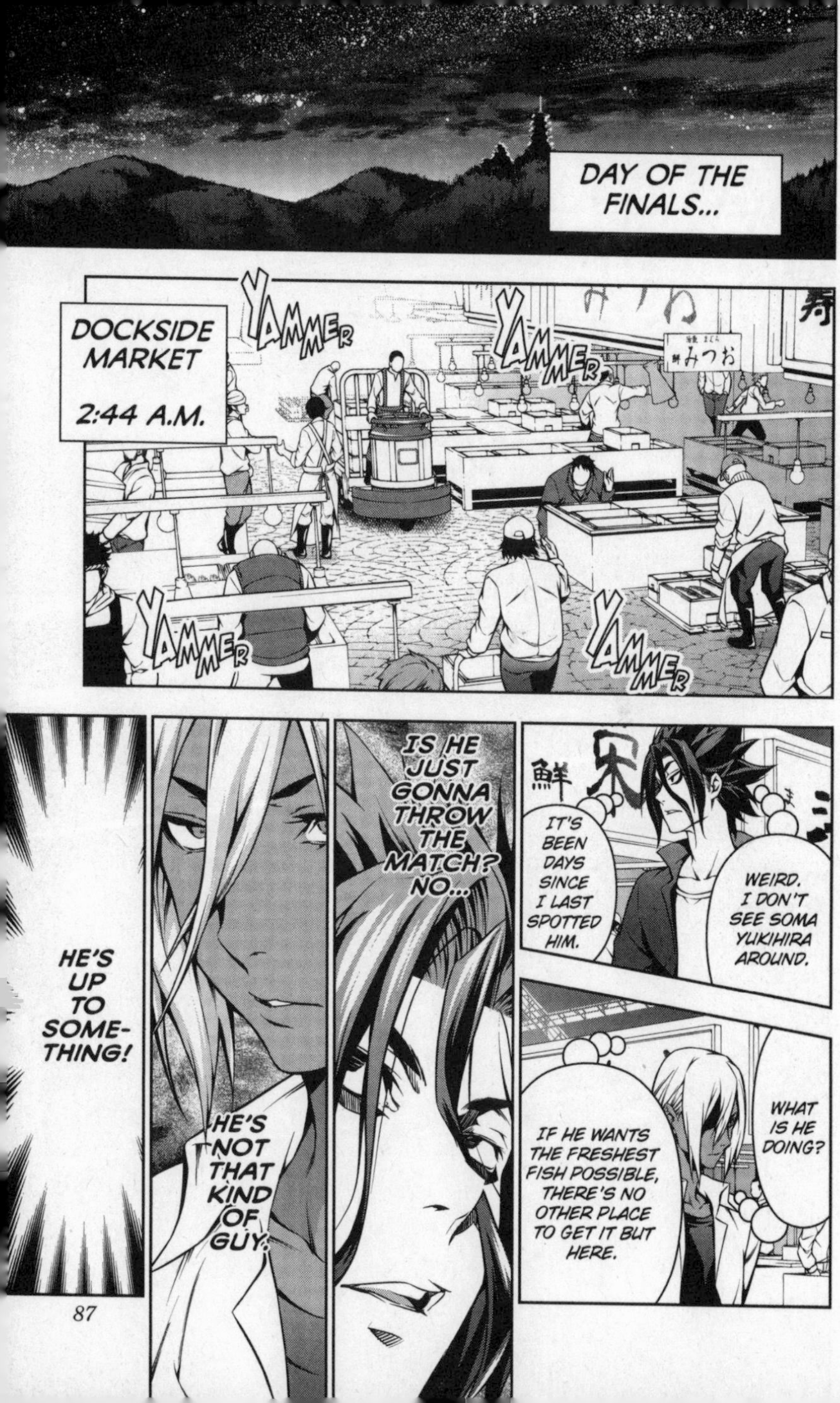
DAY OF THE FINALS...
DOCKSIDE MARKET
2:44 A.M.
YAMMER
YAMMER
YAMMER
YAMMER
みつお
WEIRD. I DON'T SEE SOMA YUKIHIRA AROUND.
IT'S BEEN DAYS SINCE I LAST SPOTTED HIM.
WHAT IS HE DOING?
IF HE WANTS THE FRESHEST FISH POSSIBLE, THERE'S NO OTHER PLACE TO GET IT BUT HERE.
IS HE JUST GONNA THROW THE MATCH? NO...
HE'S NOT THAT KIND OF GUY.
HE'S UP TO SOME-THING!

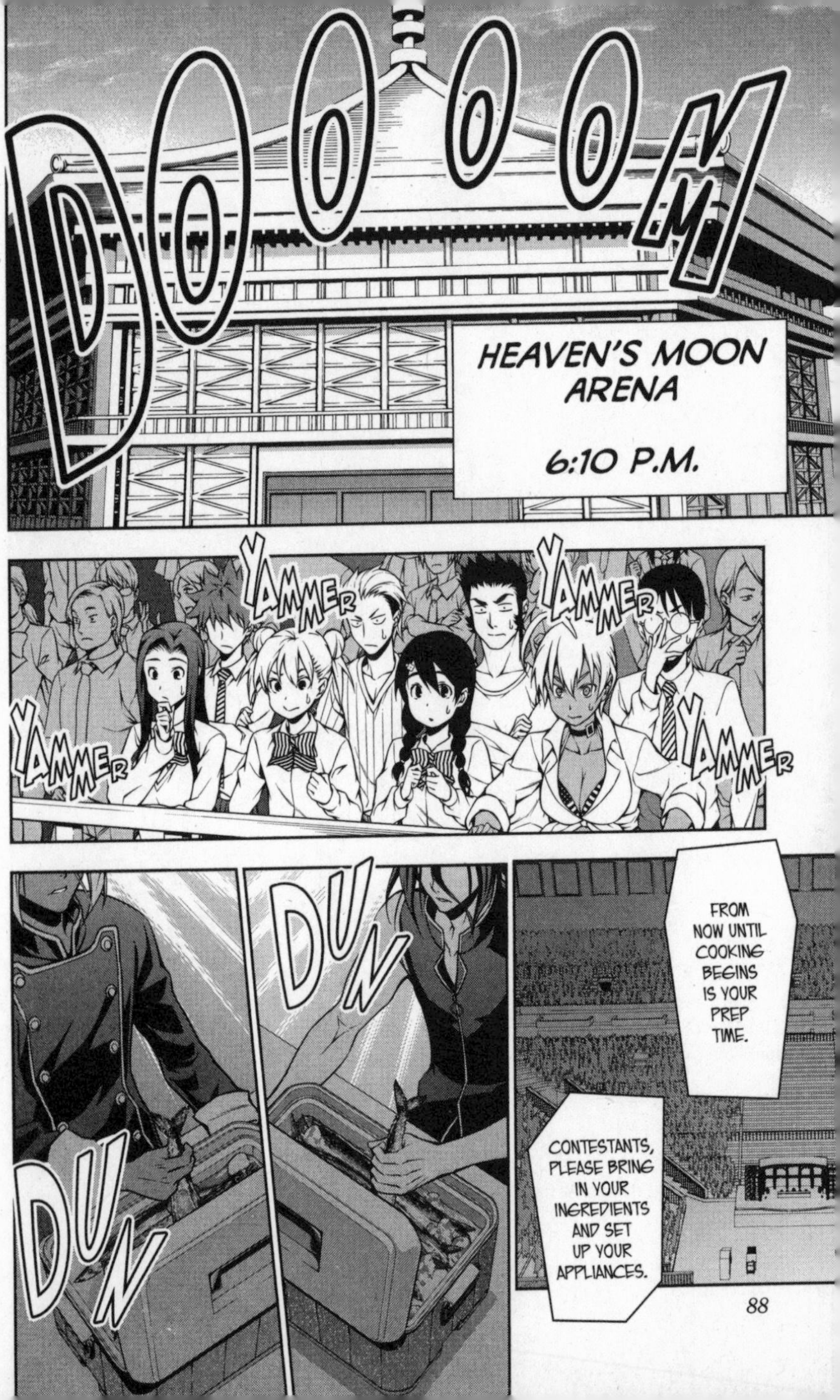
DOOOOOM
HEAVEN'S MOON ARENA
6:10 P.M.
YAMMER
YAMMER
YAMMER
YAMMER
FROM NOW UNTIL COOKING BEGINS IS YOUR PREP TIME.
CONTESTANTS, PLEASE BRING IN YOUR INGREDIENTS AND SET UP YOUR APPLIANCES.
DUN
DUN

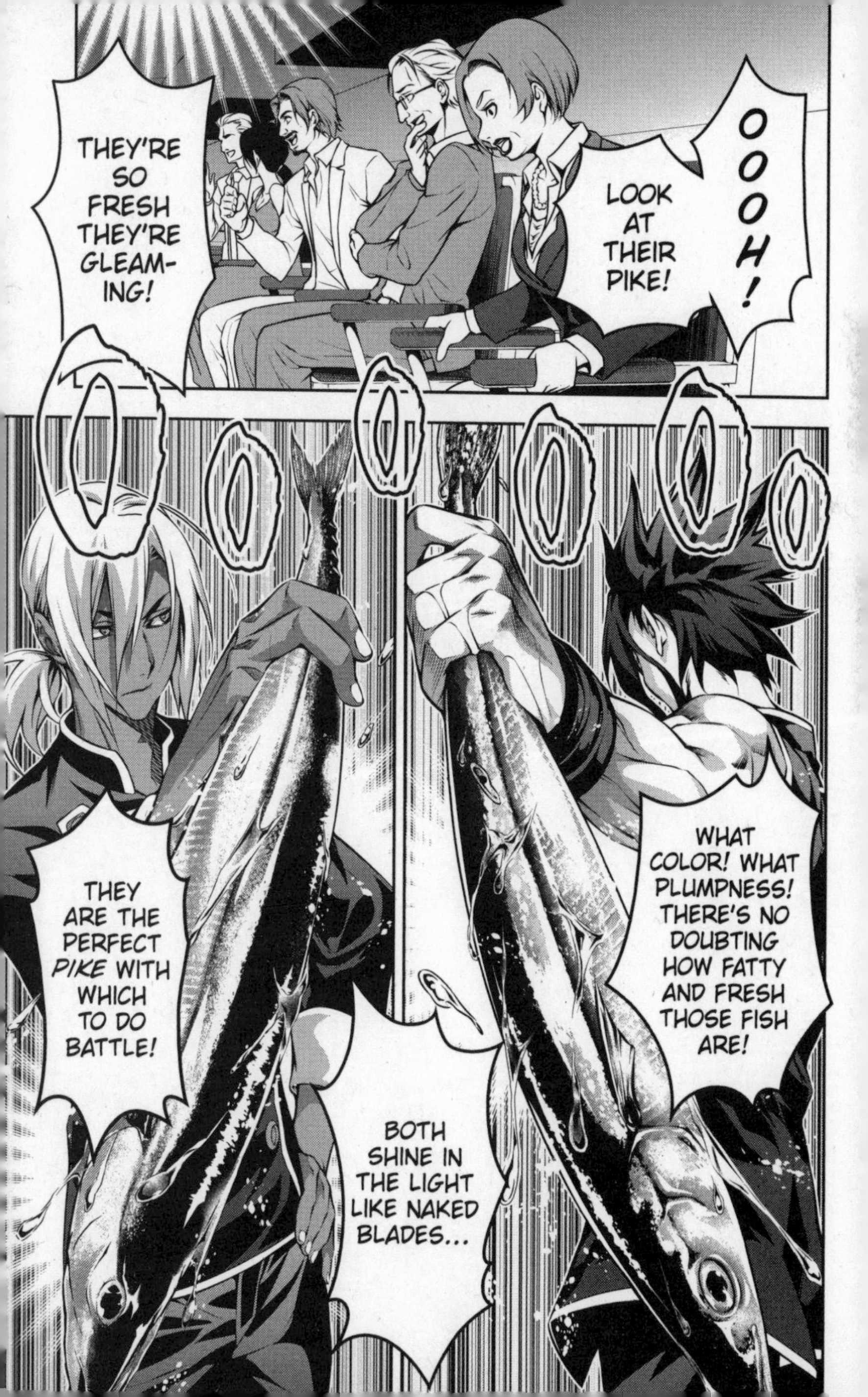
OOOOH!
LOOK AT THEIR PIKE!
THEY'RE SO FRESH THEY'RE GLEAMING!
WHAT COLOR! WHAT PLUMPNESS! THERE'S NO DOUBTING HOW FATTY AND FRESH THOSE FISH ARE!
THEY ARE THE PERFECT *PIKE* WITH WHICH TO DO BATTLE!
BOTH SHINE IN THE LIGHT LIKE NAKED BLADES...

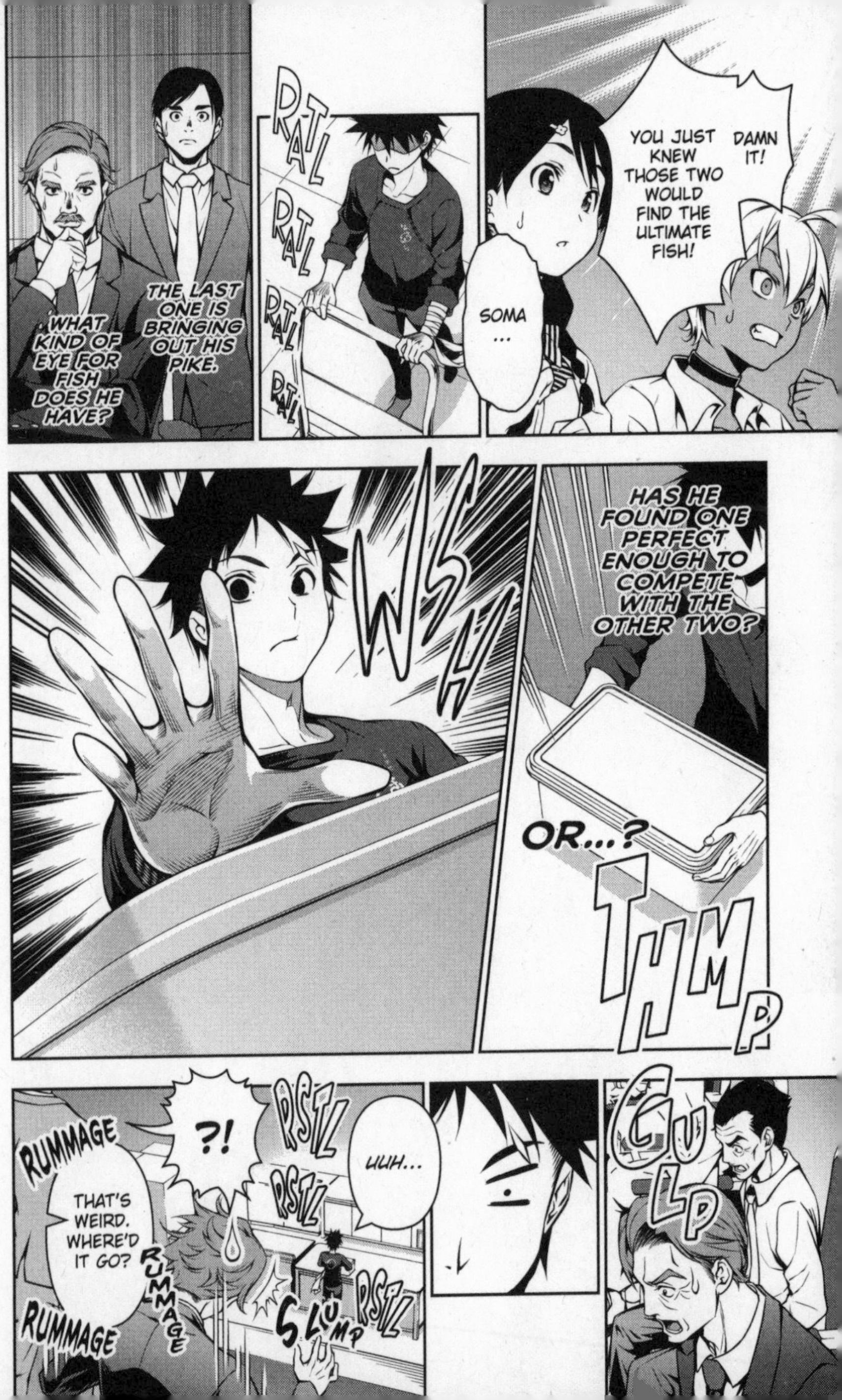
DAMN IT!
YOU JUST KNEW THOSE TWO WOULD FIND THE ULTIMATE FISH!
SOMA ...
RATL
RATL
RATL
RATL
THE LAST ONE IS BRINGING OUT HIS PIKE.
WHAT KIND OF EYE FOR FISH DOES HE HAVE?
HAS HE FOUND ONE PERFECT ENOUGH TO COMPETE WITH THE OTHER TWO?
OR...?
THMP
WSH
GULP
UUH...
RSTL
RSTL
RSTL
?!
RUMMAGE
THAT'S WEIRD. WHERE'D IT GO?
RUMMAGE
RUMMAGE
SLUMP

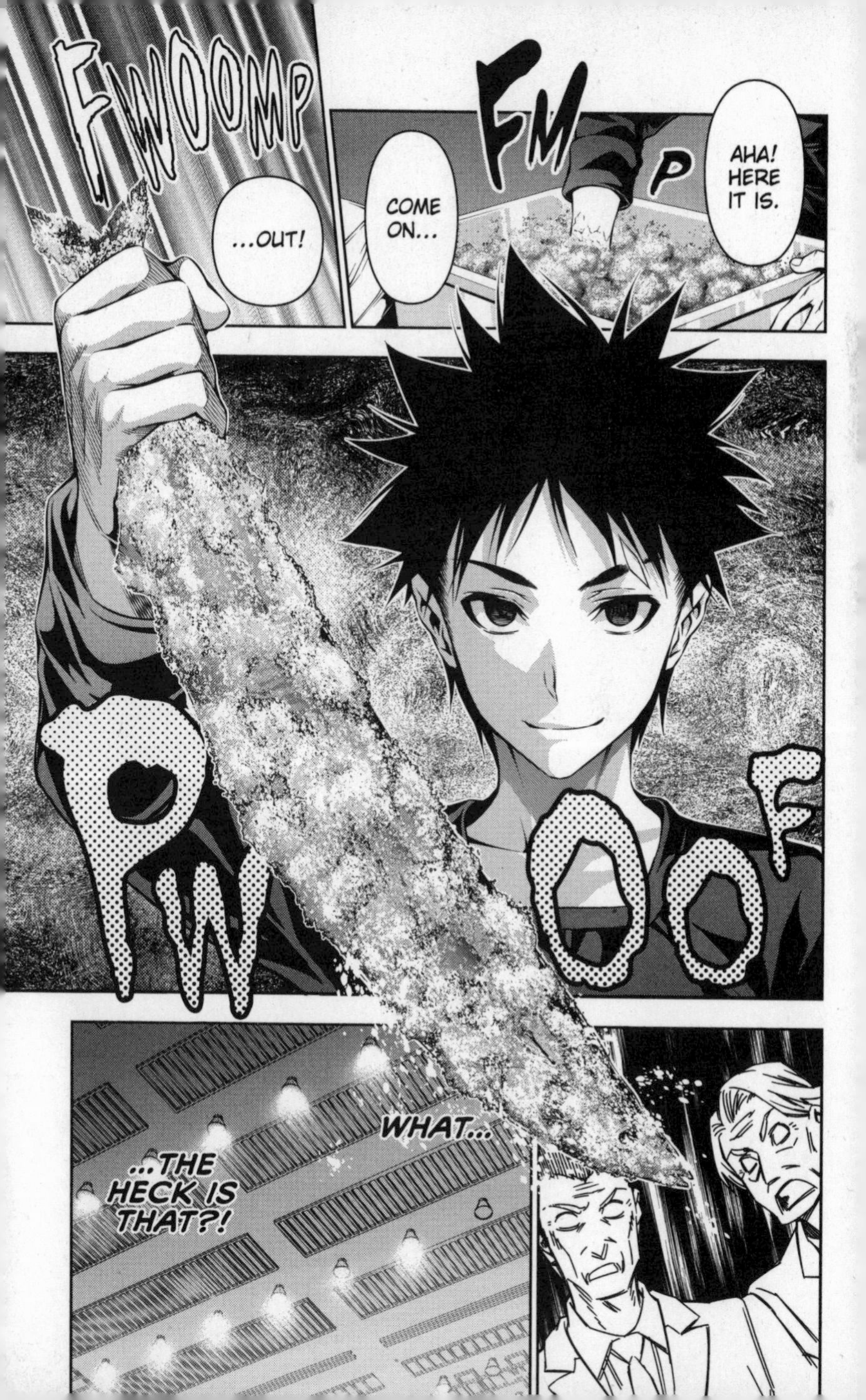
AHA! HERE IT IS.
FMP
COME ON...
FWOOMP
...OUT!
PWOOOF
WHAT...
...THE HECK IS THAT?!

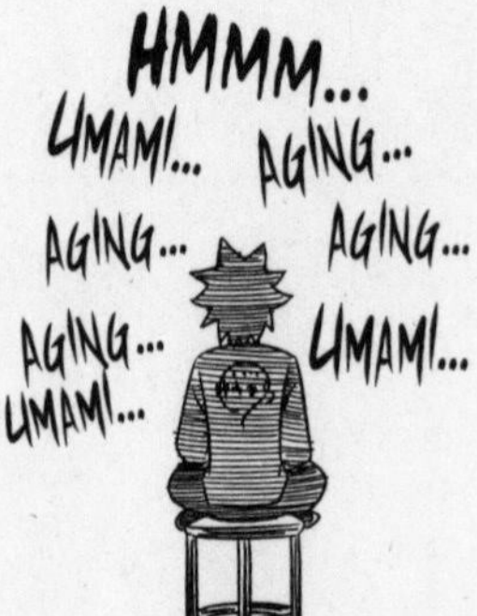
HMMM...
AGING...
UMAMI...
AGING...
AGING...
UMAMI...
AGING...
UMAMI...

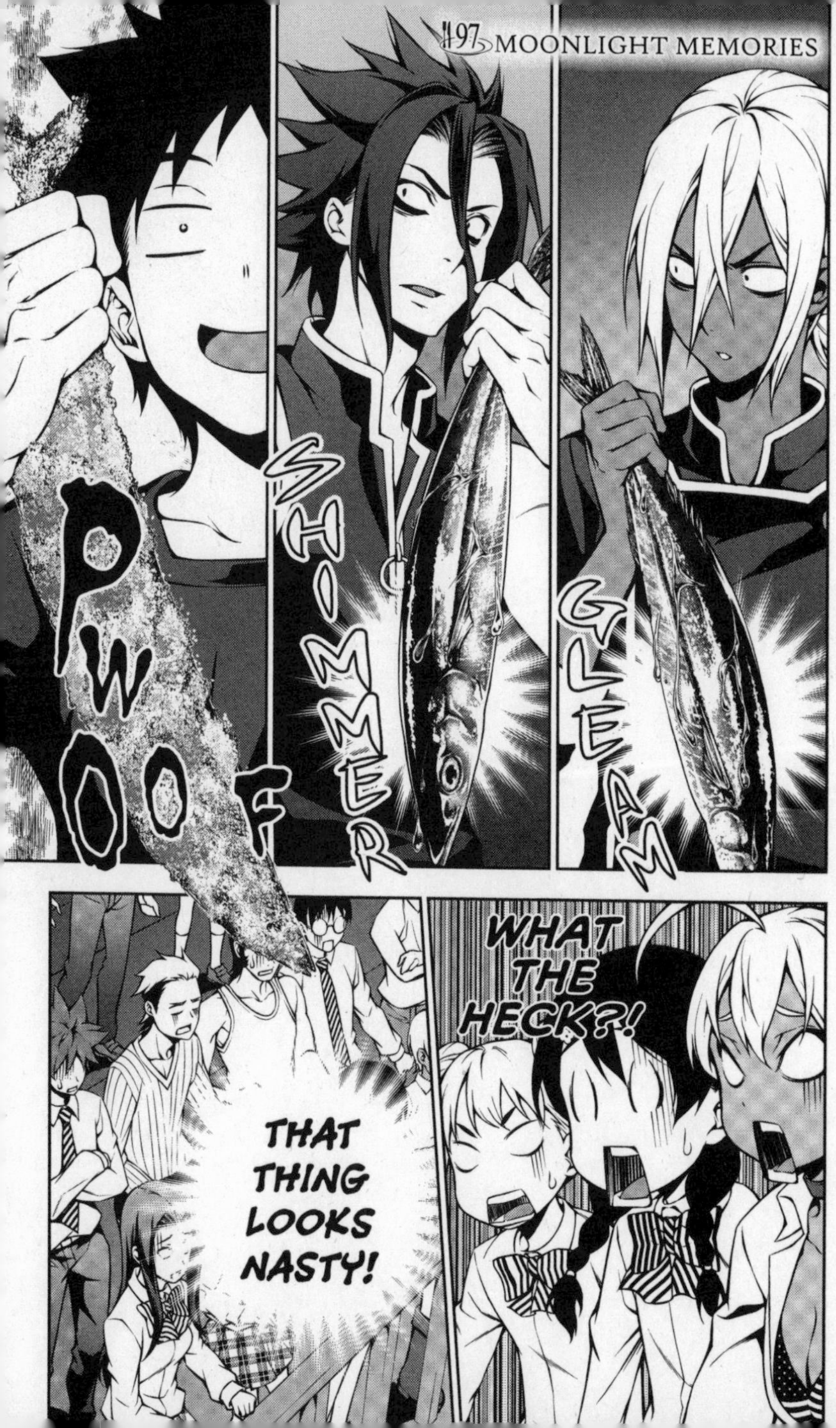

#97 MOONLIGHT MEMORIES
GLEAM
SHIMMER
PWOOF
WHAT THE HECK?!
THAT THING LOOKS NASTY!

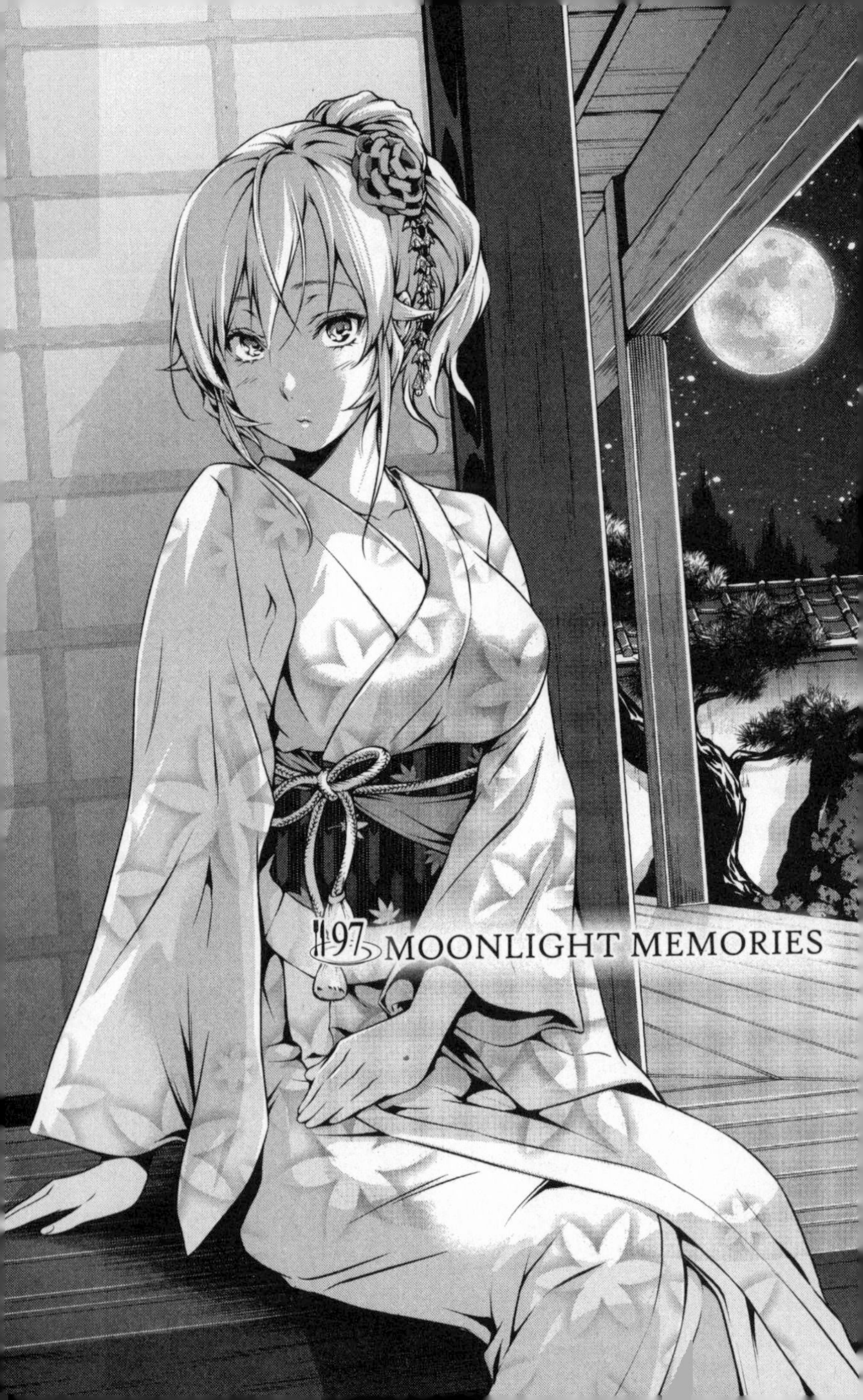
97 MOONLIGHT MEMORIES

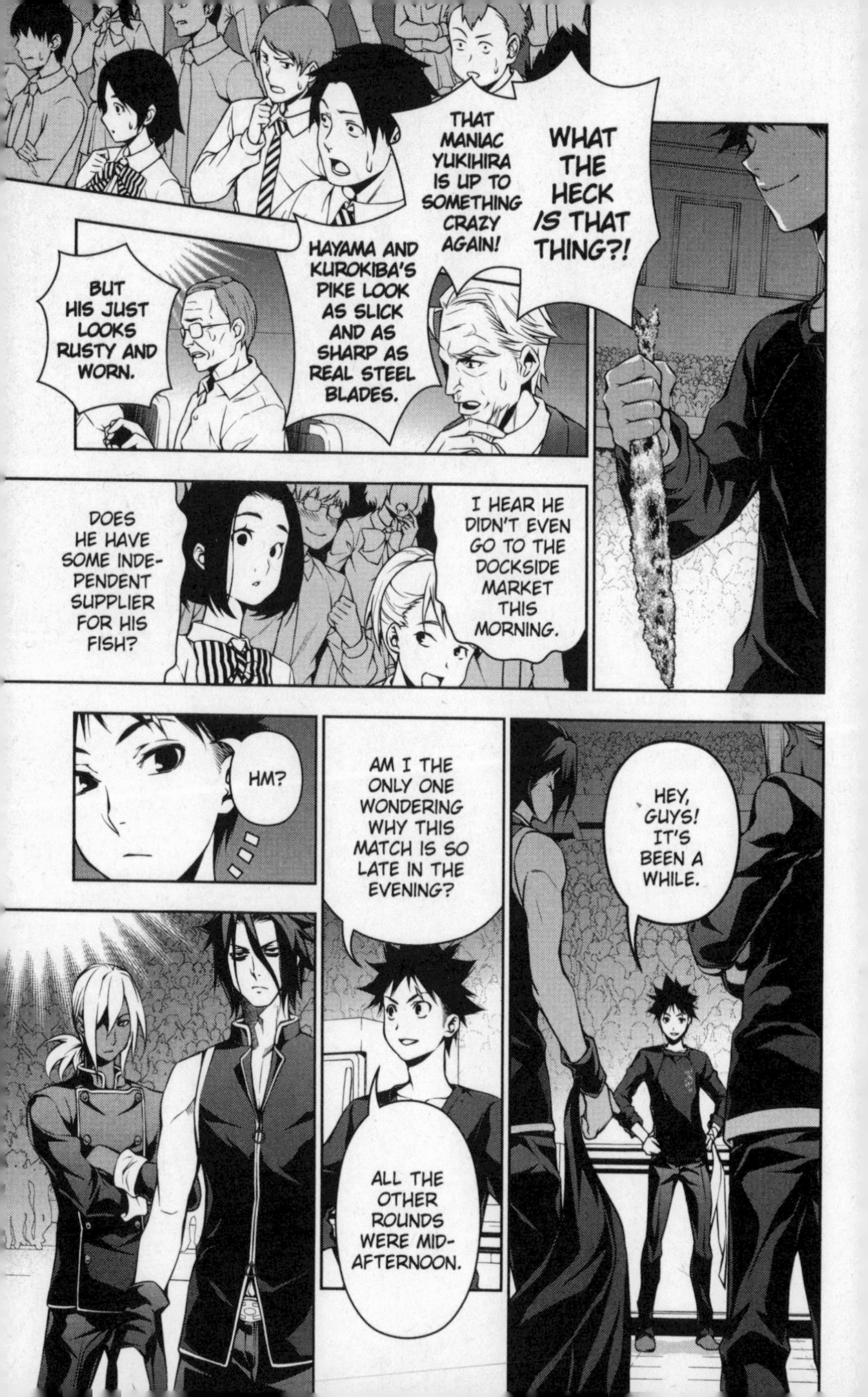
WHAT THE HECK IS THAT THING?!
THAT MANIAC YUKIHIRA IS UP TO SOMETHING CRAZY AGAIN!
HAYAMA AND KUROKIBA'S PIKE LOOK AS SLICK AND AS SHARP AS REAL STEEL BLADES.
BUT HIS JUST LOOKS RUSTY AND WORN.
I HEAR HE DIDN'T EVEN GO TO THE DOCKSIDE MARKET THIS MORNING.
DOES HE HAVE SOME INDEPENDENT SUPPLIER FOR HIS FISH?
HEY, GUYS! IT'S BEEN A WHILE.
AM I THE ONLY ONE WONDERING WHY THIS MATCH IS SO LATE IN THE EVENING?
ALL THE OTHER ROUNDS WERE MID-AFTERNOON.
HM?

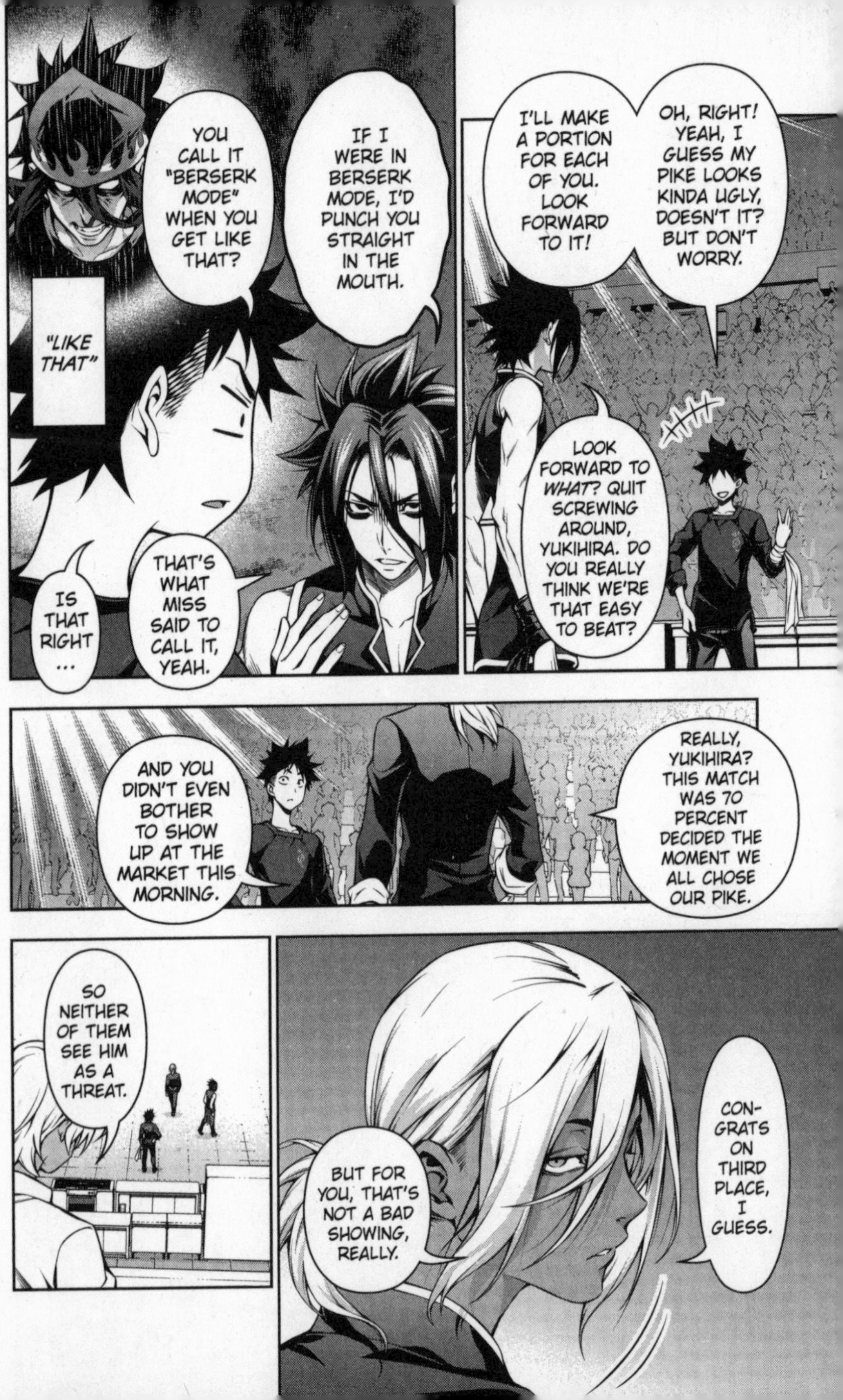
OH, RIGHT! YEAH, I GUESS MY PIKE LOOKS KINDA UGLY, DOESN'T IT? BUT DON'T WORRY.
I'LL MAKE A PORTION FOR EACH OF YOU. LOOK FORWARD TO IT!
LOOK FORWARD TO *WHAT*? QUIT SCREWING AROUND, YUKIHIRA. DO YOU REALLY THINK WE'RE THAT EASY TO BEAT?
IF I WERE IN BERSERK MODE, I'D PUNCH YOU STRAIGHT IN THE MOUTH.
YOU CALL IT "BERSERK MODE" WHEN YOU GET LIKE THAT?
"LIKE THAT"
THAT'S WHAT MISS SAID TO CALL IT, YEAH.
IS THAT RIGHT...
REALLY, YUKIHIRA? THIS MATCH WAS 70 PERCENT DECIDED THE MOMENT WE ALL CHOSE OUR PIKE.
AND YOU DIDN'T EVEN BOTHER TO SHOW UP AT THE MARKET THIS MORNING.
CON-GRATS ON THIRD PLACE, I GUESS.
BUT FOR YOU, THAT'S NOT A BAD SHOWING, REALLY.
SO NEITHER OF THEM SEE HIM AS A THREAT.

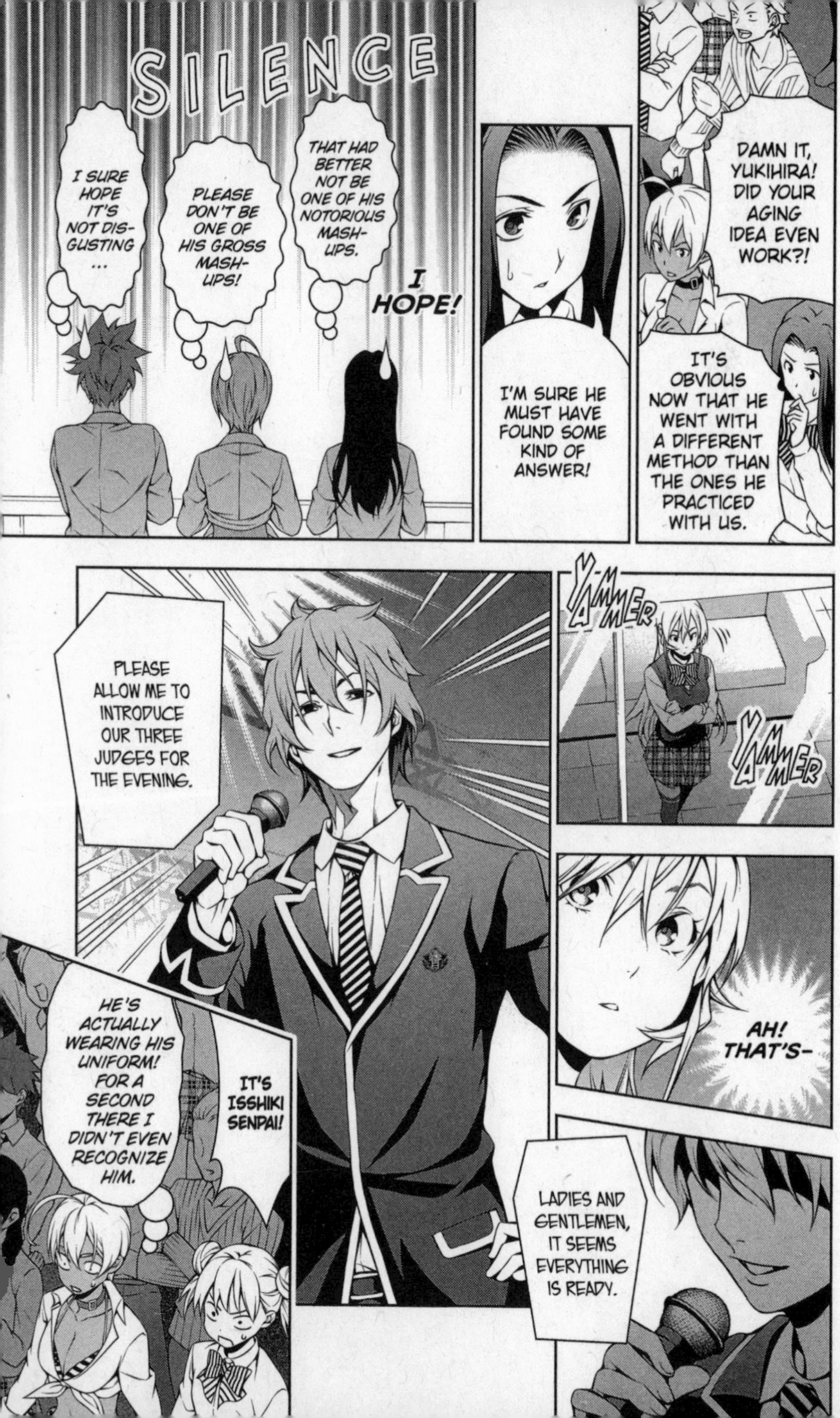
DAMN IT, YUKIHIRA! DID YOUR AGING IDEA EVEN WORK?!
IT'S OBVIOUS NOW THAT HE WENT WITH A DIFFERENT METHOD THAN THE ONES HE PRACTICED WITH US.
I'M SURE HE MUST HAVE FOUND SOME KIND OF ANSWER!
SILENCE
I HOPE!
THAT HAD BETTER NOT BE ONE OF HIS NOTORIOUS MASH-UPS.
PLEASE DON'T BE ONE OF HIS GROSS MASH-UPS!
I SURE HOPE IT'S NOT DIS-GUSTING...
YAMMER
YAMMER
AH! THAT'S-
LADIES AND GENTLEMEN, IT SEEMS EVERYTHING IS READY.
PLEASE ALLOW ME TO INTRODUCE OUR THREE JUDGES FOR THE EVENING.
IT'S ISSHIKI SENPAI!
HE'S ACTUALLY WEARING HIS UNIFORM! FOR A SECOND THERE I DIDN'T EVEN RECOGNIZE HIM.

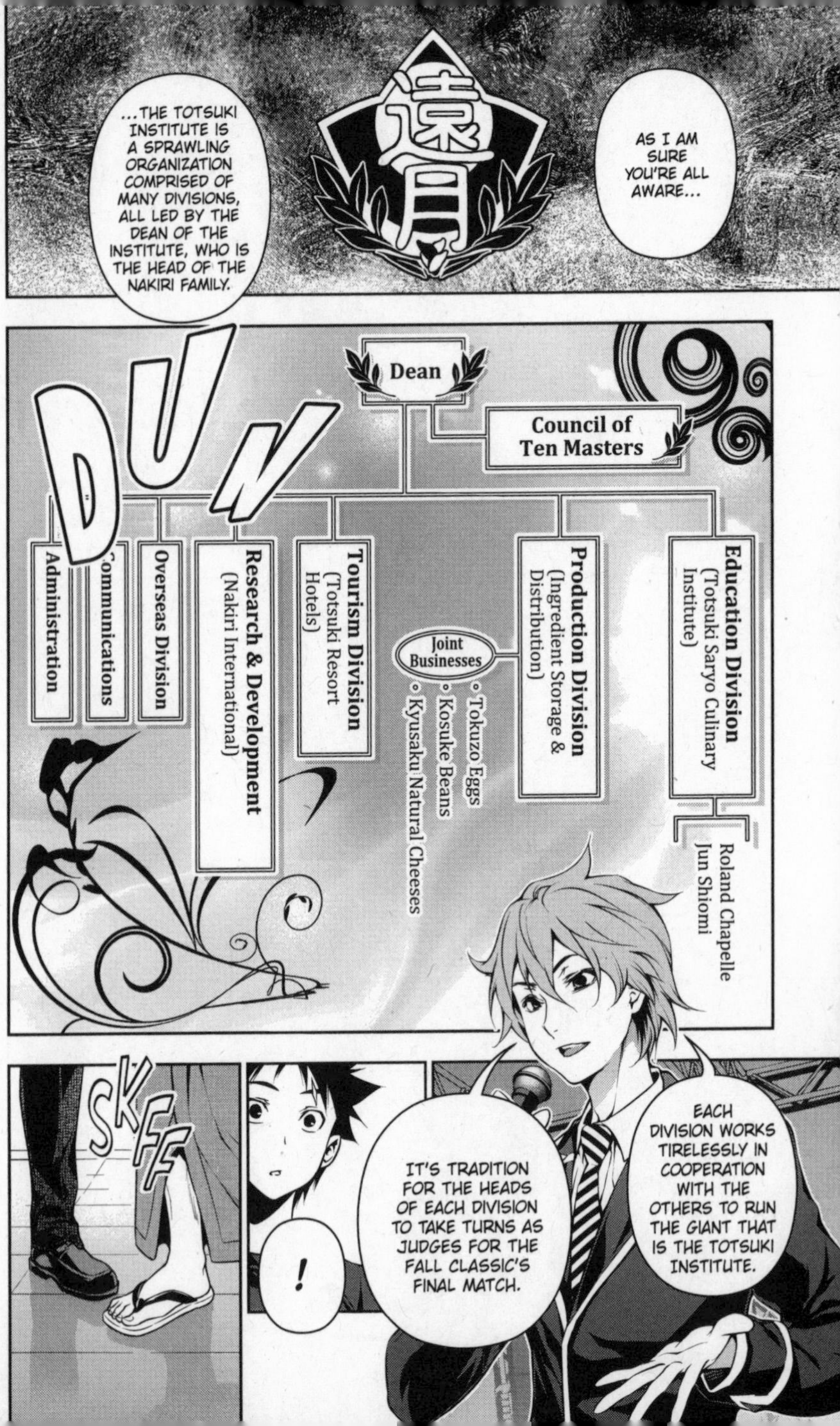
AS I AM SURE YOU'RE ALL AWARE...
遠月
...THE TOTSUKI INSTITUTE IS A SPRAWLING ORGANIZATION COMPRISED OF MANY DIVISIONS, ALL LED BY THE DEAN OF THE INSTITUTE, WHO IS THE HEAD OF THE NAKIRI FAMILY.
DUN
Dean
Council of Ten Masters
Education Division (Totsuki Saryo Culinary Institute)
Roland Chapelle
Jun Shiomi
Production Division (Ingredient Storage & Distribution)
Joint Businesses
• Tokuzo Eggs
• Kosuke Beans
• Kyusaku Natural Cheeses
Tourism Division (Totsuki Resort Hotels)
Research & Development (Nakiri International)
Overseas Division
Communications
Administration
EACH DIVISION WORKS TIRELESSLY IN COOPERATION WITH THE OTHERS TO RUN THE GIANT THAT IS THE TOTSUKI INSTITUTE.
IT'S TRADITION FOR THE HEADS OF EACH DIVISION TO TAKE TURNS AS JUDGES FOR THE FALL CLASSIC'S FINAL MATCH.
!
SKFF

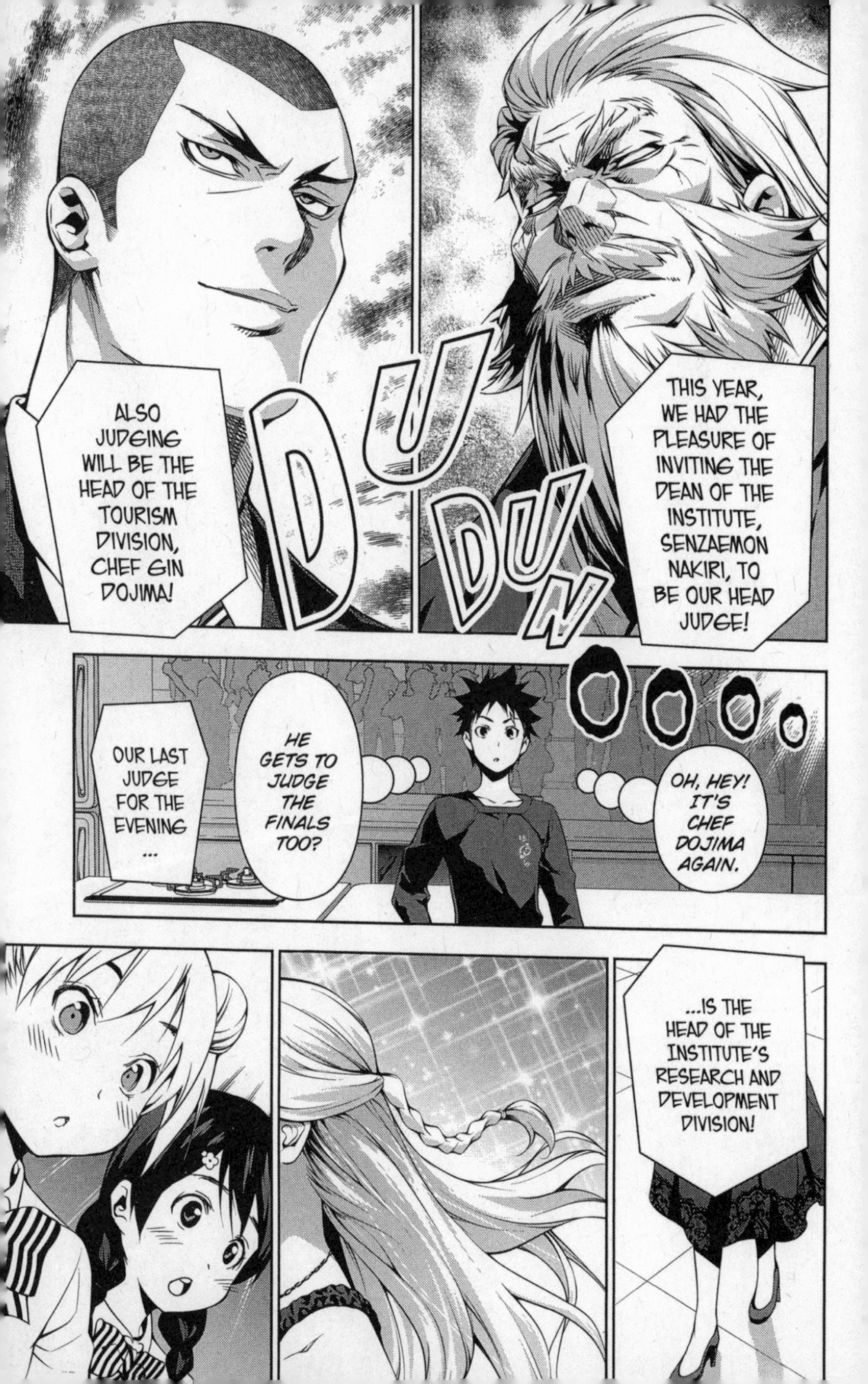
THIS YEAR, WE HAD THE PLEASURE OF INVITING THE DEAN OF THE INSTITUTE, SENZAEMON NAKIRI, TO BE OUR HEAD JUDGE!
DUDUN
ALSO JUDGING WILL BE THE HEAD OF THE TOURISM DIVISION, CHEF GIN DOJIMA!
OH, HEY! IT'S CHEF DOJIMA AGAIN.
HE GETS TO JUDGE THE FINALS TOO?
OUR LAST JUDGE FOR THE EVENING ...
...IS THE HEAD OF THE INSTITUTE'S RESEARCH AND DEVELOPMENT DIVISION!

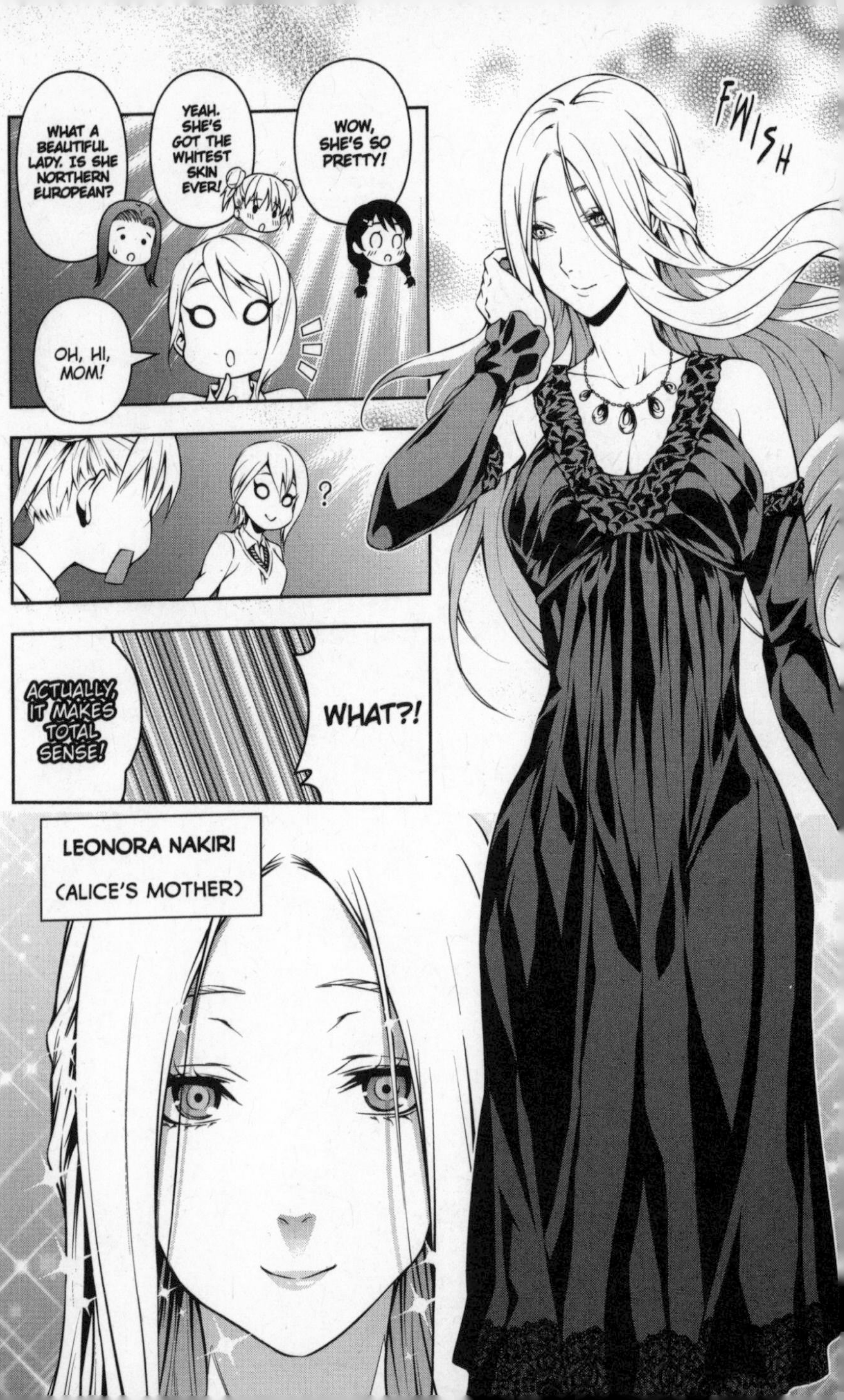
FWISH
WOW, SHE'S SO PRETTY!
YEAH. SHE'S GOT THE WHITEST SKIN EVER!
WHAT A BEAUTIFUL LADY. IS SHE NORTHERN EUROPEAN?
OH, HI, MOM!
?
WHAT?!
ACTUALLY, IT MAKES TOTAL SENSE!
LEONORA NAKIRI
(ALICE'S MOTHER)

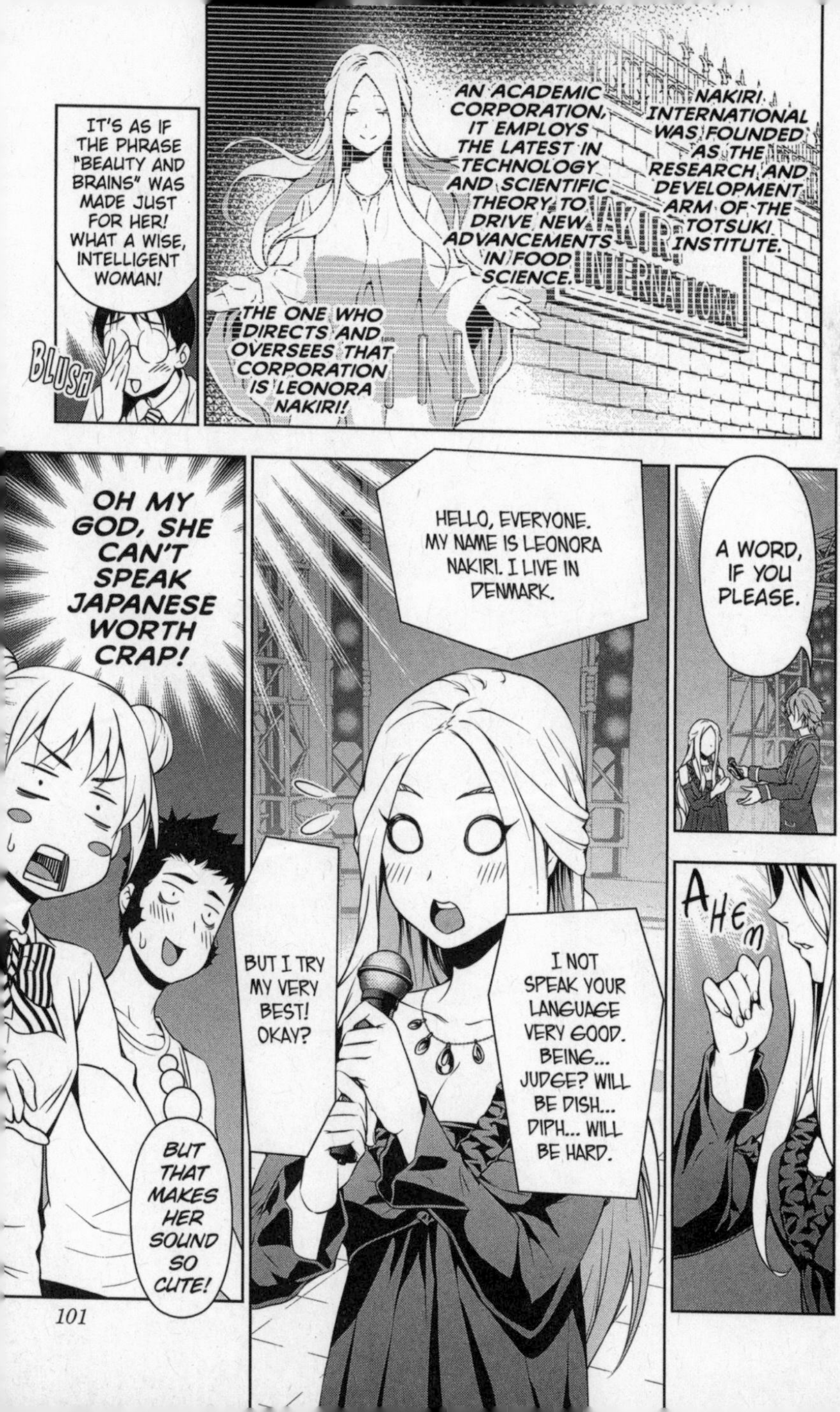
NAKIRI INTERNATIONAL WAS FOUNDED AS THE RESEARCH AND DEVELOPMENT ARM OF THE TOTSUKI INSTITUTE.
AN ACADEMIC CORPORATION, IT EMPLOYS THE LATEST IN TECHNOLOGY AND SCIENTIFIC THEORY TO DRIVE NEW ADVANCEMENTS IN FOOD SCIENCE.
THE ONE WHO DIRECTS AND OVERSEES THAT CORPORATION IS LEONORA NAKIRI!
IT'S AS IF THE PHRASE "BEAUTY AND BRAINS" WAS MADE JUST FOR HER! WHAT A WISE, INTELLIGENT WOMAN!
BLUSH
A WORD, IF YOU PLEASE.
AHEM
HELLO, EVERYONE. MY NAME IS LEONORA NAKIRI. I LIVE IN DENMARK.
I NOT SPEAK YOUR LANGUAGE VERY GOOD. BEING... JUDGE? WILL BE DISH... DIPH... WILL BE HARD.
BUT I TRY MY VERY BEST! OKAY?
OH MY GOD, SHE CAN'T SPEAK JAPANESE WORTH CRAP!
BUT THAT MAKES HER SOUND SO CUTE!

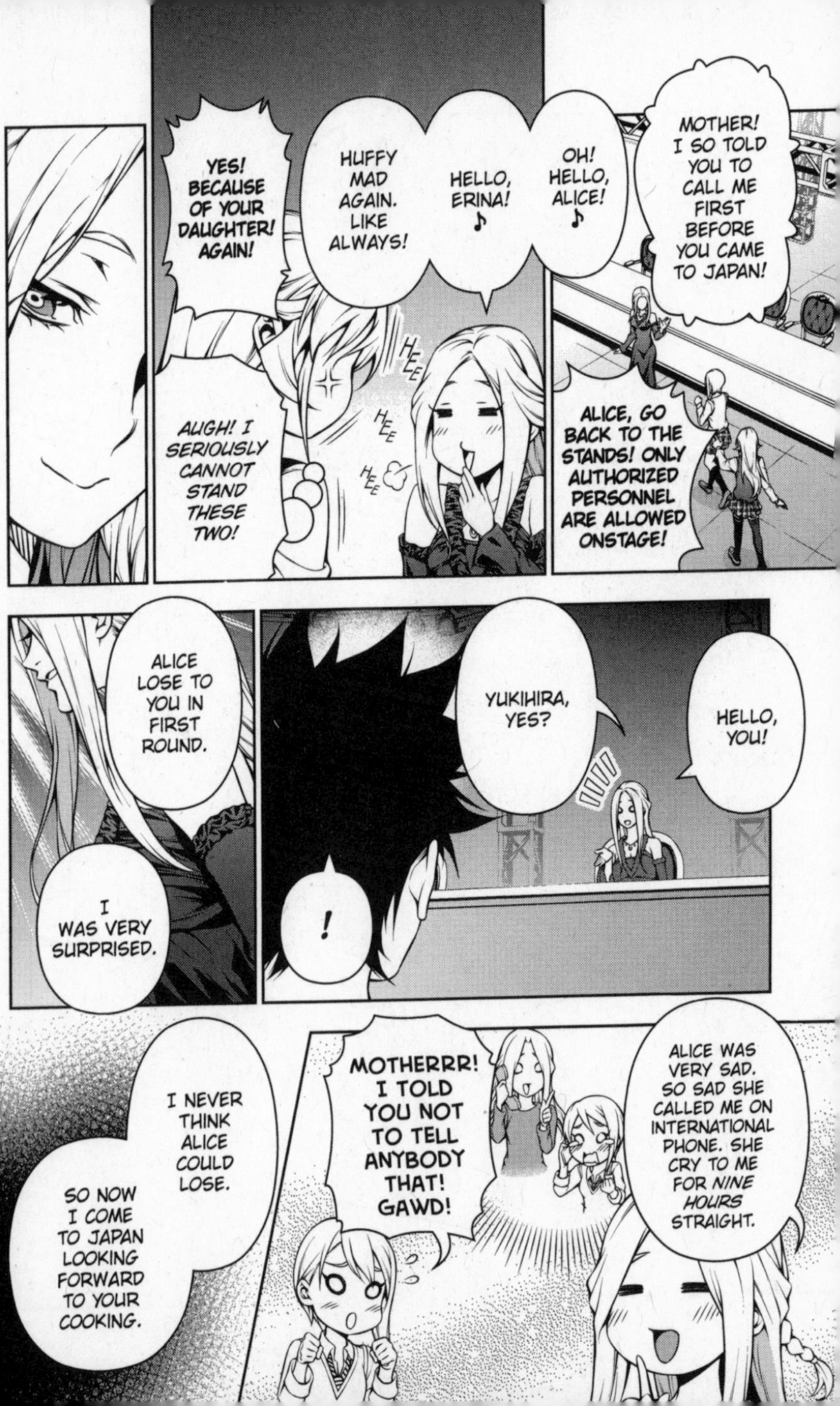
MOTHER! I SO TOLD YOU TO CALL ME FIRST BEFORE YOU CAME TO JAPAN!
ALICE, GO BACK TO THE STANDS! ONLY AUTHORIZED PERSONNEL ARE ALLOWED ONSTAGE!
OH! HELLO, ALICE! ♪
HELLO, ERINA! ♪
HUFFY MAD AGAIN. LIKE ALWAYS!
YES! BECAUSE OF YOUR DAUGHTER! AGAIN!
HEE HEE HEE
AUGH! I SERIOUSLY CANNOT STAND THESE TWO!
HELLO, YOU!
YUKIHIRA, YES?
!
ALICE LOSE TO YOU IN FIRST ROUND.
I WAS VERY SURPRISED.
ALICE WAS VERY SAD. SO SAD SHE CALLED ME ON INTERNATIONAL PHONE. SHE CRY TO ME FOR *NINE HOURS* STRAIGHT.
MOTHERRR! I TOLD YOU NOT TO TELL ANYBODY THAT! GAWD!
I NEVER THINK ALICE COULD LOSE.
SO NOW I COME TO JAPAN LOOKING FORWARD TO YOUR COOKING.

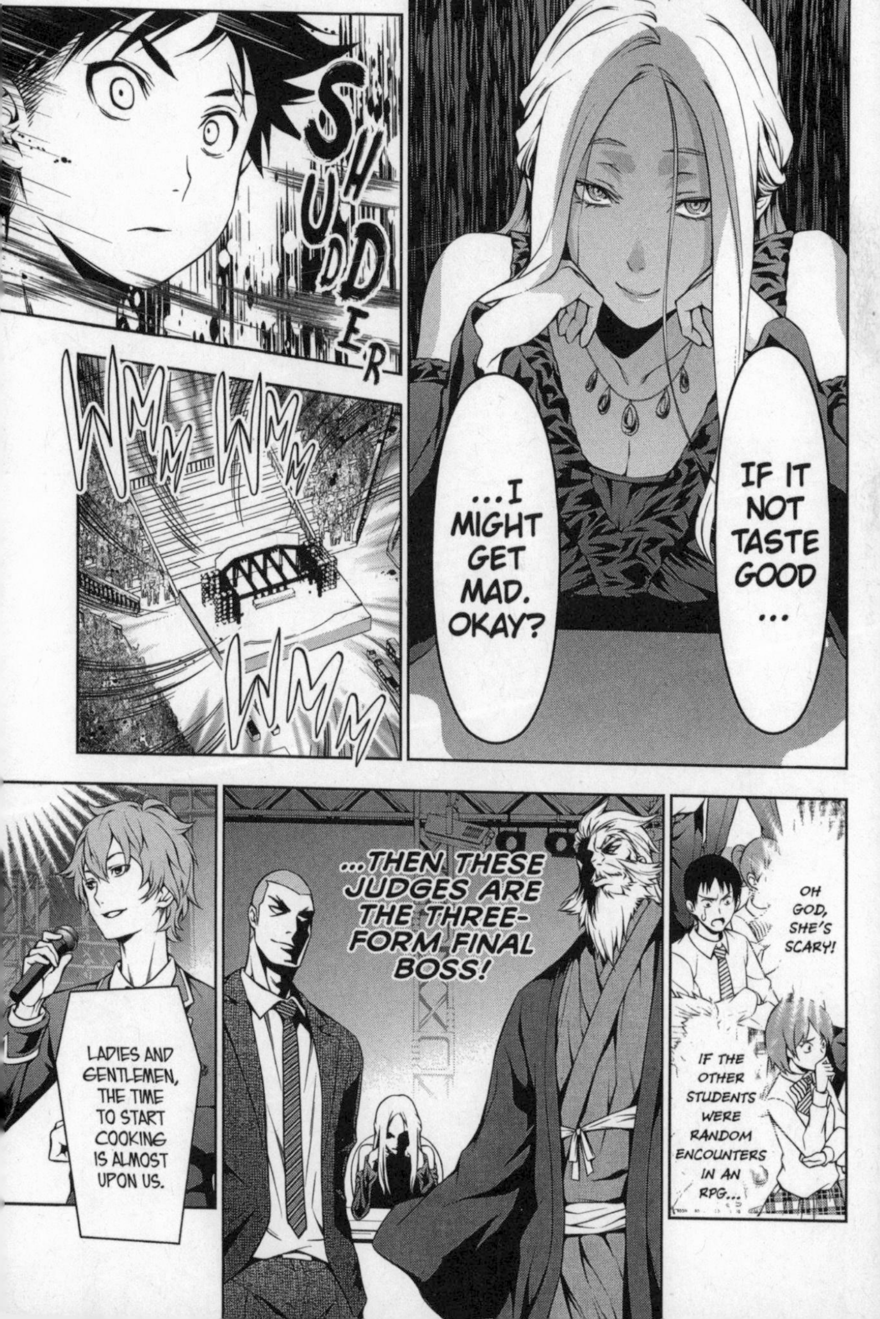
IF IT NOT TASTE GOOD...
...I MIGHT GET MAD. OKAY?
SHUDDER
WMM WMM
WMM
OH GOD, SHE'S SCARY!
IF THE OTHER STUDENTS WERE RANDOM ENCOUNTERS IN AN RPG...
...THEN THESE JUDGES ARE THE THREE-FORM FINAL BOSS!
LADIES AND GENTLEMEN, THE TIME TO START COOKING IS ALMOST UPON US.

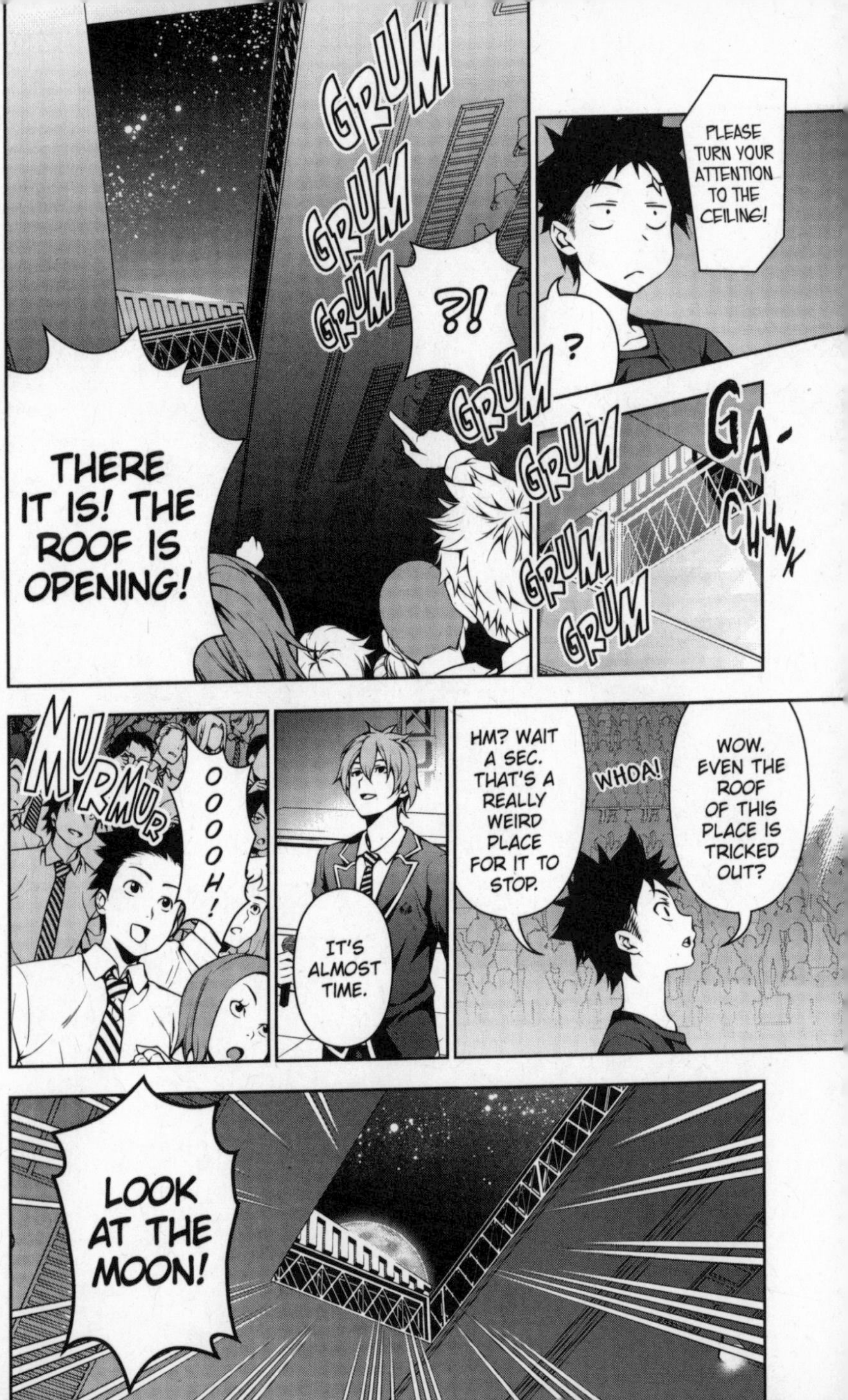
PLEASE TURN YOUR ATTENTION TO THE CEILING!
?
GRUM
GRUM
GRUM
GRUM
GA-CHUNK
GRUM
GRUM
GRUM
?!
THERE IT IS! THE ROOF IS OPENING!
WOW. EVEN THE ROOF OF THIS PLACE IS TRICKED OUT?
WHOA!
HM? WAIT A SEC. THAT'S A REALLY WEIRD PLACE FOR IT TO STOP.
IT'S ALMOST TIME.
OOOOOH!
MURMUR
LOOK AT THE MOON!

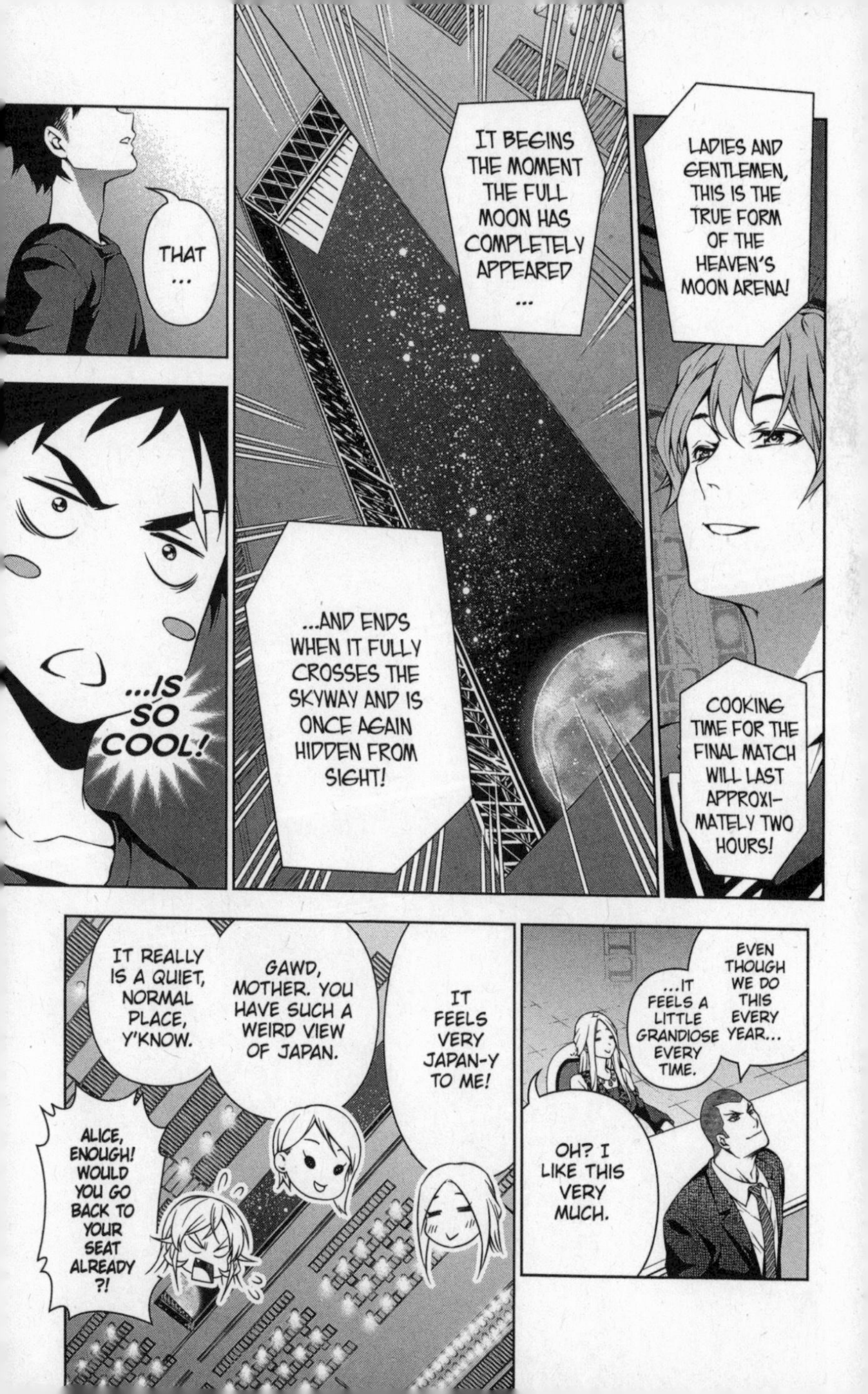
LADIES AND GENTLEMEN, THIS IS THE TRUE FORM OF THE HEAVEN'S MOON ARENA!
COOKING TIME FOR THE FINAL MATCH WILL LAST APPROXI-MATELY TWO HOURS!
IT BEGINS THE MOMENT THE FULL MOON HAS COMPLETELY APPEARED ...
...AND ENDS WHEN IT FULLY CROSSES THE SKYWAY AND IS ONCE AGAIN HIDDEN FROM SIGHT!
THAT ...
...IS SO COOL!
EVEN THOUGH WE DO THIS EVERY YEAR...
...IT FEELS A LITTLE GRANDIOSE EVERY TIME.
OH? I LIKE THIS VERY MUCH.
IT FEELS VERY JAPAN-Y TO ME!
GAWD, MOTHER. YOU HAVE SUCH A WEIRD VIEW OF JAPAN.
IT REALLY IS A QUIET, NORMAL PLACE, Y'KNOW.
ALICE, ENOUGH! WOULD YOU GO BACK TO YOUR SEAT ALREADY ?!

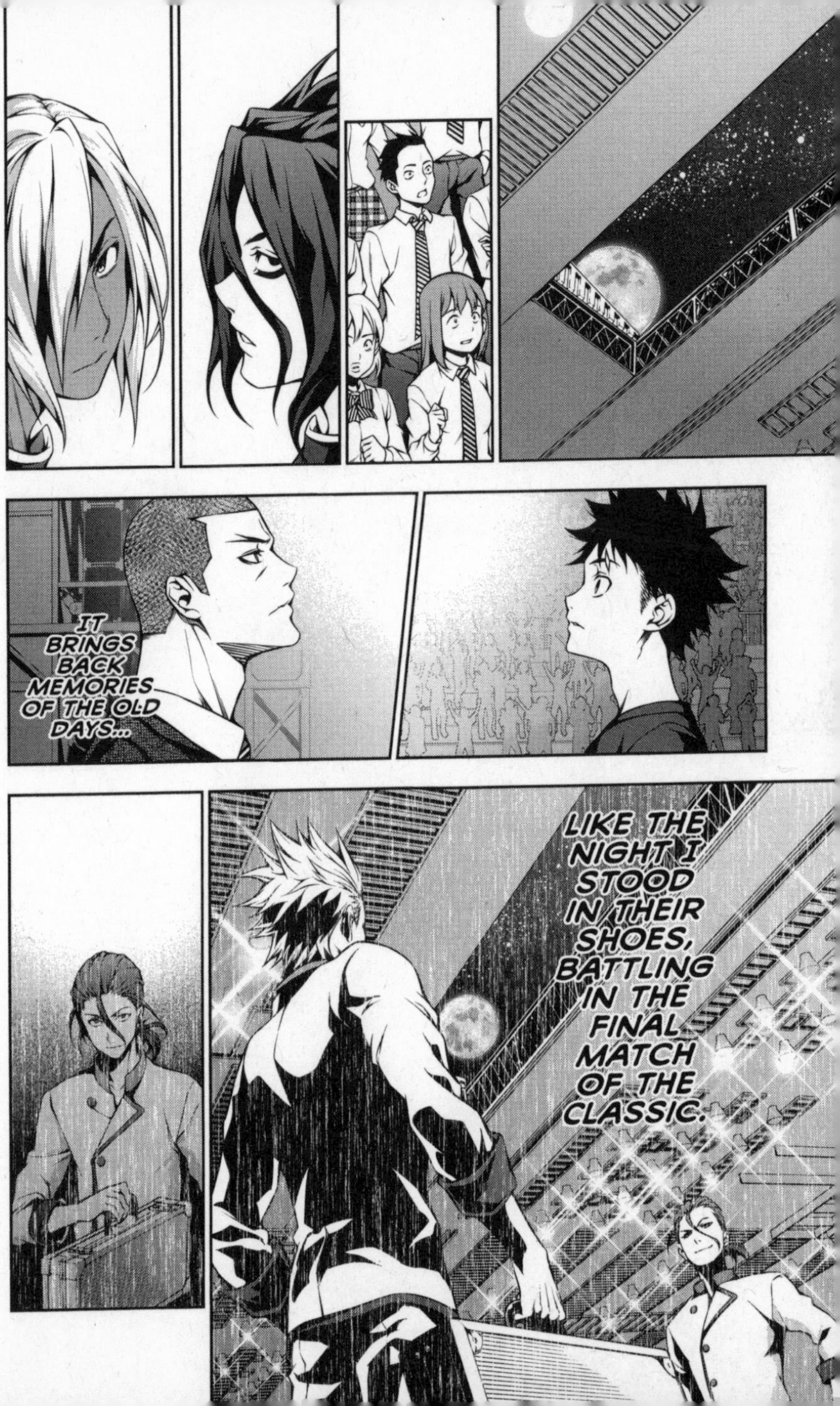
IT BRINGS BACK MEMORIES OF THE OLD DAYS...
LIKE THE NIGHT I STOOD IN THEIR SHOES, BATTLING IN THE FINAL MATCH OF THE CLASSIC.

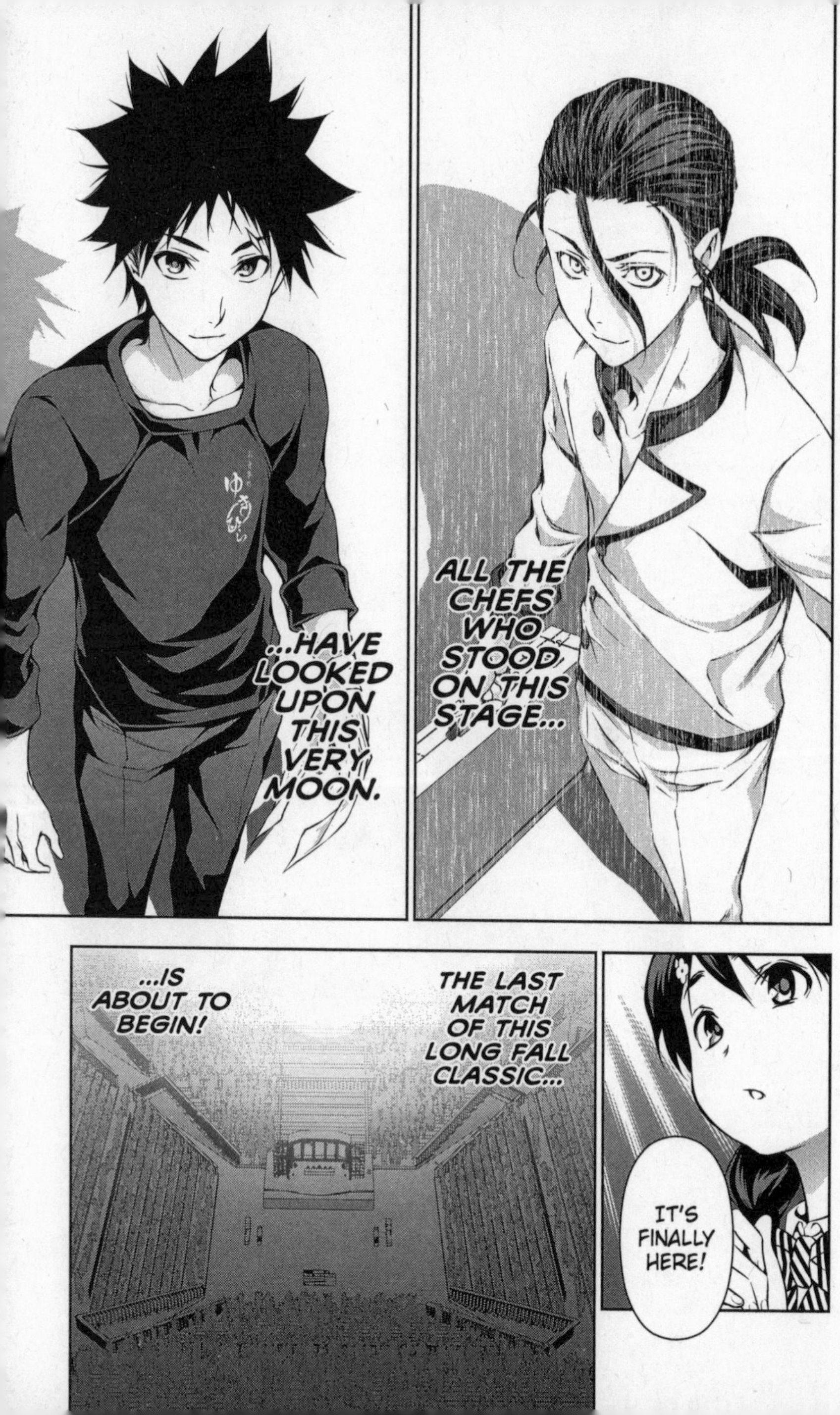
ALL THE CHEFS WHO STOOD ON THIS STAGE...
...HAVE LOOKED UPON THIS VERY MOON.
IT'S FINALLY HERE!
THE LAST MATCH OF THIS LONG FALL CLASSIC...
...IS ABOUT TO BEGIN!

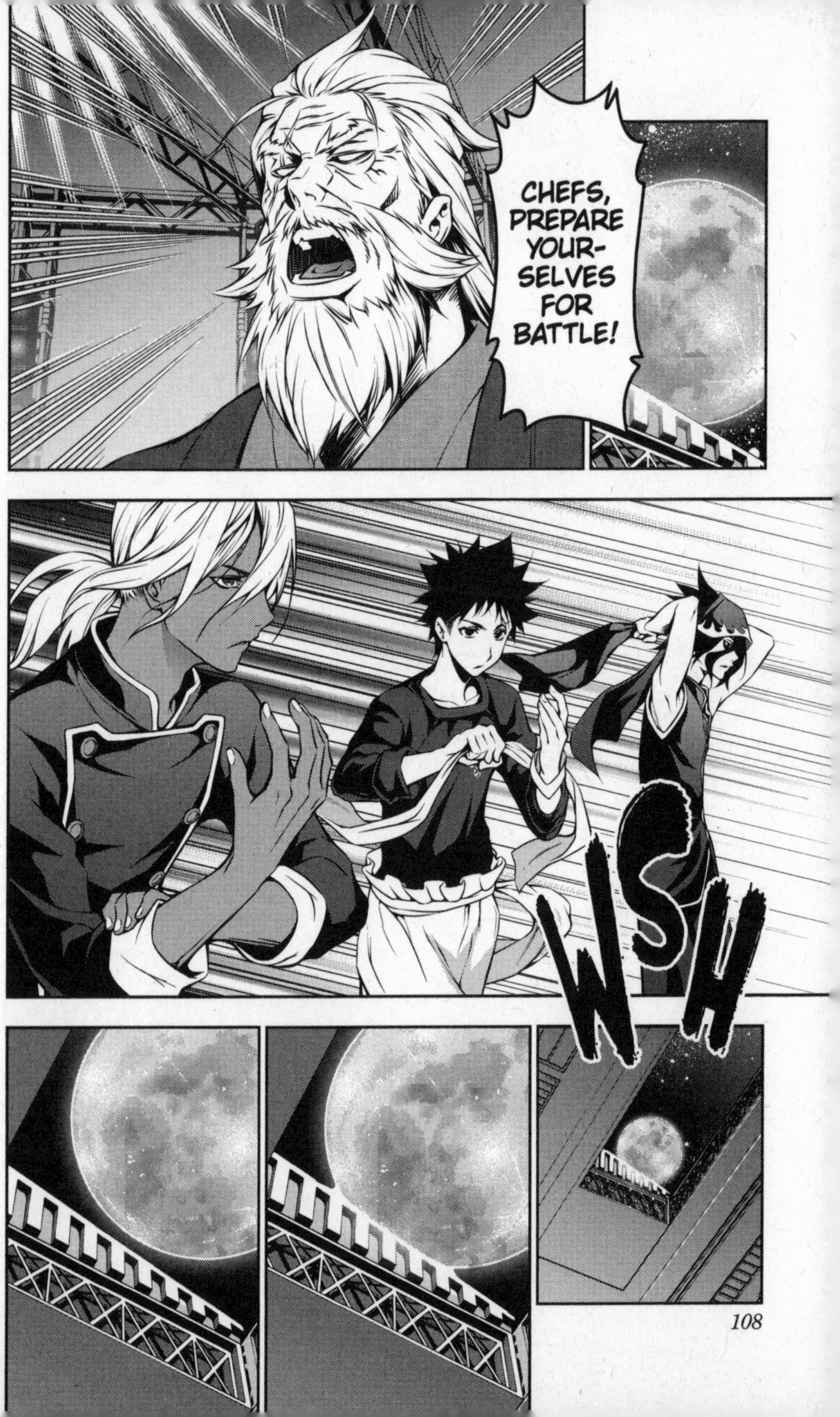
CHEFS, PREPARE YOUR-SELVES FOR BATTLE!
WSH

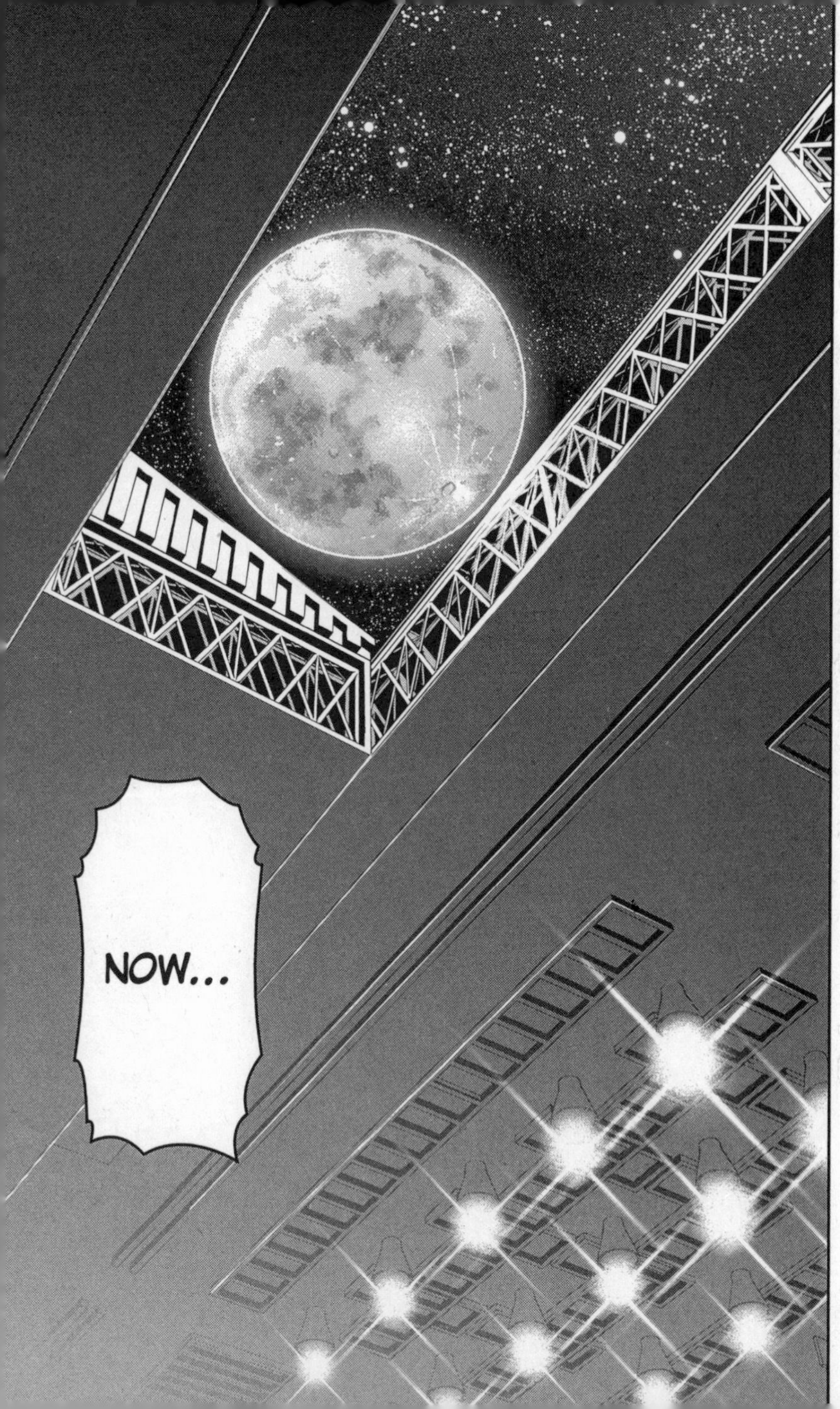
NOW...

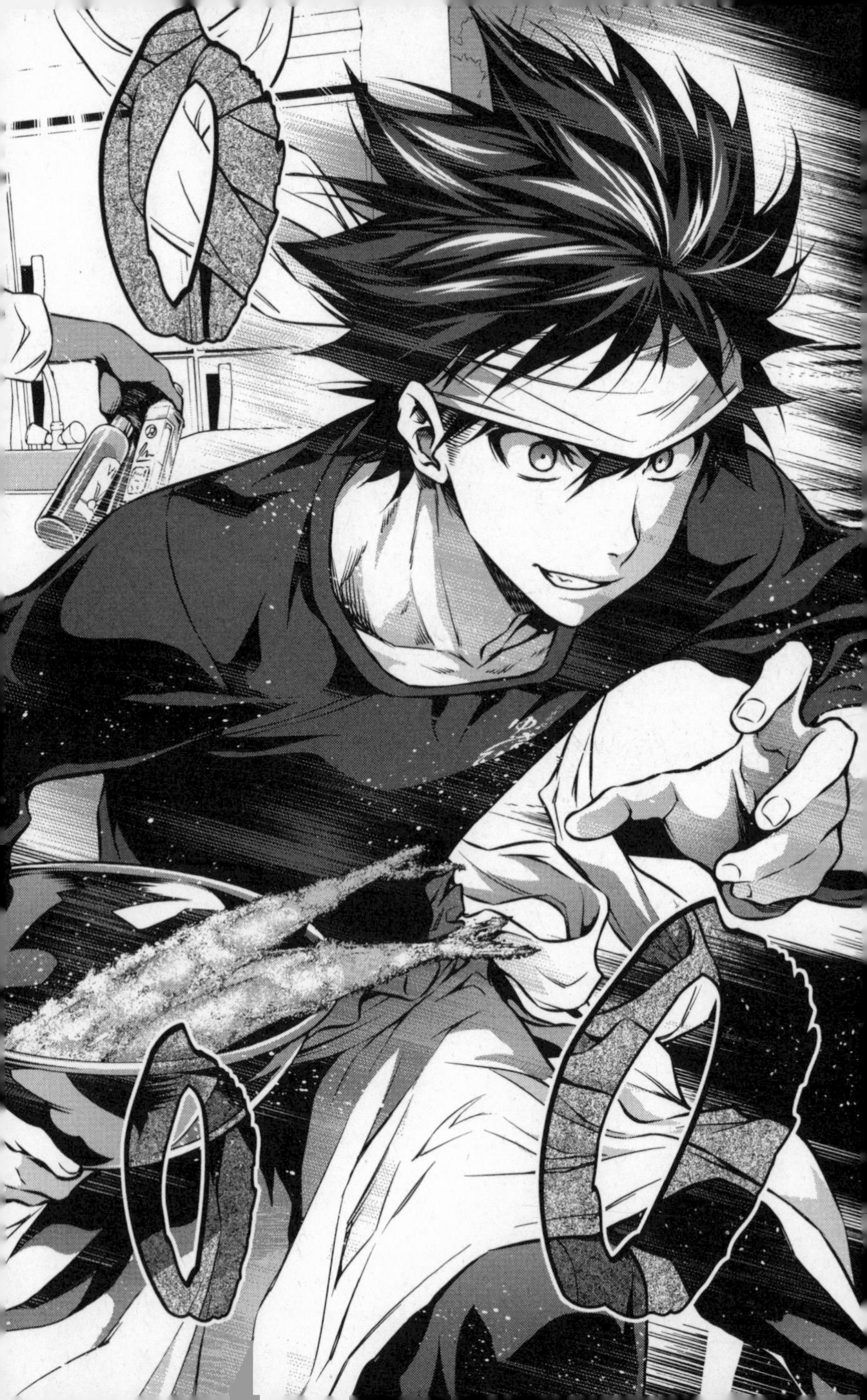

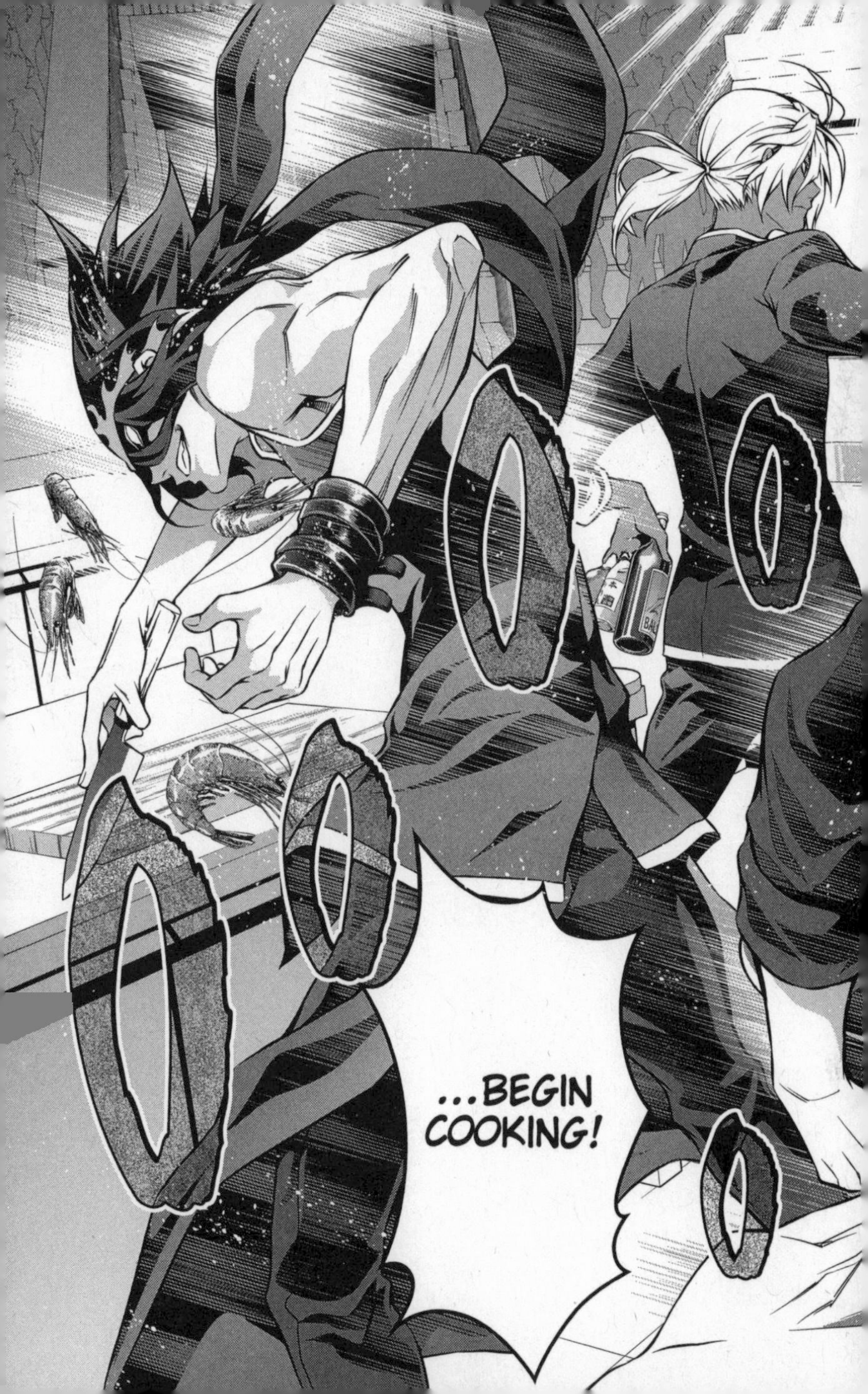
...BEGIN COOKING!

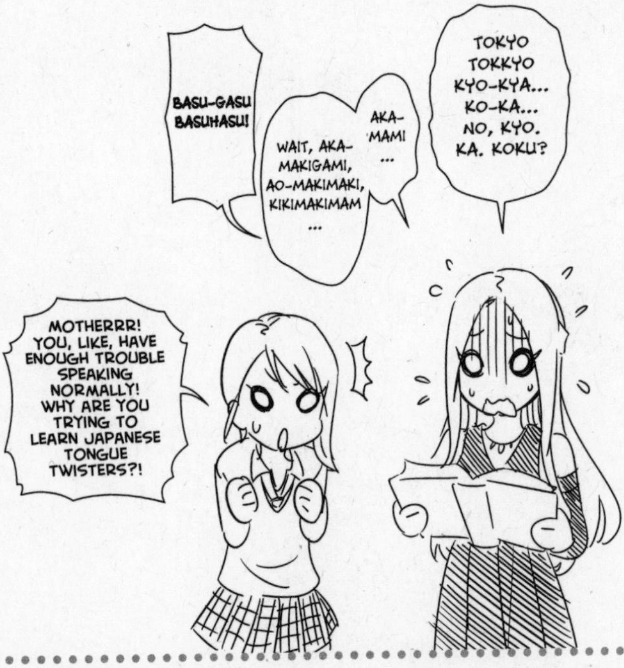
TOKYO TOKKYO KYO-KYA... KO-KA... NO, KYO. KA. KOKU?
AKA-MAMI ...
WAIT, AKA-MAKIGAMI, AO-MAKIMAKI, KIKIMAKIMAM ...
BASU-GASU BASUHASU!
MOTHERRR! YOU, LIKE, HAVE ENOUGH TROUBLE SPEAKING NORMALLY! WHY ARE YOU TRYING TO LEARN JAPANESE TONGUE TWISTERS?!

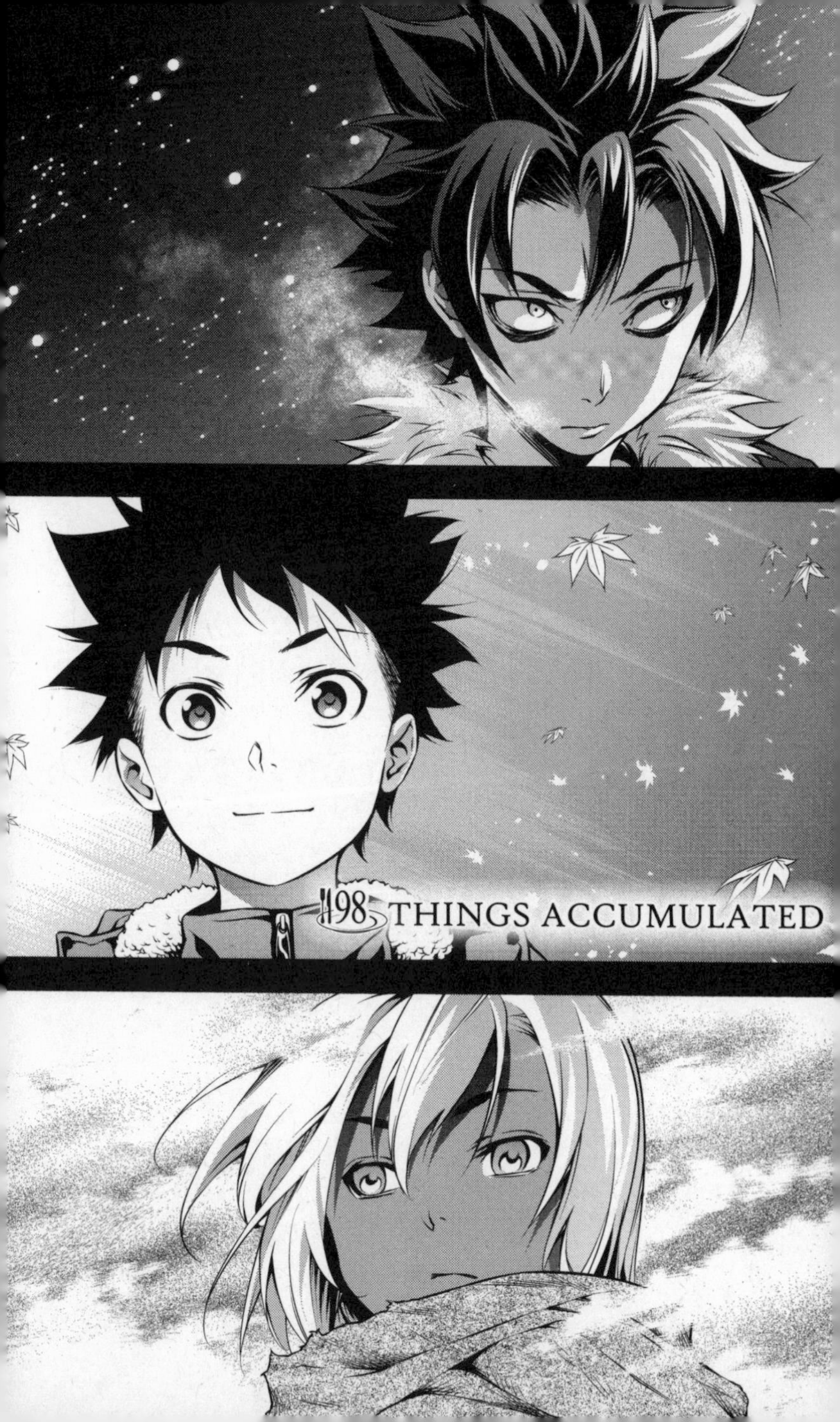
198 THINGS ACCUMULATED

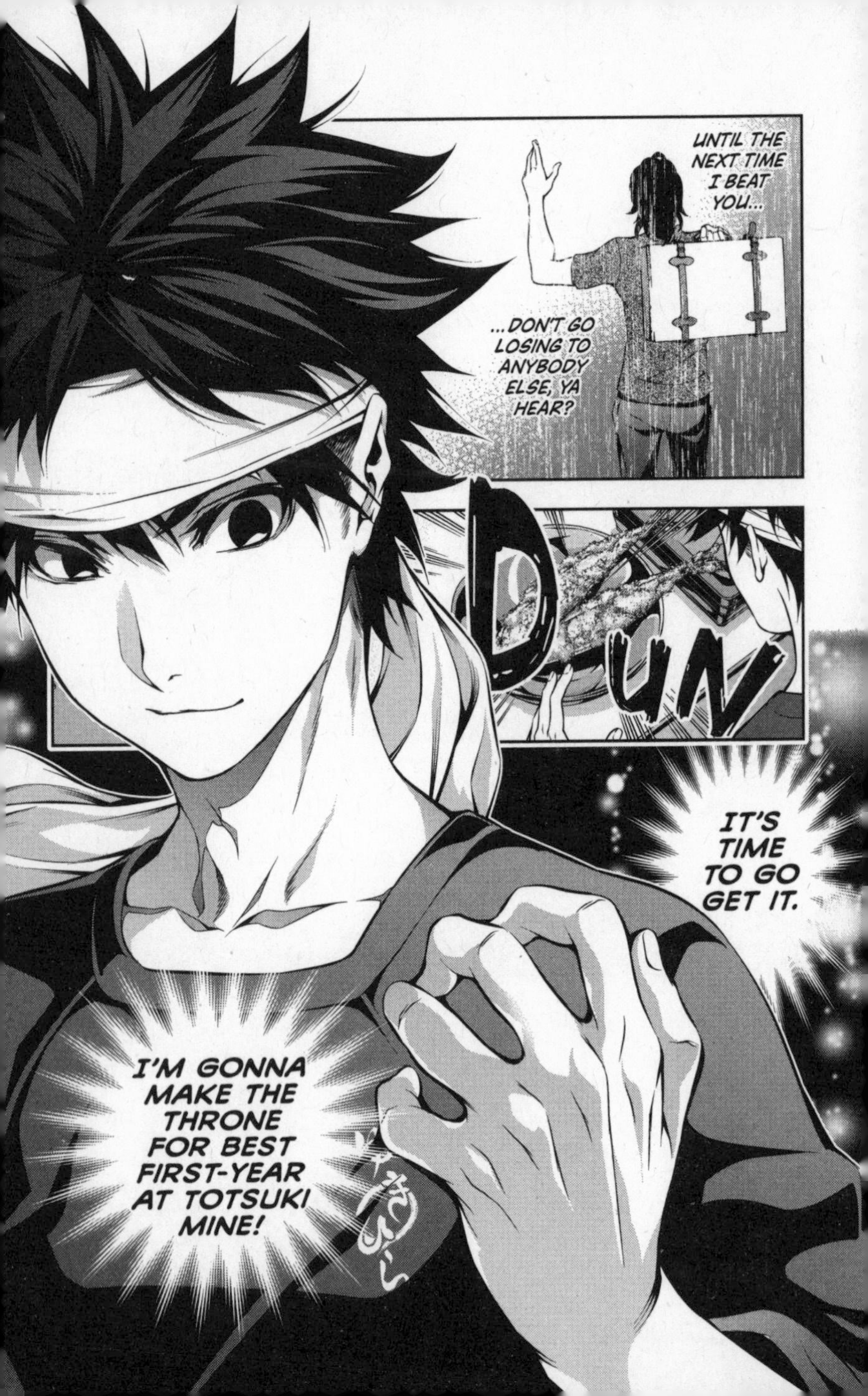
UNTIL THE NEXT TIME I BEAT YOU...
...DON'T GO LOSING TO ANYBODY ELSE, YA HEAR?
DUN
IT'S TIME TO GO GET IT.
I'M GONNA MAKE THE THRONE FOR BEST FIRST-YEAR AT TOTSUKI MINE!

WAAAAAA

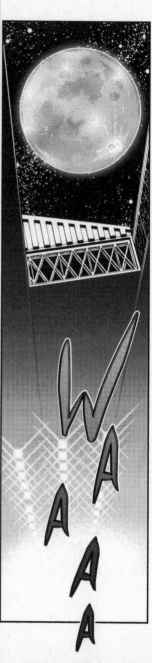

WAAAA

HM. NONE OF THE CONTESTANTS HAVE TOUCHED THEIR PIKE YET.

LOOKS LIKE THEY'RE ALL WORKING ON THE BASE PREP OF THEIR OTHER INGREDIENTS. A STANDARD MOVE.

EXCESS HANDLING MAY CAUSE THE FISH TO LOSE ITS FRESH TASTE.

EACH IS AIMING TO PRESERVE AS MUCH OF THAT FRESHNESS AS POSSIBLE.

HEE HEE! I FEEL VERY EXCITE RIGHT NOW.

AT NAKIRI INTERNATIONAL LABS IN DENMARK, THERE ARE ONLY GROWN-UP SCIENTISTS.

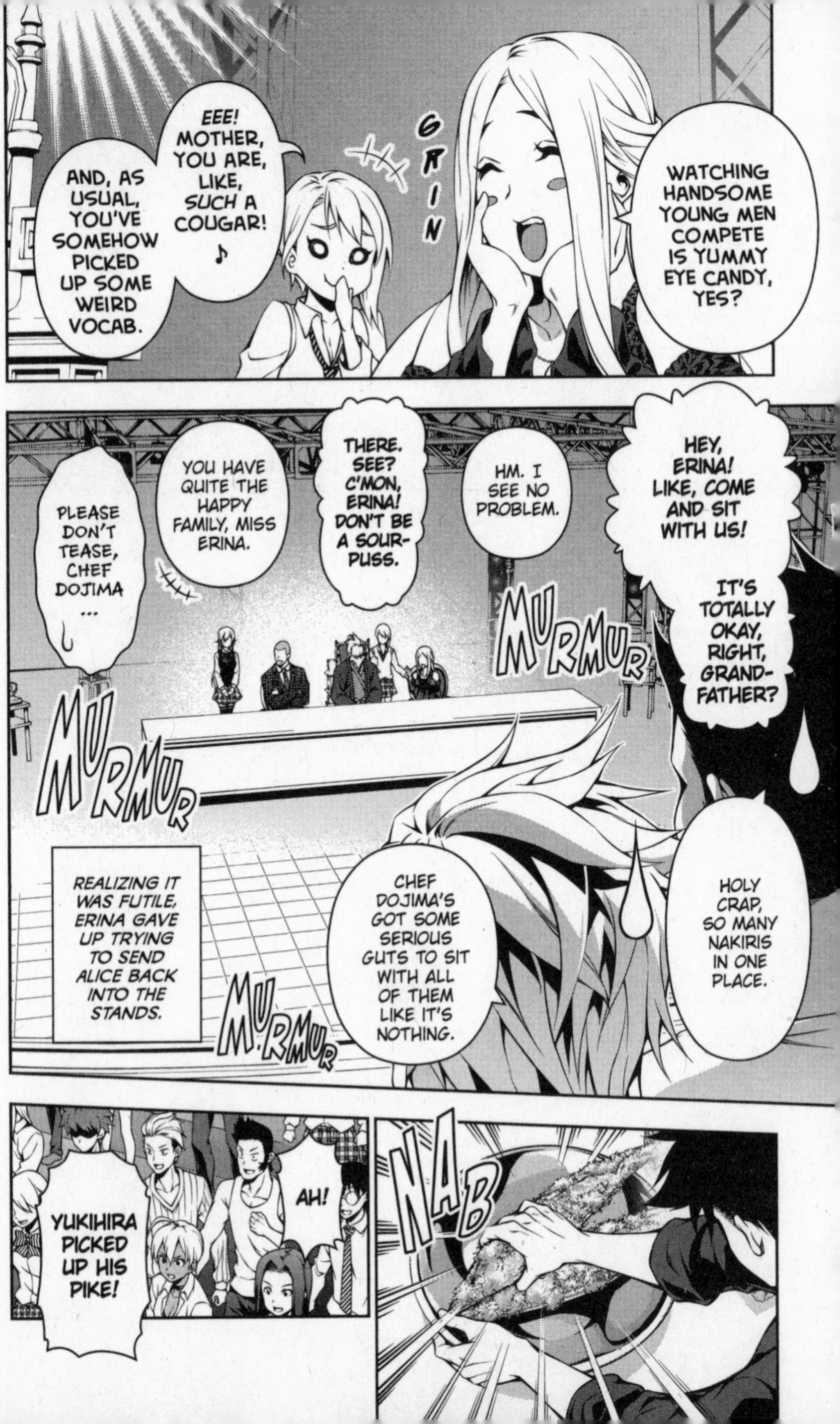
WATCHING HANDSOME YOUNG MEN COMPETE IS YUMMY EYE CANDY, YES?
GRIN
EEE! MOTHER, YOU ARE, LIKE, SUCH A COUGAR! ♪
AND, AS USUAL, YOU'VE SOMEHOW PICKED UP SOME WEIRD VOCAB.
HEY, ERINA! LIKE, COME AND SIT WITH US!
IT'S TOTALLY OKAY, RIGHT, GRANDFATHER?
HM. I SEE NO PROBLEM.
THERE. SEE? C'MON, ERINA! DON'T BE A SOUR-PUSS.
YOU HAVE QUITE THE HAPPY FAMILY, MISS ERINA.
PLEASE DON'T TEASE, CHEF DOJIMA...
MURMUR
MURMUR
HOLY CRAP, SO MANY NAKIRIS IN ONE PLACE.
CHEF DOJIMA'S GOT SOME SERIOUS GUTS TO SIT WITH ALL OF THEM LIKE IT'S NOTHING.
MURMUR
REALIZING IT WAS FUTILE, ERINA GAVE UP TRYING TO SEND ALICE BACK INTO THE STANDS.
NAB
AH!
YUKIHIRA PICKED UP HIS PIKE!

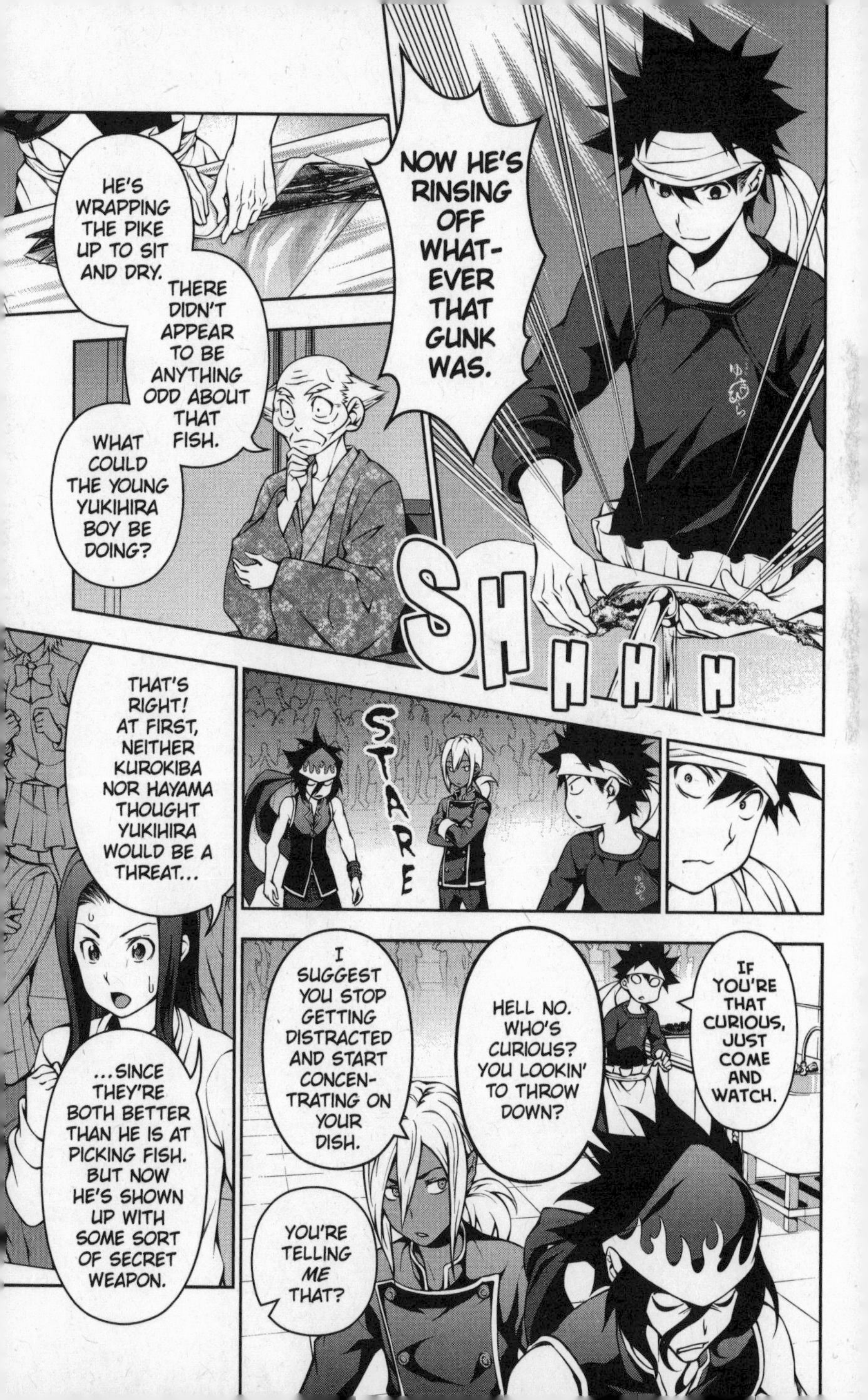

NOW HE'S RINSING OFF WHATEVER THAT GUNK WAS.
SHHHHH
HE'S WRAPPING THE PIKE UP TO SIT AND DRY.
THERE DIDN'T APPEAR TO BE ANYTHING ODD ABOUT THAT FISH.
WHAT COULD THE YOUNG YUKIHIRA BOY BE DOING?
STARE
IF YOU'RE THAT CURIOUS, JUST COME AND WATCH.
HELL NO. WHO'S CURIOUS? YOU LOOKIN' TO THROW DOWN?
I SUGGEST YOU STOP GETTING DISTRACTED AND START CONCENTRATING ON YOUR DISH.
YOU'RE TELLING *ME* THAT?
THAT'S RIGHT! AT FIRST, NEITHER KUROKIBA NOR HAYAMA THOUGHT YUKIHIRA WOULD BE A THREAT...
...SINCE THEY'RE BOTH BETTER THAN HE IS AT PICKING FISH. BUT NOW HE'S SHOWN UP WITH SOME SORT OF SECRET WEAPON.

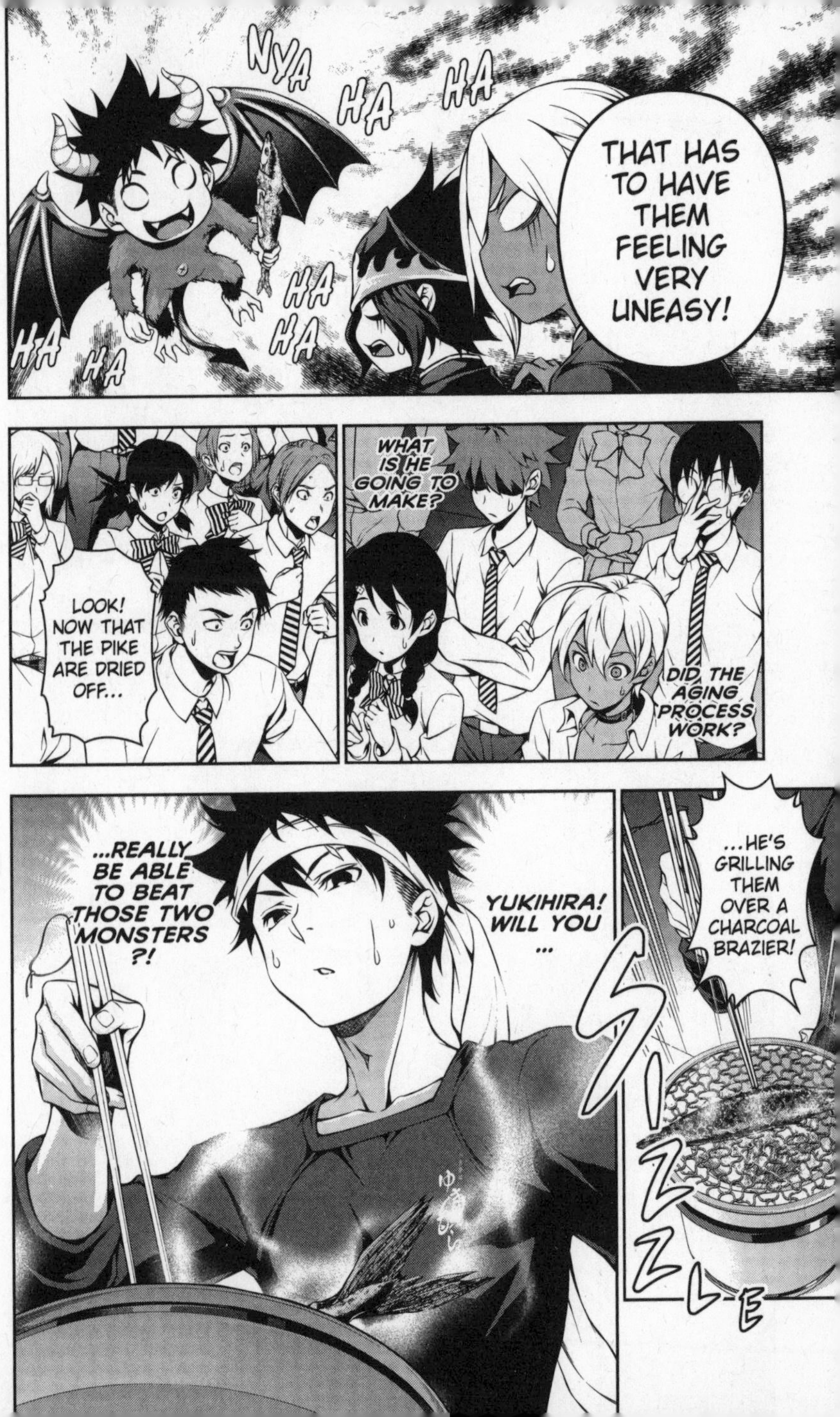
THAT HAS TO HAVE THEM FEELING VERY UNEASY!
NYA HA HA
HA HA
HA HA
WHAT IS HE GOING TO MAKE?
DID THE AGING PROCESS WORK?
LOOK! NOW THAT THE PIKE ARE DRIED OFF...
...HE'S GRILLING THEM OVER A CHARCOAL BRAZIER!
SIZZLE
YUKIHIRA! WILL YOU ...
...REALLY BE ABLE TO BEAT THOSE TWO MONSTERS?!

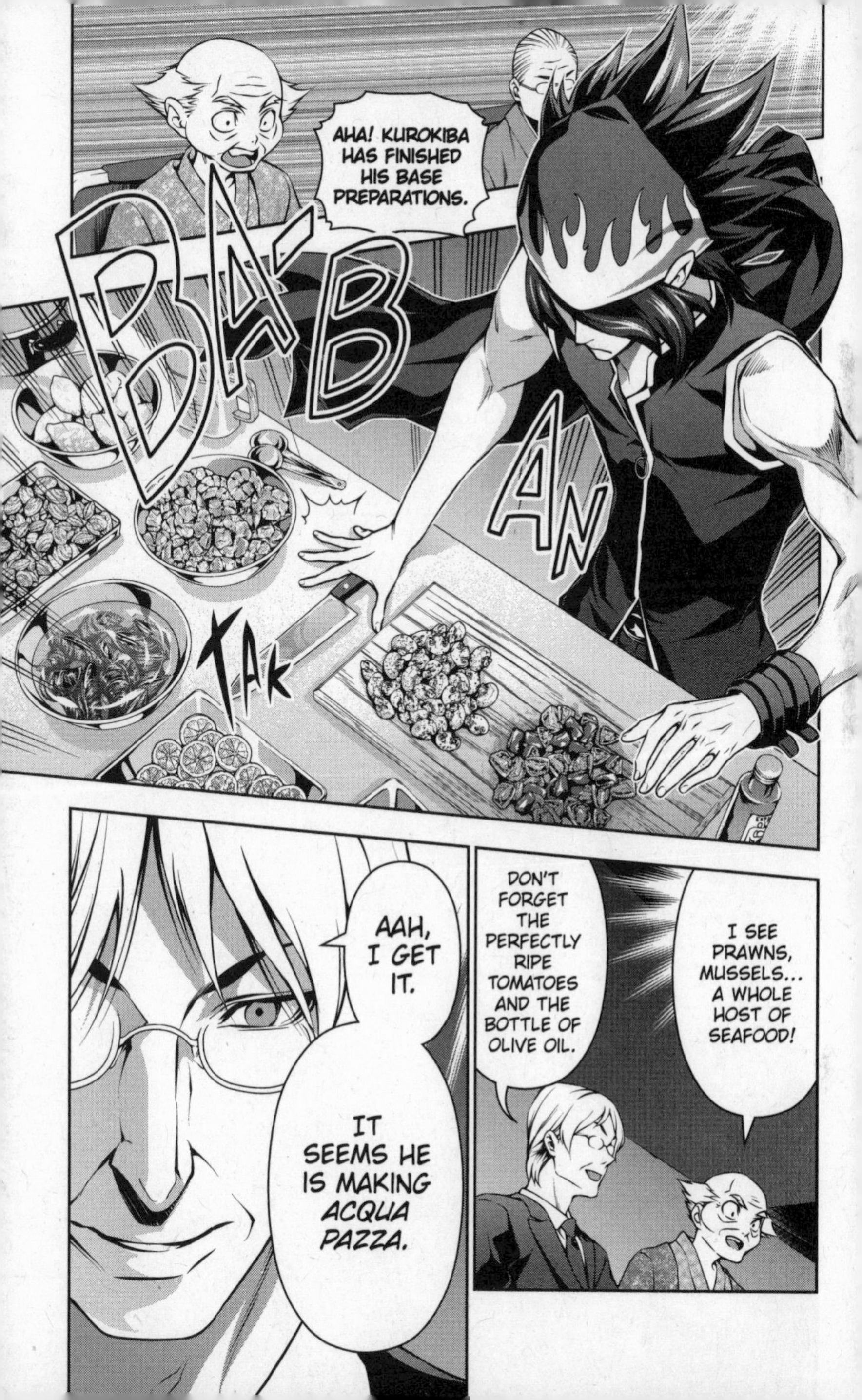

AHA! KUROKIBA HAS FINISHED HIS BASE PREPARATIONS.
BABAN
TAK
I SEE PRAWNS, MUSSELS... A WHOLE HOST OF SEAFOOD!
DON'T FORGET THE PERFECTLY RIPE TOMATOES AND THE BOTTLE OF OLIVE OIL.
AAH, I GET IT.
IT SEEMS HE IS MAKING *ACQUA PAZZA*.

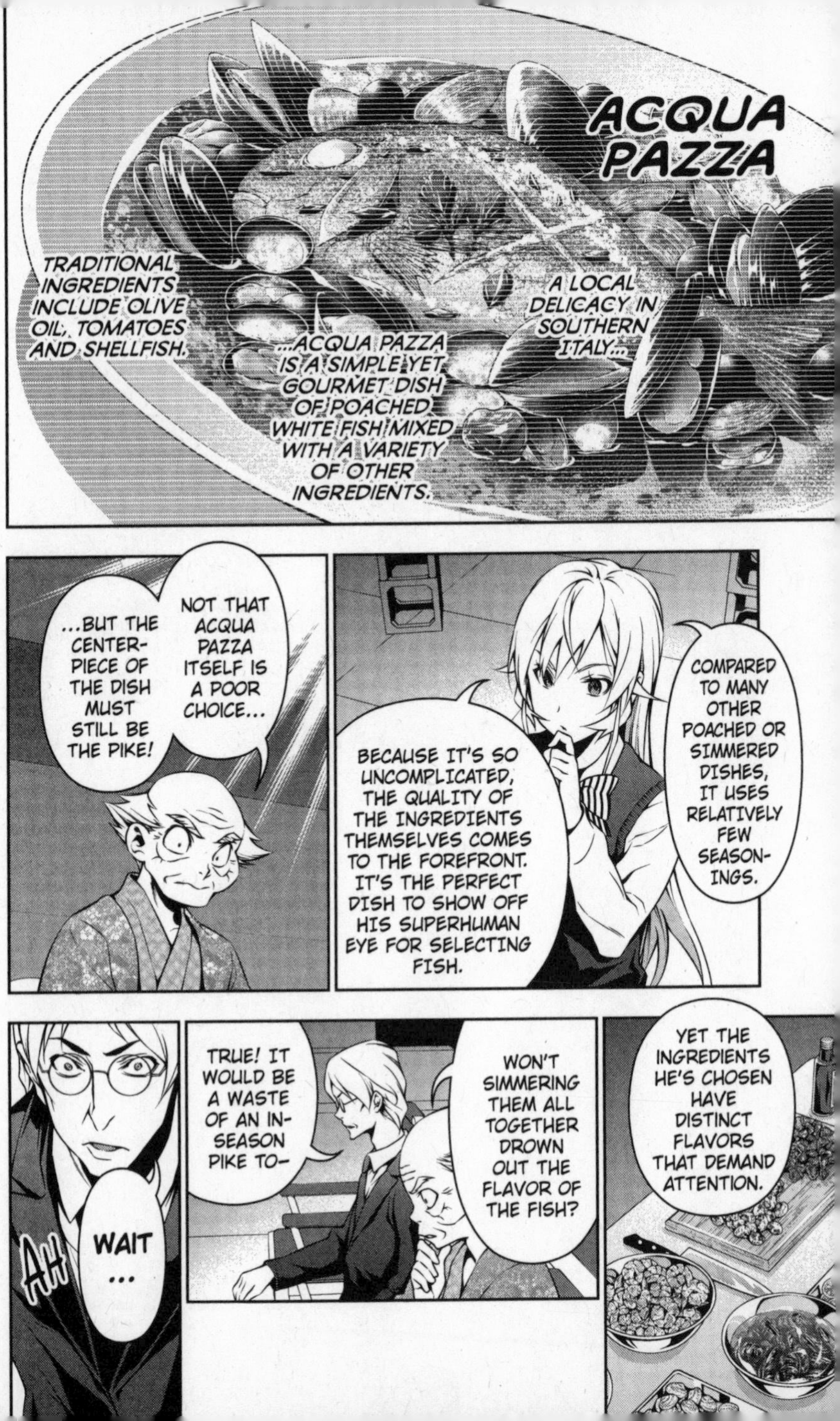
ACQUA PAZZA
A LOCAL DELICACY IN SOUTHERN ITALY...
...ACQUA PAZZA IS A SIMPLE YET GOURMET DISH OF POACHED WHITE FISH MIXED WITH A VARIETY OF OTHER INGREDIENTS.
TRADITIONAL INGREDIENTS INCLUDE OLIVE OIL, TOMATOES AND SHELLFISH.
COMPARED TO MANY OTHER POACHED OR SIMMERED DISHES, IT USES RELATIVELY FEW SEASON-INGS.
BECAUSE IT'S SO UNCOMPLICATED, THE QUALITY OF THE INGREDIENTS THEMSELVES COMES TO THE FOREFRONT. IT'S THE PERFECT DISH TO SHOW OFF HIS SUPERHUMAN EYE FOR SELECTING FISH.
NOT THAT ACQUA PAZZA ITSELF IS A POOR CHOICE...
...BUT THE CENTER-PIECE OF THE DISH MUST STILL BE THE PIKE!
YET THE INGREDIENTS HE'S CHOSEN HAVE DISTINCT FLAVORS THAT DEMAND ATTENTION.
WON'T SIMMERING THEM ALL TOGETHER DROWN OUT THE FLAVOR OF THE FISH?
TRUE! IT WOULD BE A WASTE OF AN IN-SEASON PIKE TO-
AH
WAIT ...

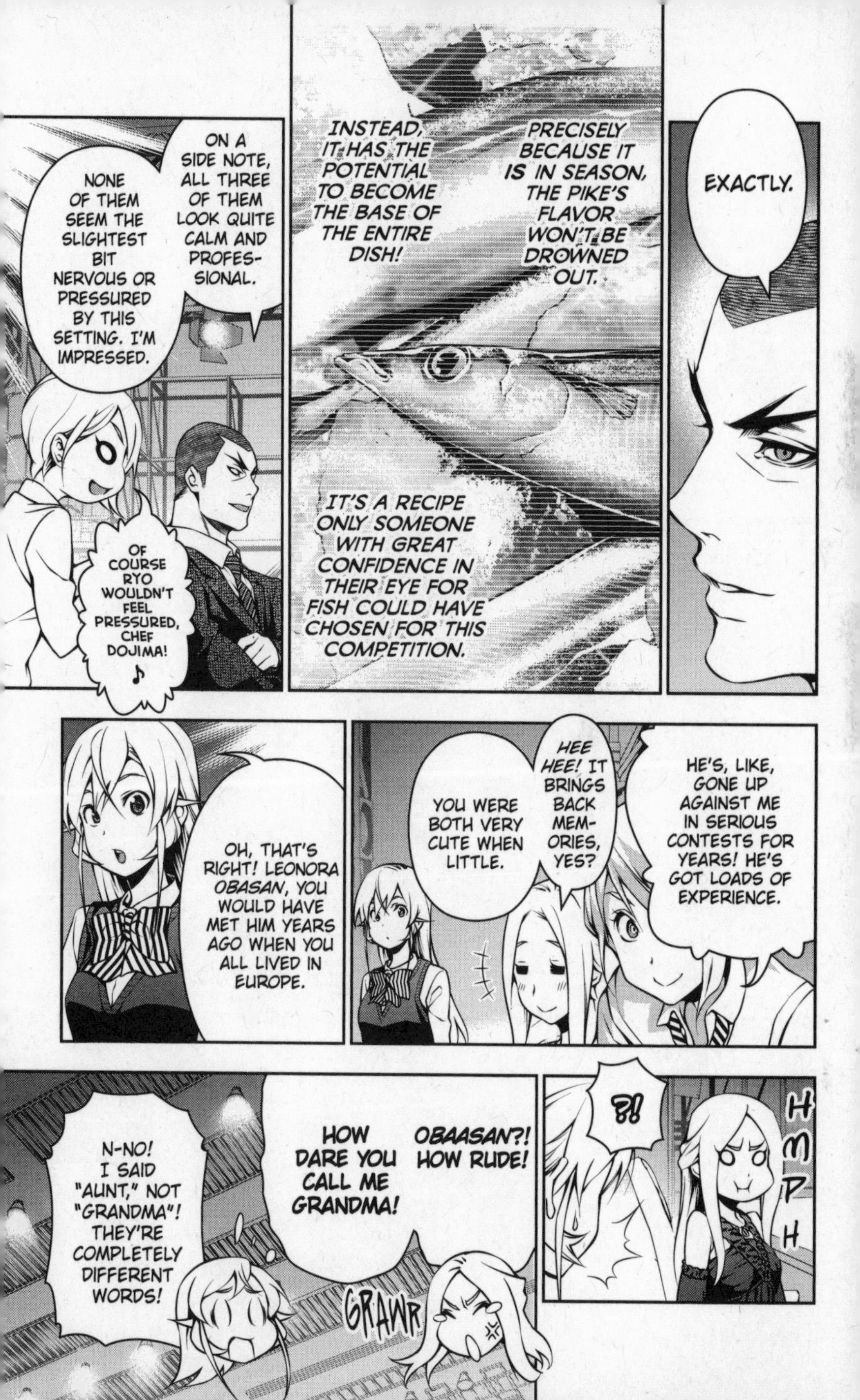
EXACTLY.
PRECISELY BECAUSE IT IS IN SEASON, THE PIKE'S FLAVOR WON'T BE DROWNED OUT.
INSTEAD, IT HAS THE POTENTIAL TO BECOME THE BASE OF THE ENTIRE DISH!
IT'S A RECIPE ONLY SOMEONE WITH GREAT CONFIDENCE IN THEIR EYE FOR FISH COULD HAVE CHOSEN FOR THIS COMPETITION.
ON A SIDE NOTE, ALL THREE OF THEM LOOK QUITE CALM AND PROFES-SIONAL.
NONE OF THEM SEEM THE SLIGHTEST BIT NERVOUS OR PRESSURED BY THIS SETTING. I'M IMPRESSED.
OF COURSE RYO WOULDN'T FEEL PRESSURED, CHEF DOJIMA! ♪
HE'S, LIKE, GONE UP AGAINST ME IN SERIOUS CONTESTS FOR YEARS! HE'S GOT LOADS OF EXPERIENCE.
HEE HEE! IT BRINGS BACK MEM-ORIES, YES?
YOU WERE BOTH VERY CUTE WHEN LITTLE.
OH, THAT'S RIGHT! LEONORA OBASAN, YOU WOULD HAVE MET HIM YEARS AGO WHEN YOU ALL LIVED IN EUROPE.
HMPH
?!
OBAASAN?! HOW RUDE!
HOW DARE YOU CALL ME GRANDMA!
N-NO! I SAID "AUNT," NOT "GRANDMA"! THEY'RE COMPLETELY DIFFERENT WORDS!
GRAWR

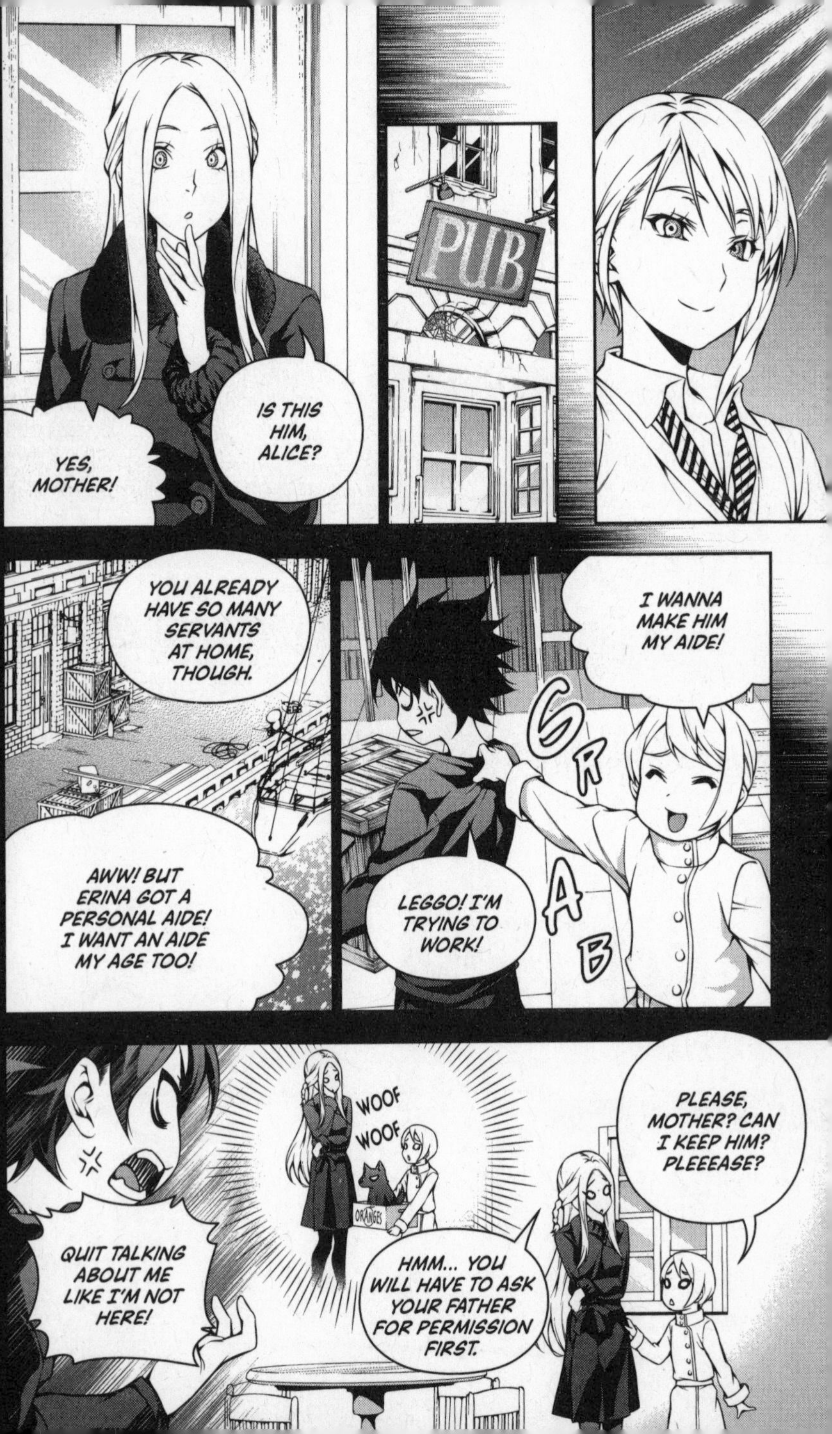
PUB
IS THIS HIM, ALICE?
YES, MOTHER!
I WANNA MAKE HIM MY AIDE!
GRAB
LEGGO! I'M TRYING TO WORK!
YOU ALREADY HAVE SO MANY SERVANTS AT HOME, THOUGH.
AWW! BUT ERINA GOT A PERSONAL AIDE! I WANT AN AIDE MY AGE TOO!
PLEASE, MOTHER? CAN I KEEP HIM? PLEEEASE?
WOOF
WOOF
ORANGES
HMM... YOU WILL HAVE TO ASK YOUR FATHER FOR PERMISSION FIRST.
QUIT TALKING ABOUT ME LIKE I'M NOT HERE!

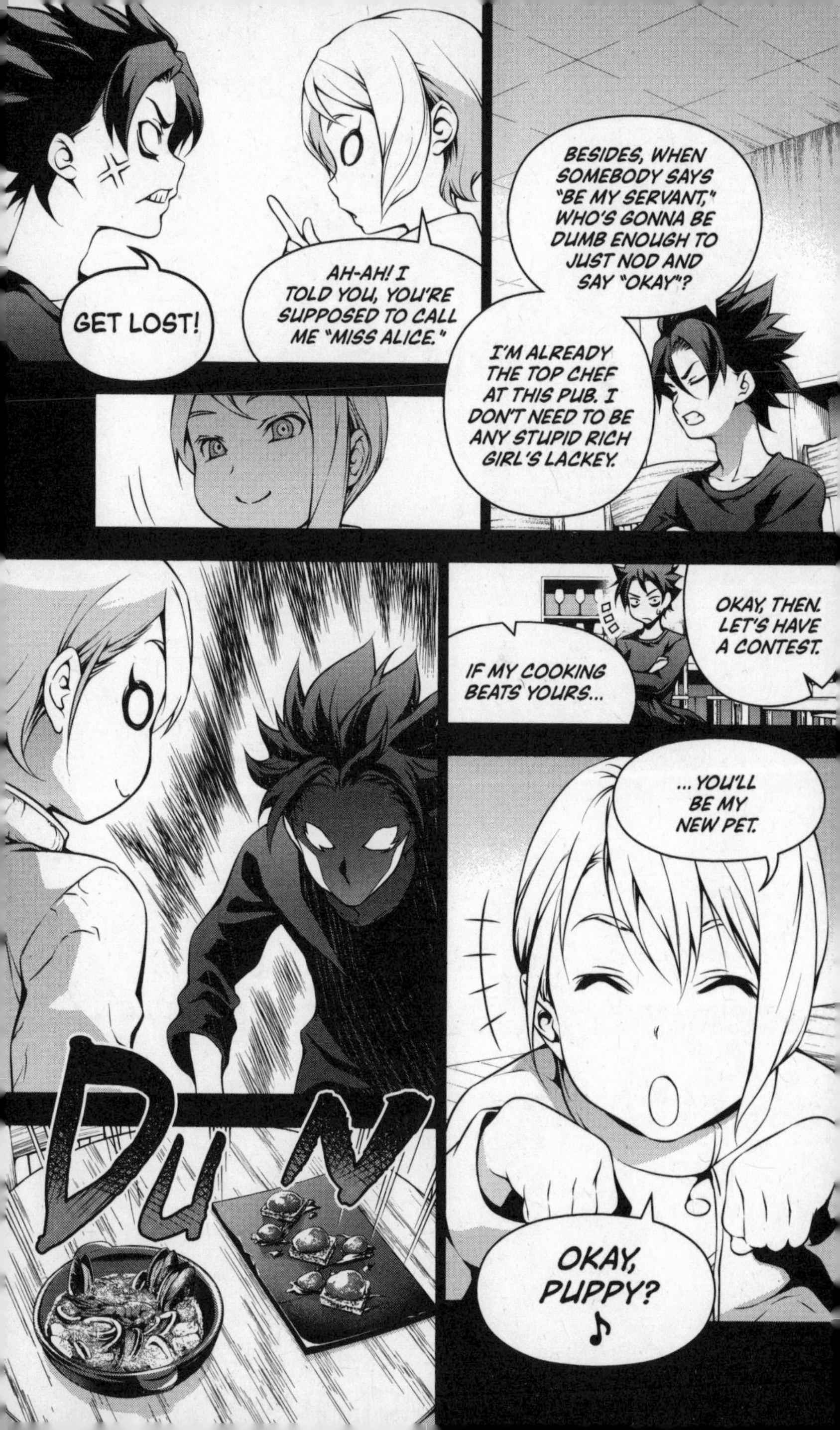
BESIDES, WHEN SOMEBODY SAYS "BE MY SERVANT," WHO'S GONNA BE DUMB ENOUGH TO JUST NOD AND SAY "OKAY"?
I'M ALREADY THE TOP CHEF AT THIS PUB. I DON'T NEED TO BE ANY STUPID RICH GIRL'S LACKEY.
AH-AH! I TOLD YOU, YOU'RE SUPPOSED TO CALL ME "MISS ALICE."
GET LOST!
OKAY, THEN. LET'S HAVE A CONTEST.
IF MY COOKING BEATS YOURS...
...YOU'LL BE MY NEW PET.
OKAY, PUPPY? ♪
DUN

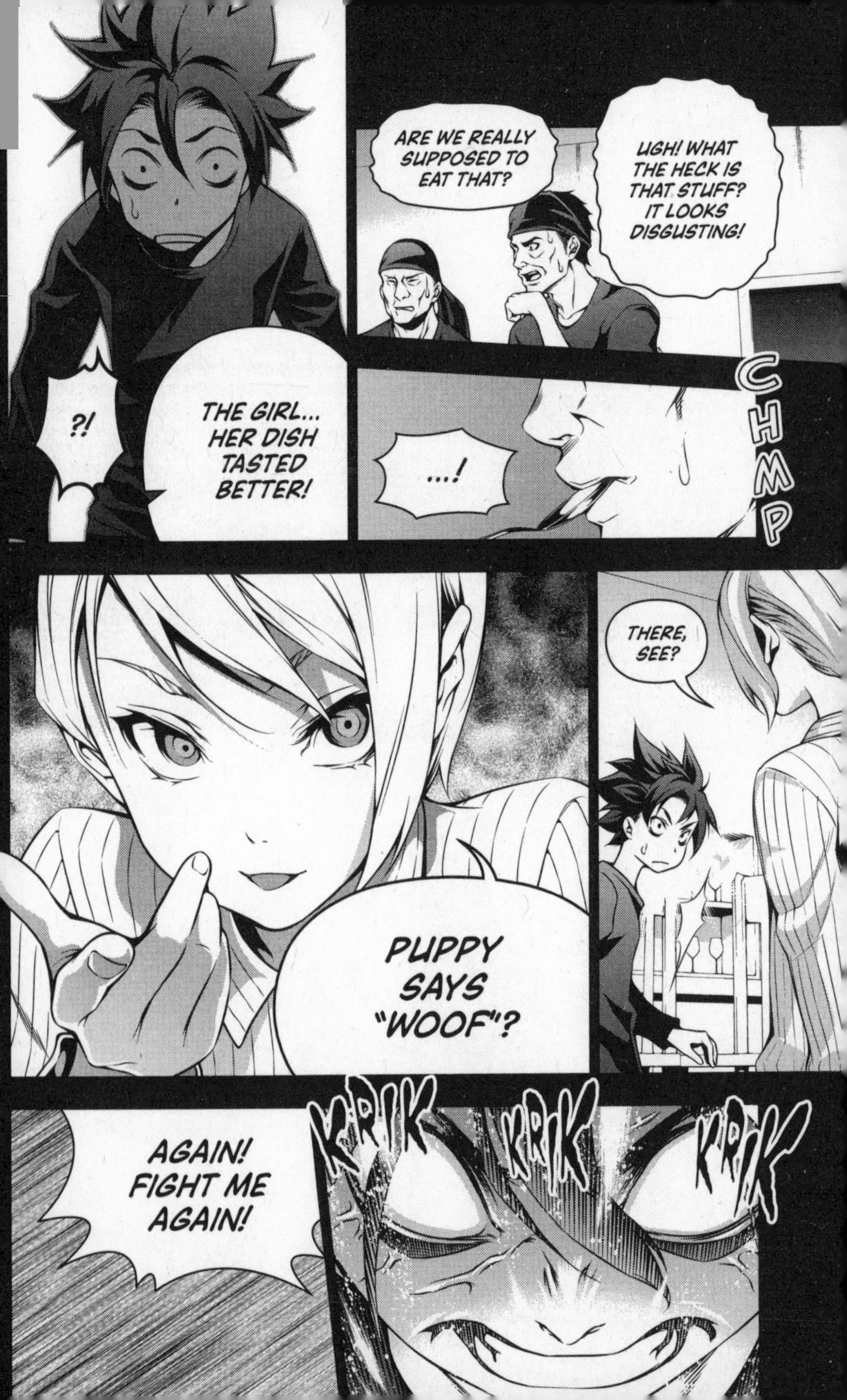
UGH! WHAT THE HECK IS THAT STUFF? IT LOOKS DISGUSTING!
ARE WE REALLY SUPPOSED TO EAT THAT?
CHMP
...!
THE GIRL... HER DISH TASTED BETTER!
?!
THERE, SEE?
PUPPY SAYS "WOOF"?
KRIK
KRIK
KRIK
AGAIN! FIGHT ME AGAIN!

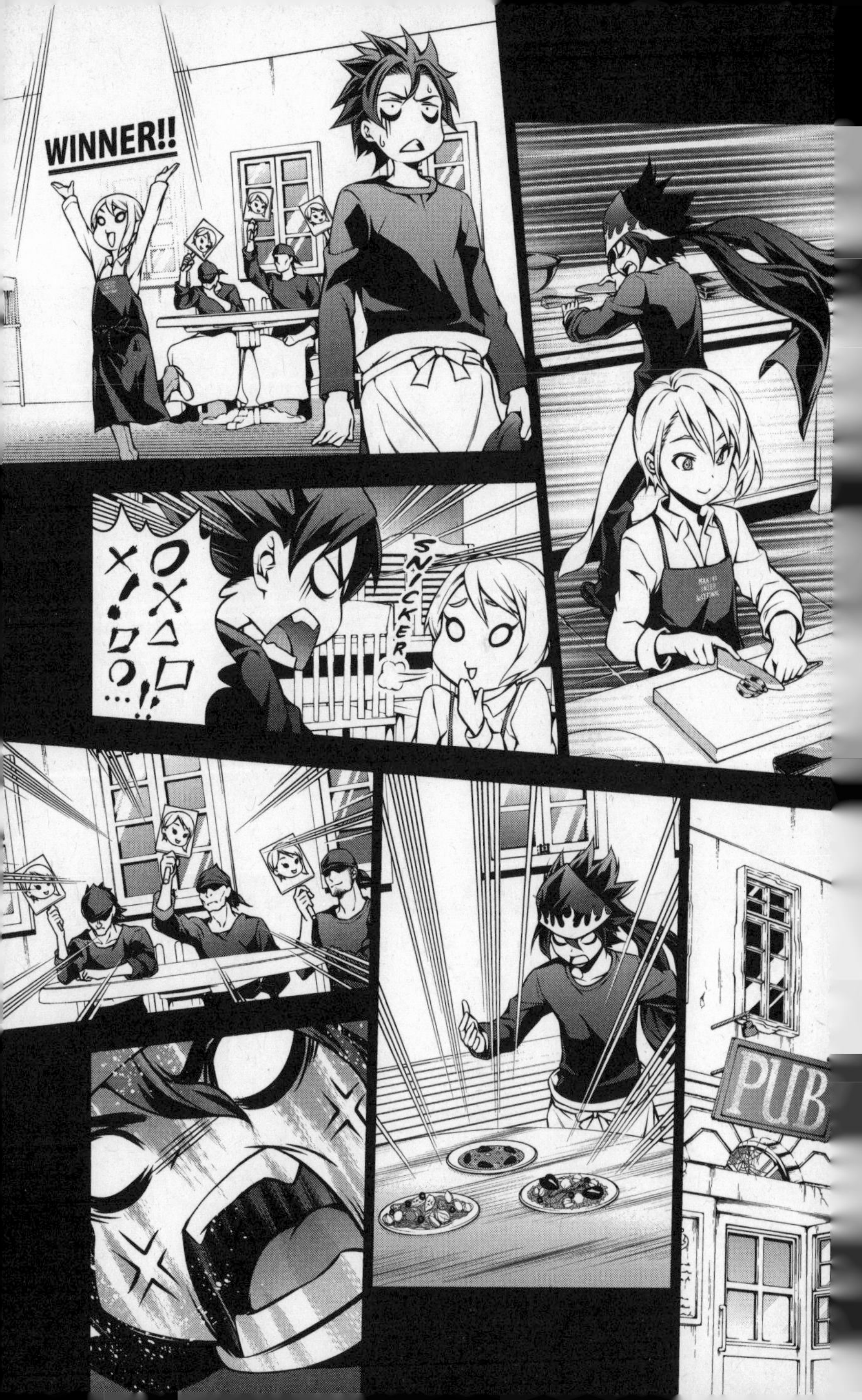
WINNER!!
○×△□
×!□○…!!
SNICKER
PUB

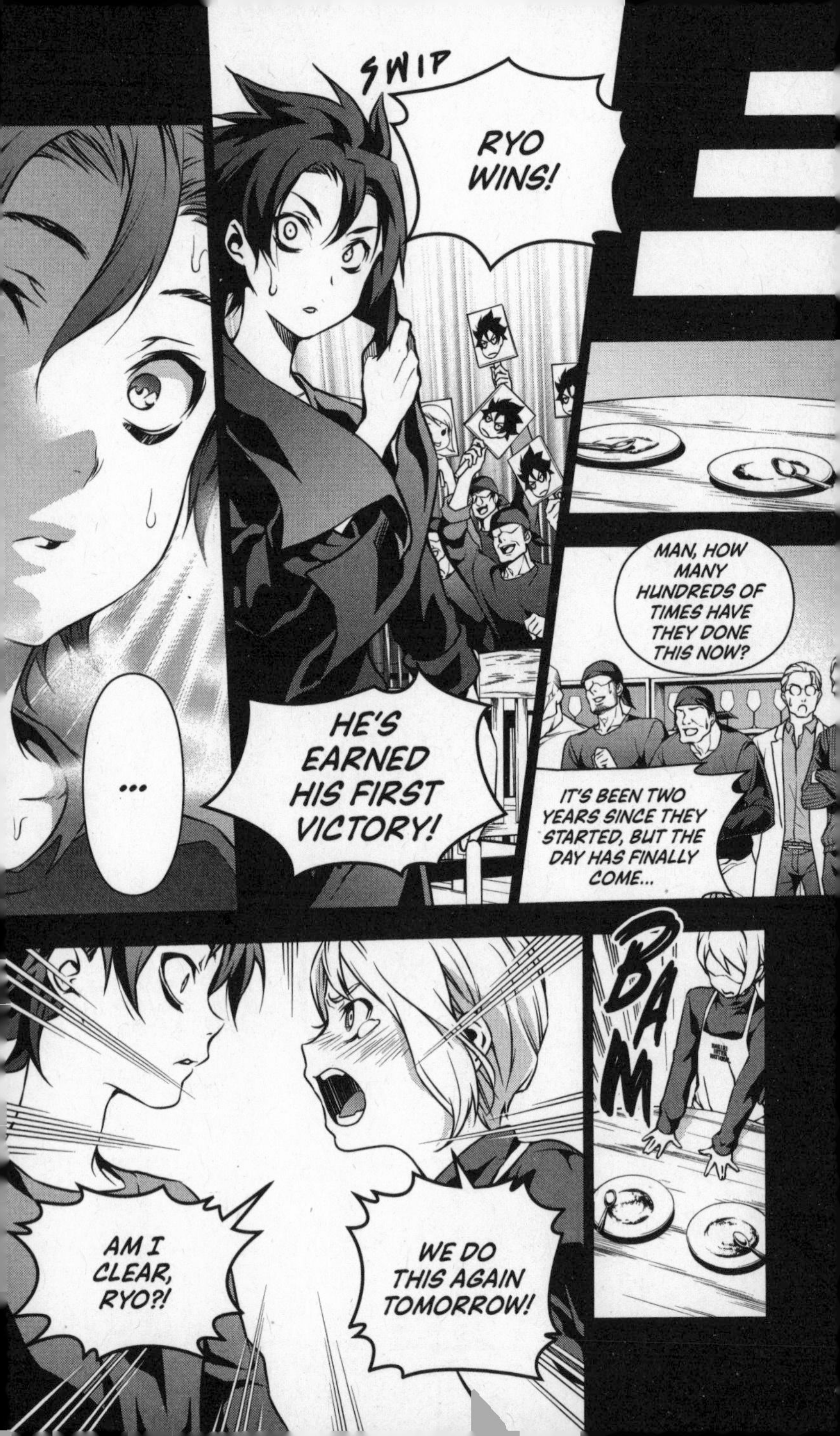

MAN, HOW MANY HUNDREDS OF TIMES HAVE THEY DONE THIS NOW?
IT'S BEEN TWO YEARS SINCE THEY STARTED, BUT THE DAY HAS FINALLY COME...
SWIP
RYO WINS!
HE'S EARNED HIS FIRST VICTORY!
...
BAM
WE DO THIS AGAIN TOMORROW!
AM I CLEAR, RYO?!

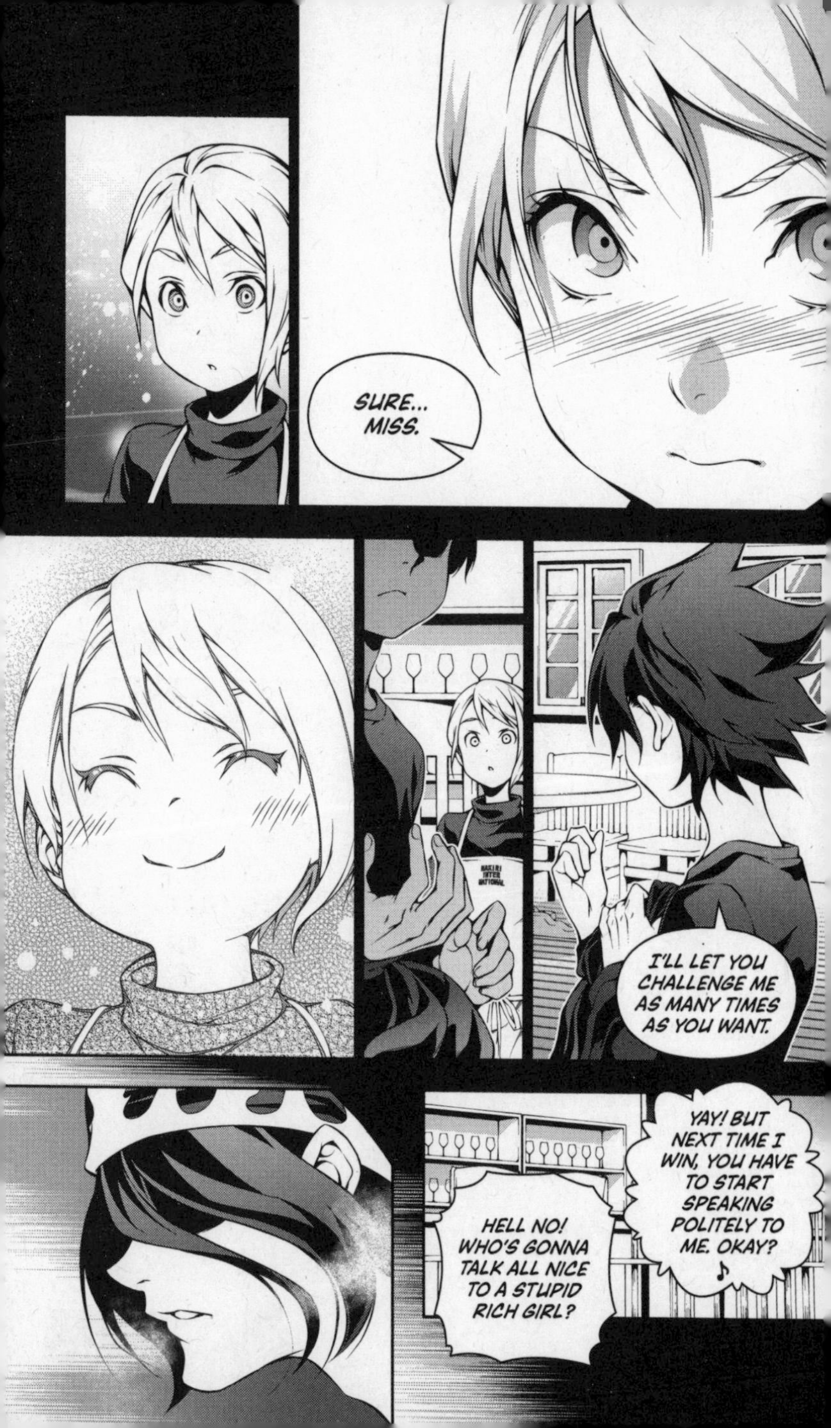
SURE... MISS.
I'LL LET YOU CHALLENGE ME AS MANY TIMES AS YOU WANT.
YAY! BUT NEXT TIME I WIN, YOU HAVE TO START SPEAKING POLITELY TO ME. OKAY? ♪
HELL NO! WHO'S GONNA TALK ALL NICE TO A STUPID RICH GIRL?

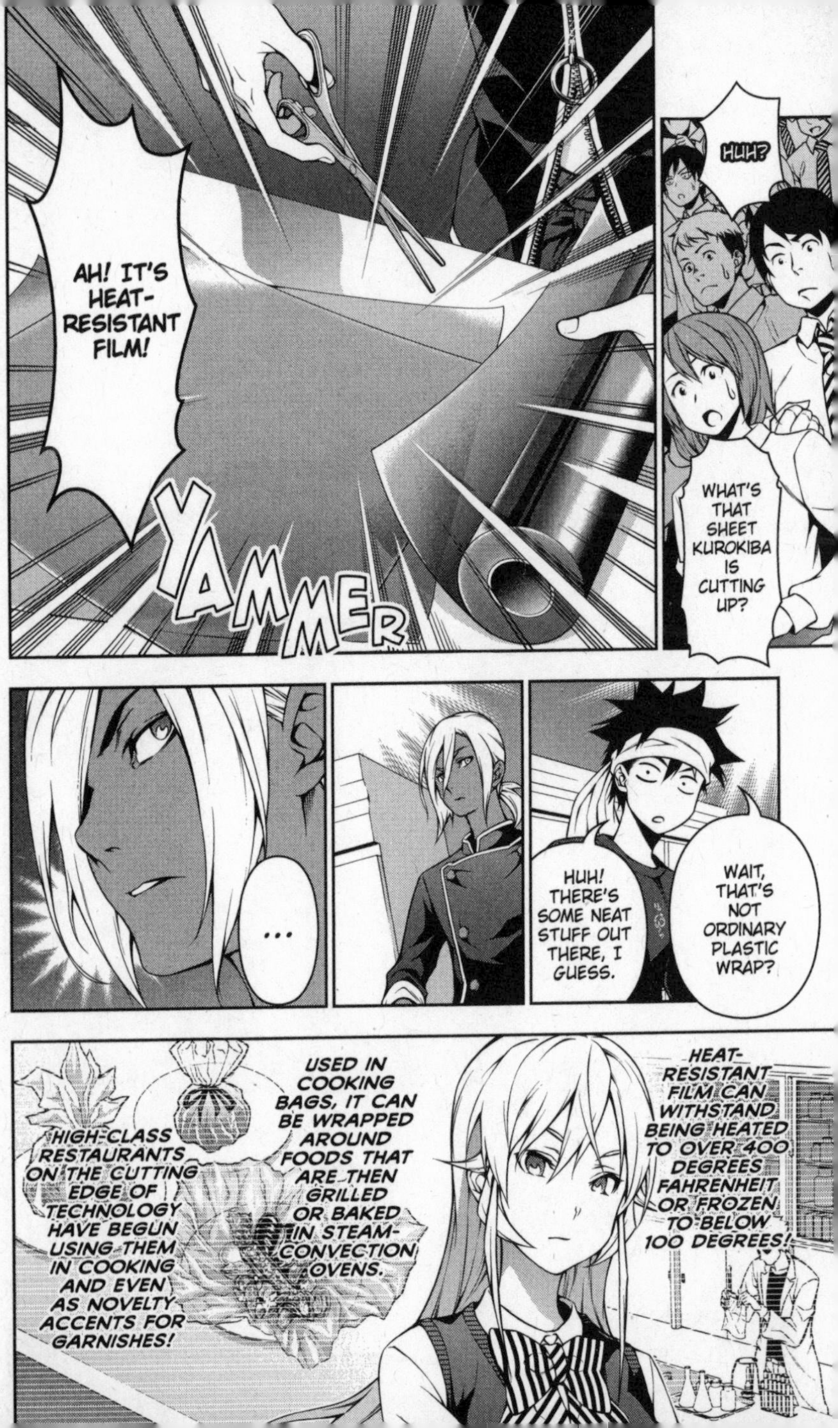
HUH?
WHAT'S THAT SHEET KUROKIBA IS CUTTING UP?
AH! IT'S HEAT-RESISTANT FILM!
YAMMER
WAIT, THAT'S NOT ORDINARY PLASTIC WRAP?
HUH! THERE'S SOME NEAT STUFF OUT THERE, I GUESS.
...
HEAT-RESISTANT FILM CAN WITHSTAND BEING HEATED TO OVER 400 DEGREES FAHRENHEIT OR FROZEN TO BELOW 100 DEGREES!
USED IN COOKING BAGS, IT CAN BE WRAPPED AROUND FOODS THAT ARE THEN GRILLED OR BAKED IN STEAM-CONVECTION OVENS.
HIGH-CLASS RESTAURANTS ON THE CUTTING EDGE OF TECHNOLOGY HAVE BEGUN USING THEM IN COOKING AND EVEN AS NOVELTY ACCENTS FOR GARNISHES!

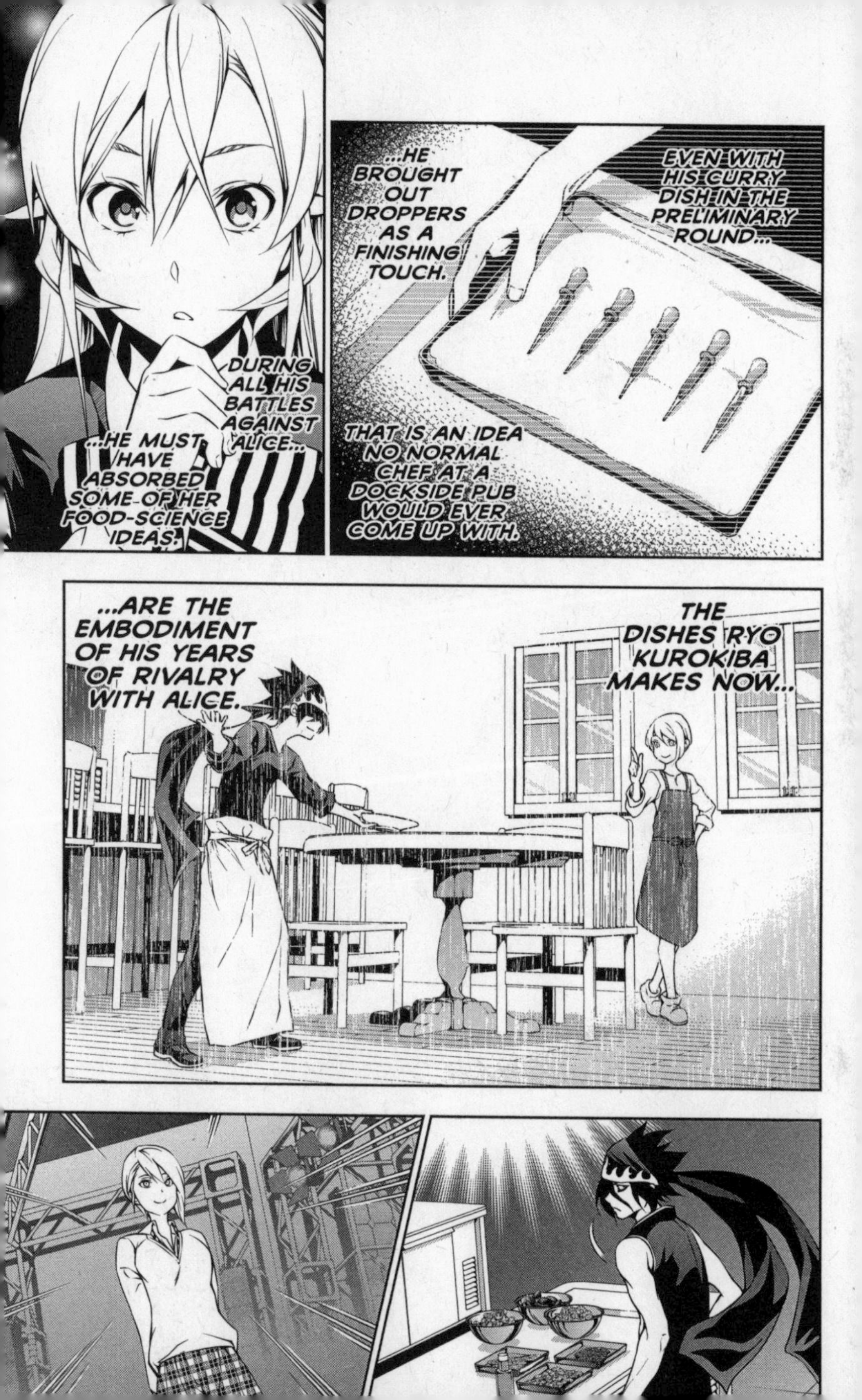
EVEN WITH HIS CURRY DISH IN THE PRELIMINARY ROUND...
...HE BROUGHT OUT DROPPERS AS A FINISHING TOUCH.
THAT IS AN IDEA NO NORMAL CHEF AT A DOCKSIDE PUB WOULD EVER COME UP WITH.
DURING ALL HIS BATTLES AGAINST ALICE...
...HE MUST HAVE ABSORBED SOME OF HER FOOD-SCIENCE IDEAS.
THE DISHES RYO KUROKIBA MAKES NOW...
...ARE THE EMBODIMENT OF HIS YEARS OF RIVALRY WITH ALICE.

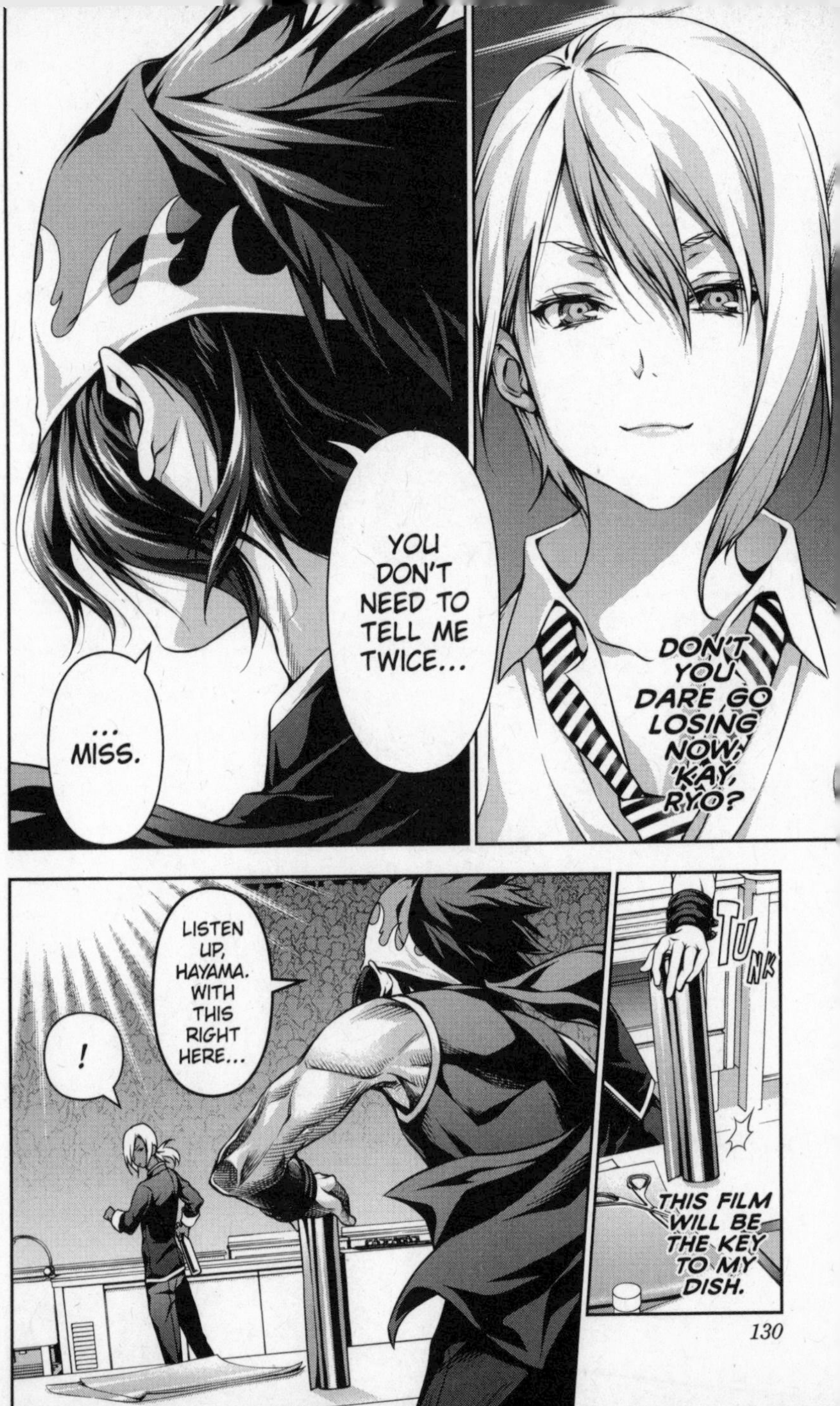
DON'T YOU DARE GO LOSING NOW, 'KAY, RYO?
YOU DON'T NEED TO TELL ME TWICE...
... MISS.
TUNK
THIS FILM WILL BE THE KEY TO MY DISH.
LISTEN UP, HAYAMA. WITH THIS RIGHT HERE...
!

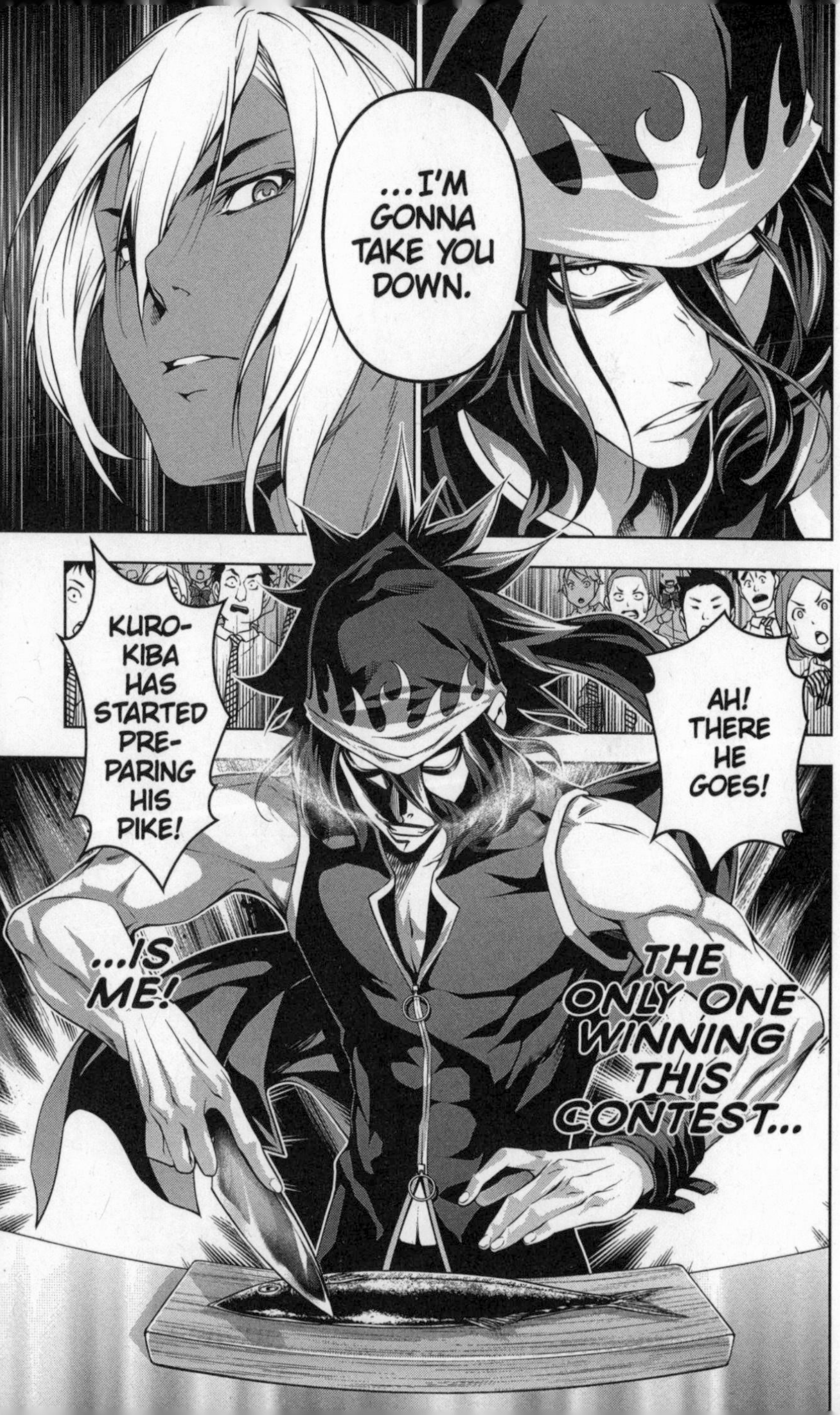
...I'M GONNA TAKE YOU DOWN.
AH! THERE HE GOES!
KURO-KIBA HAS STARTED PRE-PARING HIS PIKE!
THE ONLY ONE WINNING THIS CONTEST...
...IS ME!

MY TURN FIRST.

ORANGES

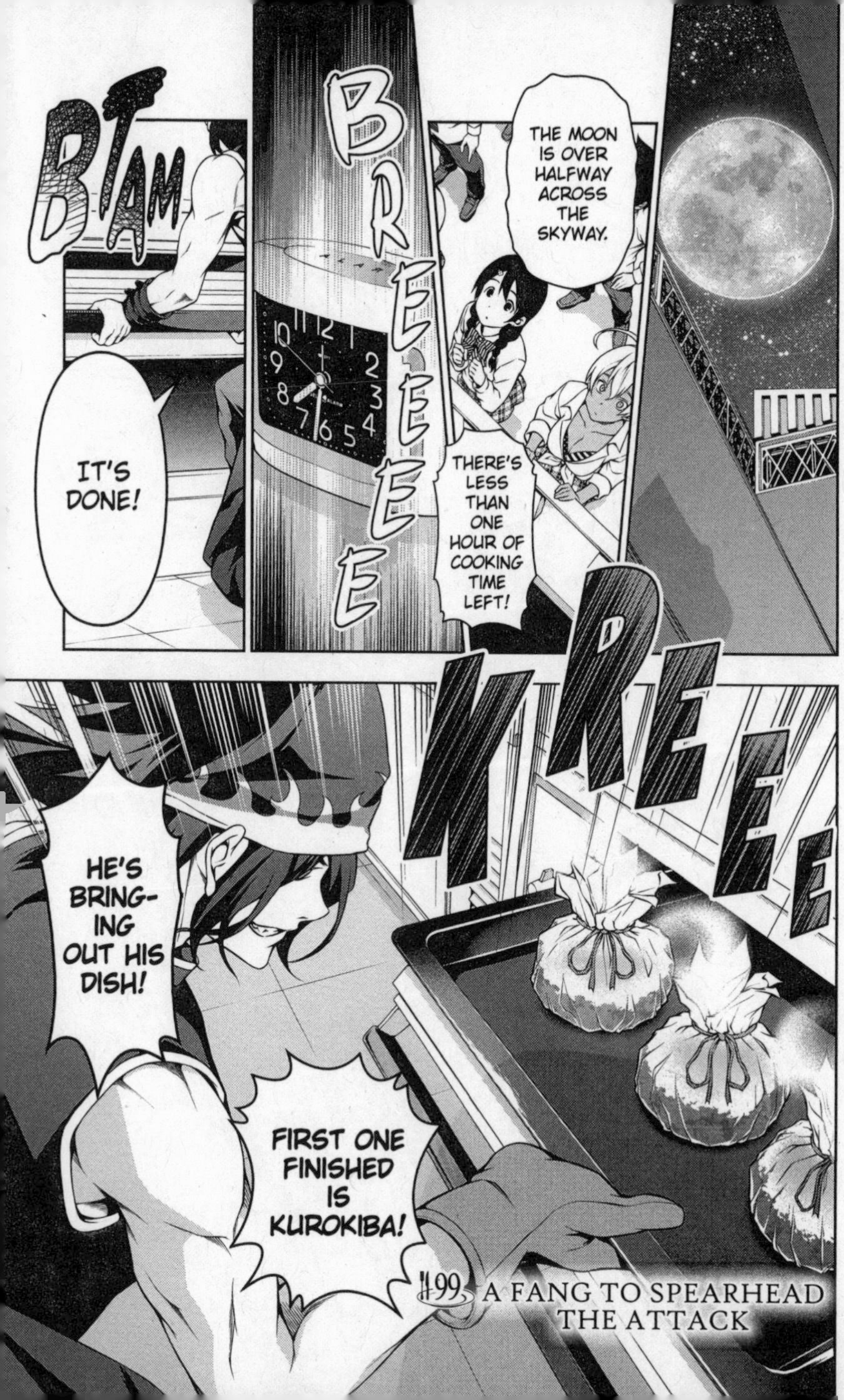
THE MOON IS OVER HALFWAY ACROSS THE SKYWAY.
THERE'S LESS THAN ONE HOUR OF COOKING TIME LEFT!
BREEEEE
BLAM
IT'S DONE!
KREEEEE
HE'S BRING-ING OUT HIS DISH!
FIRST ONE FINISHED IS KUROKIBA!
199 A FANG TO SPEARHEAD THE ATTACK

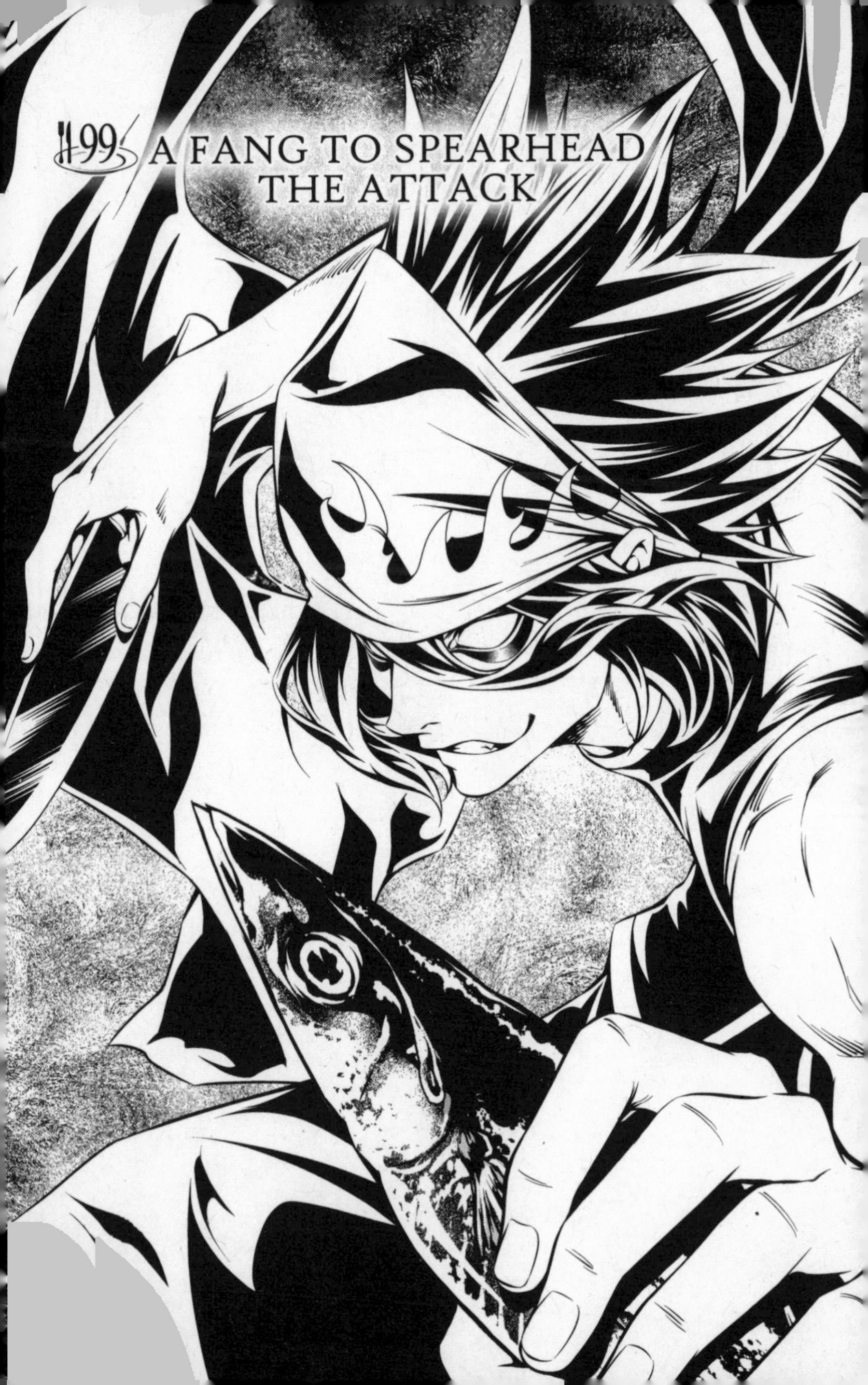
#99 A FANG TO SPEARHEAD THE ATTACK

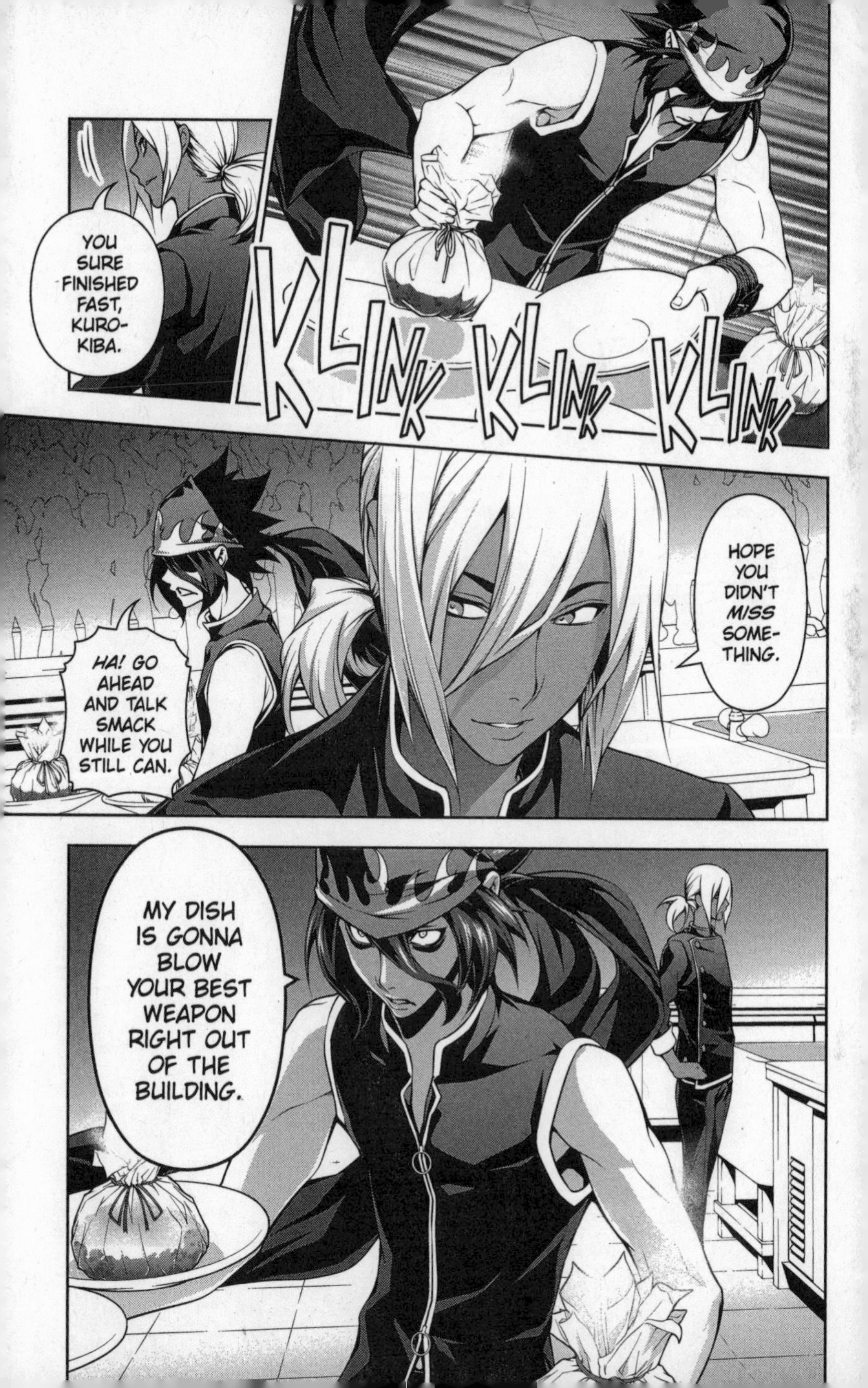
KLINK KLINK KLINK
YOU SURE FINISHED FAST, KURO-KIBA.
HOPE YOU DIDN'T *MISS* SOME-THING.
HA! GO AHEAD AND TALK SMACK WHILE YOU STILL CAN.
MY DISH IS GONNA BLOW YOUR BEST WEAPON RIGHT OUT OF THE BUILDING.

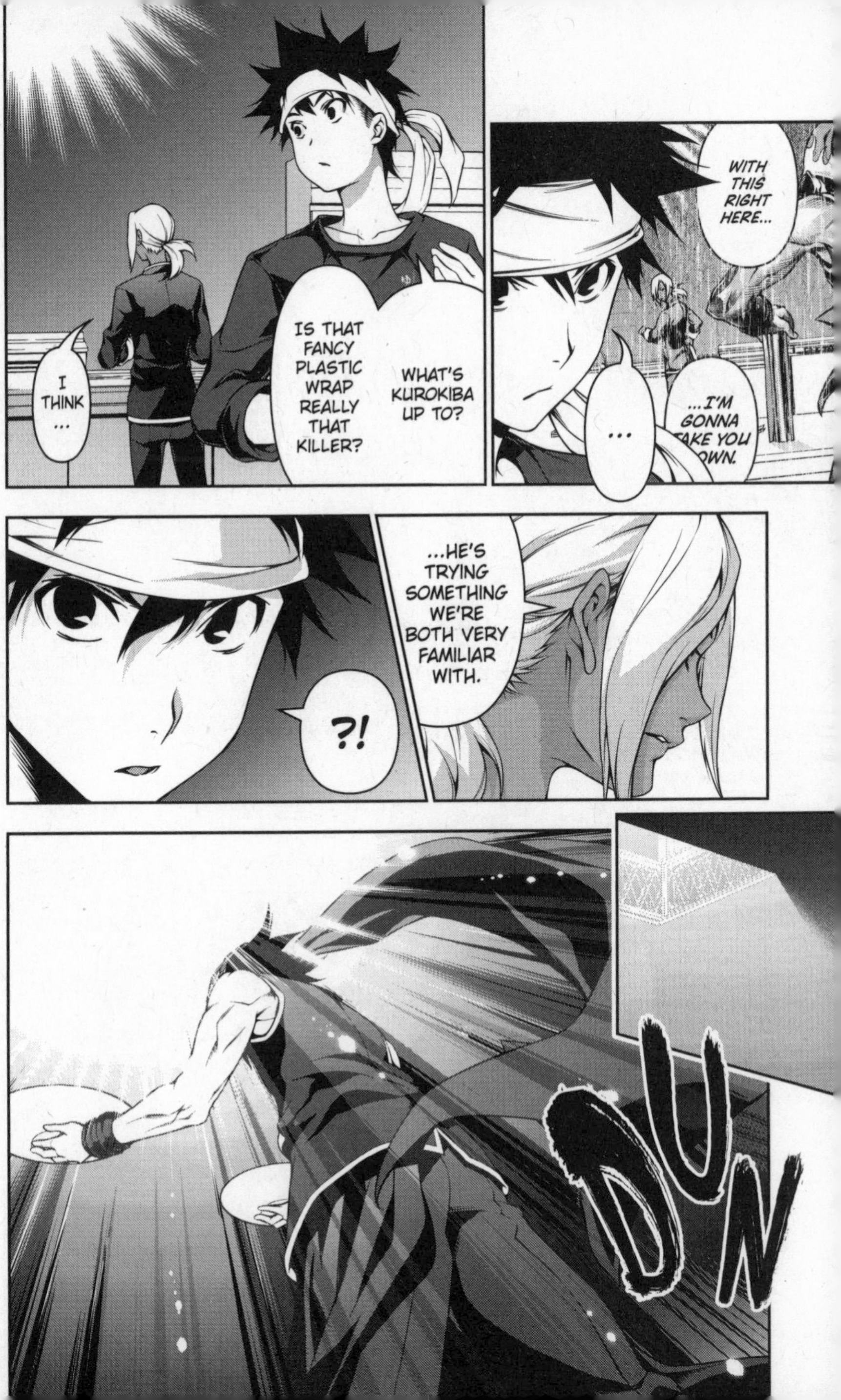
WITH THIS RIGHT HERE...
...I'M GONNA TAKE YOU DOWN.
...
WHAT'S KUROKIBA UP TO?
IS THAT FANCY PLASTIC WRAP REALLY THAT KILLER?
I THINK ...
...HE'S TRYING SOMETHING WE'RE BOTH VERY FAMILIAR WITH.
?!
DUN

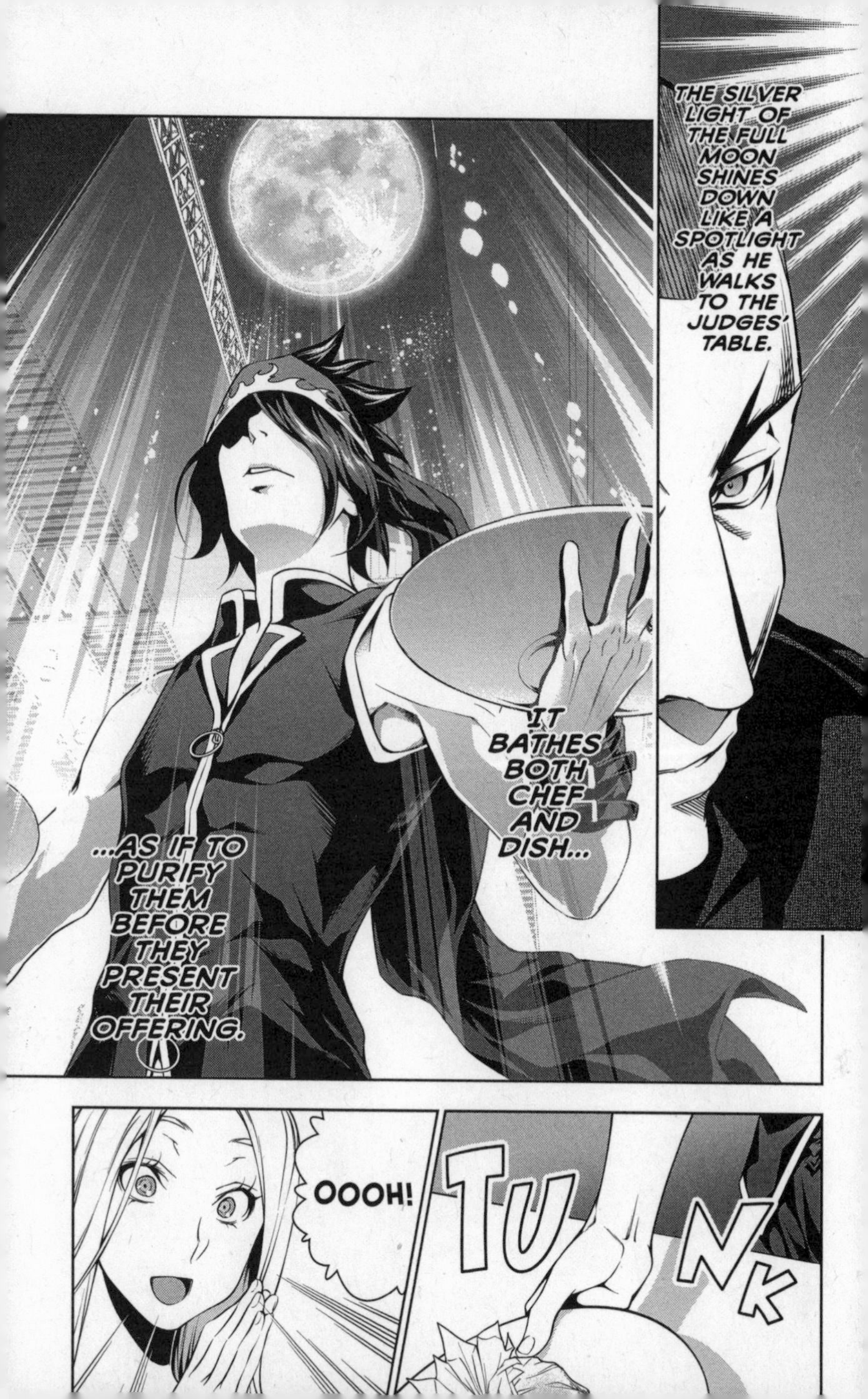
THE SILVER LIGHT OF THE FULL MOON SHINES DOWN LIKE A SPOTLIGHT AS HE WALKS TO THE JUDGES' TABLE.
IT BATHES BOTH CHEF AND DISH...
...AS IF TO PURIFY THEM BEFORE THEY PRESENT THEIR OFFERING.
TUNK
OOOH!

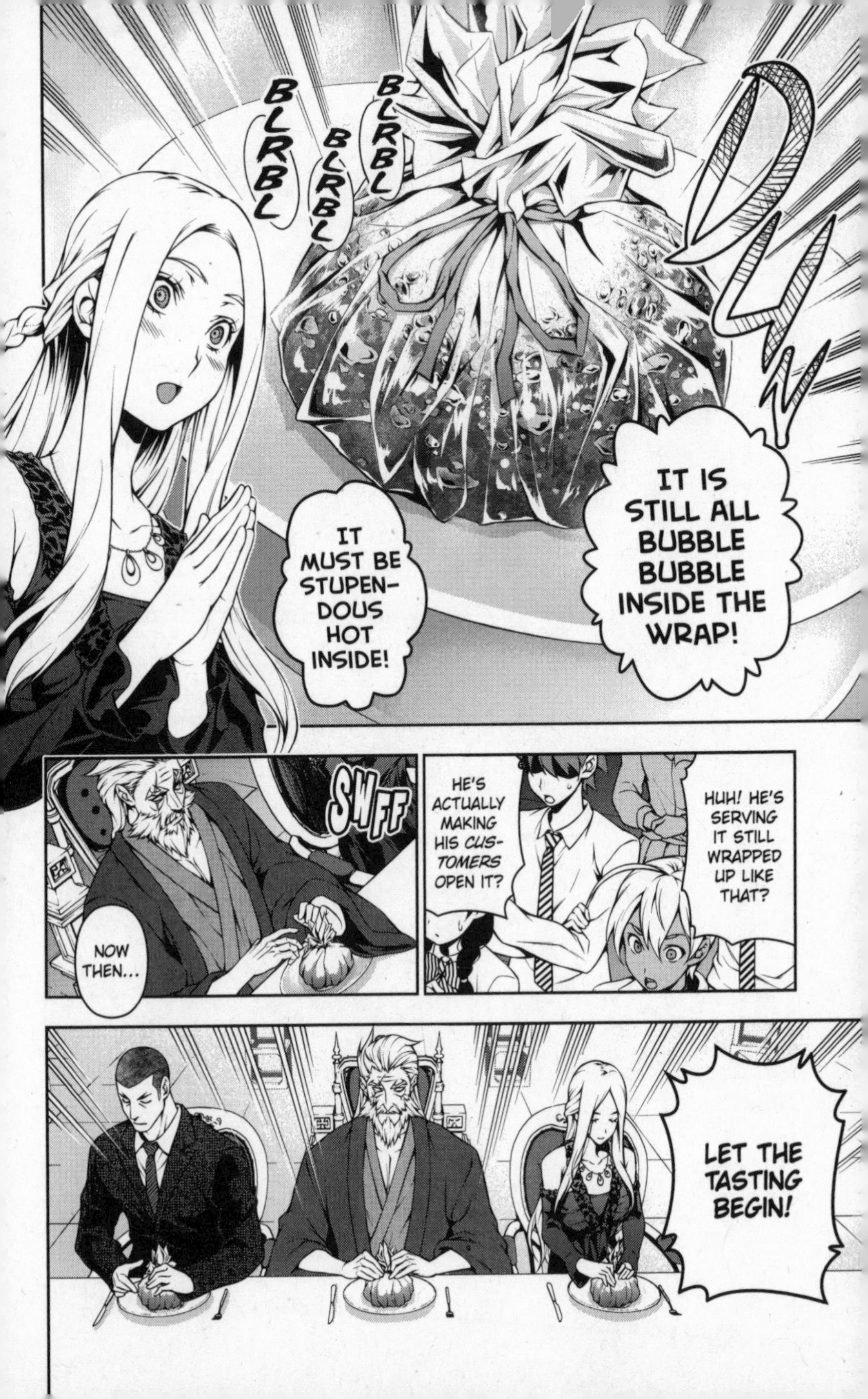
BLRBL
BLRBL
BLRBL
IT IS STILL ALL BUBBLE BUBBLE INSIDE THE WRAP!
IT MUST BE STUPEN-DOUS HOT INSIDE!
HUH! HE'S SERVING IT STILL WRAPPED UP LIKE THAT?
HE'S ACTUALLY MAKING HIS CUS-TOMERS OPEN IT?
SWFF
NOW THEN...
LET THE TASTING BEGIN!

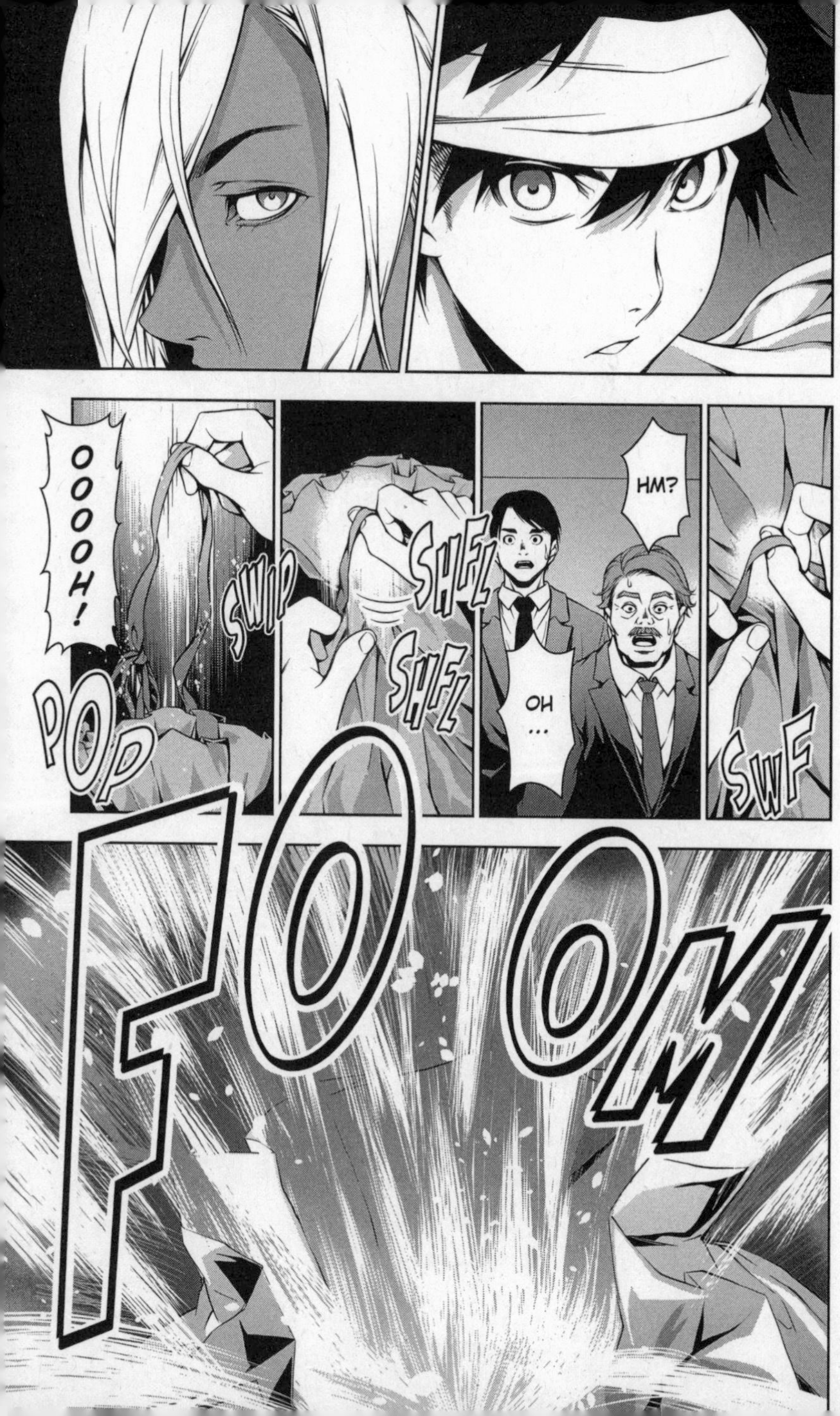
SWF
HM?
OH ...
SHFL
SHFL
OOOOOH!
SWIP
POP
FOOM

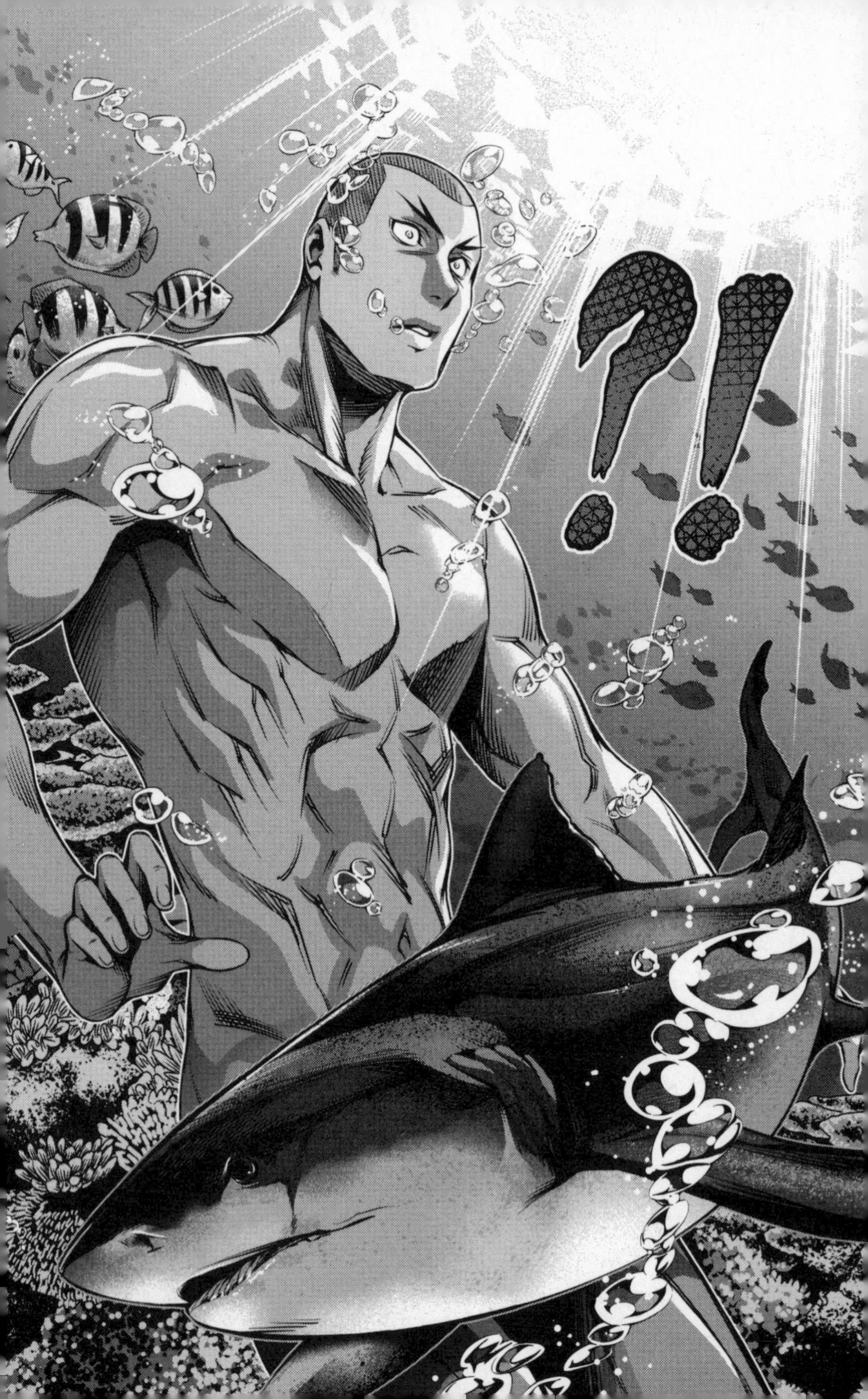
?!

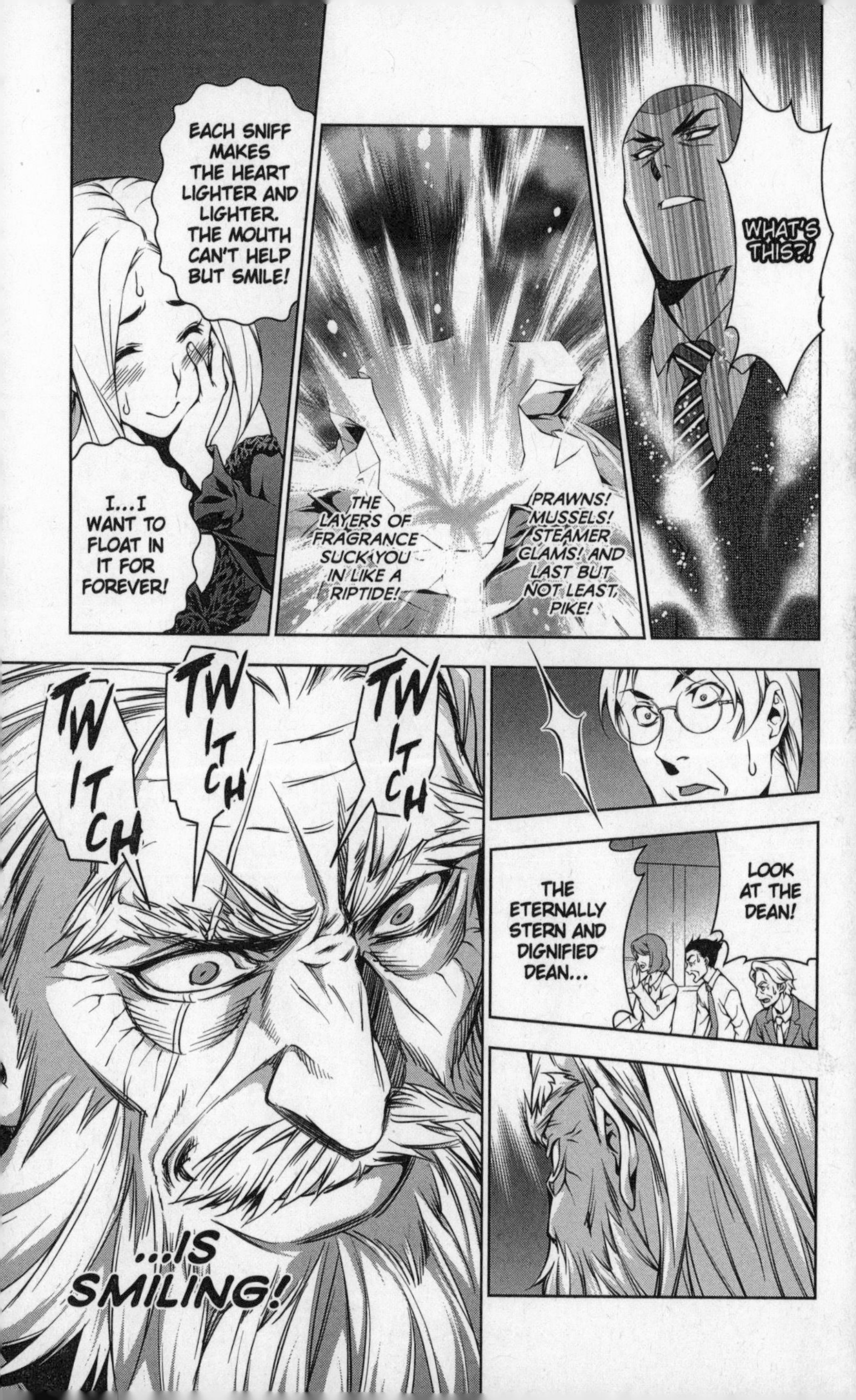
WHAT'S THIS?!
PRAWNS! MUSSELS! STEAMER CLAMS! AND LAST BUT NOT LEAST, PIKE!
THE LAYERS OF FRAGRANCE SUCK YOU IN LIKE A RIPTIDE!
EACH SNIFF MAKES THE HEART LIGHTER AND LIGHTER. THE MOUTH CAN'T HELP BUT SMILE!
I...I WANT TO FLOAT IN IT FOR FOREVER!
LOOK AT THE DEAN!
THE ETERNALLY STERN AND DIGNIFIED DEAN...
TWITCH
TWITCH
TWITCH
...IS SMILING!

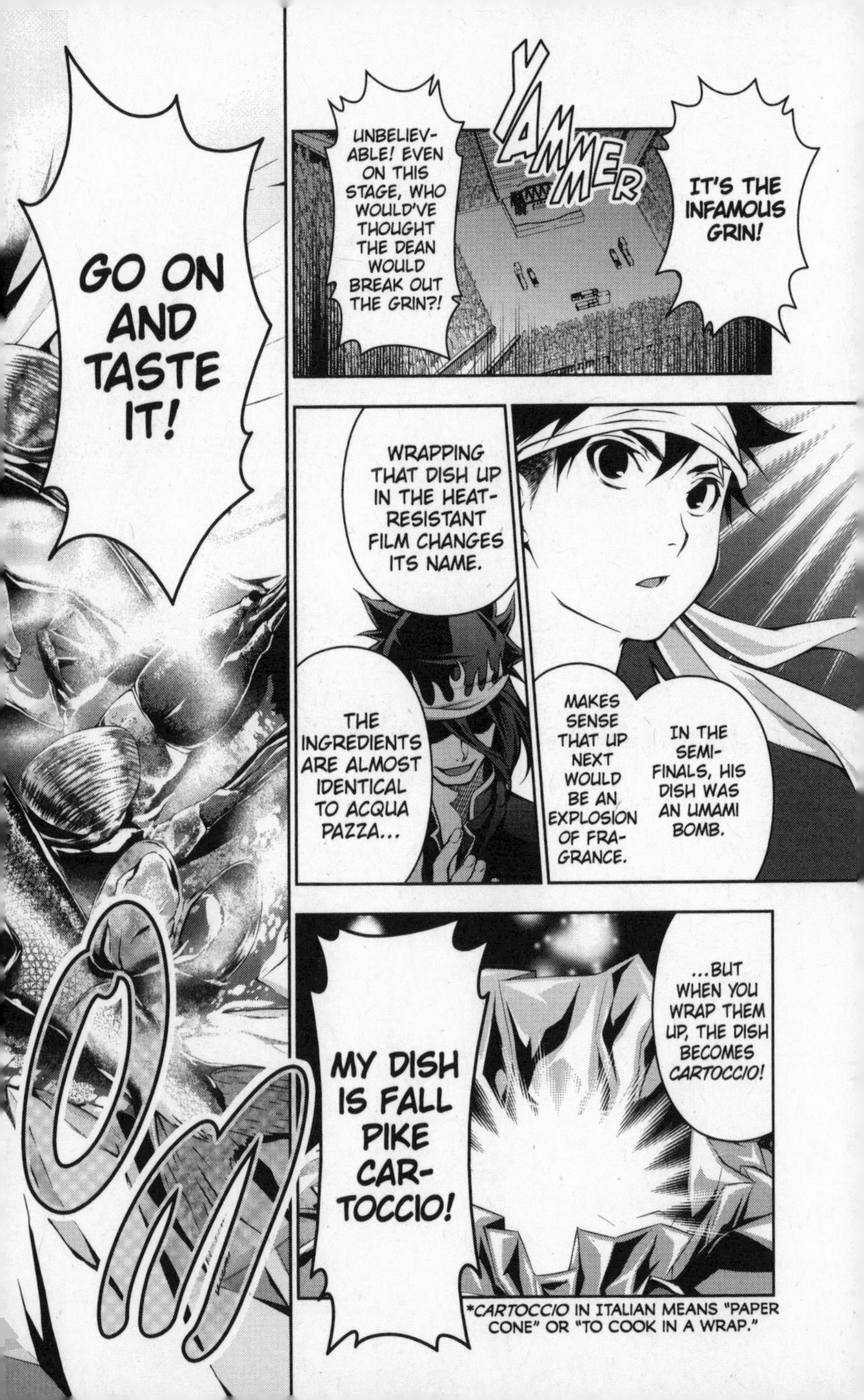
IT'S THE INFAMOUS GRIN!
YAMMER
UNBELIEVABLE! EVEN ON THIS STAGE, WHO WOULD'VE THOUGHT THE DEAN WOULD BREAK OUT THE GRIN?!
IN THE SEMI-FINALS, HIS DISH WAS AN UMAMI BOMB.
MAKES SENSE THAT UP NEXT WOULD BE AN EXPLOSION OF FRAGRANCE.
WRAPPING THAT DISH UP IN THE HEAT-RESISTANT FILM CHANGES ITS NAME.
THE INGREDIENTS ARE ALMOST IDENTICAL TO ACQUA PAZZA...
...BUT WHEN YOU WRAP THEM UP, THE DISH BECOMES *CARTOCCIO*!
MY DISH IS FALL PIKE CARTOCCIO!
**CARTOCCIO* IN ITALIAN MEANS "PAPER CONE" OR "TO COOK IN A WRAP."
GO ON AND TASTE IT!
OM

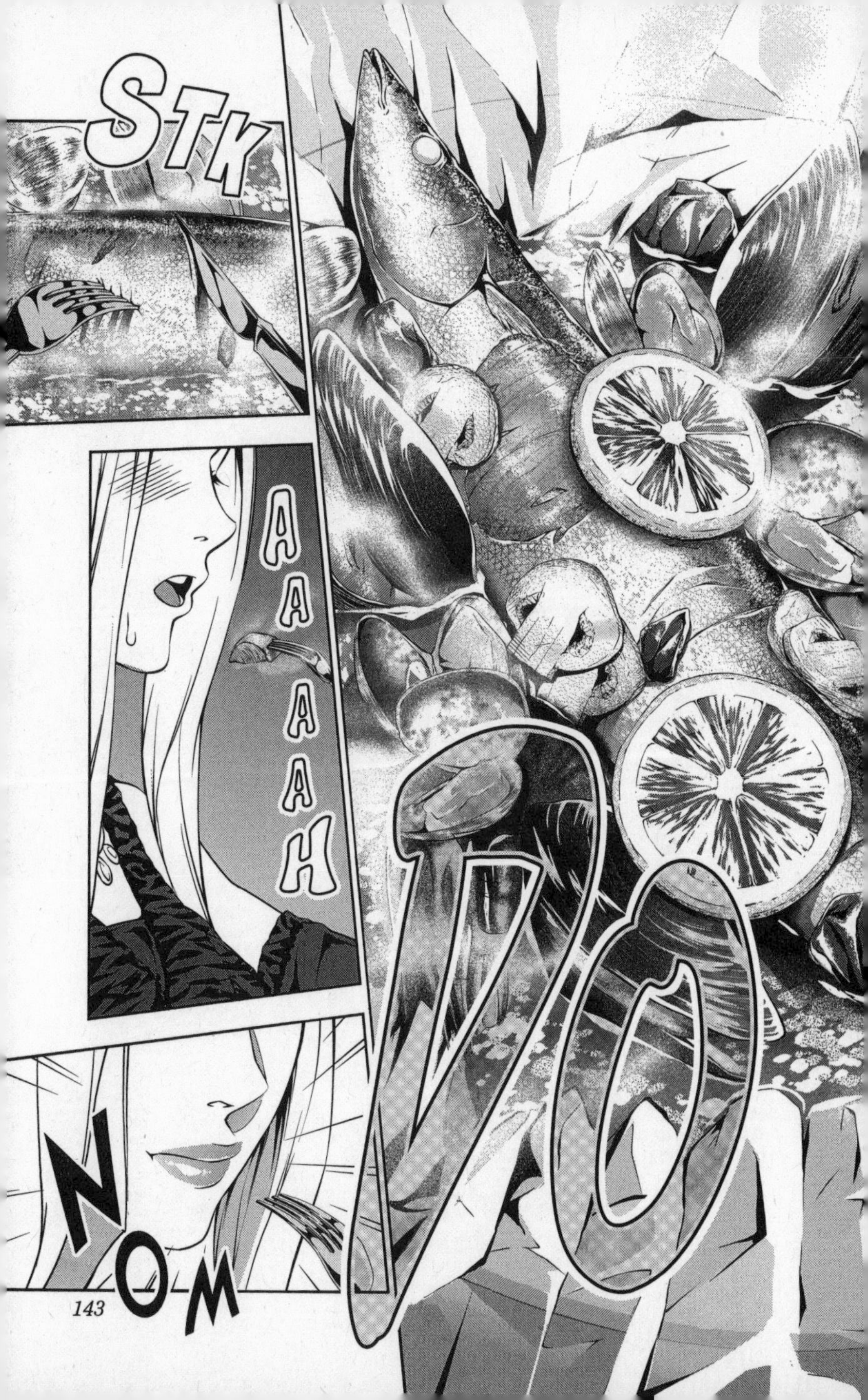
STK
AAAAAH
NOM

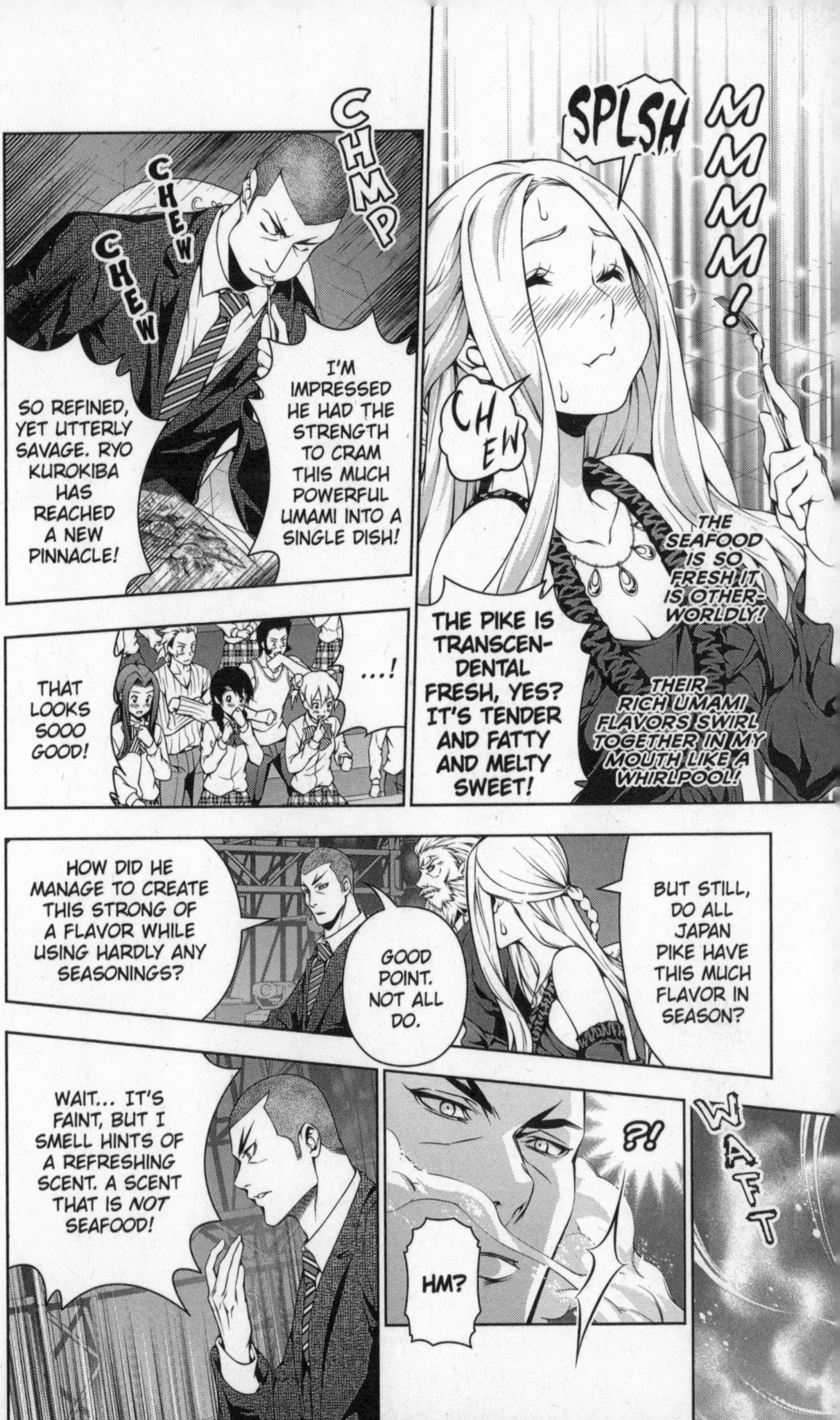
MMMMMM!
SPLSH
CHEW
THE SEAFOOD IS SO FRESH IT IS OTHER-WORLDLY!
THE PIKE IS TRANSCEN-DENTAL FRESH, YES? IT'S TENDER AND FATTY AND MELTY SWEET!
THEIR RICH UMAMI FLAVORS SWIRL TOGETHER IN MY MOUTH LIKE A WHIRLPOOL!
CHMP
CHEW
CHEW
I'M IMPRESSED HE HAD THE STRENGTH TO CRAM THIS MUCH POWERFUL UMAMI INTO A SINGLE DISH!
SO REFINED, YET UTTERLY SAVAGE. RYO KUROKIBA HAS REACHED A NEW PINNACLE!
...!
THAT LOOKS SOOO GOOD!
BUT STILL, DO ALL JAPAN PIKE HAVE THIS MUCH FLAVOR IN SEASON?
GOOD POINT. NOT ALL DO.
HOW DID HE MANAGE TO CREATE THIS STRONG OF A FLAVOR WHILE USING HARDLY ANY SEASONINGS?
WAFT
?!
HM?
WAIT... IT'S FAINT, BUT I SMELL HINTS OF A REFRESHING SCENT. A SCENT THAT IS *NOT* SEAFOOD!

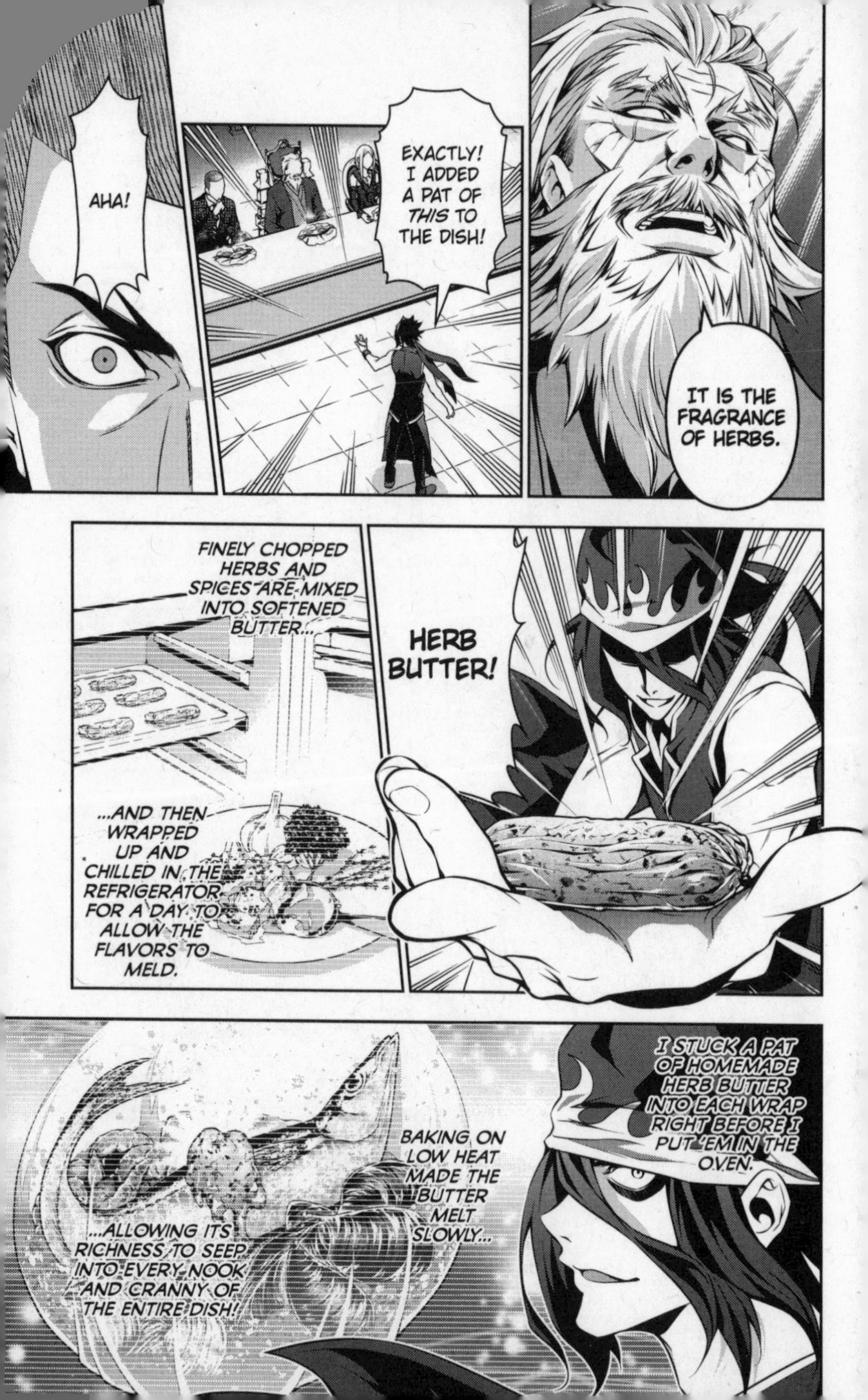
IT IS THE FRAGRANCE OF HERBS.
EXACTLY! I ADDED A PAT OF *THIS* TO THE DISH!
AHA!
HERB BUTTER!
FINELY CHOPPED HERBS AND SPICES ARE MIXED INTO SOFTENED BUTTER...
...AND THEN WRAPPED UP AND CHILLED IN THE REFRIGERATOR FOR A DAY TO ALLOW THE FLAVORS TO MELD.
I STUCK A PAT OF HOMEMADE HERB BUTTER INTO EACH WRAP RIGHT BEFORE I PUT 'EM IN THE OVEN.
BAKING ON LOW HEAT MADE THE BUTTER MELT SLOWLY...
...ALLOWING ITS RICHNESS TO SEEP INTO EVERY NOOK AND CRANNY OF THE ENTIRE DISH!

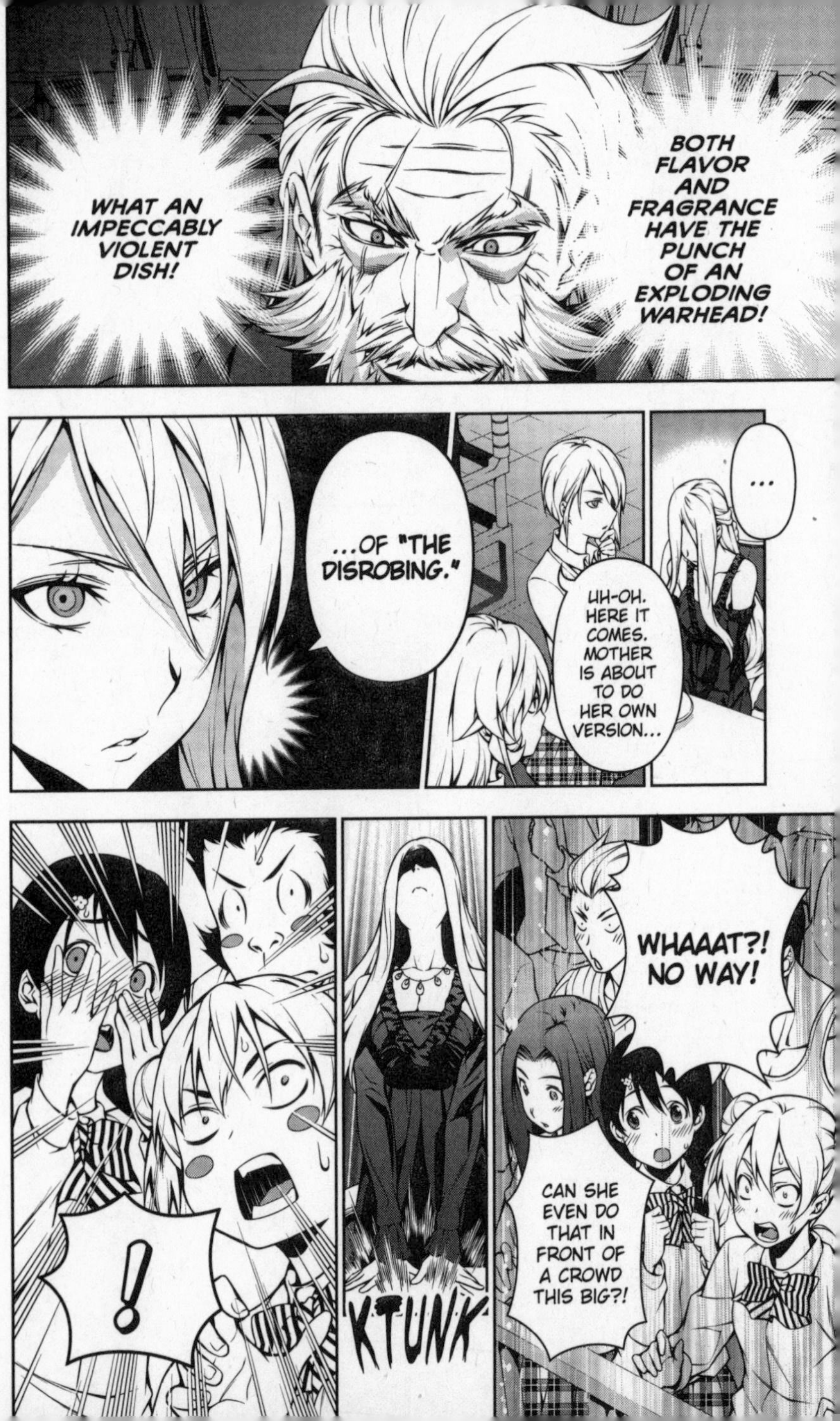
BOTH FLAVOR AND FRAGRANCE HAVE THE PUNCH OF AN EXPLODING WARHEAD!
WHAT AN IMPECCABLY VIOLENT DISH!
...
UH-OH. HERE IT COMES. MOTHER IS ABOUT TO DO HER OWN VERSION...
...OF "THE DISROBING."
WHAAAT?! NO WAY!
CAN SHE EVEN DO THAT IN FRONT OF A CROWD THIS BIG?!
KTUNK
!

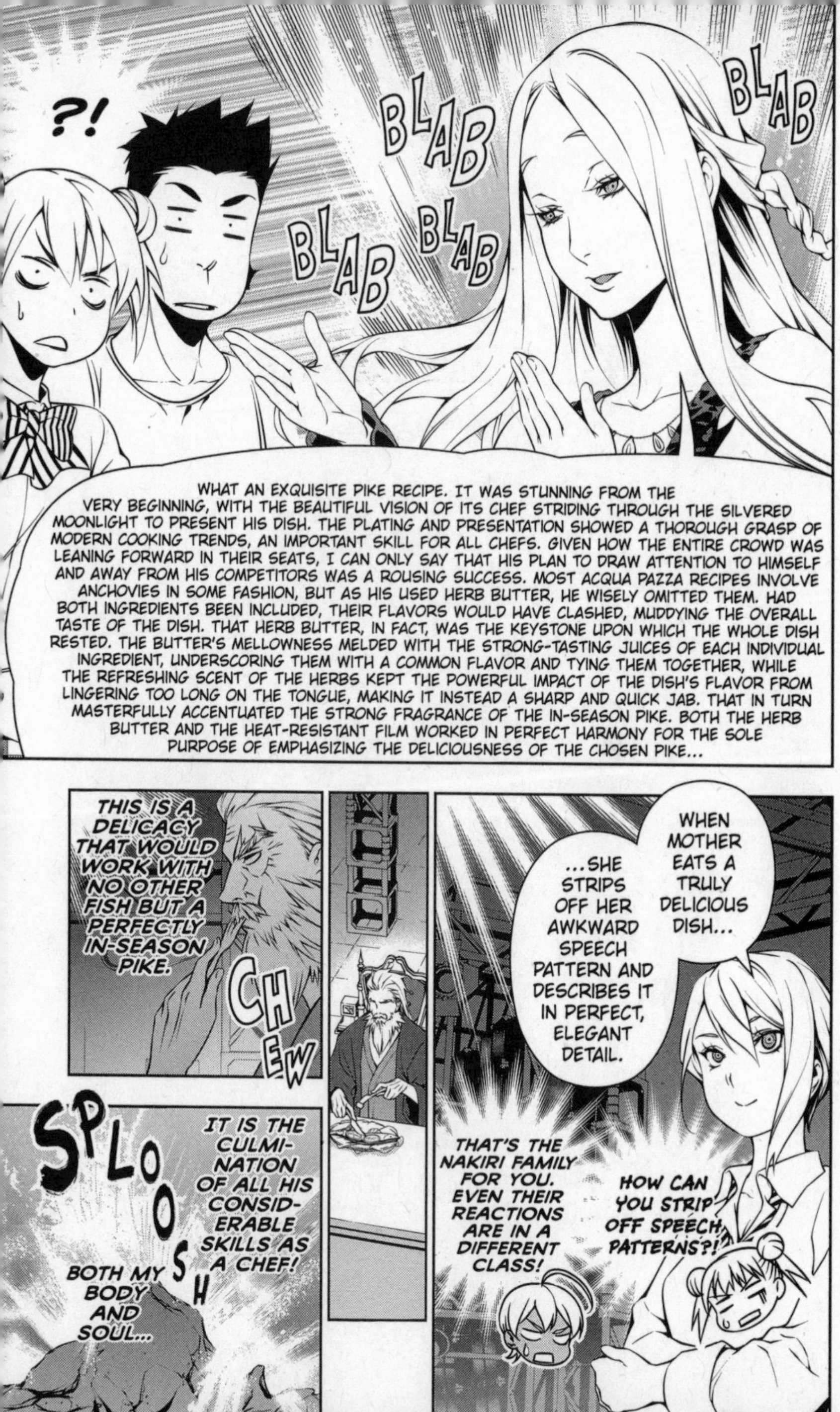
BLAB
BLAB
BLAB
BLAB
?!
WHAT AN EXQUISITE PIKE RECIPE. IT WAS STUNNING FROM THE VERY BEGINNING, WITH THE BEAUTIFUL VISION OF ITS CHEF STRIDING THROUGH THE SILVERED MOONLIGHT TO PRESENT HIS DISH. THE PLATING AND PRESENTATION SHOWED A THOROUGH GRASP OF MODERN COOKING TRENDS, AN IMPORTANT SKILL FOR ALL CHEFS. GIVEN HOW THE ENTIRE CROWD WAS LEANING FORWARD IN THEIR SEATS, I CAN ONLY SAY THAT HIS PLAN TO DRAW ATTENTION TO HIMSELF AND AWAY FROM HIS COMPETITORS WAS A ROUSING SUCCESS. MOST ACQUA PAZZA RECIPES INVOLVE ANCHOVIES IN SOME FASHION, BUT AS HIS USED HERB BUTTER, HE WISELY OMITTED THEM. HAD BOTH INGREDIENTS BEEN INCLUDED, THEIR FLAVORS WOULD HAVE CLASHED, MUDDYING THE OVERALL TASTE OF THE DISH. THAT HERB BUTTER, IN FACT, WAS THE KEYSTONE UPON WHICH THE WHOLE DISH RESTED. THE BUTTER'S MELLOWNESS MELDED WITH THE STRONG-TASTING JUICES OF EACH INDIVIDUAL INGREDIENT, UNDERSCORING THEM WITH A COMMON FLAVOR AND TYING THEM TOGETHER, WHILE THE REFRESHING SCENT OF THE HERBS KEPT THE POWERFUL IMPACT OF THE DISH'S FLAVOR FROM LINGERING TOO LONG ON THE TONGUE, MAKING IT INSTEAD A SHARP AND QUICK JAB. THAT IN TURN MASTERFULLY ACCENTUATED THE STRONG FRAGRANCE OF THE IN-SEASON PIKE. BOTH THE HERB BUTTER AND THE HEAT-RESISTANT FILM WORKED IN PERFECT HARMONY FOR THE SOLE PURPOSE OF EMPHASIZING THE DELICIOUSNESS OF THE CHOSEN PIKE...
WHEN MOTHER EATS A TRULY DELICIOUS DISH...
...SHE STRIPS OFF HER AWKWARD SPEECH PATTERN AND DESCRIBES IT IN PERFECT, ELEGANT DETAIL.
HOW CAN YOU STRIP OFF SPEECH PATTERNS?!
THAT'S THE NAKIRI FAMILY FOR YOU. EVEN THEIR REACTIONS ARE IN A DIFFERENT CLASS!
THIS IS A DELICACY THAT WOULD WORK WITH NO OTHER FISH BUT A PERFECTLY IN-SEASON PIKE.
CHEW
IT IS THE CULMINATION OF ALL HIS CONSIDERABLE SKILLS AS A CHEF!
SPLOOSH
BOTH MY BODY AND SOUL...

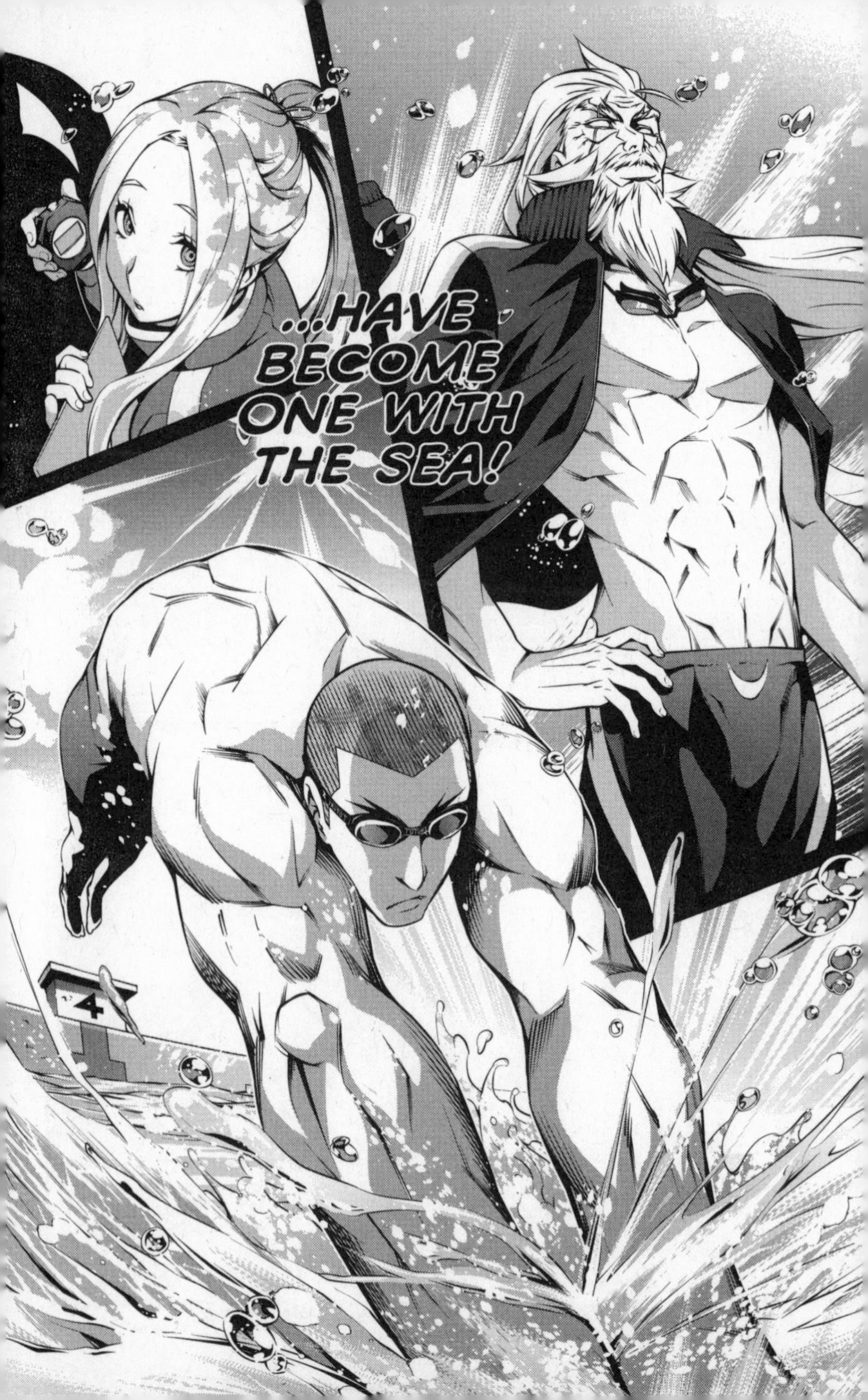
...HAVE BECOME ONE WITH THE SEA!
4

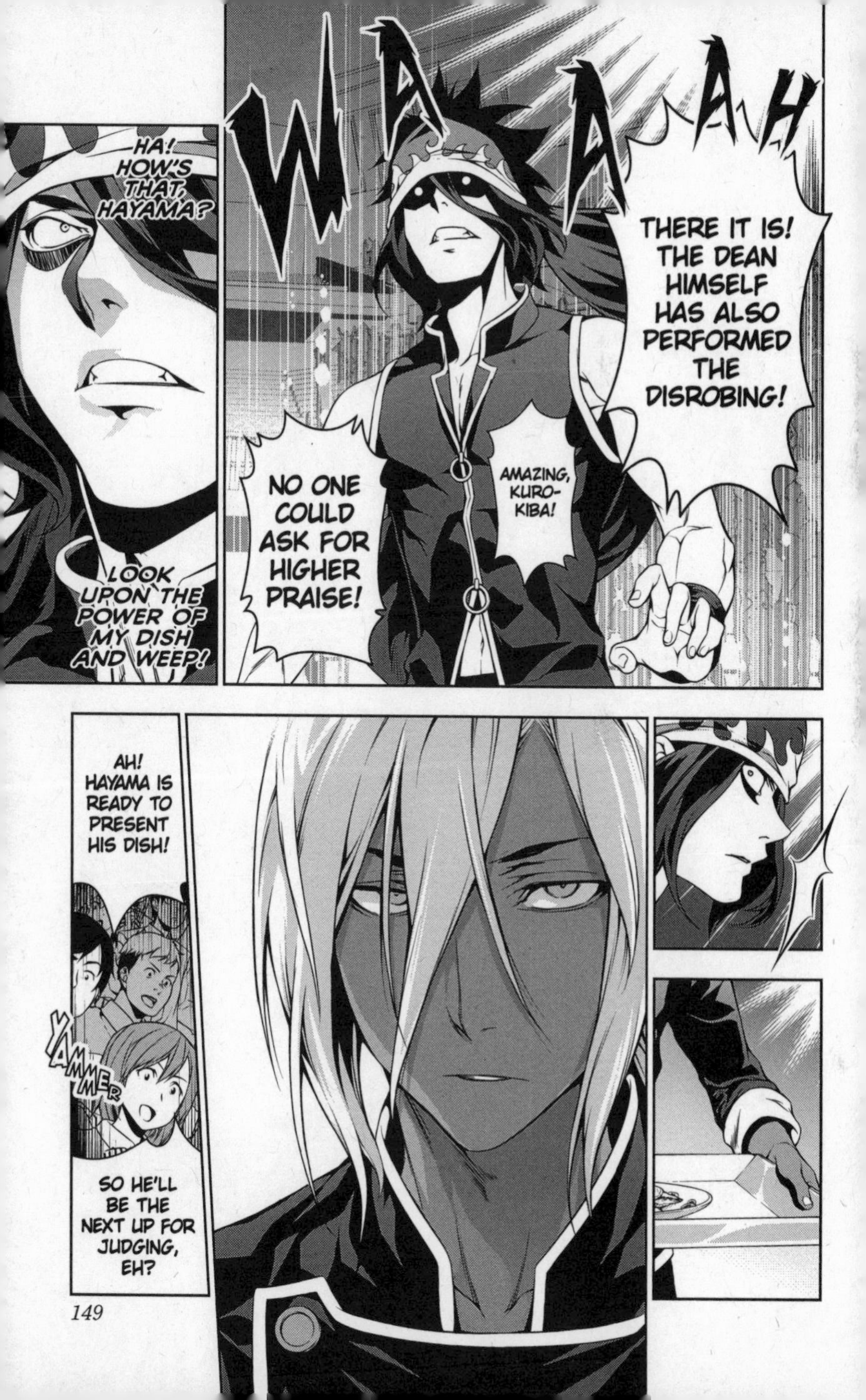
WAAAAH
THERE IT IS! THE DEAN HIMSELF HAS ALSO PERFORMED THE DISROBING!
AMAZING, KURO-KIBA!
NO ONE COULD ASK FOR HIGHER PRAISE!
HA! HOW'S THAT, HAYAMA?
LOOK UPON THE POWER OF MY DISH AND WEEP!
AH! HAYAMA IS READY TO PRESENT HIS DISH!
YAMMER
SO HE'LL BE THE NEXT UP FOR JUDGING, EH?

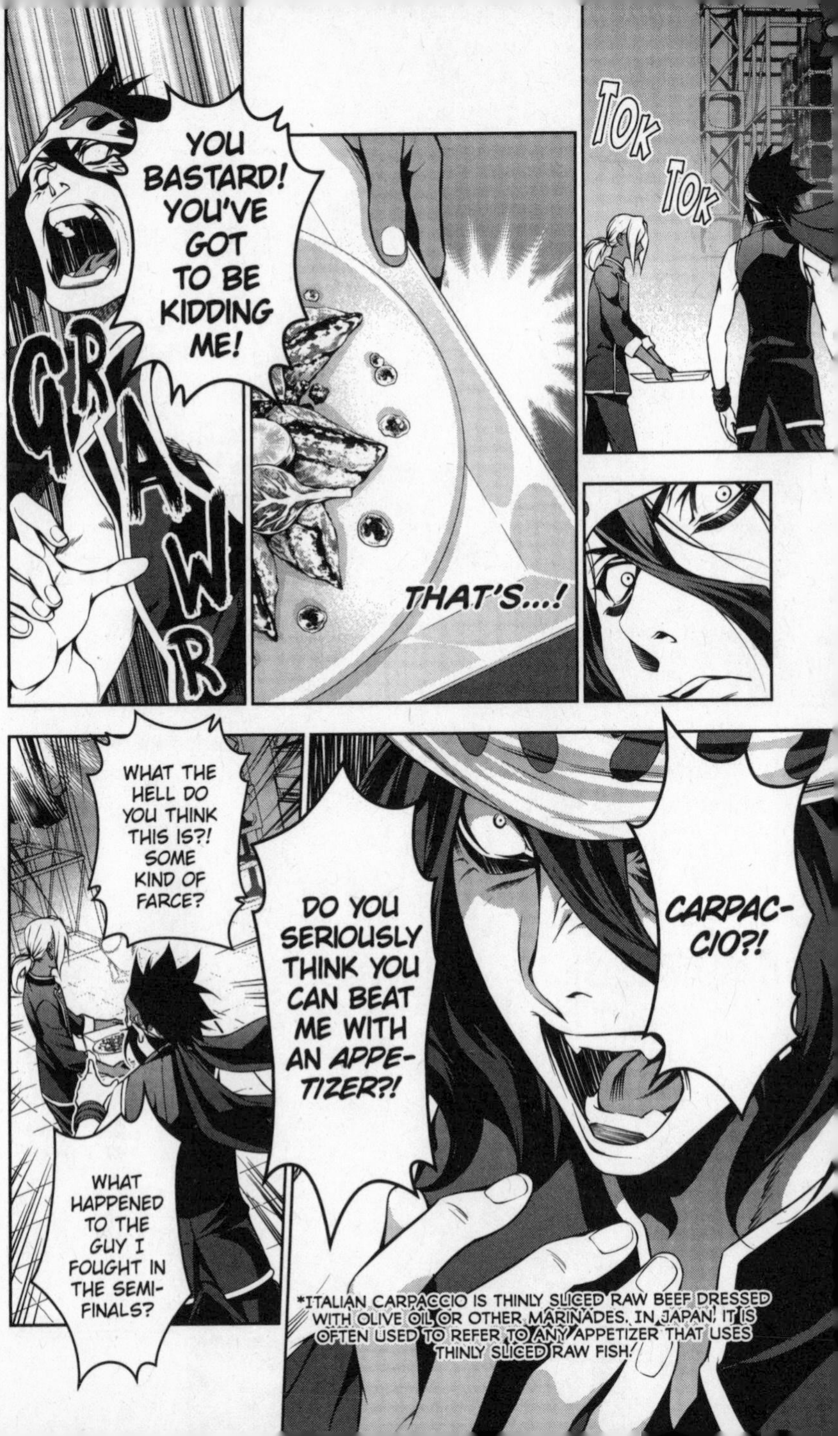
TOK TOK
THAT'S...!
YOU BASTARD! YOU'VE GOT TO BE KIDDING ME!
GRAWR
CARPAC-CIO?!
DO YOU SERIOUSLY THINK YOU CAN BEAT ME WITH AN *APPE-TIZER*?!
*ITALIAN CARPACCIO IS THINLY SLICED RAW BEEF DRESSED WITH OLIVE OIL OR OTHER MARINADES. IN JAPAN, IT IS OFTEN USED TO REFER TO ANY APPETIZER THAT USES THINLY SLICED RAW FISH.
WHAT THE HELL DO YOU THINK THIS IS?! SOME KIND OF FARCE?
WHAT HAPPENED TO THE GUY I FOUGHT IN THE SEMI-FINALS?

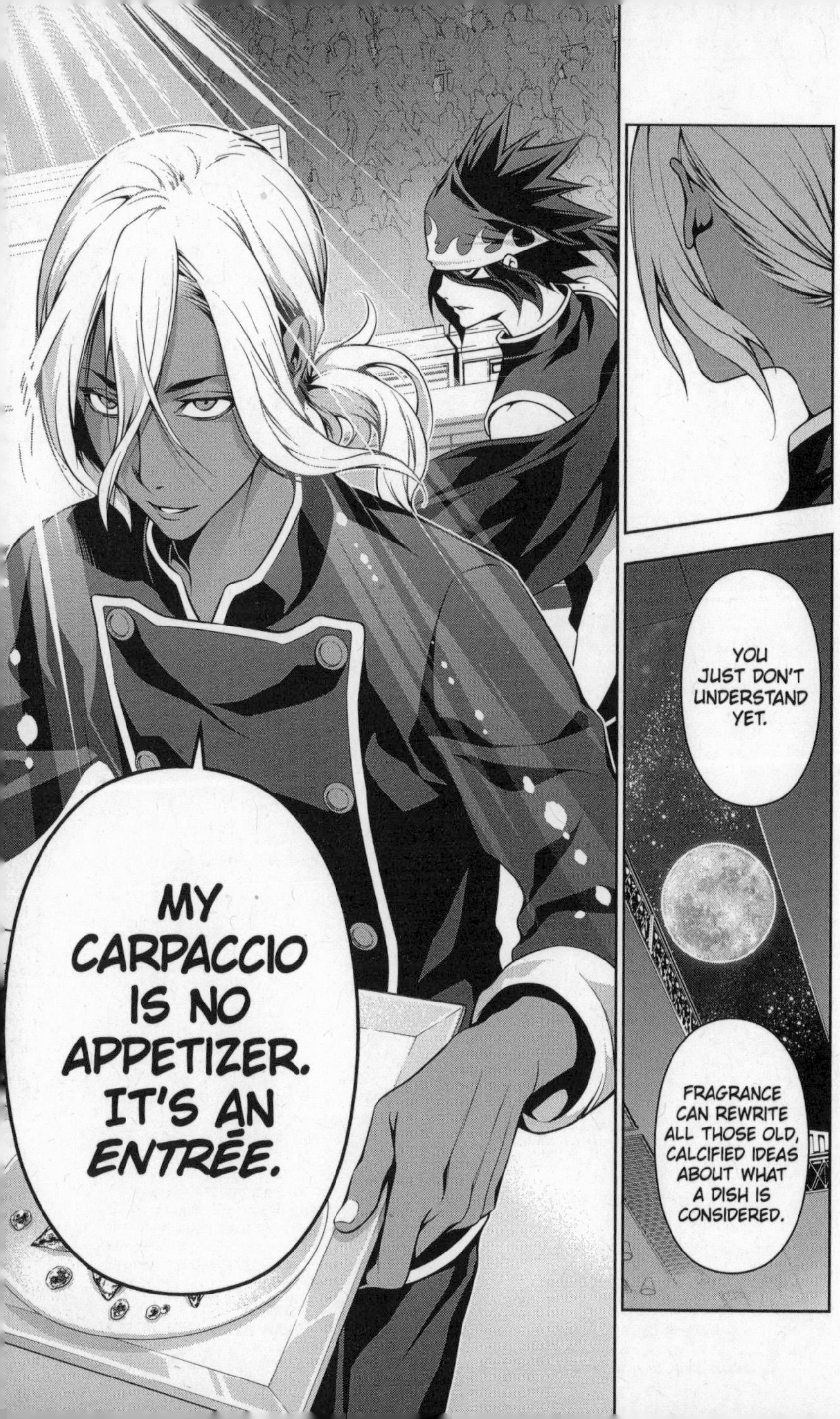
YOU JUST DON'T UNDERSTAND YET.
FRAGRANCE CAN REWRITE ALL THOSE OLD, CALCIFIED IDEAS ABOUT WHAT A DISH IS CONSIDERED.
MY CARPACCIO IS NO APPETIZER. IT'S AN ENTRÉE.

ARTIST: YUTO TSUKUDA RECIPE BY: YUKI MORISAKI

VOLUME 12
SPECIAL SUPPLEMENT!

PRACTICAL RECIPE #1

CARTOCCIO

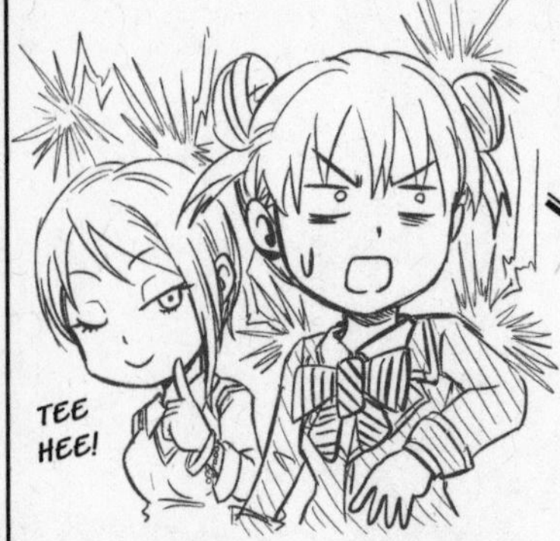
I STILL SAY STRIPPING OFF A SPEECH PATTERN IS WEIRD!
TEE HEE!
OH, IT'S HARDLY SURPRISING TO DEVELOP SOMETHING LIKE THAT WHEN YOU MARRY INTO THE NAKIRI FAMILY. ♪

INGREDIENTS
(SERVES 2)

2 PIKE FILLETS (CAN BE SUBSTITUTED WITH OTHER WHITE FISH, SUCH AS SEA BREAM, SEA BASS OR COD)
4 SHRIMP, PEELED
8 STEAMER CLAMS
6 CHERRY TOMATOES
4 MUSHROOMS
40 GRAMS BUTTER

LEMON, SALT, PEPPER

A [1 TEASPOON GRATED GARLIC
¼ TEASPOON EACH DRIED PARSLEY, THYME

2 16-INCH SHEETS OF PARCHMENT PAPER

1

WARM THE BUTTER TO ROOM TEMPERATURE. MIX IN (A). WRAP IN PLASTIC WRAP AND SET IN THE FREEZER TO CHILL.

2

CUT THE CHERRY TOMATOES IN HALF. SLICE THE MUSHROOMS. MAKE A SLIT ALONG THE BACK OF THE SHRIMP AND DEVEIN THEM.

3

SPRINKLE THE FISH FILLETS WITH SALT AND LET SIT FOR TEN MINUTES. PAT WITH A PAPER TOWEL TO REMOVE EXCESS MOISTURE.

4

IN THE CENTER OF A SHEET OF PARCHMENT PAPER, PLACE HALF EACH OF (2), (3) AND THE STEAMER CLAMS. SPRINKLE LIGHTLY WITH SALT AND PEPPER. CUT HALF OF THE BUTTER FROM (1) INTO CHUNKS AND PLACE ON TOP. MAKE A SECOND PORTION WITH THE REMAINING HALF OF THE INGREDIENTS ON THE SECOND SHEET OF PARCHMENT PAPER. CAREFULLY WRAP THE PARCHMENT PAPER FIRMLY CLOSED, AND BAKE IN THE OVEN AT 400°F FOR TWENTY MINUTES. REMOVE FROM THE OVEN, OPEN THE WRAP, SIDE WITH LEMON SLICES AND... DONE!

*IF PIKE IS NOT IN SEASON, TRY MAKING THIS WITH OTHER WHITE FISH INSTEAD!

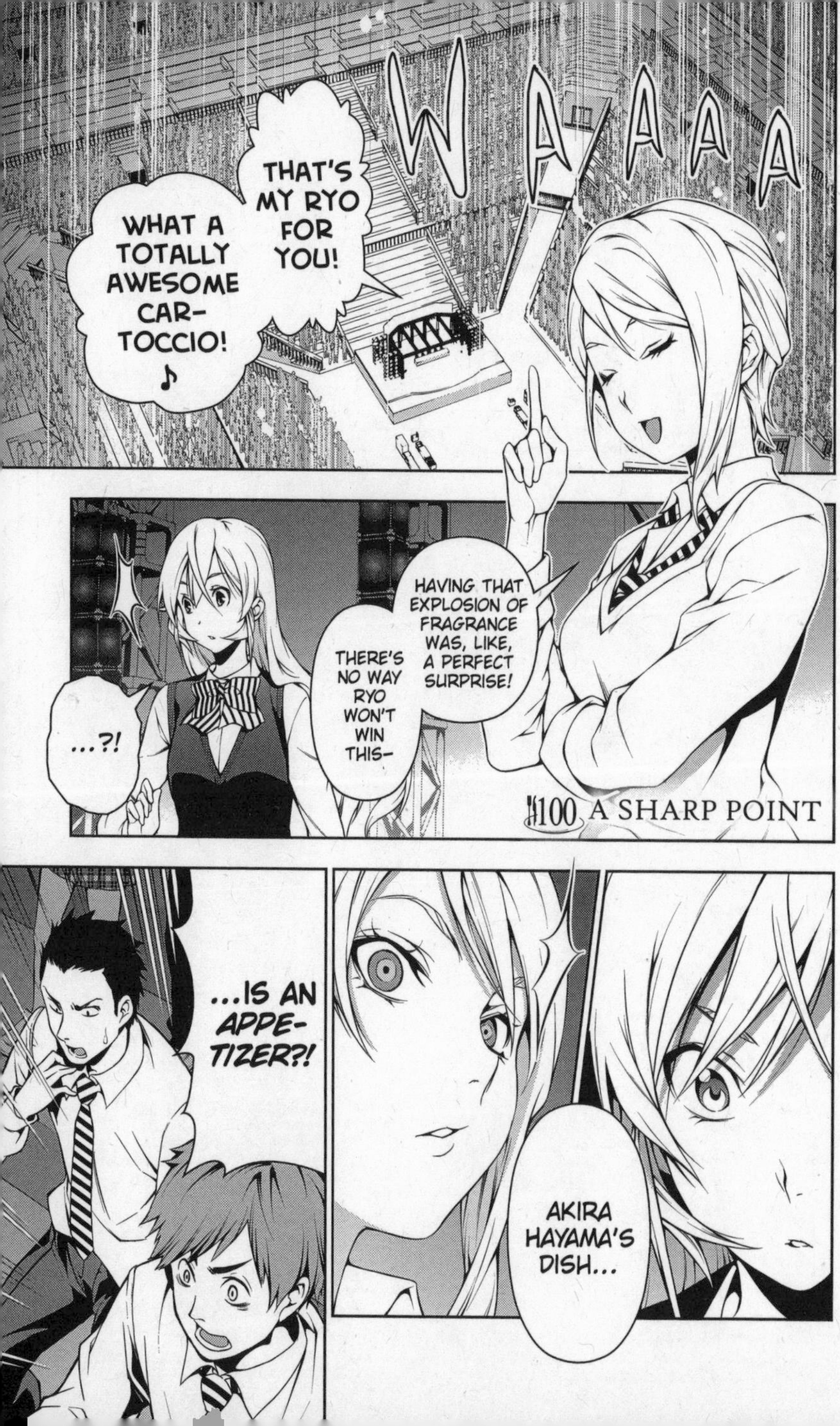
WAAAA
THAT'S MY RYO FOR YOU!
WHAT A TOTALLY AWESOME CAR-TOCCIO! ♪
HAVING THAT EXPLOSION OF FRAGRANCE WAS, LIKE, A PERFECT SURPRISE!
THERE'S NO WAY RYO WON'T WIN THIS–
...?!
#100 A SHARP POINT
AKIRA HAYAMA'S DISH...
...IS AN APPE-TIZER?!

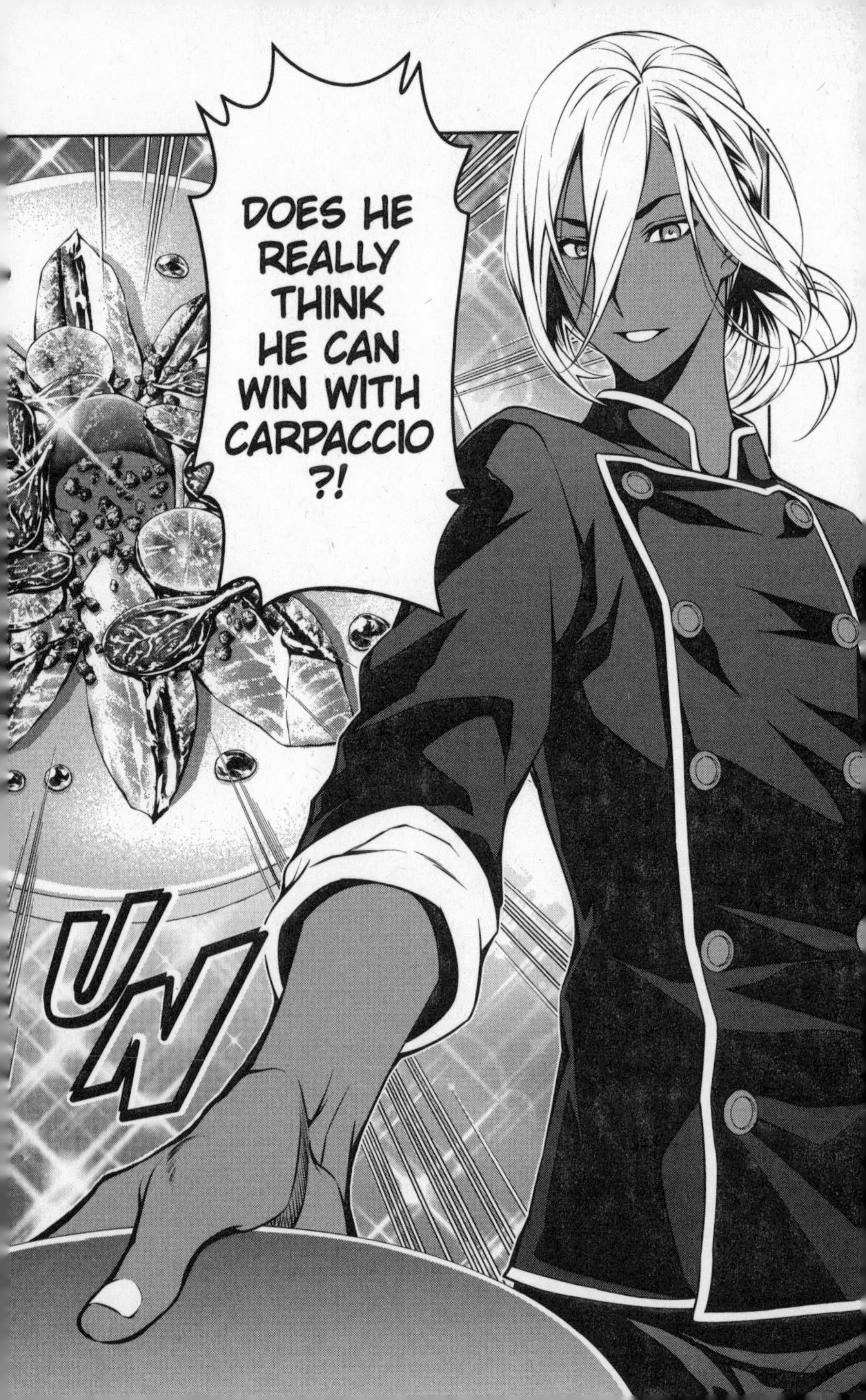
DOES HE REALLY THINK HE CAN WIN WITH CARPACCIO ?!
UN

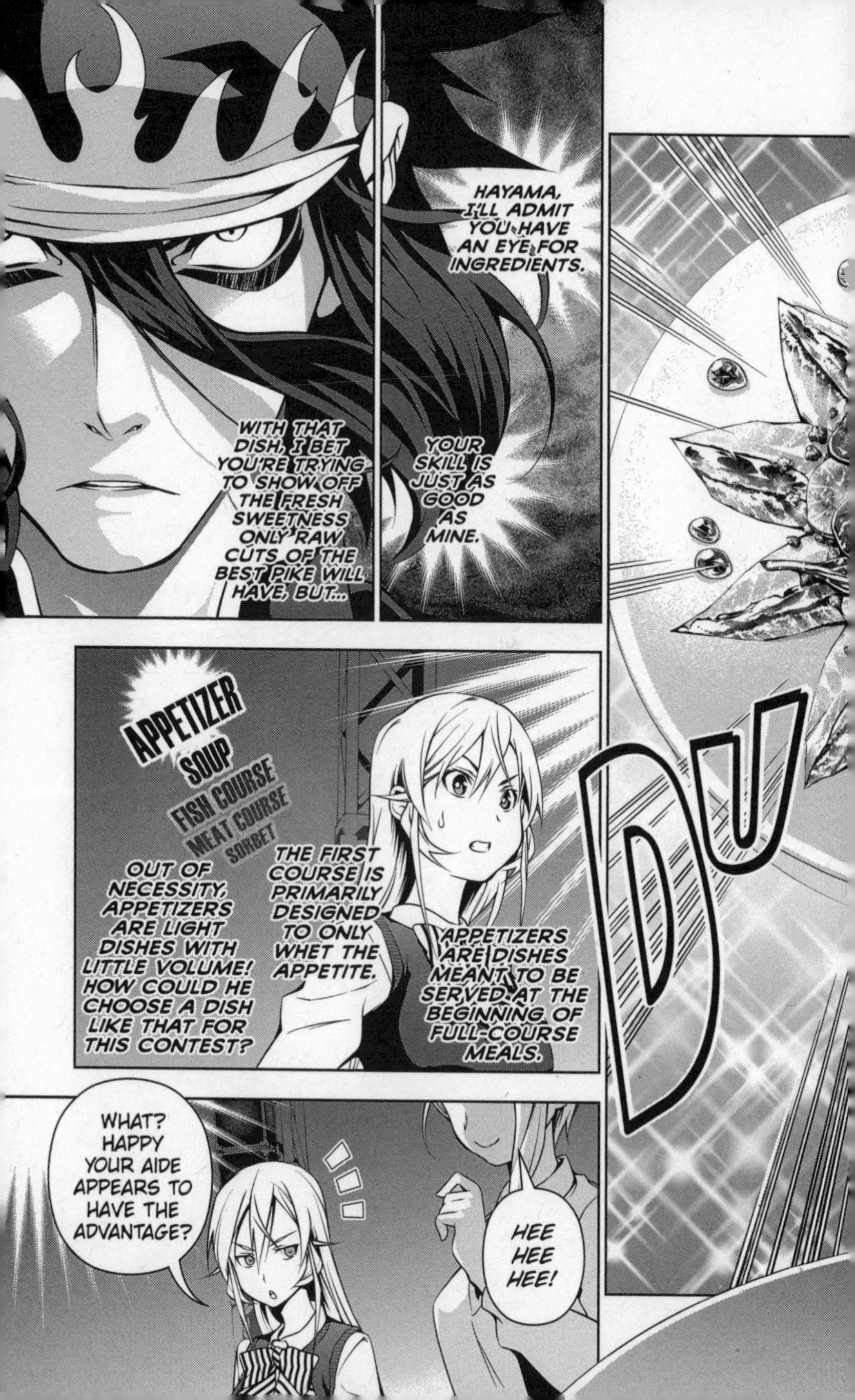
DU
HAYAMA, I'LL ADMIT YOU HAVE AN EYE FOR INGREDIENTS.
YOUR SKILL IS JUST AS GOOD AS MINE.
WITH THAT DISH, I BET YOU'RE TRYING TO SHOW OFF THE FRESH SWEETNESS ONLY RAW CUTS OF THE BEST PIKE WILL HAVE, BUT...
APPETIZER
SOUP
FISH COURSE
MEAT COURSE
SORBET
APPETIZERS ARE DISHES MEANT TO BE SERVED AT THE BEGINNING OF FULL-COURSE MEALS.
THE FIRST COURSE IS PRIMARILY DESIGNED TO ONLY WHET THE APPETITE.
OUT OF NECESSITY, APPETIZERS ARE LIGHT DISHES WITH LITTLE VOLUME! HOW COULD HE CHOOSE A DISH LIKE THAT FOR THIS CONTEST?
HEE HEE HEE!
WHAT? HAPPY YOUR AIDE APPEARS TO HAVE THE ADVANTAGE?

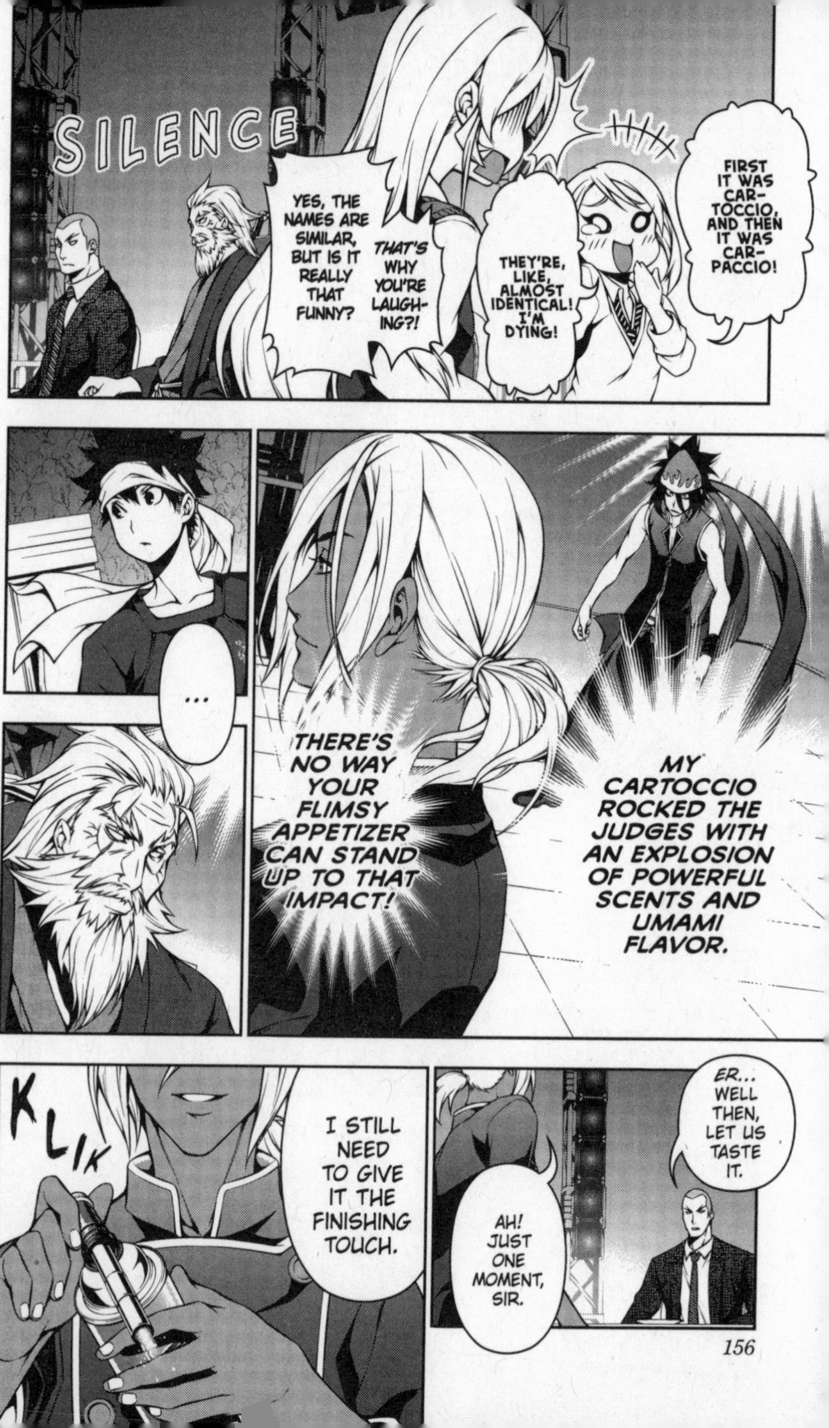
FIRST IT WAS CAR-TOCCIO, AND THEN IT WAS CAR-PACCIO!
THEY'RE, LIKE, ALMOST IDENTICAL! I'M DYING!
THAT'S WHY YOU'RE LAUGH-ING?!
YES, THE NAMES ARE SIMILAR, BUT IS IT REALLY THAT FUNNY?
SILENCE
MY CARTOCCIO ROCKED THE JUDGES WITH AN EXPLOSION OF POWERFUL SCENTS AND UMAMI FLAVOR.
THERE'S NO WAY YOUR FLIMSY APPETIZER CAN STAND UP TO THAT IMPACT!
...
ER... WELL THEN, LET US TASTE IT.
AH! JUST ONE MOMENT, SIR.
I STILL NEED TO GIVE IT THE FINISHING TOUCH.
KLIK

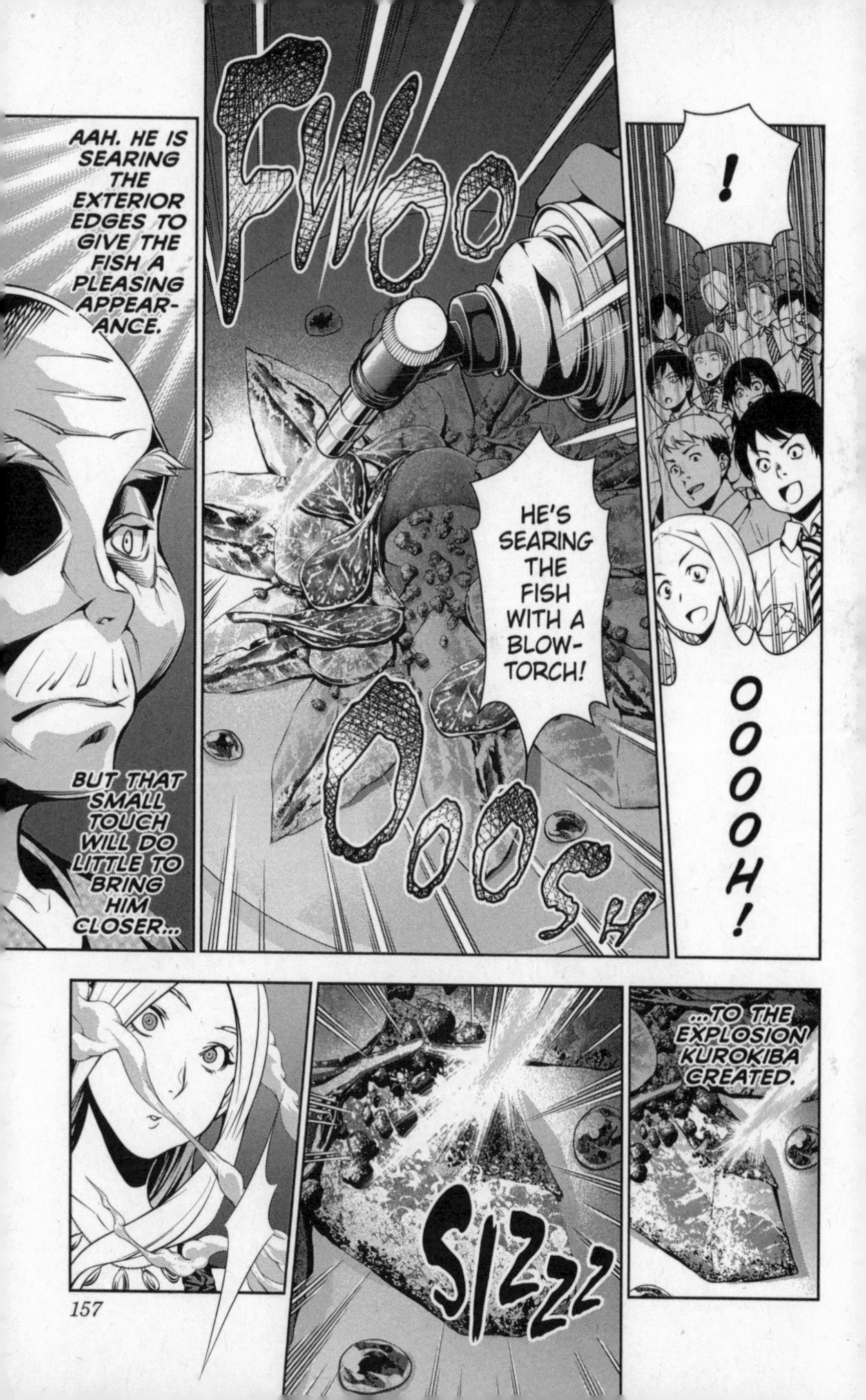
!
OOOOOH!
FWOO
OOOSH
HE'S SEARING THE FISH WITH A BLOW-TORCH!
AAH. HE IS SEARING THE EXTERIOR EDGES TO GIVE THE FISH A PLEASING APPEAR-ANCE.
BUT THAT SMALL TOUCH WILL DO LITTLE TO BRING HIM CLOSER...
...TO THE EXPLOSION KUROKIBA CREATED.
SIZZZ

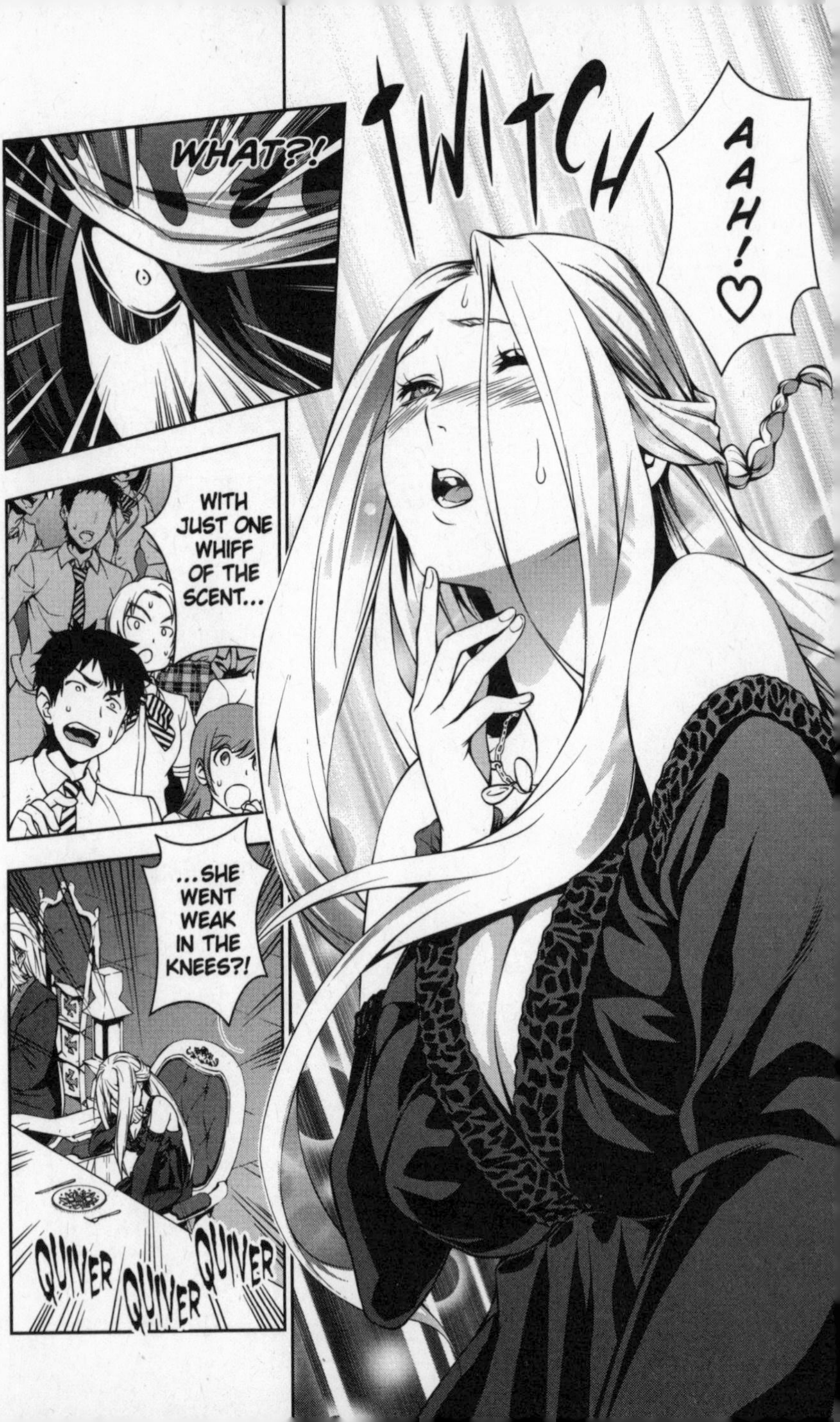
TWITCH
AAH! ♥
WHAT?!
WITH JUST ONE WHIFF OF THE SCENT...
...SHE WENT WEAK IN THE KNEES?!
QUIVER QUIVER QUIVER

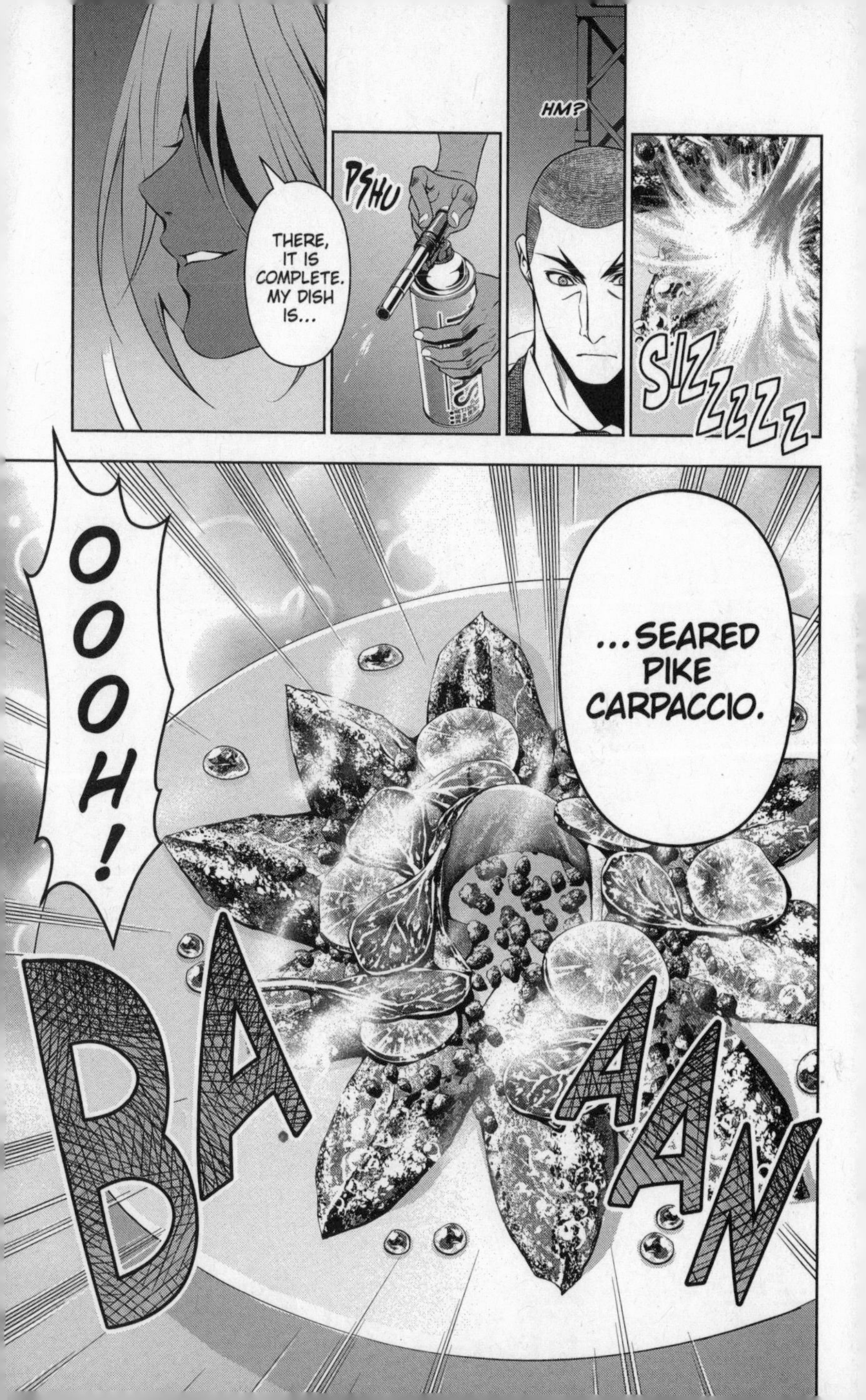
SIZZZZZ
HM?
PSHU
THERE, IT IS COMPLETE. MY DISH IS...
...SEARED PIKE CARPACCIO.
OOOOH!
BAAAN

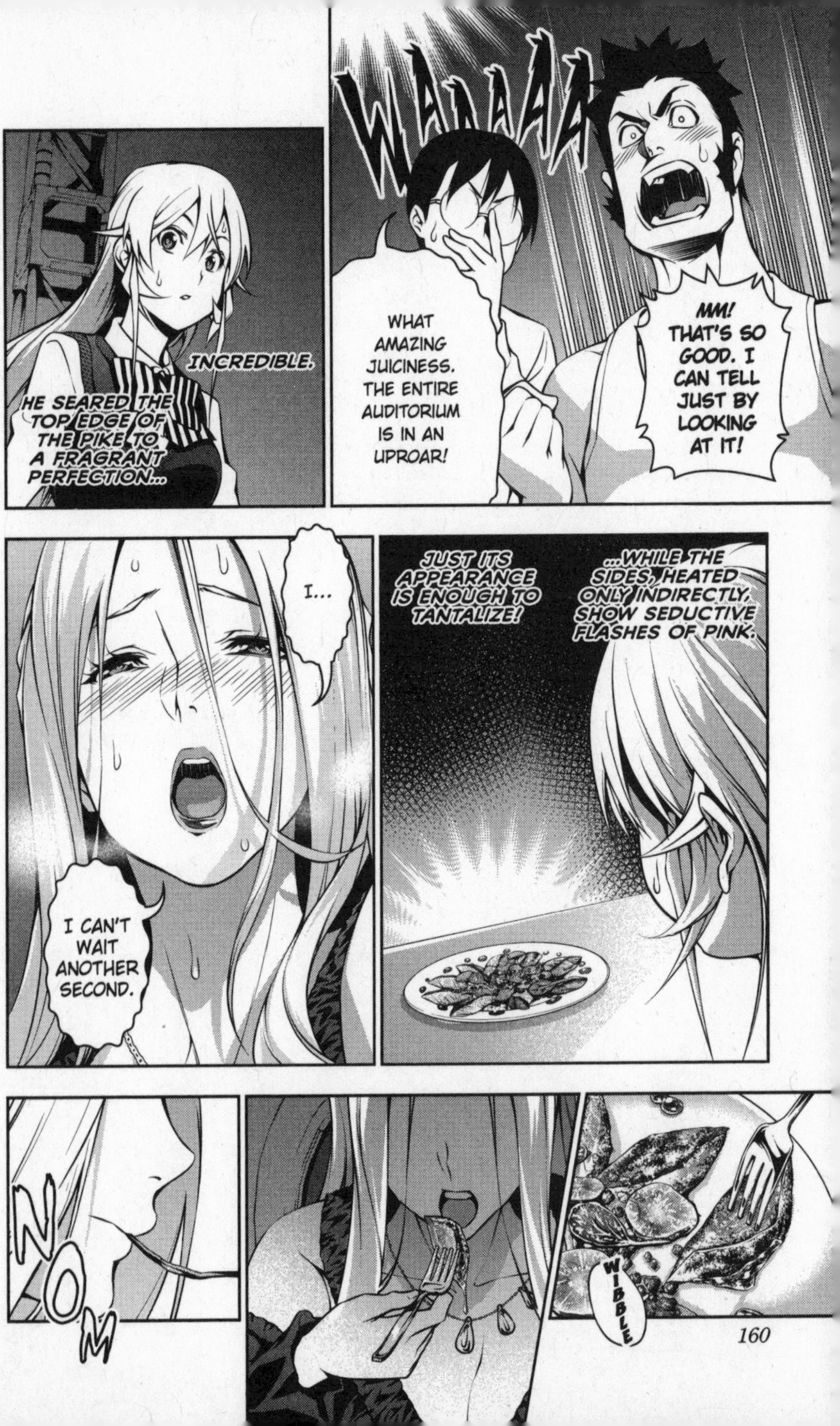
WAAAAA
MM! THAT'S SO GOOD. I CAN TELL JUST BY LOOKING AT IT!
WHAT AMAZING JUICINESS. THE ENTIRE AUDITORIUM IS IN AN UPROAR!
INCREDIBLE.
HE SEARED THE TOP EDGE OF THE PIKE TO A FRAGRANT PERFECTION...
...WHILE THE SIDES, HEATED ONLY INDIRECTLY, SHOW SEDUCTIVE FLASHES OF PINK.
JUST ITS APPEARANCE IS ENOUGH TO TANTALIZE!
I...
I CAN'T WAIT ANOTHER SECOND.
WIBBLE
NOM

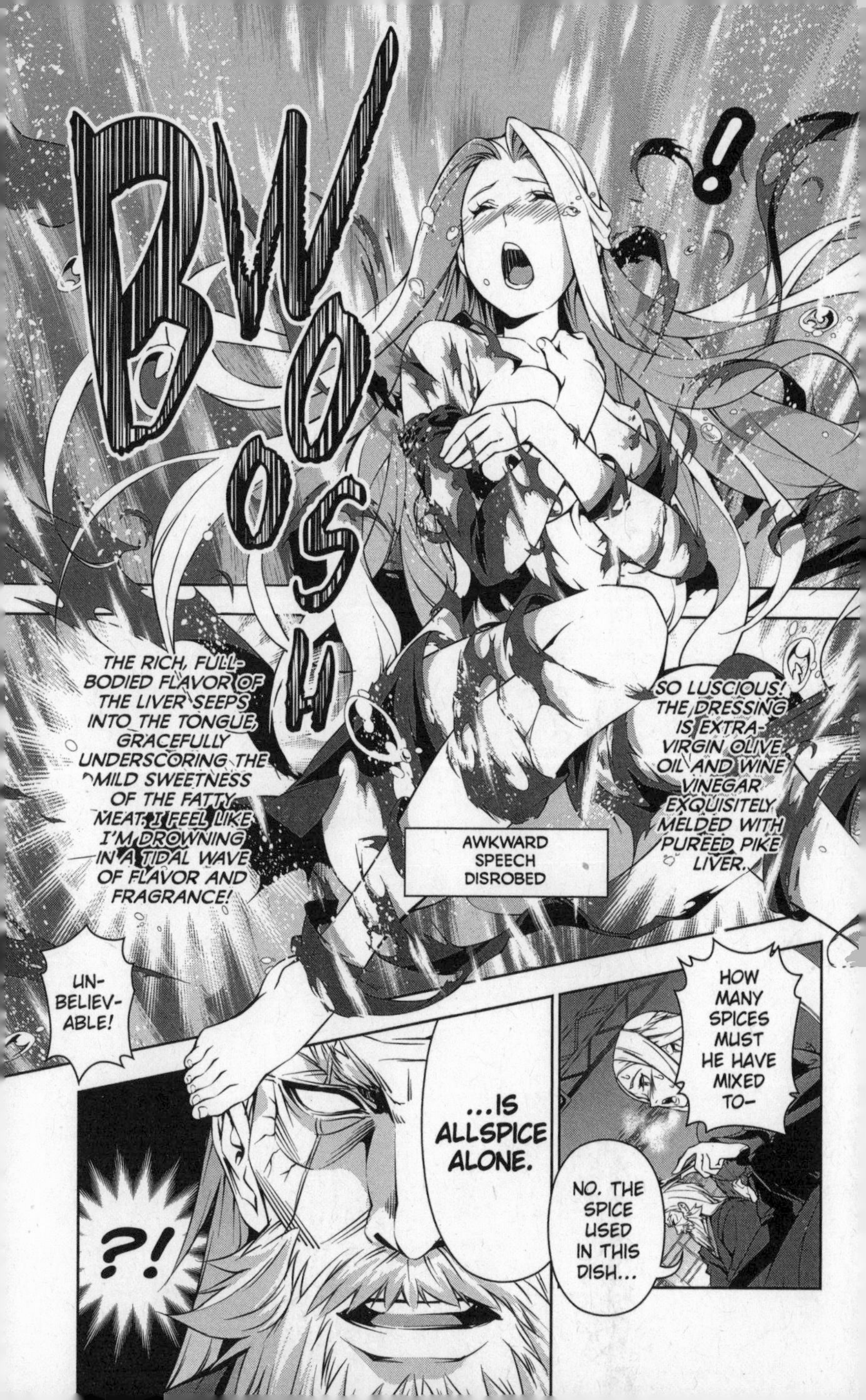
!
BWOOOSH!!
SO LUSCIOUS! THE DRESSING IS EXTRA-VIRGIN OLIVE OIL AND WINE VINEGAR EXQUISITELY MELDED WITH PUREED PIKE LIVER.
THE RICH, FULL-BODIED FLAVOR OF THE LIVER SEEPS INTO THE TONGUE, GRACEFULLY UNDERSCORING THE MILD SWEETNESS OF THE FATTY MEAT. I FEEL LIKE I'M DROWNING IN A TIDAL WAVE OF FLAVOR AND FRAGRANCE!
AWKWARD SPEECH DISROBED
UN-BELIEV-ABLE!
HOW MANY SPICES MUST HE HAVE MIXED TO-
NO. THE SPICE USED IN THIS DISH...
...IS ALLSPICE ALONE.
?!

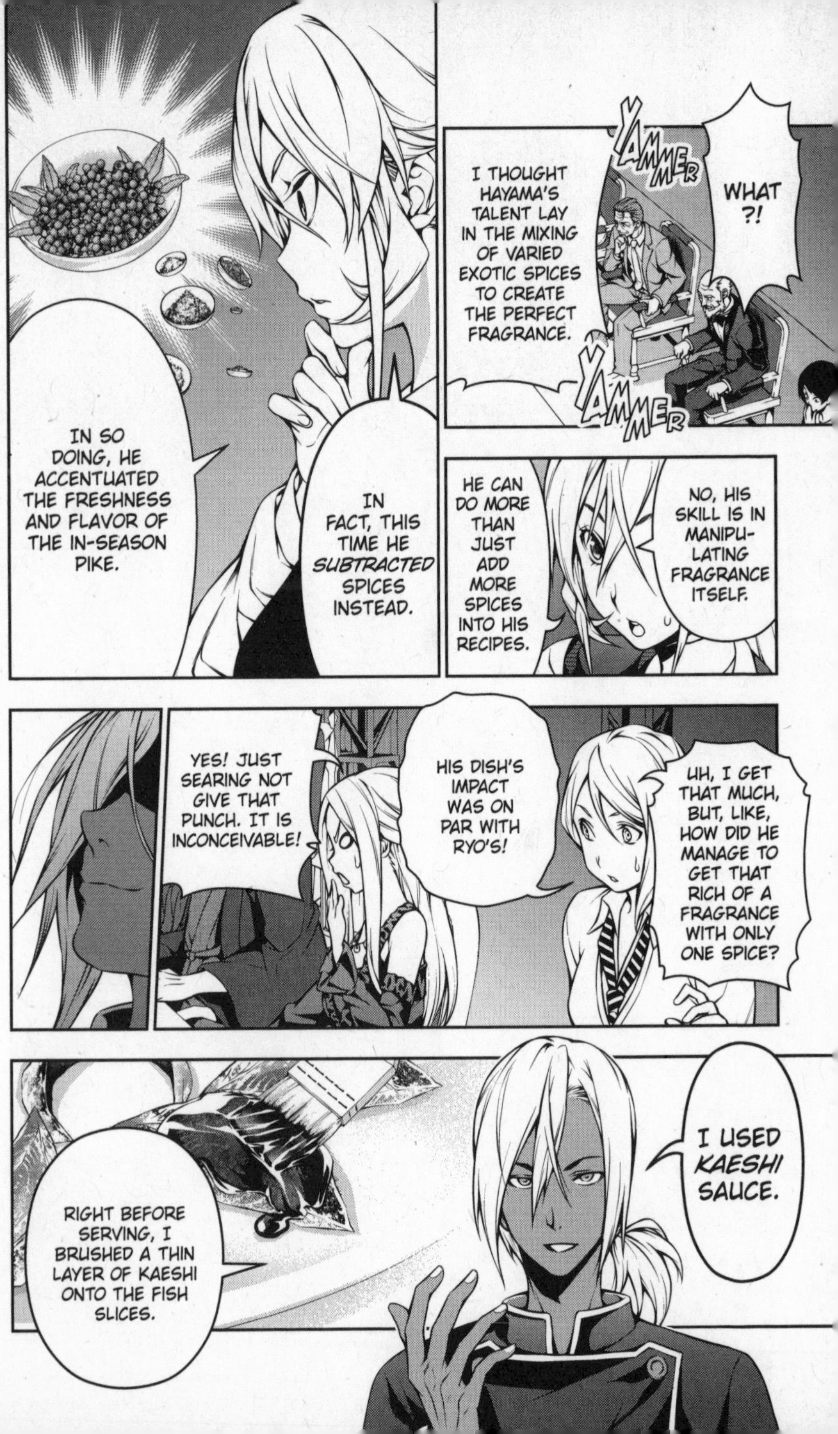
WHAT ?!
YAMMER
I THOUGHT HAYAMA'S TALENT LAY IN THE MIXING OF VARIED EXOTIC SPICES TO CREATE THE PERFECT FRAGRANCE.
YAMMER
NO, HIS SKILL IS IN MANIPULATING FRAGRANCE ITSELF.
HE CAN DO MORE THAN JUST ADD MORE SPICES INTO HIS RECIPES.
IN FACT, THIS TIME HE *SUBTRACTED* SPICES INSTEAD.
IN SO DOING, HE ACCENTUATED THE FRESHNESS AND FLAVOR OF THE IN-SEASON PIKE.
UH, I GET THAT MUCH, BUT, LIKE, HOW DID HE MANAGE TO GET THAT RICH OF A FRAGRANCE WITH ONLY ONE SPICE?
HIS DISH'S IMPACT WAS ON PAR WITH RYO'S!
YES! JUST SEARING NOT GIVE THAT PUNCH. IT IS INCONCEIVABLE!
I USED *KAESHI* SAUCE.
RIGHT BEFORE SERVING, I BRUSHED A THIN LAYER OF KAESHI ONTO THE FISH SLICES.

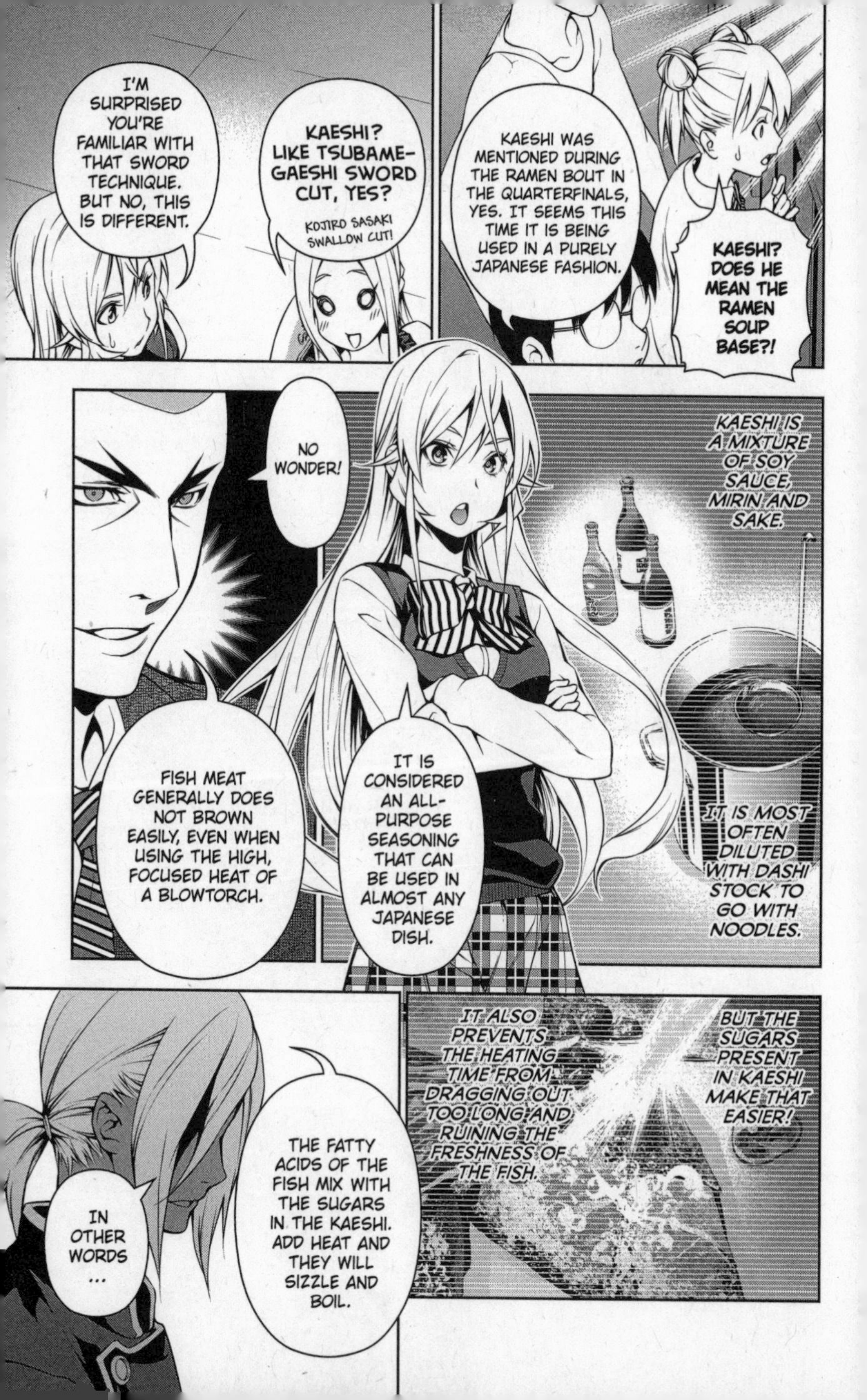
KAESHI? DOES HE MEAN THE RAMEN SOUP BASE?!
KAESHI WAS MENTIONED DURING THE RAMEN BOUT IN THE QUARTERFINALS, YES. IT SEEMS THIS TIME IT IS BEING USED IN A PURELY JAPANESE FASHION.
KAESHI? LIKE TSUBAME-GAESHI SWORD CUT, YES?
KOJIRO SASAKI SWALLOW CUT!
I'M SURPRISED YOU'RE FAMILIAR WITH THAT SWORD TECHNIQUE. BUT NO, THIS IS DIFFERENT.
KAESHI IS A MIXTURE OF SOY SAUCE, MIRIN AND SAKE.
IT IS MOST OFTEN DILUTED WITH DASHI STOCK TO GO WITH NOODLES.
IT IS CONSIDERED AN ALL-PURPOSE SEASONING THAT CAN BE USED IN ALMOST ANY JAPANESE DISH.
NO WONDER!
FISH MEAT GENERALLY DOES NOT BROWN EASILY, EVEN WHEN USING THE HIGH, FOCUSED HEAT OF A BLOWTORCH.
BUT THE SUGARS PRESENT IN KAESHI MAKE THAT EASIER!
IT ALSO PREVENTS THE HEATING TIME FROM DRAGGING OUT TOO LONG AND RUINING THE FRESHNESS OF THE FISH.
THE FATTY ACIDS OF THE FISH MIX WITH THE SUGARS IN THE KAESHI. ADD HEAT AND THEY WILL SIZZLE AND BOIL.
IN OTHER WORDS ...

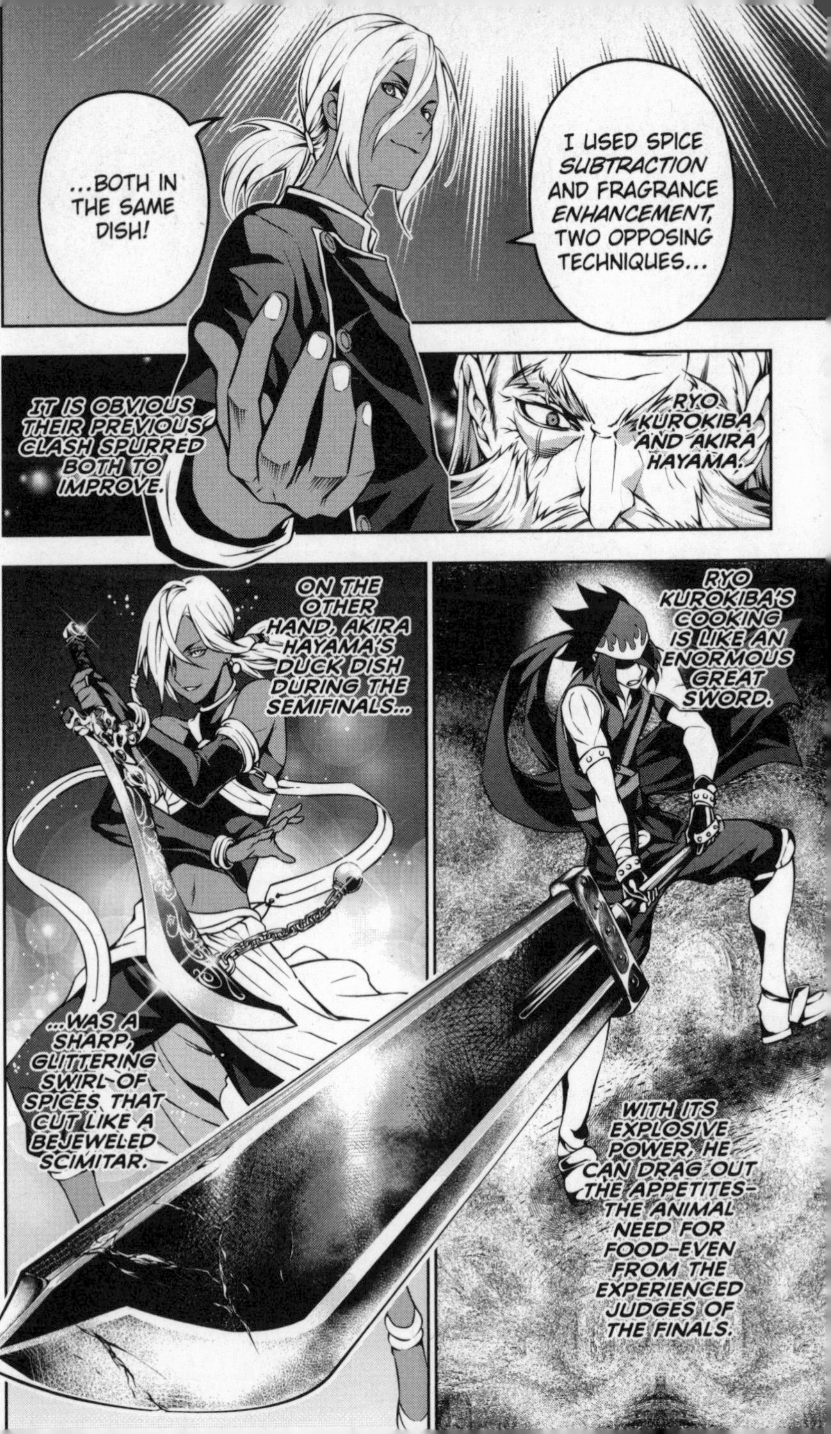
I USED SPICE SUBTRACTION AND FRAGRANCE ENHANCEMENT, TWO OPPOSING TECHNIQUES...
...BOTH IN THE SAME DISH!
RYO KUROKIBA AND AKIRA HAYAMA.
IT IS OBVIOUS THEIR PREVIOUS CLASH SPURRED BOTH TO IMPROVE.
RYO KUROKIBA'S COOKING IS LIKE AN ENORMOUS GREAT SWORD.
WITH ITS EXPLOSIVE POWER, HE CAN DRAG OUT THE APPETITES—THE ANIMAL NEED FOR FOOD—EVEN FROM THE EXPERIENCED JUDGES OF THE FINALS.
ON THE OTHER HAND, AKIRA HAYAMA'S DUCK DISH DURING THE SEMIFINALS...
...WAS A SHARP, GLITTERING SWIRL OF SPICES THAT CUT LIKE A BEJEWELED SCIMITAR.

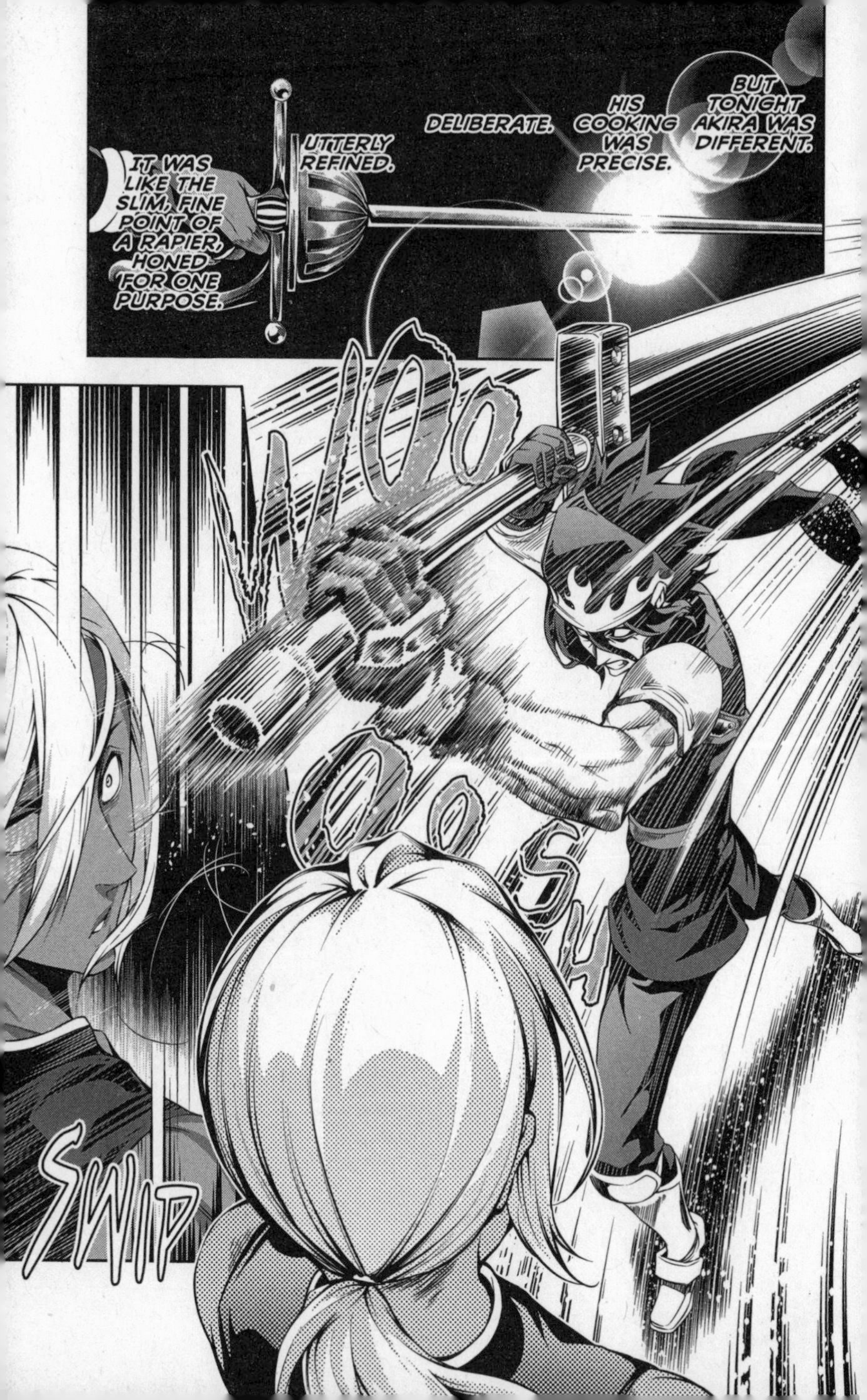
BUT TONIGHT AKIRA WAS DIFFERENT.
HIS COOKING WAS PRECISE.
DELIBERATE.
UTTERLY REFINED.
IT WAS LIKE THE SLIM, FINE POINT OF A RAPIER, HONED FOR ONE PURPOSE.
WHOOOSH
SWIP

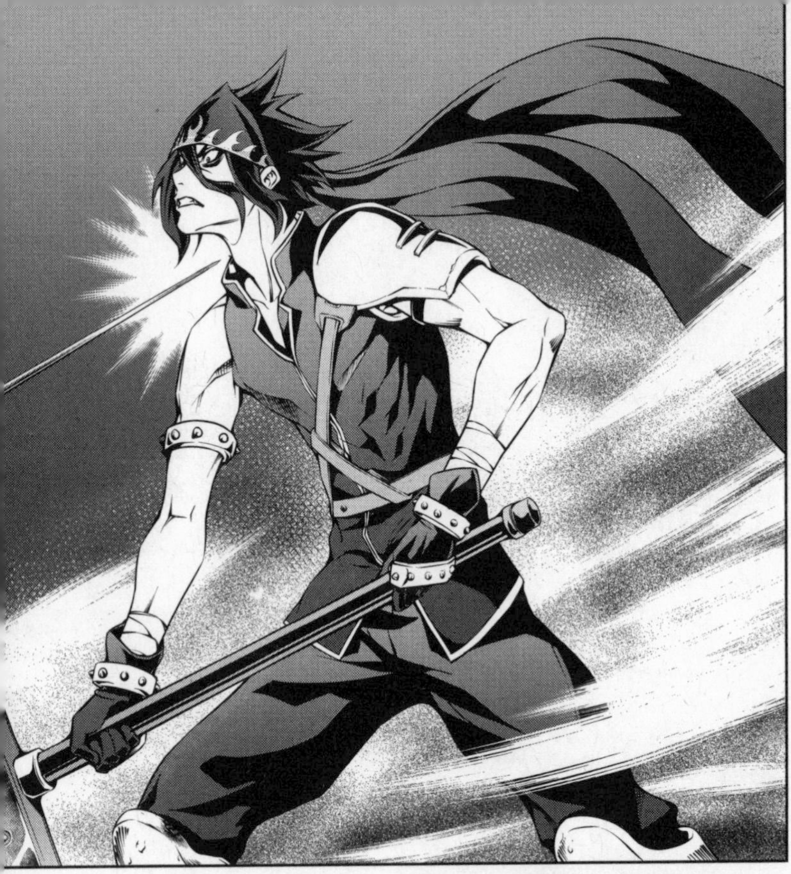

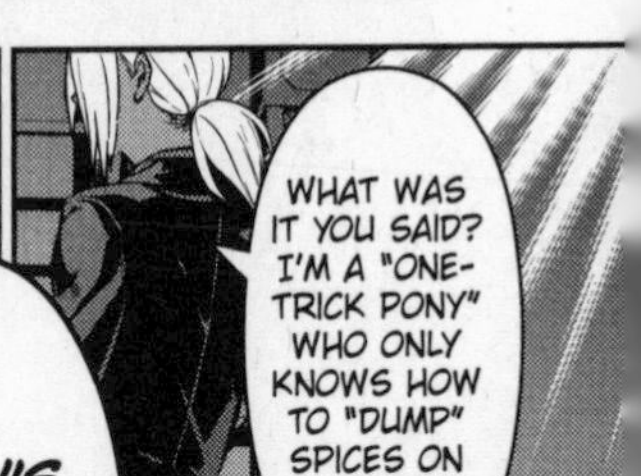
WHAT WAS IT YOU SAID? I'M A "ONE-TRICK PONY" WHO ONLY KNOWS HOW TO "DUMP" SPICES ON THINGS?

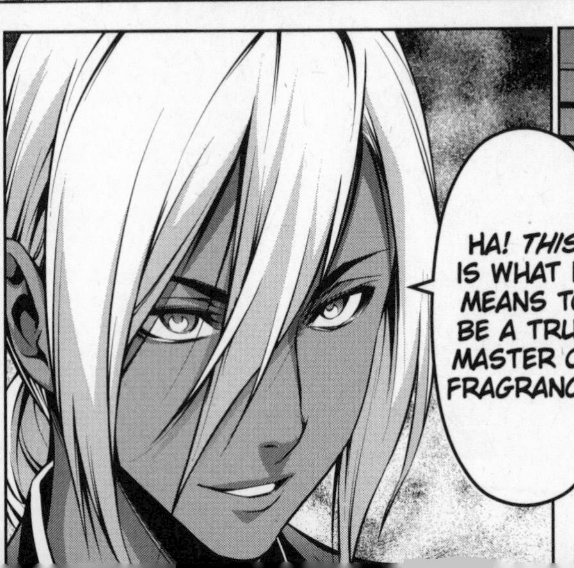
HA! *THIS* IS WHAT IT MEANS TO BE A TRUE MASTER OF FRAGRANCE.

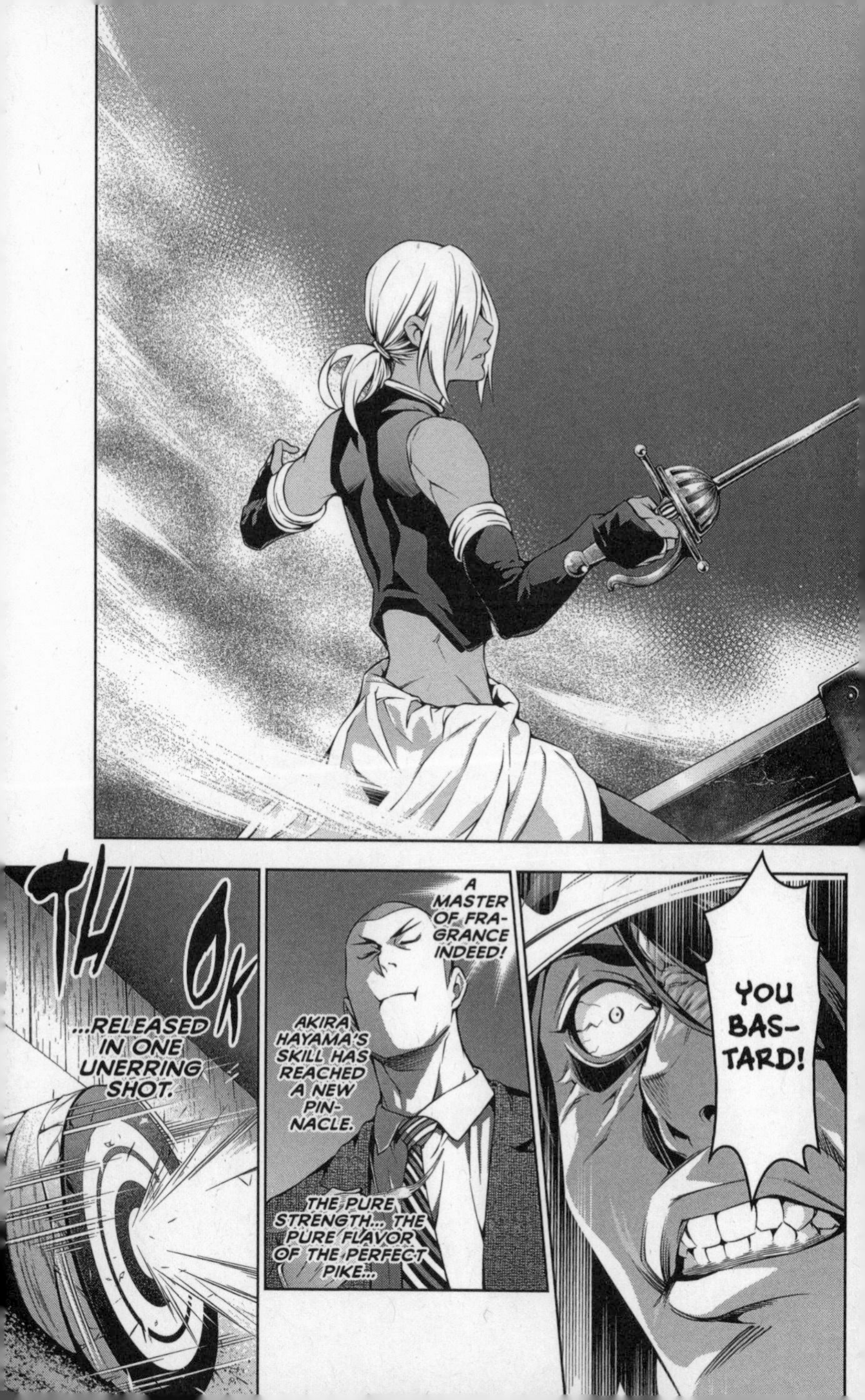
YOU BAS-TARD!
A MASTER OF FRA-GRANCE INDEED!
AKIRA HAYAMA'S SKILL HAS REACHED A NEW PIN-NACLE.
THE PURE STRENGTH... THE PURE FLAVOR OF THE PERFECT PIKE...
THOK
...RELEASED IN ONE UNERRING SHOT.

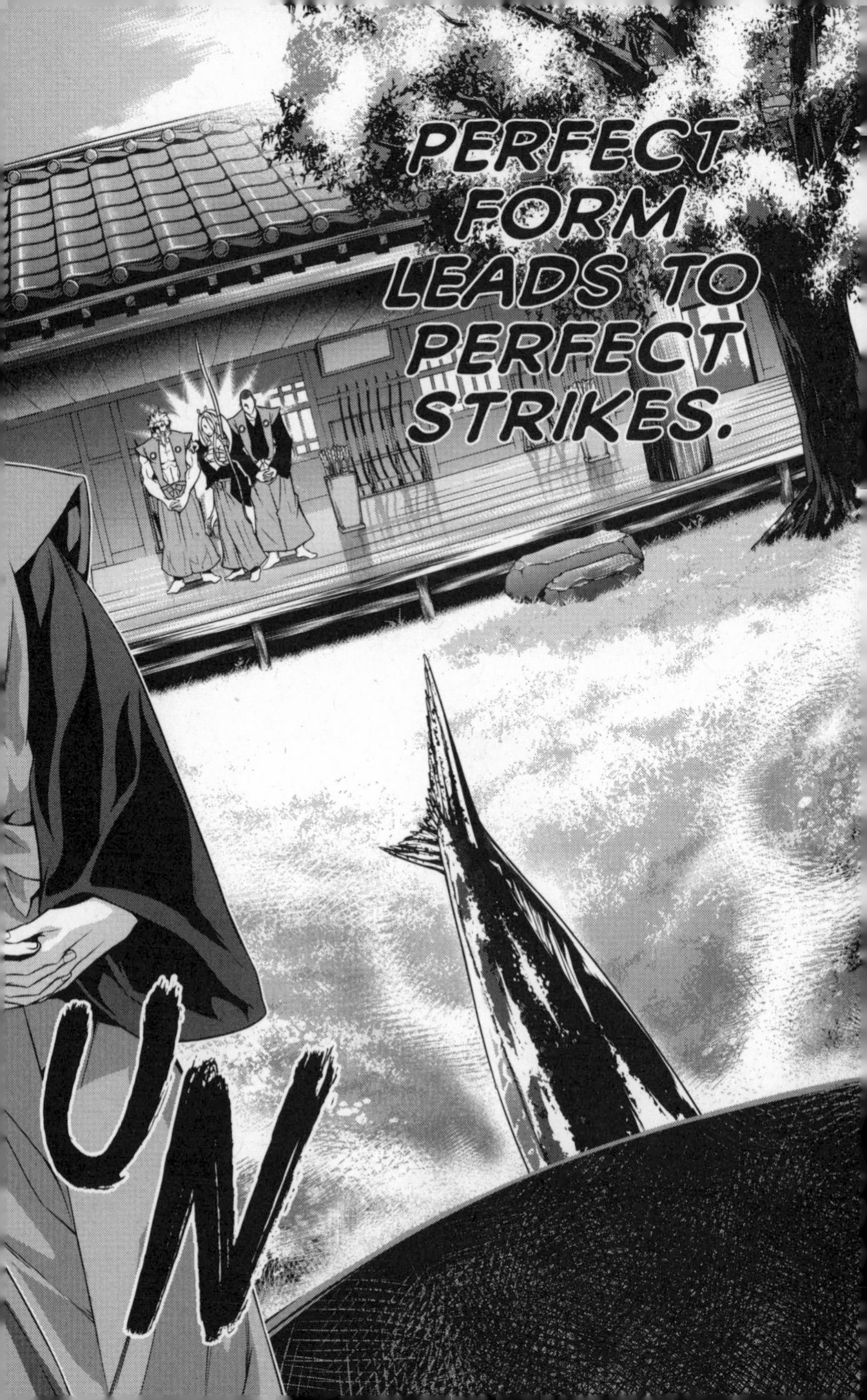
PERFECT FORM LEADS TO PERFECT STRIKES.
UN

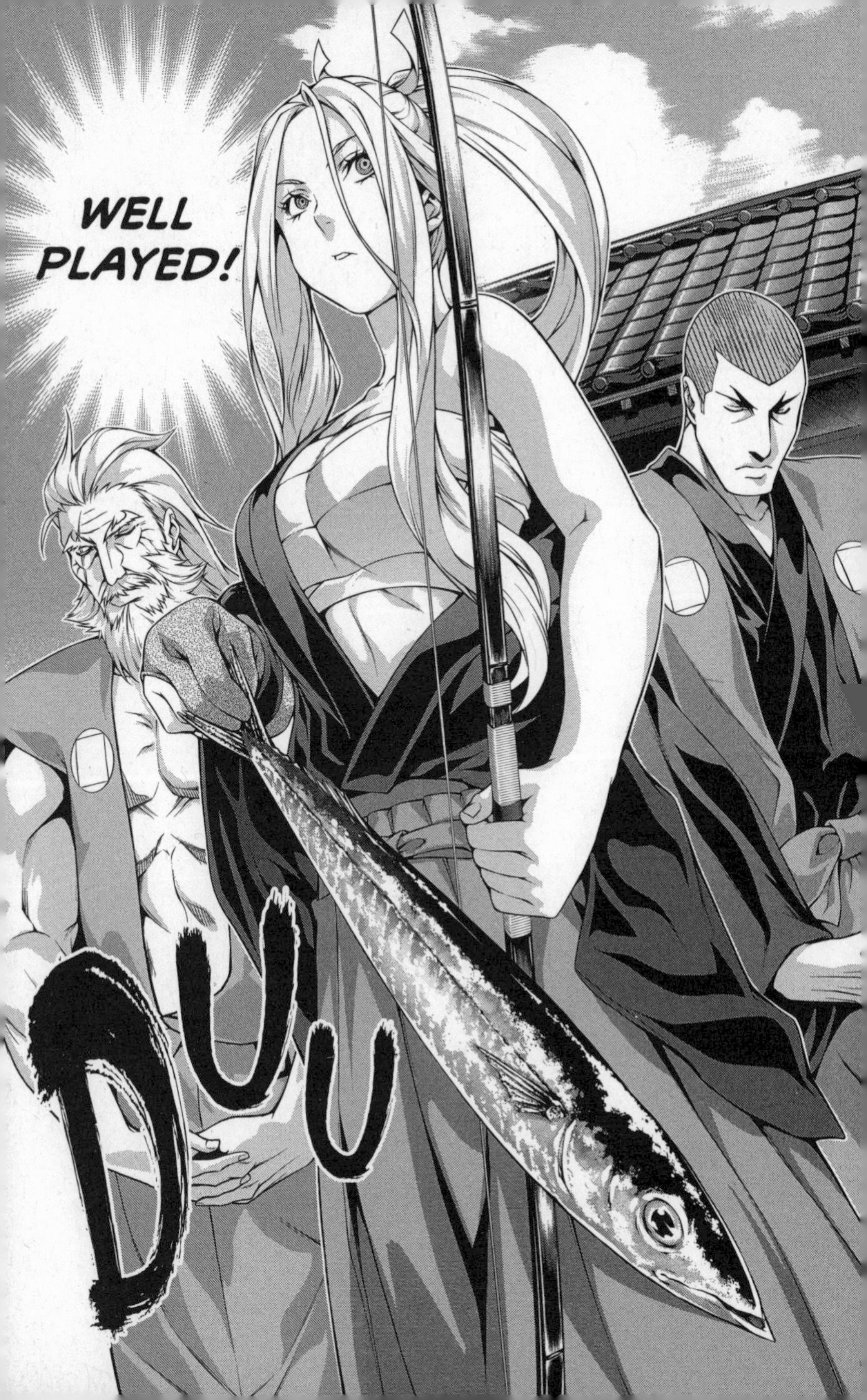
WELL PLAYED!

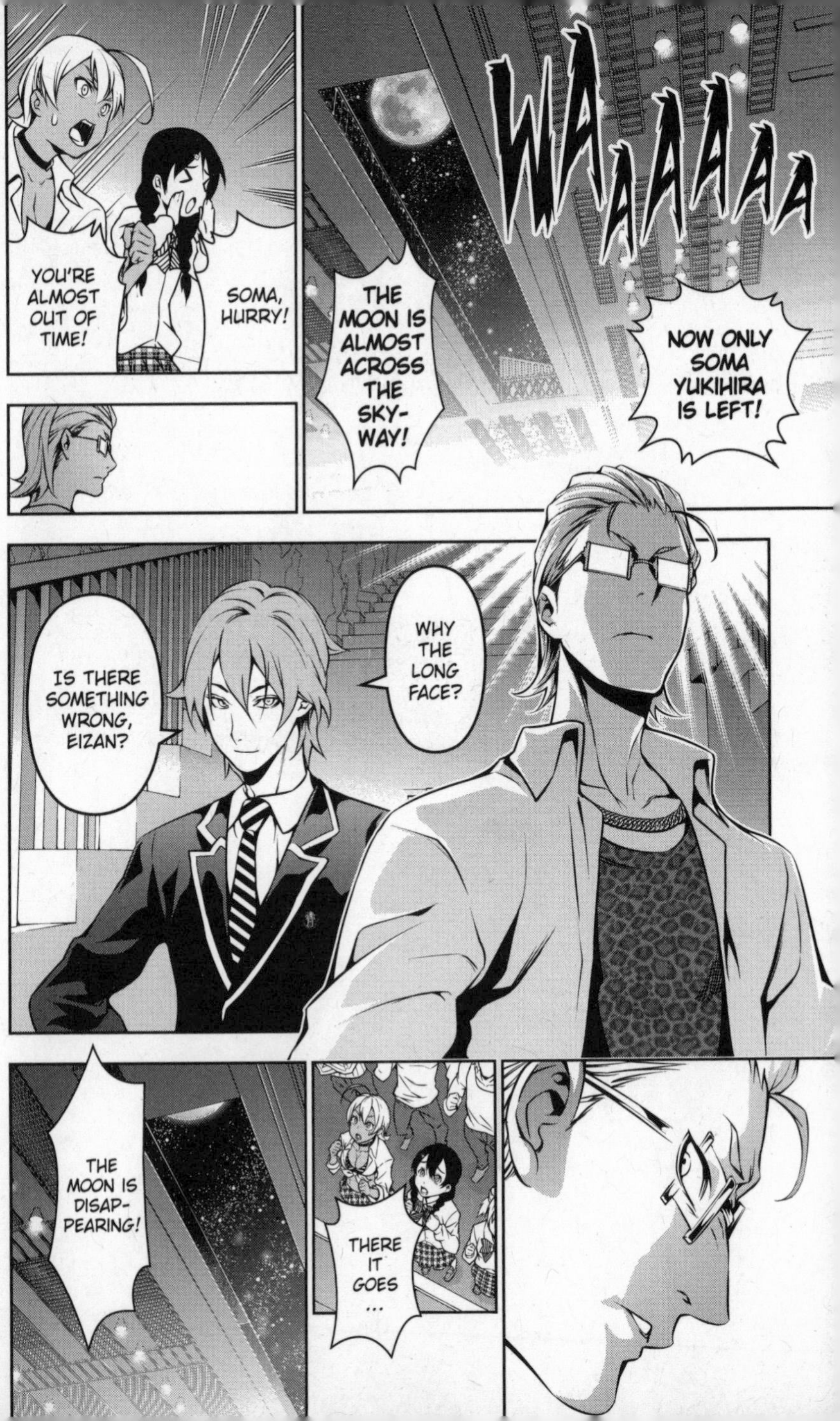
WAAAAAAA
NOW ONLY SOMA YUKIHIRA IS LEFT!
THE MOON IS ALMOST ACROSS THE SKY-WAY!
SOMA, HURRY!
YOU'RE ALMOST OUT OF TIME!
WHY THE LONG FACE?
IS THERE SOMETHING WRONG, EIZAN?
THERE IT GOES ...
THE MOON IS DISAP-PEARING!

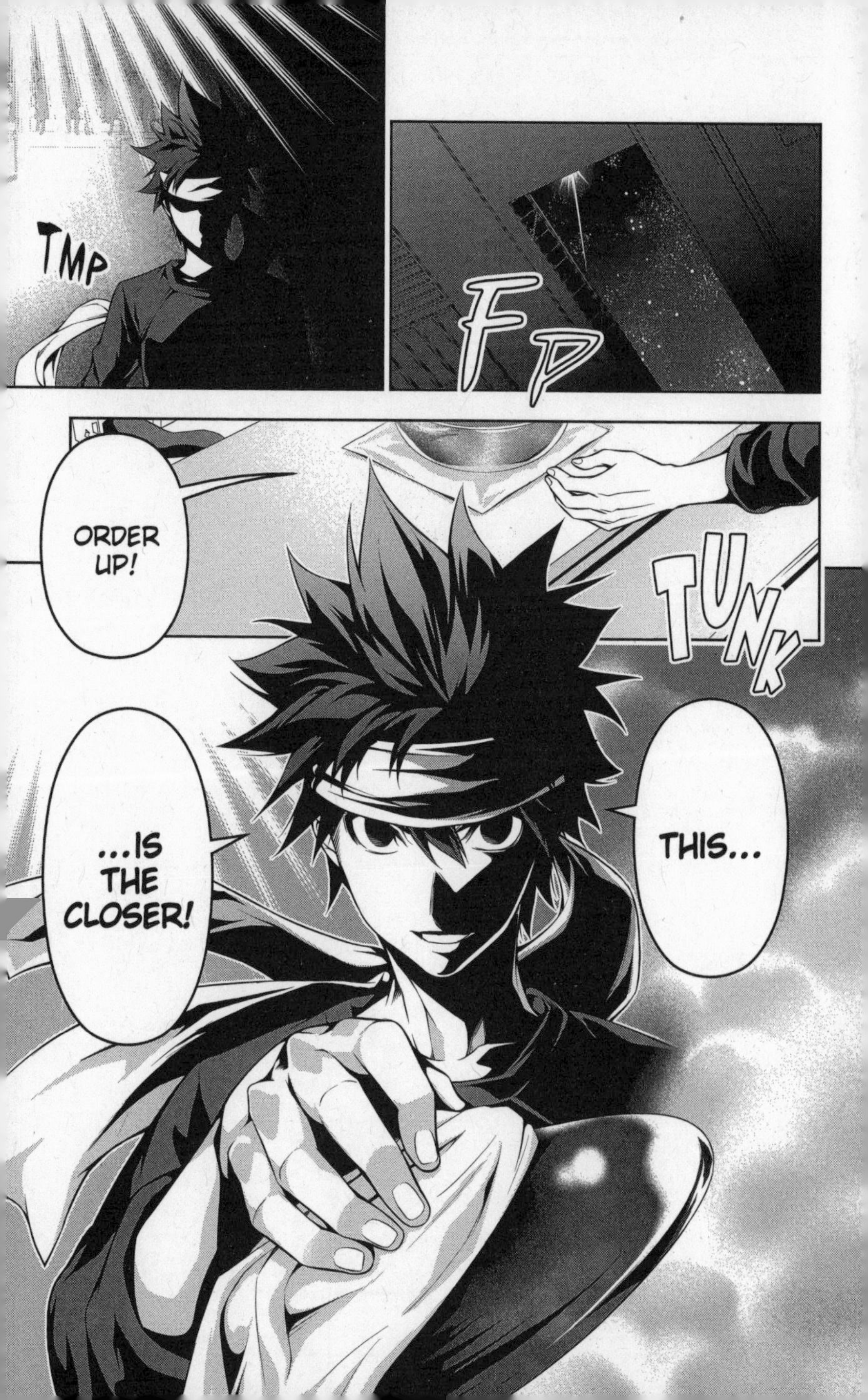
FP
TMP
TUNK
ORDER UP!
THIS...
...IS THE CLOSER!

ARTIST: YUTO TSUKUDA RECIPE BY: YUKI MORISAKI

PRACTICAL RECIPE #2

VOLUME 12 SPECIAL SUPPLEMENT!

PIKE CARPACCIO

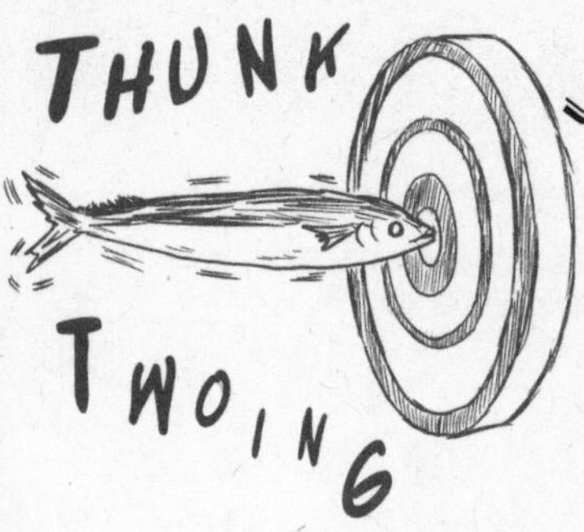
THUNK
TWOING

INGREDIENTS
(SERVES 2)

1 PIKE (OR YOUR FAVORITE SASHIMI)
BABY ARUGULA
RADISH WEDGES

A 2 TABLESPOONS EACH SOY SAUCE, MIRIN, SAKE

B 2 TABLESPOONS EXTRA-VIRGIN OLIVE OIL
1 TABLESPOON WINE VINEGAR
ALLSPICE, SALT, PEPPER

1. FILLET THE PIKE. CUT OFF ITS HEAD JUST BEHIND THE GILLS, AND THEN GUT AND DEBONE IT. SET THE INNARDS ASIDE. SLICE THE FILLETS INTO ¼-INCH-THICK SASHIMI SLICES.

2. TAKE THE FISH INNARDS FROM (1) AND SMASH THEM WITH THE FLAT OF A KNIFE. MIX THOROUGHLY TOGETHER WITH (A) AND PUT THEM IN A SMALL POT TO BOIL. AS SOON AS THE POT BOILS, REMOVE CONTENTS FROM THE HEAT AND CHILL.

3. PUT (B) INTO A BOWL AND ADD (2). MIX TOGETHER TO MAKE A DRESSING.

4. PLACE THE SASHIMI SLICES IN A CIRCLE PATTERN ON A PLATE. ADD SOME BABY ARUGULA LEAVES IN THE MIDDLE FOR DECORATION. DRIZZLE GENEROUSLY WITH (3) AND DONE!

*YOU CAN ENJOY THE PIKE SASHIMI AS IS, OR YOU CAN LIGHTLY SEAR IT WITH A BLOWTORCH. (IF YOU DO NOT HAVE A COOKING BLOWTORCH AVAILABLE, SIMPLY SEAR QUICKLY ON A TEFLON FRYING PAN.) IF PIKE ISN'T IN SEASON, TRY MAKING THIS WITH YOUR FAVORITE SASHIMI INSTEAD. ♪

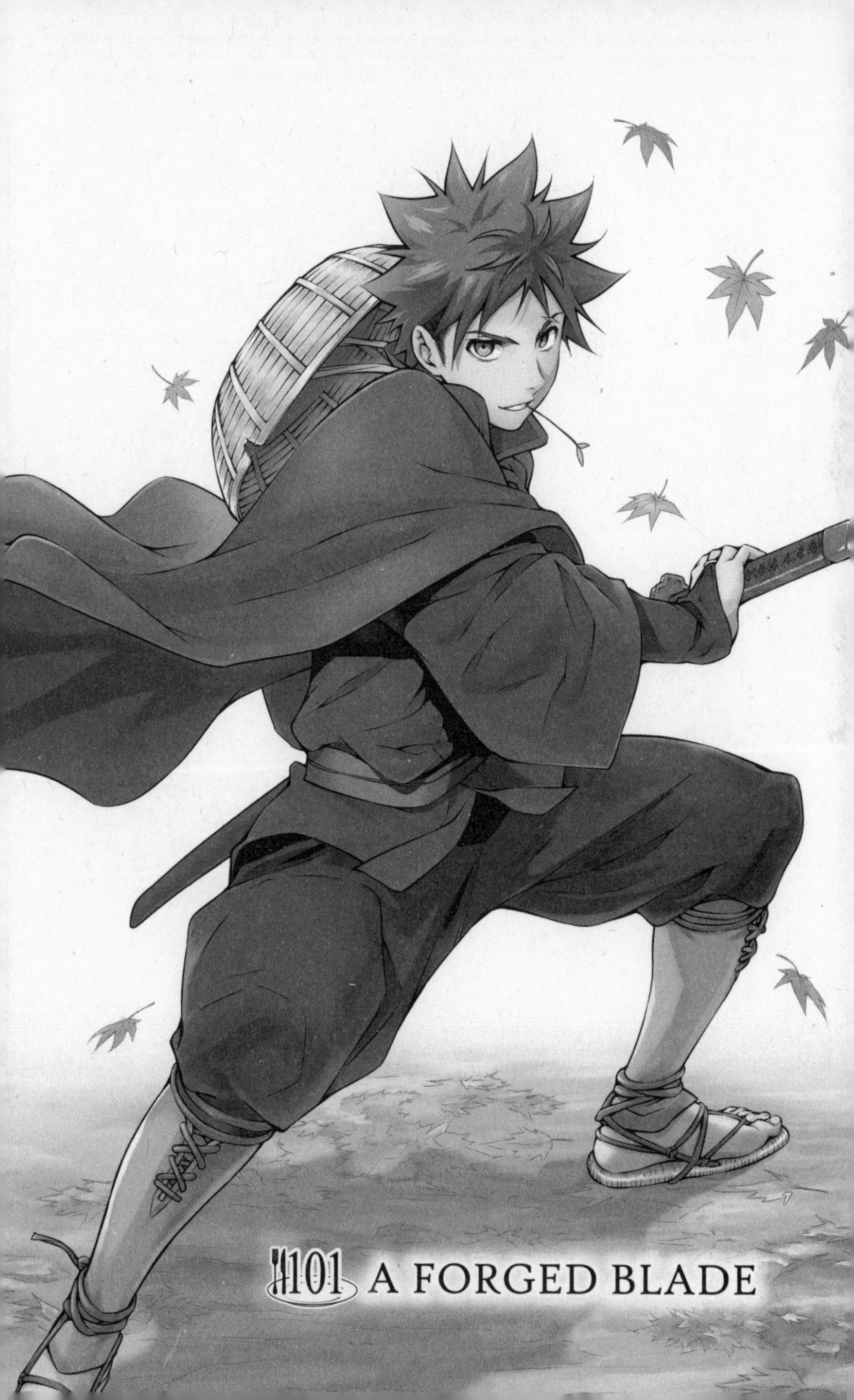
101 A FORGED BLADE

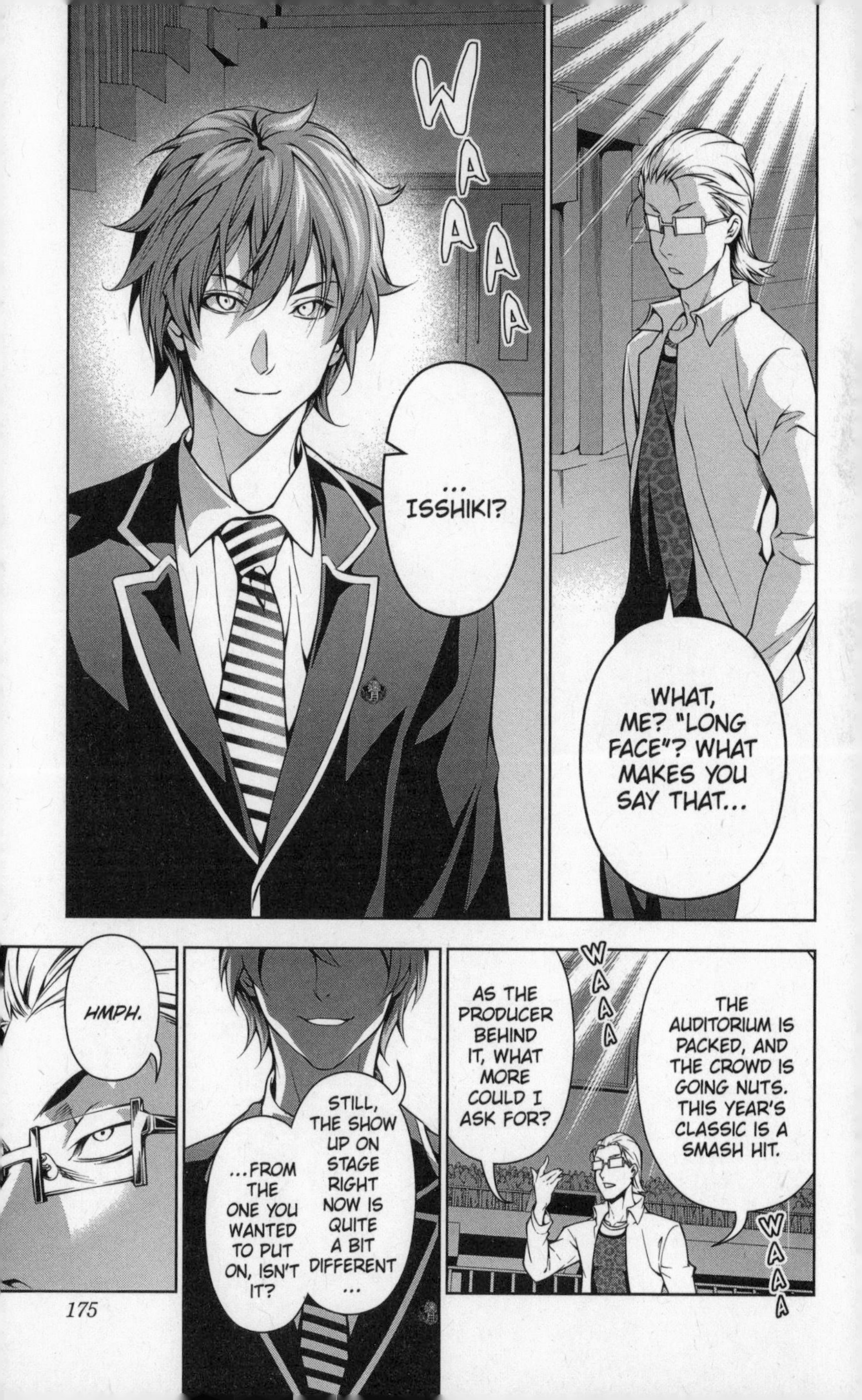
WHAT, ME? "LONG FACE"? WHAT MAKES YOU SAY THAT...
WAAAAAA
... ISSHIKI?
WAAA
THE AUDITORIUM IS PACKED, AND THE CROWD IS GOING NUTS. THIS YEAR'S CLASSIC IS A SMASH HIT.
WAAA
AS THE PRODUCER BEHIND IT, WHAT MORE COULD I ASK FOR?
STILL, THE SHOW UP ON STAGE RIGHT NOW IS QUITE A BIT DIFFERENT ...
...FROM THE ONE YOU WANTED TO PUT ON, ISN'T IT?
HMPH.

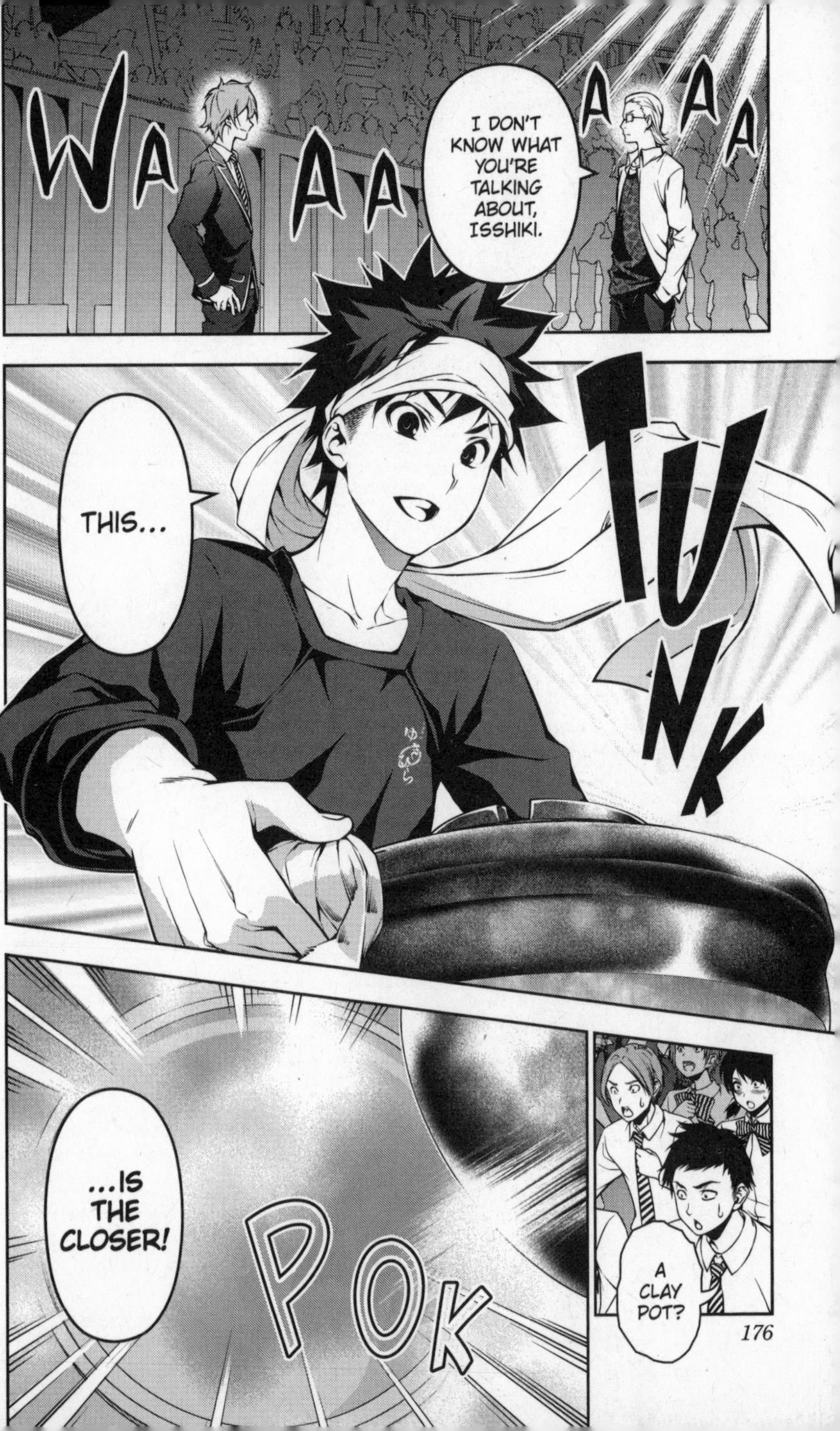
WAAAAAAA
I DON'T KNOW WHAT YOU'RE TALKING ABOUT, ISSHIKI.
TUNK
THIS...
A CLAY POT?
...IS THE CLOSER!
POK

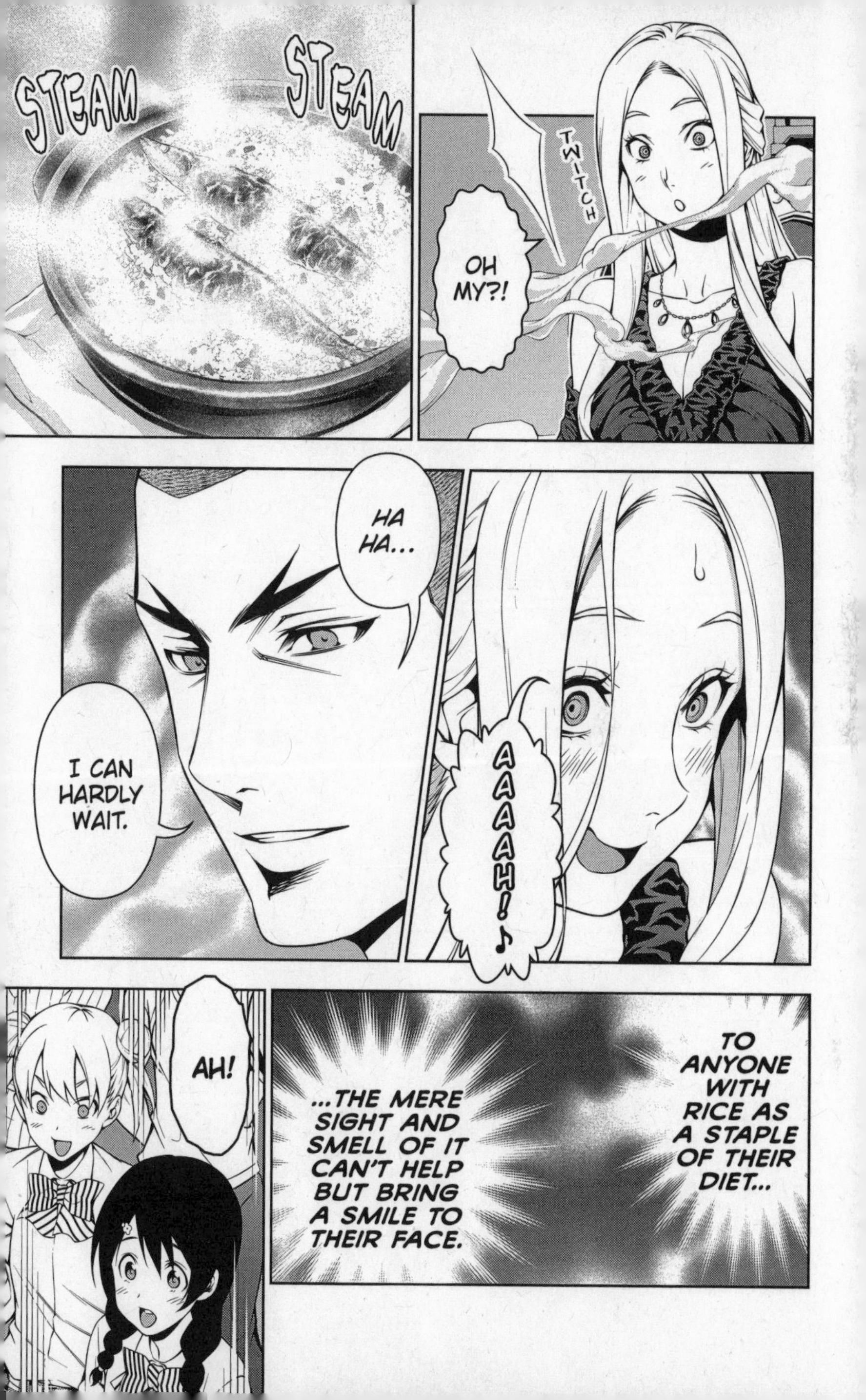

TWITCH
OH MY?!
STEAM
STEAM
HA HA...
AAAAAH!♪
I CAN HARDLY WAIT.
TO ANYONE WITH RICE AS A STAPLE OF THEIR DIET...
...THE MERE SIGHT AND SMELL OF IT CAN'T HELP BUT BRING A SMILE TO THEIR FACE.
AH!

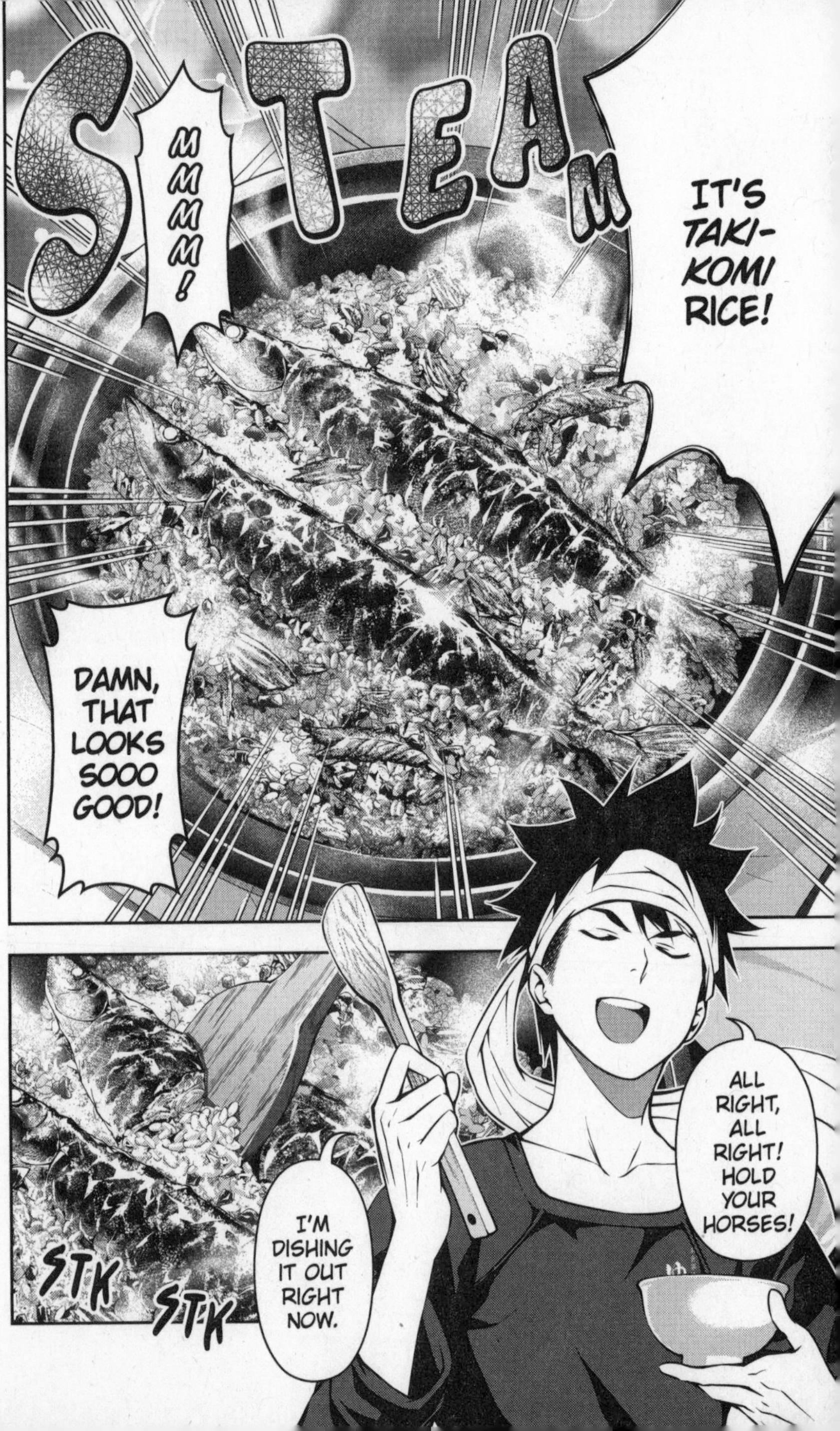
IT'S TAKI-KOMI RICE!
STEAM
MMMMM!
DAMN, THAT LOOKS SOOO GOOD!
ALL RIGHT, ALL RIGHT! HOLD YOUR HORSES!
I'M DISHING IT OUT RIGHT NOW.
STK STK

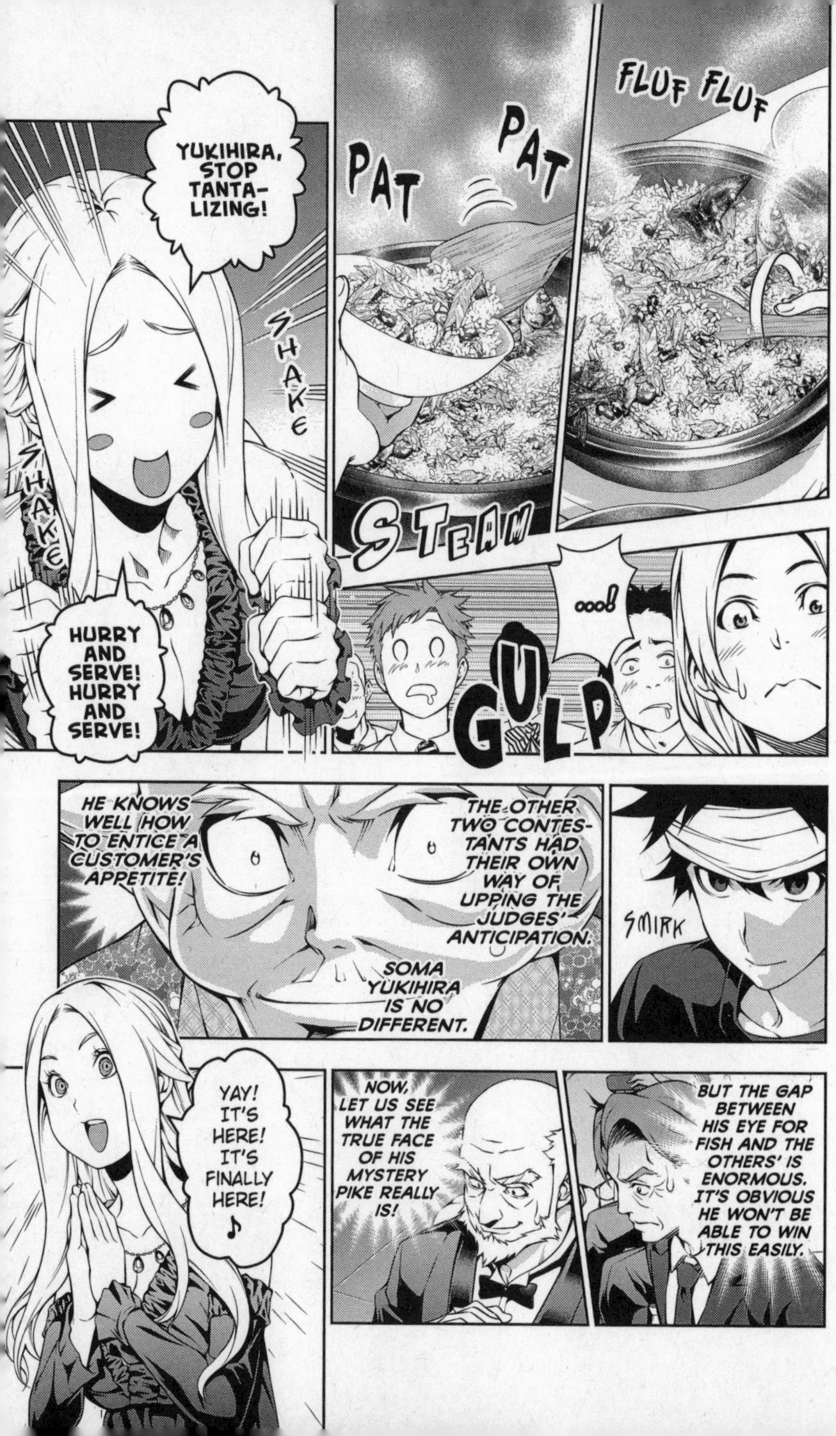
FLUF FLUF
PAT
PAT
STEAM
...!
GULP
YUKIHIRA, STOP TANTALIZING!
SHAKE
SHAKE
HURRY AND SERVE! HURRY AND SERVE!
SMIRK
THE OTHER TWO CONTESTANTS HAD THEIR OWN WAY OF UPPING THE JUDGES' ANTICIPATION.
HE KNOWS WELL HOW TO ENTICE A CUSTOMER'S APPETITE!
SOMA YUKIHIRA IS NO DIFFERENT.
BUT THE GAP BETWEEN HIS EYE FOR FISH AND THE OTHERS' IS ENORMOUS. IT'S OBVIOUS HE WON'T BE ABLE TO WIN THIS EASILY.
NOW, LET US SEE WHAT THE TRUE FACE OF HIS MYSTERY PIKE REALLY IS!
YAY! IT'S HERE! IT'S FINALLY HERE! ♪

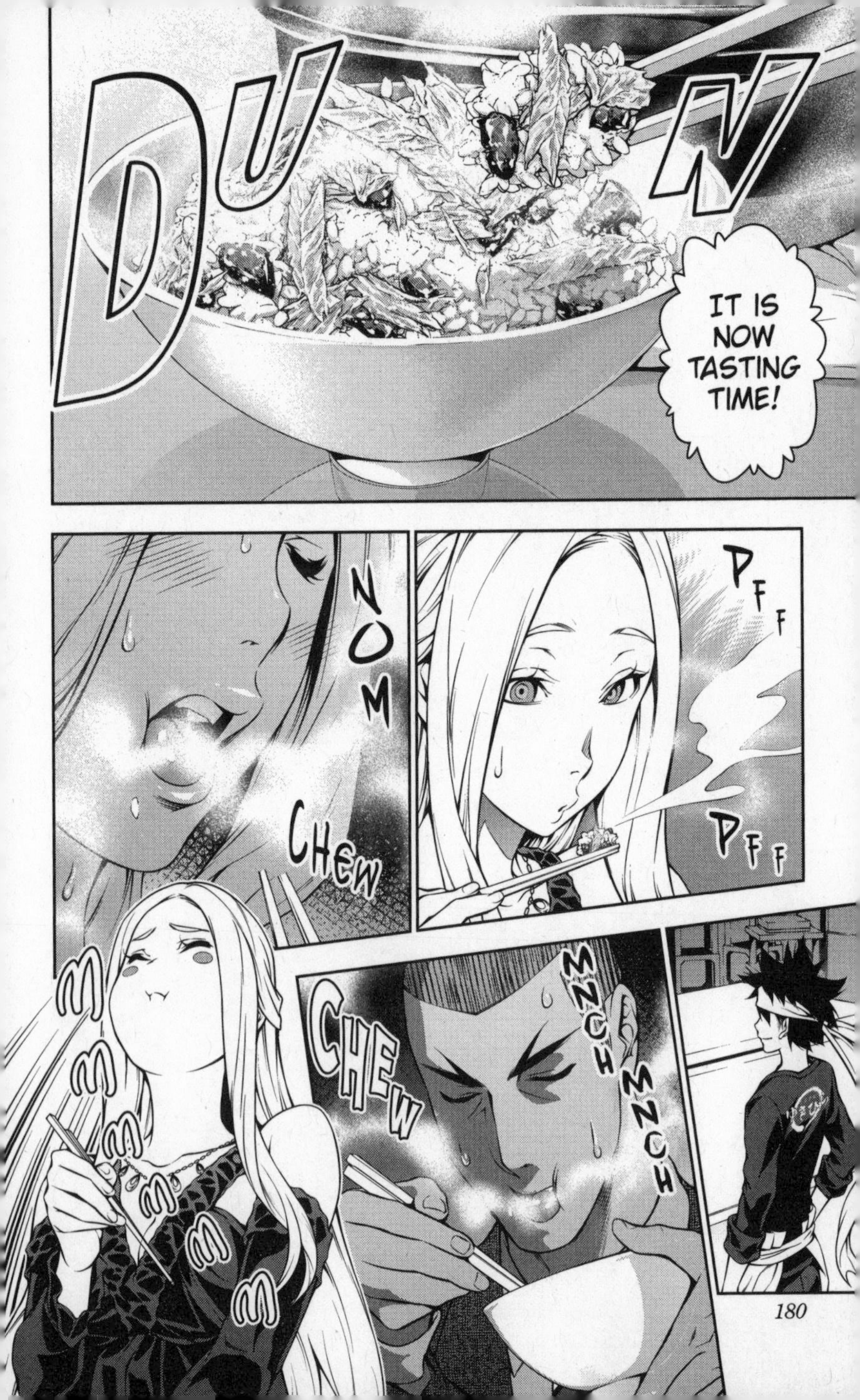
DUN
IT IS NOW TASTING TIME!
PFF
PFF
NOM
CHEW
MNCH
MNCH
CHEW
MMMMMMMMMM

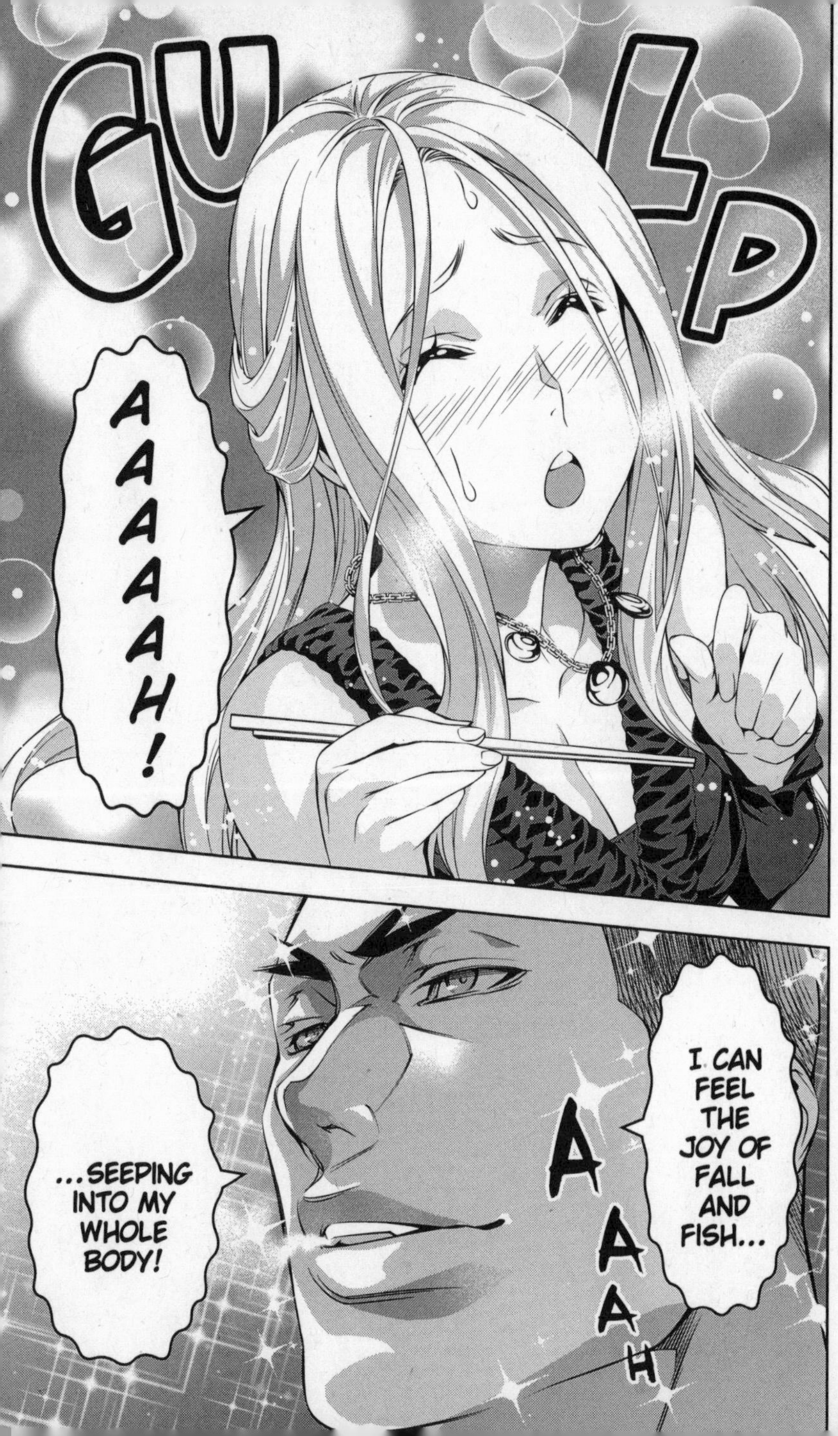
GU LP
AAAAAAH!
I CAN FEEL THE JOY OF FALL AND FISH...
AAAH
...SEEPING INTO MY WHOLE BODY!

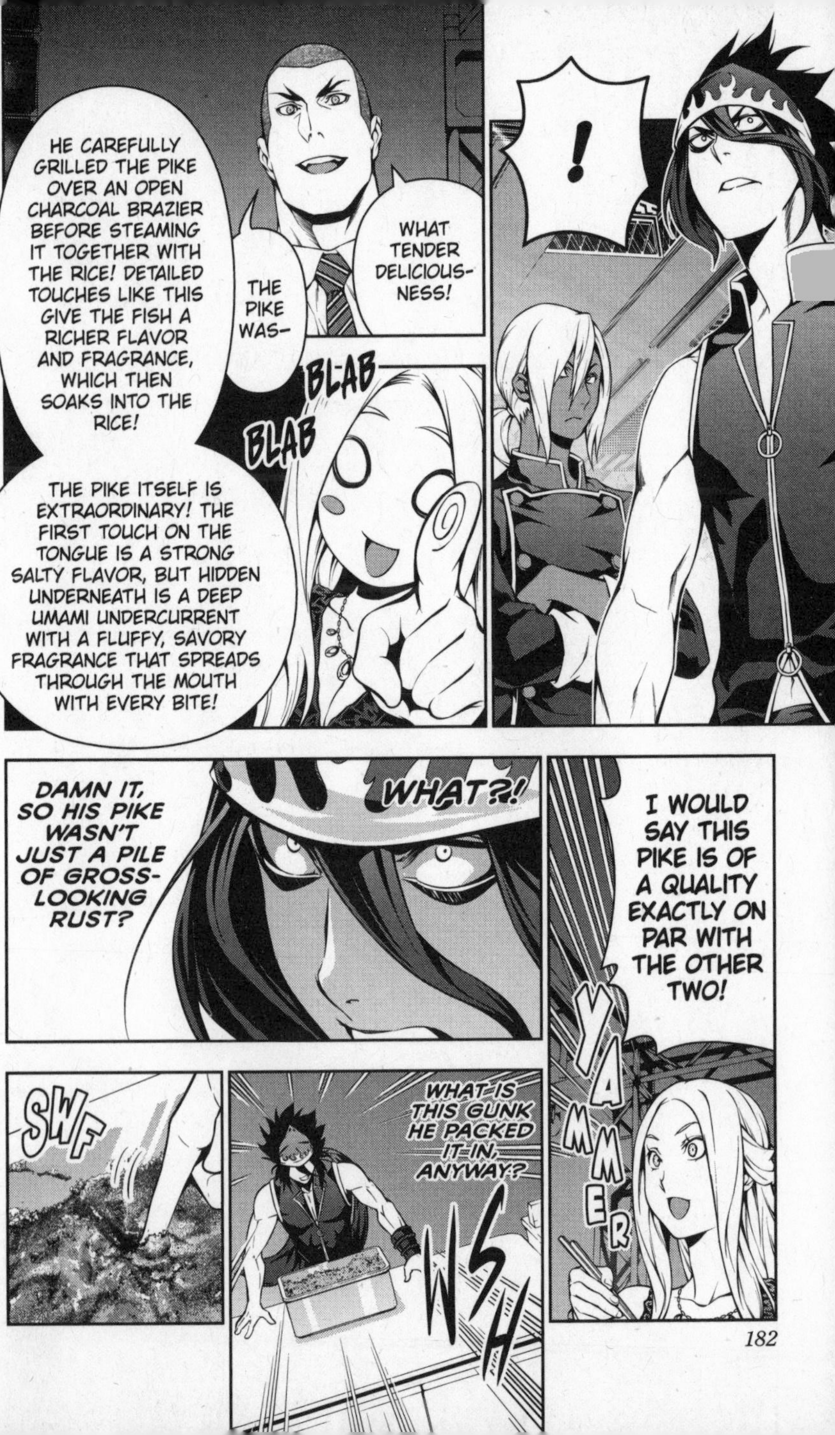
!
WHAT TENDER DELICIOUSNESS!
THE PIKE WAS-
HE CAREFULLY GRILLED THE PIKE OVER AN OPEN CHARCOAL BRAZIER BEFORE STEAMING IT TOGETHER WITH THE RICE! DETAILED TOUCHES LIKE THIS GIVE THE FISH A RICHER FLAVOR AND FRAGRANCE, WHICH THEN SOAKS INTO THE RICE!
BLAB BLAB
THE PIKE ITSELF IS EXTRAORDINARY! THE FIRST TOUCH ON THE TONGUE IS A STRONG SALTY FLAVOR, BUT HIDDEN UNDERNEATH IS A DEEP UMAMI UNDERCURRENT WITH A FLUFFY, SAVORY FRAGRANCE THAT SPREADS THROUGH THE MOUTH WITH EVERY BITE!
I WOULD SAY THIS PIKE IS OF A QUALITY EXACTLY ON PAR WITH THE OTHER TWO!
YAMMMMER
WHAT?!
DAMN IT, SO HIS PIKE WASN'T JUST A PILE OF GROSS-LOOKING RUST?
WHAT IS THIS GUNK HE PACKED IT IN, ANYWAY?
WSH
SWF

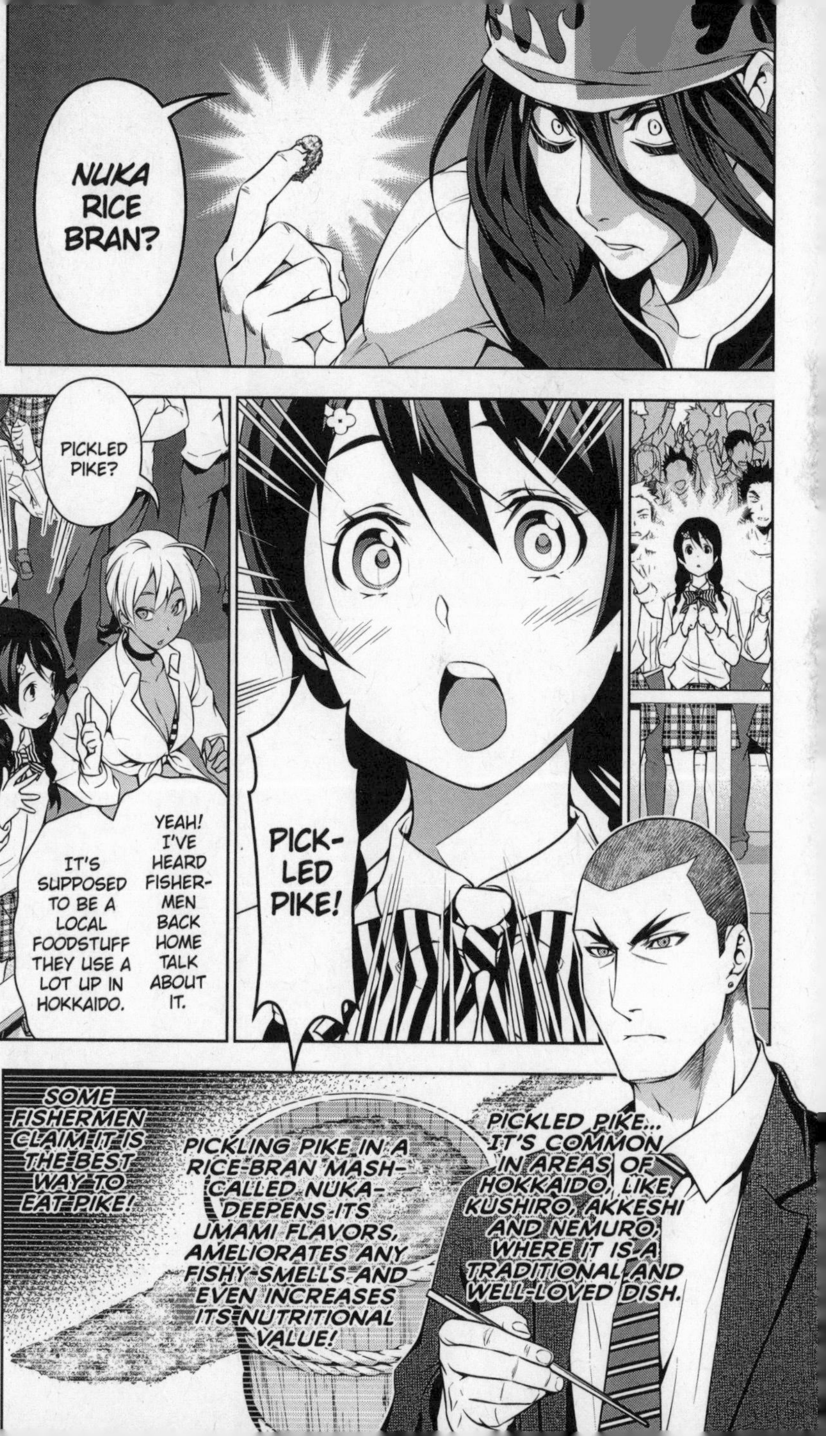
NUKA RICE BRAN?
PICK-LED PIKE!
PICKLED PIKE?
YEAH! I'VE HEARD FISHER-MEN BACK HOME TALK ABOUT IT.
IT'S SUPPOSED TO BE A LOCAL FOODSTUFF THEY USE A LOT UP IN HOKKAIDO.
PICKLED PIKE... IT'S COMMON IN AREAS OF HOKKAIDO, LIKE KUSHIRO, AKKESHI AND NEMURO, WHERE IT IS A TRADITIONAL AND WELL-LOVED DISH.
PICKLING PIKE IN A RICE-BRAN MASH–CALLED NUKA–DEEPENS ITS UMAMI FLAVORS, AMELIORATES ANY FISHY SMELLS AND EVEN INCREASES ITS NUTRITIONAL VALUE!
SOME FISHERMEN CLAIM IT IS THE BEST WAY TO EAT PIKE!

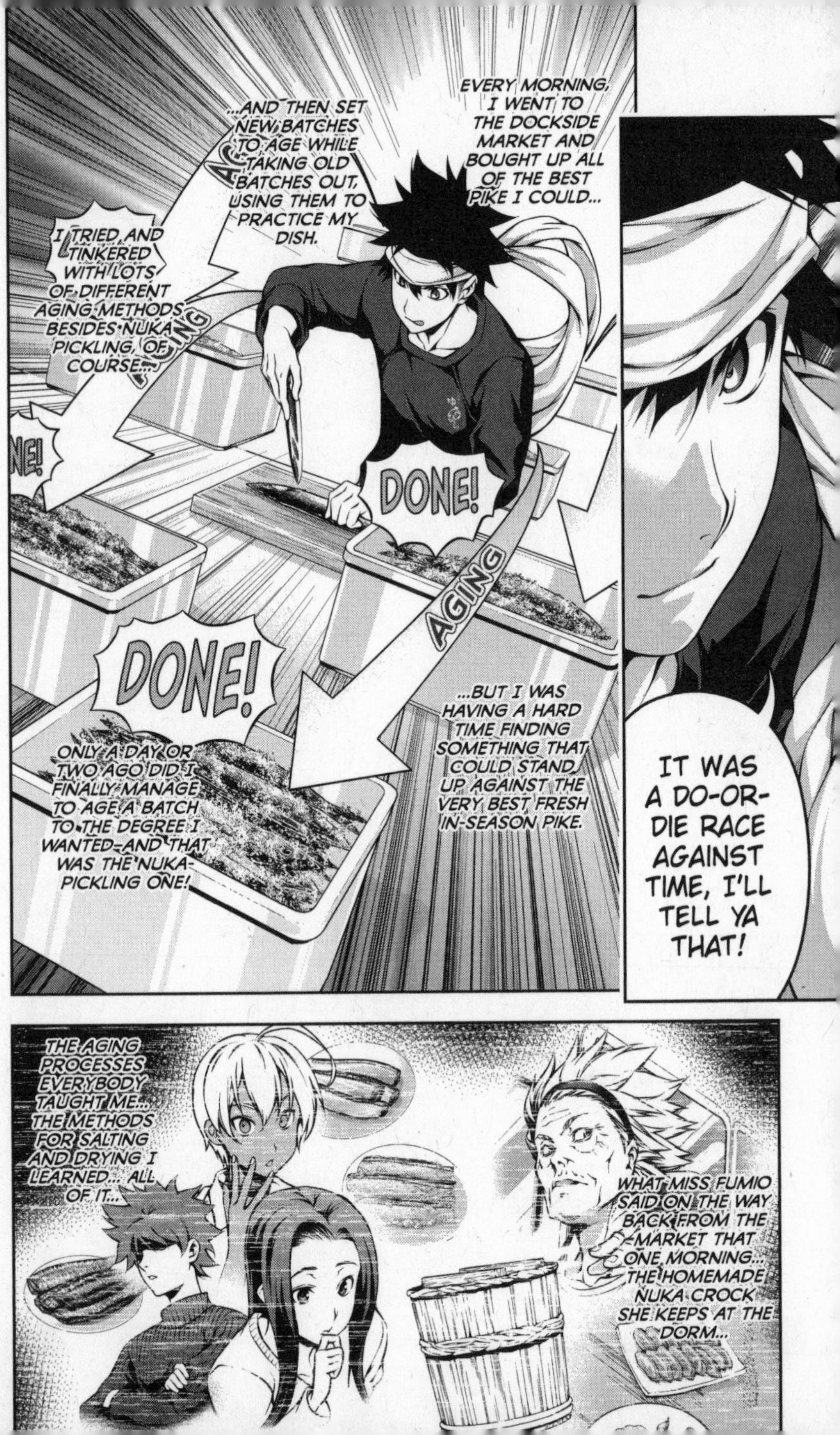
IT WAS A DO-OR-DIE RACE AGAINST TIME, I'LL TELL YA THAT!
EVERY MORNING, I WENT TO THE DOCKSIDE MARKET AND BOUGHT UP ALL OF THE BEST PIKE I COULD...
...AND THEN SET NEW BATCHES TO AGE WHILE TAKING OLD BATCHES OUT, USING THEM TO PRACTICE MY DISH.
I TRIED AND TINKERED WITH LOTS OF DIFFERENT AGING METHODS BESIDES NUKA PICKLING, OF COURSE...
AGING
DONE!
AGING
AGING
DONE!
...BUT I WAS HAVING A HARD TIME FINDING SOMETHING THAT COULD STAND UP AGAINST THE VERY BEST FRESH IN-SEASON PIKE.
ONLY A DAY OR TWO AGO DID I FINALLY MANAGE TO AGE A BATCH TO THE DEGREE I WANTED-AND THAT WAS THE NUKA-PICKLING ONE!
WHAT MISS FUMIO SAID ON THE WAY BACK FROM THE MARKET THAT ONE MORNING... THE HOMEMADE NUKA CROCK SHE KEEPS AT THE DORM...
THE AGING PROCESSES EVERYBODY TAUGHT ME... THE METHODS FOR SALTING AND DRYING I LEARNED... ALL OF IT...

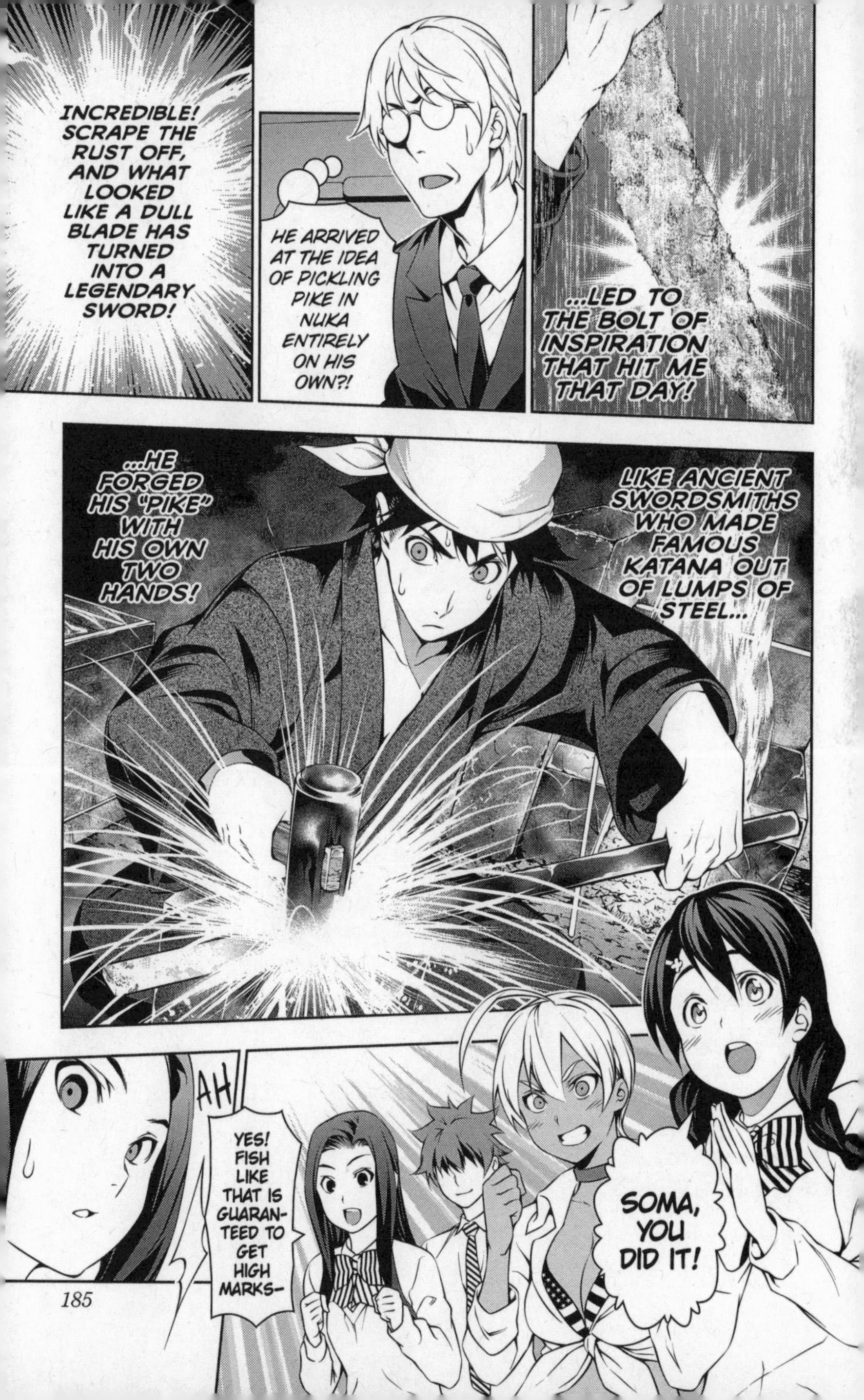
...LED TO THE BOLT OF INSPIRATION THAT HIT ME THAT DAY!
HE ARRIVED AT THE IDEA OF PICKLING PIKE IN NUKA ENTIRELY ON HIS OWN?!
INCREDIBLE! SCRAPE THE RUST OFF, AND WHAT LOOKED LIKE A DULL BLADE HAS TURNED INTO A LEGENDARY SWORD!
LIKE ANCIENT SWORDSMITHS WHO MADE FAMOUS KATANA OUT OF LUMPS OF STEEL...
...HE FORGED HIS "PIKE" WITH HIS OWN TWO HANDS!
SOMA, YOU DID IT!
YES! FISH LIKE THAT IS GUARAN-TEED TO GET HIGH MARKS-
AH

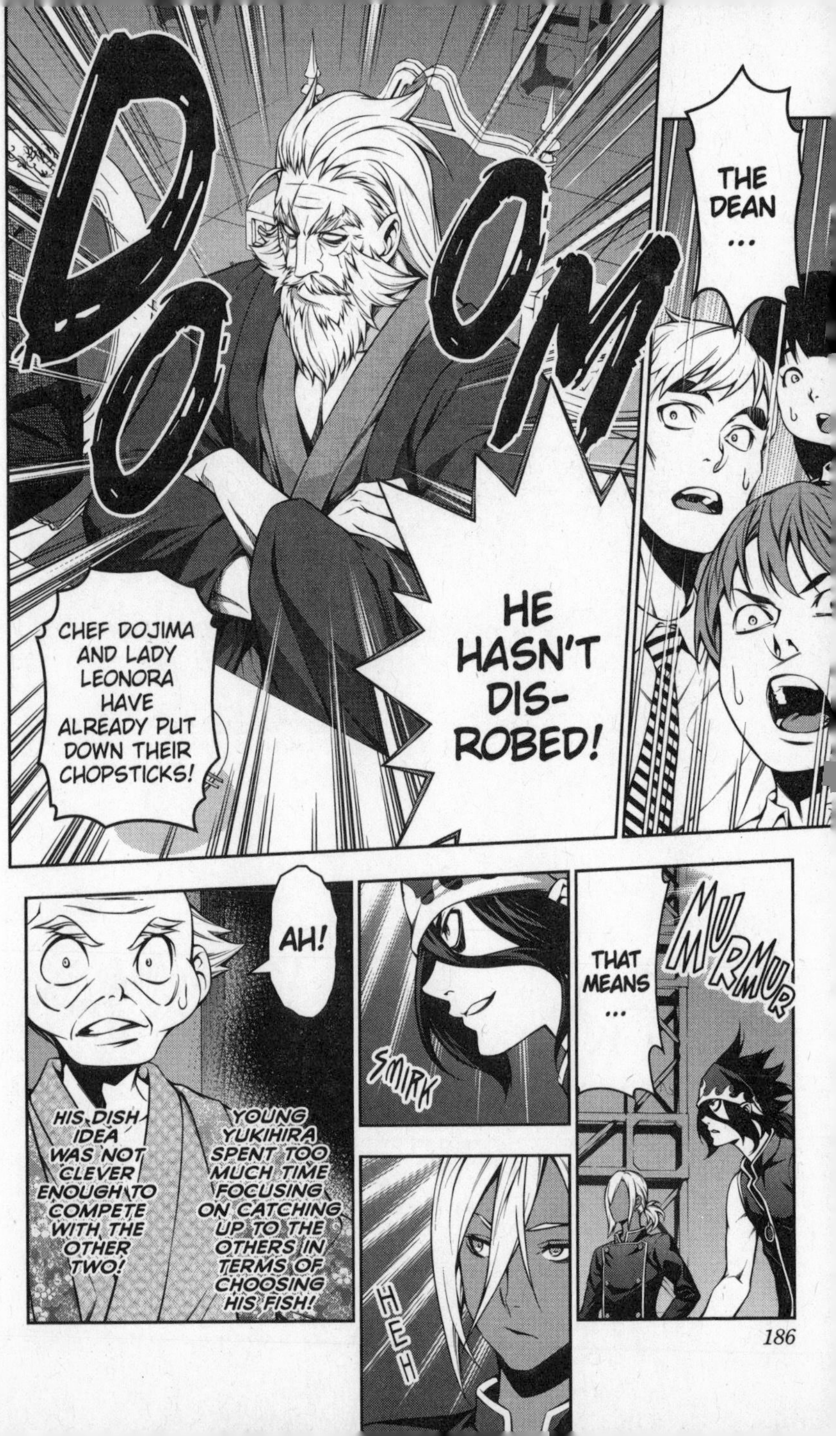
THE DEAN ...
DOOM
HE HASN'T DIS-ROBED!
CHEF DOJIMA AND LADY LEONORA HAVE ALREADY PUT DOWN THEIR CHOPSTICKS!
MURMUR MURMUR
THAT MEANS ...
SMIRK
HEH
AH!
YOUNG YUKIHIRA SPENT TOO MUCH TIME FOCUSING ON CATCHING UP TO THE OTHERS IN TERMS OF CHOOSING HIS FISH!
HIS DISH IDEA WAS NOT CLEVER ENOUGH TO COMPETE WITH THE OTHER TWO!

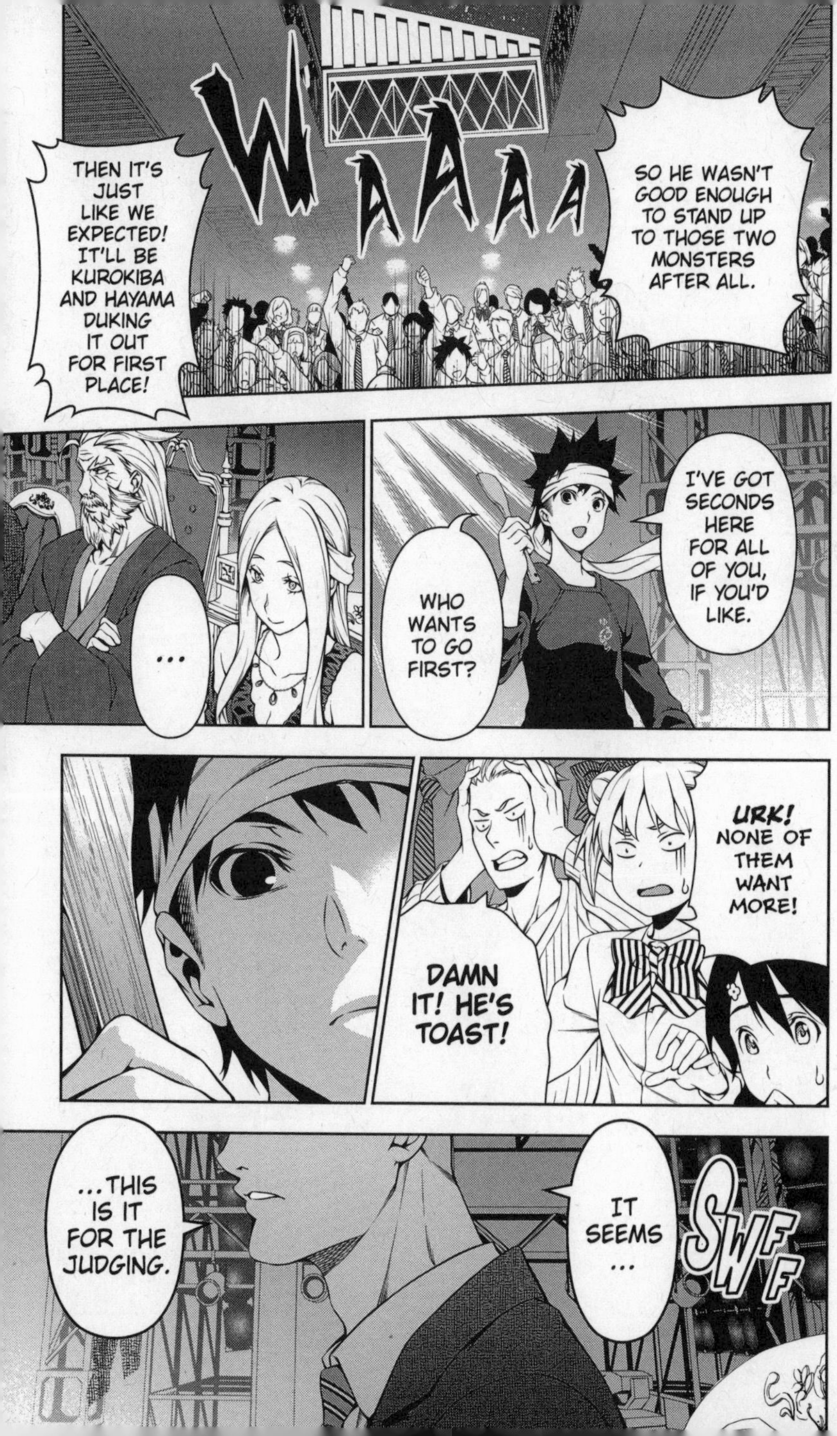
WAAAA
SO HE WASN'T GOOD ENOUGH TO STAND UP TO THOSE TWO MONSTERS AFTER ALL.
THEN IT'S JUST LIKE WE EXPECTED! IT'LL BE KUROKIBA AND HAYAMA DUKING IT OUT FOR FIRST PLACE!
I'VE GOT SECONDS HERE FOR ALL OF YOU, IF YOU'D LIKE.
WHO WANTS TO GO FIRST?
...
URK! NONE OF THEM WANT MORE!
DAMN IT! HE'S TOAST!
SWFF
IT SEEMS...
...THIS IS IT FOR THE JUDGING.

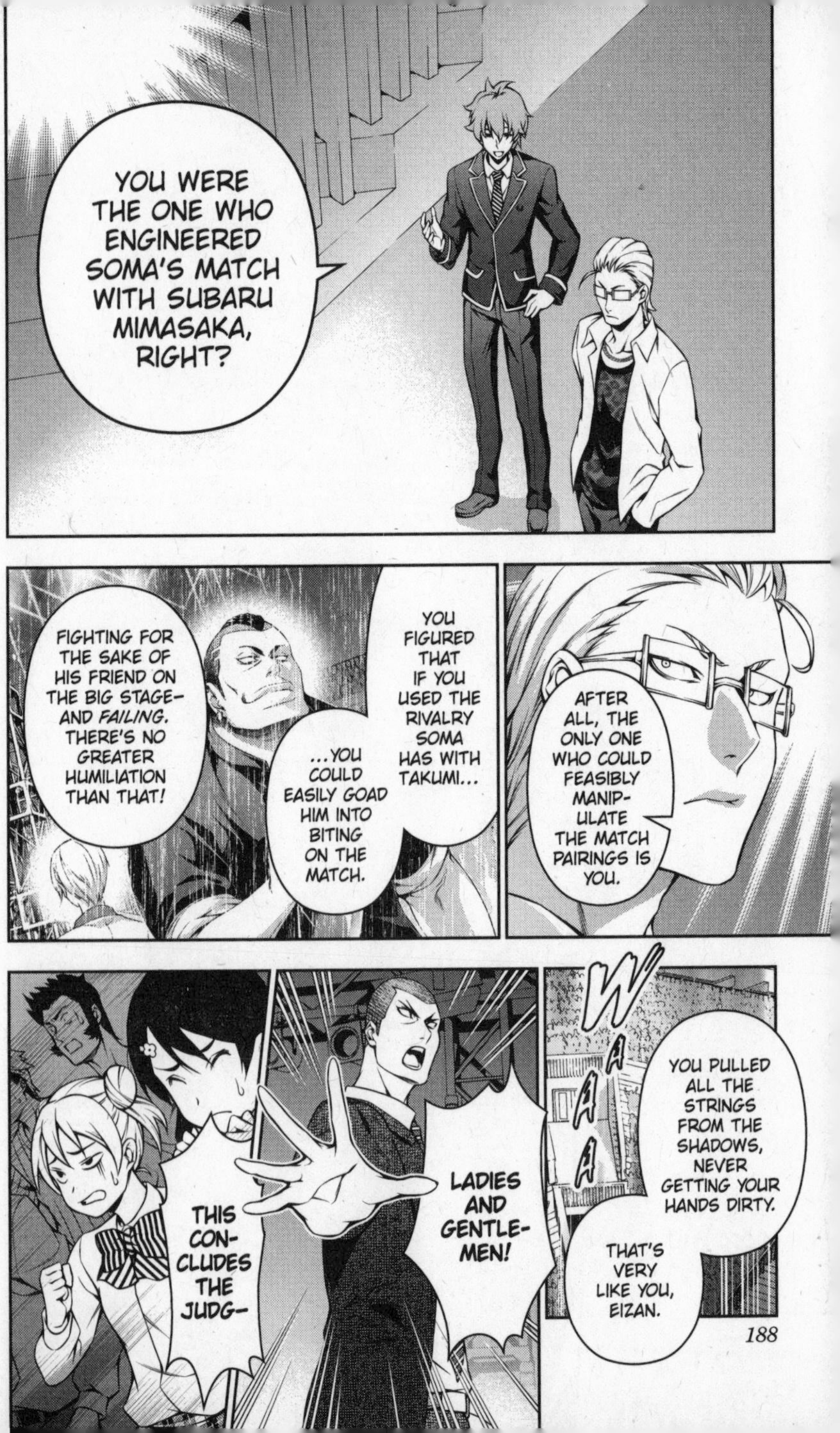
YOU WERE THE ONE WHO ENGINEERED SOMA'S MATCH WITH SUBARU MIMASAKA, RIGHT?
AFTER ALL, THE ONLY ONE WHO COULD FEASIBLY MANIP-ULATE THE MATCH PAIRINGS IS YOU.
YOU FIGURED THAT IF YOU USED THE RIVALRY SOMA HAS WITH TAKUMI...
...YOU COULD EASILY GOAD HIM INTO BITING ON THE MATCH.
FIGHTING FOR THE SAKE OF HIS FRIEND ON THE BIG STAGE—AND *FAILING*. THERE'S NO GREATER HUMILIATION THAN THAT!
WAAAA
YOU PULLED ALL THE STRINGS FROM THE SHADOWS, NEVER GETTING YOUR HANDS DIRTY.
THAT'S VERY LIKE YOU, EIZAN.
LADIES AND GENTLE-MEN!
THIS CON-CLUDES THE JUDG-

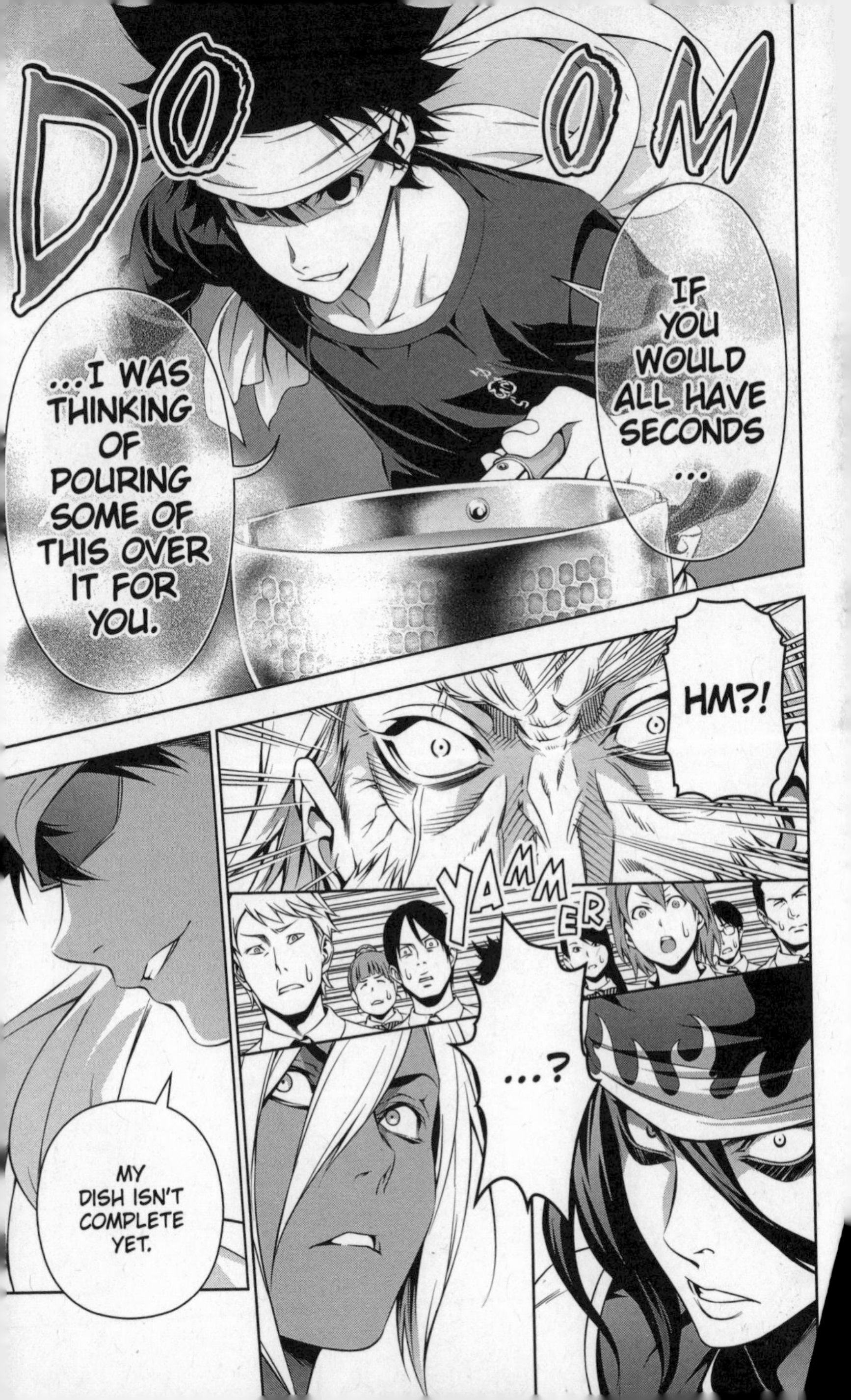
DOOM
IF YOU WOULD ALL HAVE SECONDS...
...I WAS THINKING OF POURING SOME OF THIS OVER IT FOR YOU.
HM?!
YAMMER
...?
MY DISH ISN'T COMPLETE YET.

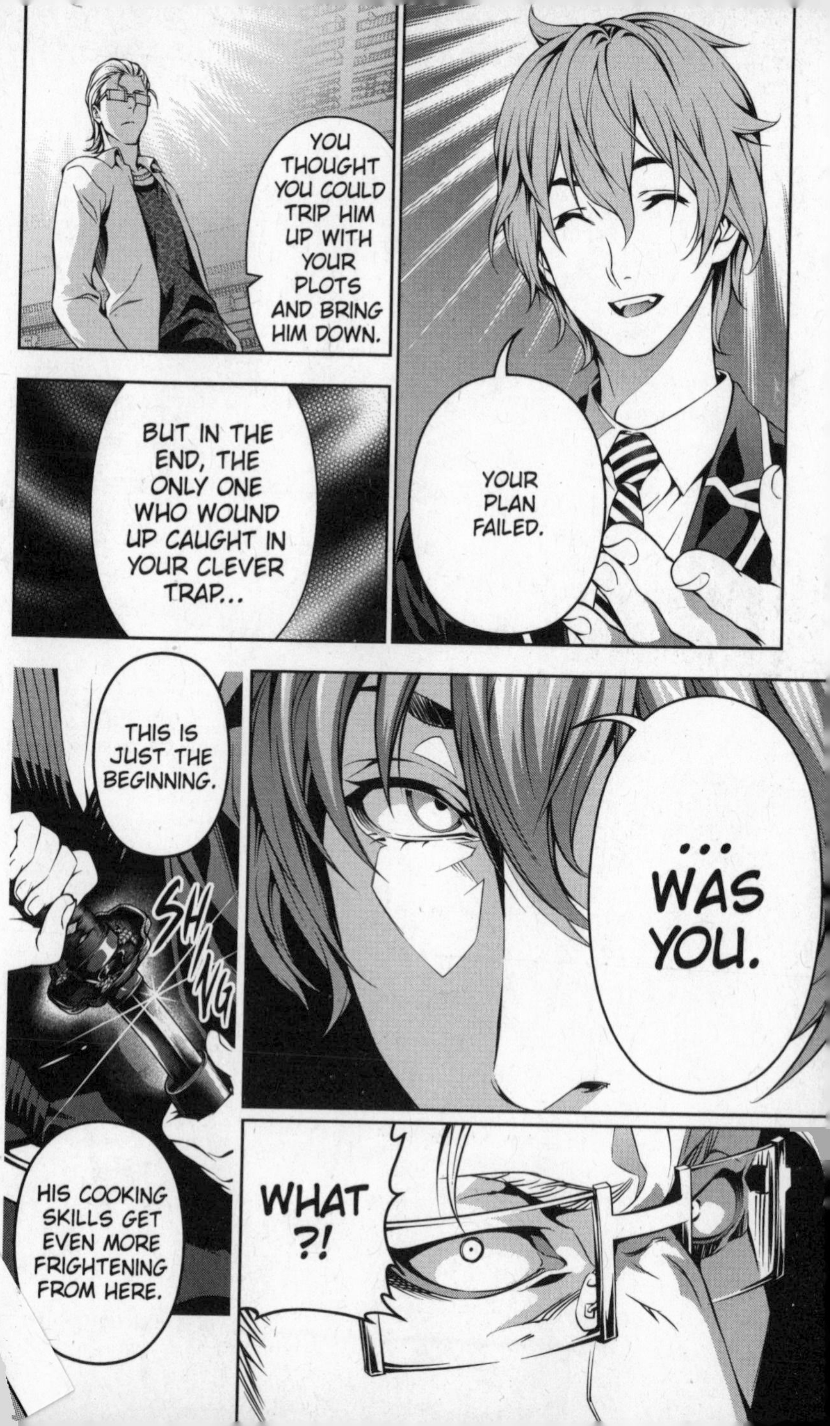
YOUR PLAN FAILED.
YOU THOUGHT YOU COULD TRIP HIM UP WITH YOUR PLOTS AND BRING HIM DOWN.
BUT IN THE END, THE ONLY ONE WHO WOUND UP CAUGHT IN YOUR CLEVER TRAP...
...WAS YOU.
WHAT ?!
THIS IS JUST THE BEGINNING.
SHING
HIS COOKING SKILLS GET EVEN MORE FRIGHTENING FROM HERE.

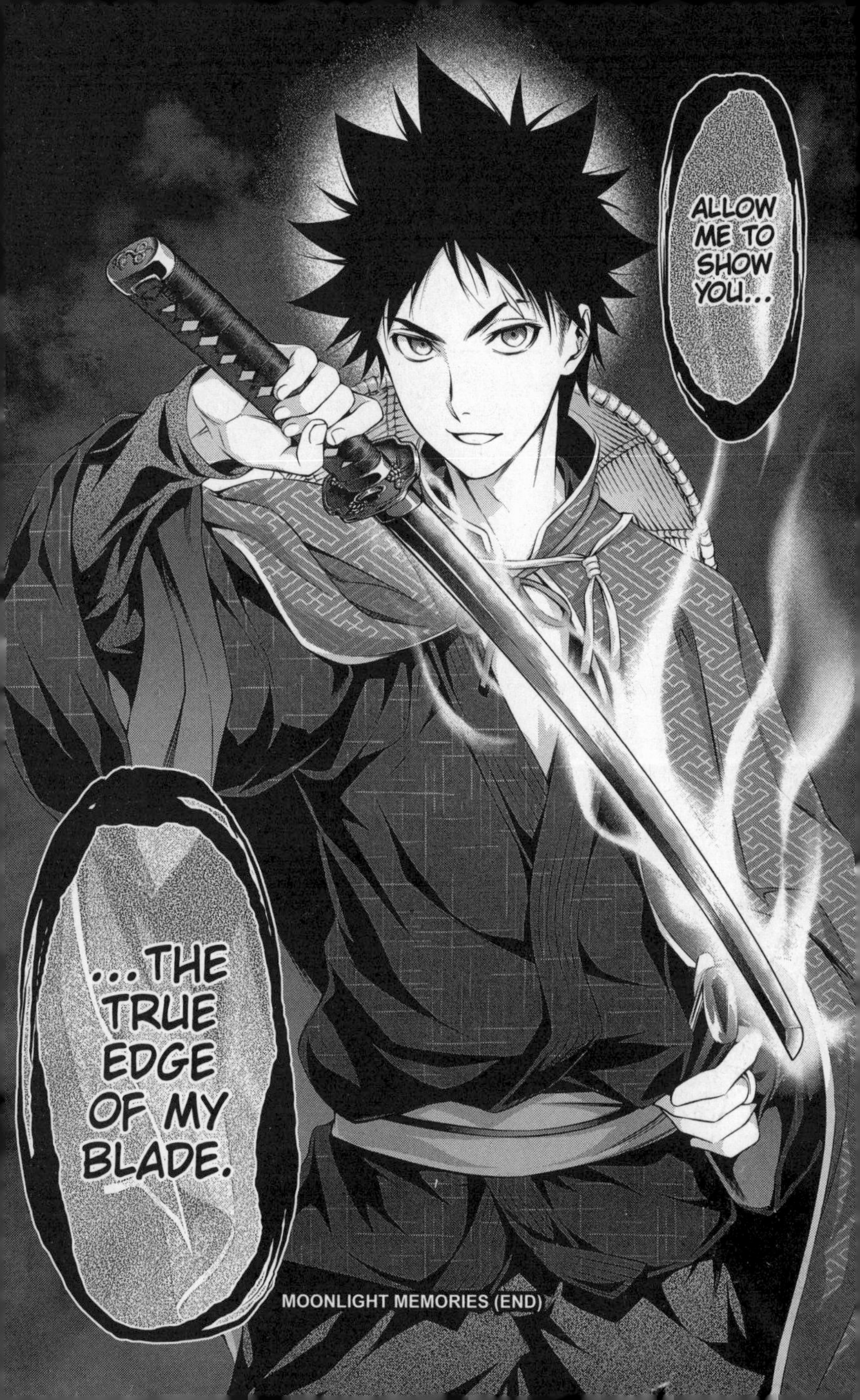
ALLOW ME TO SHOW YOU...
...THE TRUE EDGE OF MY BLADE.
MOONLIGHT MEMORIES (END)

You're Reading in the Wrong Direction!!

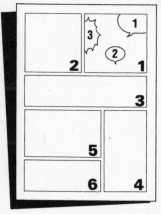

Whoops! Guess what? You're starting at the wrong end of the comic!

...It's true! In keeping with the original Japanese format, **Food Wars!** is meant to be read from right to left, starting in the upper-right corner.

Unlike English, which is read from left to right, Japanese is read from right to left, meaning that action, sound effects and word-balloon order are completely reversed... something which can make readers unfamiliar with Japanese feel pretty backwards themselves. For this reason, manga or Japanese comics published in the U.S. in English have sometimes been published "flopped"—that is, printed in exact reverse order, as though seen from the other side of a mirror.

By flopping pages, U.S. publishers can avoid confusing readers, but the compromise is not without its downside. For one thing, a character in a flopped manga series who once wore in the original Japanese version a T-shirt emblazoned with "M A Y" (as in "the merry month of") now wears one which reads "Y A M"! Additionally, many manga creators in Japan are themselves unhappy with the process, as some feel the mirror-imaging of their art skews their original intentions.

EEE! MOTHER, YOU SURE DO LOOK HOT!

We are proud to bring you Yuto Tsukuda and Shun Saeki's **Food Wars!** in the original unflopped format.

For now, though, turn to the other side of the book and let the adventure begin...!

—Editor